RELIGIONS OF THE CONST

Religions of the Constantinian Empire

MARK EDWARDS

OXFORD UNIVERSITY PRESS

Great Clarendon Street, Oxford, OX2 6DP,
United Kingdom

Oxford University Press is a department of the University of Oxford.
It furthers the University's objective of excellence in research, scholarship,
and education by publishing worldwide. Oxford is a registered trade mark of
Oxford University Press in the UK and in certain other countries

First published 2015
First published in paperback 2018

Published in the United States of America by Oxford University Press
198 Madison Avenue, New York, NY 10016, United States of America

British Library Cataloguing in Publication Data
Data available

Library of Congress Cataloging in Publication Data
Data available

ISBN 978–0–19–968772–5 (Hbk.)
ISBN 978–0–19–878524–8 (Pbk.)

In memoriam Bernard Green

Preface

The year 2006 marked the seventeenth centenary of Constantine's assumption of the title Augustus; this was followed in 2012 by the seventeenth centenary of his conversion, or more precisely of the date traditionally assigned to it. These anniversaries stimulated the writing of new books which offered subtle, rounded, and sometimes novel answers to the questions which have been debated ever since Jacob Burckhardt first threw doubt on the sincerity of Constantine's religion.[1] Was his Christianity feigned? Did he understand that it excluded other cults? Did he attempt to impose his own creed on the empire? Did he engage a general suppression of pagan worship? Did his measures pacify or inflame the intestinal discords of the church? Alongside this body of literature there has grown up another in which the theological causes of these intestinal discords are discussed in a more detached and analytical manner than was customary when the only purpose of studying the 'fathers' was to vindicate the orthodoxy of one's own communion. For the most part these historians of doctrine have taken little account of political history, except when trying to understand the outcome of the Council of Nicaea in 325; and while there are, by contrast, a number of political historians who are admirably conversant with the doctrinal controversies of this era, there are others who continue to write 'here be dragons' whenever their research has brought them to the frontiers of theology. A third and equally salutary development is an acknowledgement that philosophy did not die with Plotinus: tirades against the decadence of the Roman mind no longer go proxy for sober exploration of the writings of Iamblichus, and Christians are perceived to have been creators of systems, not only iconoclasts to the systems of others. At the same time, most historians of philosophy remain indifferent, not only to the political environment of philosophy in this era, but to the constraints that scripture and hermeneutic tradition imposed on the Christian appropriation of Platonism. One could almost forget that the interval between the Great Persecution and Constantine's death was nearly coterminous with that portion of the life of Athanasius which preceded his first exile and with the years that separate the death of Porphyry from that of his hostile amanuensis, Bishop Eusebius of Caesarea.

The consequences of this dispersal of interest will be more evident if we consider how differently the 'question of sacrifice' in the late Roman world might be phrased by students in each of these three disciplines. Political

[1] Burckhardt (1853).

historians will canvass the effects of its atrophy or abolition on the economy of the empire and the practice of religion.[2] The historian of philosophy is more interested in the innovatory arguments that were advanced against this linchpin of classical piety by some Platonists and in the equally novel arguments which were advanced by other Platonists in its defence. In the meantime theologians know nothing of the end of sacrifice as they discuss the origins of the cultic vocabulary which transformed the Eucharist into a ritual offering and its celebrant into a priest. The exponent of a fourth, much younger discipline, the history of religions, may protest that all three have failed to pose the right question, namely: What was the structural element in the Christianity of the later empire that replaced the civic altar?[3] The fact that Eusebius would be the principal witness for all four disputants illustrates the desirability of a more holistic approach. Our failure to cultivate such an approach cannot be blamed entirely on the modern rage for specialization, though it is certainly true that this often leaves us not so much 'knowing more and more about less and less' as knowing less about anything at all. In this case, even a general knowledge would be no more than a cluster of specialisms, as the sources do not lend themselves to an integrated narrative. Accordingly, no narrative will be attempted in the present book, which offers instead a conspectus of the phenomena between the years 300 and 340 that might reasonably be brought under the heading of 'religion'.

I have divided the present study into three parts. The first takes for its subject the efforts of Christians to construct their own philosophy, and their own patterns of the philosophic life, in opposition to Platonism. The second assembles evidence of survival, variation, or decay in religious practices which were never compulsory under Roman law. The third reviews the changes, both within the church and in the public sphere, which were undeniably prompted by the accession of a Christian monarch. The material in the first will be most familiar to the historian of philosophy, that of the second to the historian of religion, and that of the third to the theologian. Since all history is political history, all three sections will make reference to such factors as the persecution under Diocletian, the so-called edict of Milan, the subsequent legislation of Constantine and the summoning of the Council of Nicaea. It will not be maintained, however, that the religious and philosophical innovations of this period were mere by-products of political revolution; indeed, we shall often have reason to observe that Christianity was more revolutionary in its expectations than any sovereign could afford to be in his acts.

The title of Part I, 'Philosophical Variations', embraces a number of figures who would not find their way into a conventional history of philosophy. Yet if this compliment is paid to Origen and Clement of Alexandria, it cannot be

[2] See Trombley (2001), ix–x and 1–2. [3] Stroumsa (2009).

withheld from Eusebius, whose apologetic treatises are at least equally systematic and far more copious in citation from the philosophical writings of his own contemporaries. The works of his African counterparts Arnobius and Lactantius are more voluminous than those of any precursor in the Latin world, and more attentive to the prevailing currents of Greek thought. No doubt for this reason, both are sufficiently estranged from Roman society to challenge its pretensions to antiquity, the legitimacy of its conquests, and the moral utility of its classic texts. It is possible that all three took the Platonist Porphyry of Tyre as an interlocutor, and I may appear to have shown in Chapter 3 that they imbibed more from him than the Platonists who succeeded him cared to imbibe from Christianity. In Chapter 4, however, I have argued that Iamblichus, who had certainly read at least one Gnostic text, betrays his acquaintance with the Gospel of John in his treatise *On the Pythagorean Life*. Reciprocal imitation of Iamblichus (or his antecedents) has been detected in the *Life of Antony*, and the readiness of some Christians to adapt the arts that others shunned is illustrated, also in Chapter 4, by the juxtaposition of Firmicus Maternus with the author of the tract *Against Hierocles*. Nevertheless, I maintain in Chapter 5 that the flight of Antony from the world was more complete than that of any Pythagorean, and that even the Pachomian communities were governed by other laws than those that underwrote Greek culture and Roman power.

The 'religious plurality' of Part II includes those cults which are represented as demonic burlesques of the sacraments by Firmicus Maternus. As the sixth chapter demonstrates, however, none of them was sufficiently like Christianity to be counted among its rivals; nor do the paltry relics of devotion from this epoch suggest that any of them was adding to its numbers, even before the accession of Constantine. On the other hand, there are evident signs of vigour in the 'religions of transformation' which are examined in Chapter 7. Manichaeism became suddenly conspicuous, Gnostic texts were transcribed with solicitude, Hermes was named in the same breath as Plato, alchemy was attested for the first time. Since all these movements promised immortality as the consequence of internal transformation, all were doomed to compete in vain with Christianity; yet all in a fashion survived in symbiosis with the catholic tradition while the cults of Isis, Mithras, and Bacchus perished. The Jews have not fared so well at Christian hands, and those who trace the origin of this fraternal persecution to Constantine point out that he can scarcely use the term 'Jew' in a legal enactment without an ebullition of pious animosity. But if this is his 'bark', as A. H. M. Jones expressed it,[4] his 'bite', as we see in Chapter 8, took the form of severe reprisals against defectors to the synagogue, and against Jews who punished converts to Christianity or imposed

[4] Jones (1966), 47.

circumcision on their Gentile slaves. Such legislation was not unprecedented, and its aim was to ensure, with all the menaces at Constantine's disposal, that no one would become a Jew who had not been born a Jew.

In Part III, 'Christian Polyphony', I pass on from this deliberate petrifaction of Judaism to the profound shift in relations between the church and the civic cult that followed the emperor's choice of a new divine protector. I shall hope to show in Chapter 9 that, while he was neither a hypocrite nor a syncretist, his zeal for the propagation of Christianity was tempered by his sense of a ruler's duty to his subjects and the limits of his own power. In Chapter 10 we shall find that the abolition of sacrifice—certainly a result of Constantine's measures, if not one of them—was justified in this period by Christian propaganda which was itself an amplified echo of pagan scruples. I shall also maintain, in answer to the historian of religion, that the Eucharist was as much a structural as a symbolic equivalent to the pagan institution. In the Great Persecution Christian refusal to sacrifice had been avenged by the burning of the scriptures: we shall see in Chapter 11 that, although Constantine promoted the distribution of the New Testament, its contents were not determined by his own fiat or that of a council, since they had already been established, with few exceptions, by the consensus of the episcopate. We shall also see that readings of the Old Testament which would now be considered fantastic by the majority of scholars were forced upon the early Christians by their unwavering literalism. Chapter 12 examines the attempts of two such literalists to resolve the apparent discord in the gospels. Eusebius claims to uphold the plain sense of the text against the heretic, to vindicate the competence and integrity of its authors and to demonstrate the absurdity of the comparisons drawn by pagans between the Christian saviour and their own wonder-workers; the poet Juvencus sets out to give Christianity its own Virgil, thus enabling the cultured Roman to embrace the religion of the new Augustus without disparaging the fruits of his own education. In Chapter 13 I address the theological controversies on which Eusebius is often thought to have taken a heterodox position, first in defence of Origen, then in support of Arius, and lastly against Marcellus. My conclusion will be that, while the same points were subject to debate in both the Origenist and the Arian controversies, it was not true that a point in favour of Origen was always a vote for Arius. It is certainly not true, as a matter of history, that Eusebius was obliged to recant his earlier teachings either to escape deposition at the Nicene Council or to gain a polemical victory over Marcellus. His panegyric on Constantine which I take as the preface to my fourteenth chapter was thus delivered in 336 with an easy conscience; this chapter, however, will also illustrate the growth of ecclesiastical discord, the resentment of the pagans and the discontent of those for whom the very existence of the pagan cults was an insult to Christ.

Everything changes; everything persists. That Constantine transformed the world and that Constantine left the world much as he found it would be equally valid, and equally inadequate, conclusions from the evidence that remains to us. The present study does not propound a new theory that could be recapitulated in half a paragraph: it is rather, as I have said above, a conspectus of change and persistence, which does not belie but throws into high relief the ambiguity, the complexity, and the heterogeneity of the facts that have been brought under review.

Contents

Part I

Philosophical Variations

1

Christian versus Pagan in Eusebius of Caesarea

It is fitting that the subject of the first chapter in this book should be a man who will figure in almost every chapter. It is equally fitting that we should meet him first through his labours as an apologist, though it might be said that we could hardly do otherwise, for the spirit of advocacy is never absent from his numerous essays in exegesis, history, biography, or the exposition of dogma. In contrast to his precursors, however, he had some notion of apologetic as a genre, for it was he who gave it a name and who drew up the first canon of its Greek exemplars.[1] When he added himself to the canon he aimed to be more than an imitator: no practitioner of an ancient genre is merely a copyist, and Eusebius—Eusebius of Caesarea, as we call him after his bishopric—was the first apologist who achieved double eminence as a scholar and as a churchman. He set out to polish, not merely to preserve, the lamp of truth by which he was pointing out the way to an increasingly cultured public of Christian readers and an increasingly bellicose audience of pagans. Old arguments had ossified while new critics remained unanswered; Christian numbers were growing, but the gospel was being proclaimed in the dominant language of a polytheistic world to which no single text was holy but Homer and Plato were divine. The project that took shape in the *Preparation for the Gospel* and its sequel, the *Demonstration*, was at once more eclectic and more synoptic, more combative and more urbane than any of its Greek models. It was not, for all that, unique in its generation, for we shall see in Chapter 2 that two Latin contemporaries of Eusebius were equally responsive to the new temper (or distemper) of the age.

Few authors who wrote so copiously have hidden themselves so well. We know that Eusebius succeeded Agapius as Bishop of Caesarea in 313, and that he lived to write the biography of Constantine, who died in 337. He seems not

[1] Frede (1999), 227 notes that Eusebius applies the term 'apologetic' to the oration of the martyr Apollonius (*Church History* 5.21.2–5) and the treatises by Quadratus (4.3.1), Aristides (4.3.1), Justin Martyr (4.5.3), Miltiades (5.17.3), Melito and Apollonius (4.26).

to have been alive at the time of the council of Antioch in 341, but he was present at the Council of Nicaea in 325 and left with his bishopric intact, having signed the creed. Some months before, it appears that he had been condemned, though not deposed, at a synod held in Antioch; the fact that his name appears fifth in the list of Palestinian signatories to the creed of 325 (although his bishopric was the metropolis of Palestine) suggests that he put his hand to the document with some hesitation. He was later to decline the see of Antioch when it was offered to him by Constantine; the deposed incumbent, Eustathius, had accused Eusebius of bad faith in his subscription to the Creed. His admirer Jerome adds only that he was a diligent student of the holy scriptures under Pamphilus of Caesarea, who died in the persecution of Maximinus (*Of Illustrious Men* 81). The corpus of works ascribed to him by Jerome includes the *Preparation for the Gospel* in fifteen books, the *Demonstration* in twenty, the *Theophany* in five, the *Commentary on Isaiah* in ten, the *Ecclesiastical History* in ten, the *Apology for Origen* (begun by Pamphilus) in six, the *Life of Pamphilus* in three, commentaries on all the Psalms, a work on the disagreements between the gospels, a *Chronicle*, a work *On Places*, and (according to report) a refutation of Porphyry the Neoplatonist in thirty books, of which Jerome has seen but twenty. He adds that there are many more: the longest that has come down to us is a commentary on Luke.

Eusebius was not a common name in pagan circles; it rose in popularity as Christian parents grew reluctant to give their children the names of fictitious gods.[2] Since Eusebius of Caesarea was not known by any other appellation, it is reasonable to conclude that he was a Christian by nurture. Unlike apologists of the second century who had been converts, he never slights Greek culture or the Greek language; although he impugns the Greek claim to pre-eminence in wisdom, he does not represent Christianity as the religion of barbarians. Instead he followed Origen, whose library he inherited, in reckoning scholarship among the virtues of a Christian theologian.

PRELIMINARIES

Although the word *apologia* strictly signifies a defensive speech, the earliest Christian specimens date from an era of persecution, and hence move easily from remonstrance to polemic. Against those who accused them of sedition, the authors protested that they offered prayers on the emperor's behalf, though not to the emperor himself. Against the charge of illiteracy, they retorted that, barbarians as they were, they had read enough to know that

[2] See further Harnack (1908), 422–30.

the Greeks had no monopoly of wisdom. In answer to both their political and their intellectual critics they contended that, as the true legatees of Moses, they had as much right to deference and immunity as the Jews. Some made use of the gospels, or related texts, to prove that Jesus of Nazareth was the Messiah of whom the Jews grasped only the shadow in their scriptures; others, handling mysteries with more reticence, were content to maintain the unity of God and denounce the futility of idols. They employed the forms of rhetoric, but with little art; in poetry they had neither taste nor learning, and in philosophy they were at best dilettanti. No pagan intellectual was likely to be moved by a threadbare attempt to show that Plato had stolen from Moses, a brief excursus on the creation of matter, an allegorical reading of the six days in the opening chapter of Genesis or a second-hand catena of lampoons on the personal vices of the great philosophers.[3] Clement of Alexandria was the first Christian—and then only in his *Stromateis*, not his *Protrepticus*—whom an educated Greek might have regarded as his peer. The purpose of his incomplete compendium remains uncertain, but its method is to demonstrate a harmony in first principles between the best fruits of reason and the teaching of the church. For all his admiration of the Greeks, and especially Plato, Clement insists repeatedly that they are junior to Moses by some centuries and often in his debt. While it may be their merit to have said clearly what was vouchsafed to the prophets in cipher, they are apt to forget that such truths must be revealed before they are known, and they are as guilty as the Jews of spurning the truth when it is manifested in the incarnate Word.

Yet even Clement barely has a Christology, a doctrine which explains how one being can be both God and man. Perhaps it was only when Christ's claims to divinity had been impugned by a pagan satirist that Christians came to see this as a mandatory element in apologetic. In his *True Logos* (*c.*170) Celsus also pressed the charge that Christians had apostatized, not only from pagan cults but from the Jews whom they had adopted as their fathers; furthermore he denied that the puerile representations of God in the Jewish scriptures could be redeemed by allegory, and argued that, as militants on behalf of another kingdom, Christians could not be good citizens of the empire.[4] Origen's refutation of these strictures ran to eight books, and set a pattern for future apologies in content if not in structure. In his magnum opus, which comprises the *Preparation for the Gospel* and *Demonstration of the Gospel*, Eusebius undertakes to prove the antiquity of the Christian faith, the coherence of its theology, the superiority of the Jewish scriptures to any Greek system and the necessity of reading them with an eye to the deeper meaning

[3] Justin, *First Apology* 60; Athenagoras, *Embassy* 4 and 15; Theophilus, *To Autolycus* 2.11–19; Tatian, *Oration to the Greeks* 2.

[4] See Origen, *Against Celsus* 1.28 and 32 etc.; 4.38; 8.55.

that has been made plain in Christ.[5] The *Preparation* puts one in mind of Clement rather than Origen in its prolixity and the polyphonic character of materials; it has in common with Origen, however, that it takes as its most frequent interlocutor a pagan author of recent times, who had come to be seen as the church's most dangerous enemy to date. Porphyry owes this reputation chiefly to the burning of his books by Constantine and to a letter by Augustine which implies that his name was likely to attach itself to objections that a Christian found especially perplexing.[6] The *Suda*, a Byzantine lexicon, enumerates fifteen *logoi* or discourses against the Christians in a catalogue of his writings; yet five allusions in the *Preparation for the Gospel* to a 'tract against us' afford the most cogent evidence of his having written a work against the Christians, distinct from the many others which Eusebius cites as proof of his inconsistency and his willingness to collude with the very powers whose maleficence he had exposed.[7]

But what in fact had Porphyry written?[8] Jerome records, with his usual acerbity, that Porphyry had impugned the antiquity of the Book of Daniel, maintaining that, where accurate, it was written after the events that it purports to foresee.[9] Since he is quoting a detailed rejoinder to Porphyry by Eusebius, we need not doubt that he is well informed, although we have reason to doubt the existence of the *Chronicle* in which Porphyry was once thought to have hurled his barbs at the prophet.[10] The *Suda*, as we have noted, ascribes to him fifteen *logoi* against the Christians: the term *logoi* would normally signify more than one book, and a monumental work in fifteen books is not attested in earlier sources.[11] Again it is true that the six objections which Augustine rebuts in his 102nd letter are attached to the name of Porphyry, but Augustine does not say expressly that he was the author of them or that they were all contained in a single work. Harnack enlarged his collection of testimonia and fragments by identifying Porphyry with the 'Hellene' who combs the New Testament for absurdities and contradictions in a fictitious dialogue by Macarius Magnes; as Barnes and others have demonstrated, however, this is merely a conjecture, which has little to recommend it but its economy in the postulation of sources for Macarius.[12] According to Lactantius, a philosopher

[5] On his 'ambivalent' relation to Greek culture see Frede (1999), 243.

[6] Bochet (2011); Magny (2014), 99–118.

[7] The search for new fragments has been indefatigable: see Nautin (1950); Cook (1998); Morlet (2008); Morlet (2010); Goulet (2010).

[8] For another discussion of this question see now Schott (2013a), 277–86.

[9] It has been assumed since Harnack (1916) that these strictures appeared in Porphyry's *Chronicle* rather than his work *Against the Christians*.

[10] See Croke (1983) and Barnes (1994).

[11] See further Berchman (2005).

[12] So Barnes (1973a), with the support of Meredith (1980), 1126–7. On the possible identity of the Hellene see Digeser (2002). Munnich (2011) concludes that criticisms originating in pagan invective have undergone redaction either in Macarius or in his pagan sources.

whom he forbears to name had aggravated the sufferings of the church under persecution by composing a polemic in three books; the hypothesis that this was the *Philosophy from Oracles* is not improbable, though by no means proven.[13] It cannot be maintained, however, that the *Philosophy from Oracles* was Porphyry's only assault on Christianity, for if that were so Eusebius would not have said that its author had also been the author of 'the writing against us'.[14] In short, we know only that there was such a writing, and that its reputation was such that the pagan orator Libanius, on reading the Emperor Julian's lucubration *Against the Galileans*, congratulated him on having outdone 'the old man of Tyre' (*Oration* 18.173)

Jerome assigns both twenty-five and thirty books to the work *Against Porphyry*, which is now lost.[15] In his commentary on Daniel he says that Porphyry's strictures on this book have been refuted by Eusebius in the eighteenth, the nineteenth, and the twentieth books of an unnamed treatise. It is possible that the writing to which he alludes was the *Demonstration of the Gospel*, which is said in his catalogue to have run to twenty books, though only ten survive today. This conjecture accrues weight from the one surviving fragment of the lost half of the *Demonstration*, an elucidation of Nebuchadnezzar's vision in the Book of Daniel, taken (as the scribe tells us) from Book 15.[16] Nevertheless, in the manuscripts followed by Heikel (p. 492), the tenth would appear to be the final book of the *Demonstration*, as it is the only one that does not end with a sentence introducing the contents of the next. If, then, we surmise that the original edition contained only ten books, it is possible that the twenty-five books *Against Porphyry* (some of which Jerome does not profess to have seen) consisted of the *Preparation* and the ten books of the *Demonstration* in its original form.[17]

THE *PREPARATION FOR THE GOSPEL*

Whatever has perished, the extant corpus of writings by Eusebius exceeds that of any Christian contemporary or predecessor with the exception of Origen. The apologetic corpus alone includes not two but three substantial works: the *Theophany*, which now exists only in Syriac, will be discussed together with the *Demonstration of the Gospel* in Chapter 12. It is often regarded as one of his earlier writings, though a scientific chronology of literature from this

[13] Lactantius, *Divine Institutes* 5.2. See Edwards (2007b), 117–20 on Barnes's attempt to prove that it cannot be Porphyry.
[14] *Pace* Beatrice (1989) see Eusebius, *Preparation* 5.5 and 5.36.2.
[15] Jerome, *On Famous Men* 81; Letters 70.3.
[16] See Heikel's edition of the *Demonstration* (Bibliography A), 493–8.
[17] For a more circumspect version of this theory see Stevenson (1929), 37 and 63.

period has yet to be constructed. The date of the *Preparation*, if a date could be assigned to it, would throw much light on the intellectual history of the author. The one hard piece of evidence, however, is the dedication to Theodotus of Laodicea, which, since he held his bishopric from 310 to 333, leaves a margin of twenty-three years.[18] The exultation with which it proclaims the universal triumph of Christianity seems hardly to be compatible with an era of persecution; on the other hand, since nothing is said of martial victories, the boast would have been credible some years before Constantine's accession to the eastern throne in 324. If the *Preparation* refers to the execution of former agents of Maximinus Daia this proves only what we might have guessed, that this work was not complete before 313.[19] An allusion to the persecution of Christians by 'rulers, nations and kings' has been detected in its sequel, the *Demonstration of the Gospel*, but until it is shown that these oppressors were acting within the Roman Empire,[20] no date of composition can be inferred. Some scholars have maintained that it could not have been written after 325 because its teaching on the relation of the Son to the Father bears too close a resemblance to that of Arius, which was anathematized in that year at the Council of Nicaea.[21] It does not, however, teach any of the positions that were formally anathematized, and, in the absence of any official decree, we must be wary of assuming that we know what tenets Eusebius might have been compelled to abandon at the Council. It is arguing in a circle to deduce the date of a writing from its putative heterodoxy if we have already made an assumption about its date when we pronounced it heterodox.

Explaining his task to Theodotus, Eusebius asseverates that the light of the Gospel has filled the world, that Greeks and barbarians in their multitudes have become its disciples (1.1.6), that under its corrective tutelage Scythians have ceased to eat human flesh and Persians now abstain from intercourse with their mothers (1.4.6). Although the Word of God rejects no one, it is no more capable than the best physicians of healing those who do not confess that they are sick. Among these are the Greek detractors of Christianity, who assume that it is always wrong to break with ancestral tradition, as though the truth or falsity of the tradition counted for nothing. At the same time they

[18] Morlet (2009), 80–93 believes that the date cannot be fixed with any more precision.

[19] *Preparation* 4.2.11, cited most recently by Johnson (2014), 19. The names of the pagans whose false pretensions to sorcery were exposed under torture are not given in this passage. On p. liv of his edition of the *Preparation* (Bibliography A), Mras purports to discern a 'fresh' recollection of the exposure of Theotecnus, related by Eusebius, *Church History* 9.2; this argument is hardly substantial enough to require an answer.

[20] Johnson (2014), quoting *Demonstration* 4.16. Constantine's letter to Shapur of Persia at Eusebius, *Life of Constantine* 4.13 implies some fear for the safety of Christians under that ruler; cf. Gelasius of Cyzicus, *Church History* 3.10.26–27 on his reasons for refraining from war against Persia in the last months of his reign.

[21] See Johnson (2014), on the contradictions which result when one attempts to date the writings of Eusebius by this criterion.

charge Christians with duplicity to their own fathers because they claim for themselves the barbarian philosophy of Moses, yet revile living Jews as stiff-necked traitors to God (1.2.3). In answer to this indictment it is necessary to show that, while the Israelites excelled all other races of antiquity in their knowledge of God, they received the truth in ciphers which have proved illegible to their blind descendants (1.2.5–8). Accepting that the Greeks, if not the oldest, are the best-informed of nations, Eusebius states (without any named authority[22]) that the Phoenicians were the first to make gods of the sun and moon, enthroning the creature in place of the Creator (1.6.1). They were followed by the Egyptians (1.6.4), who, according to Diodorus Siculus (*History* 1.6–8), entertained a purely physiological—that is, godless and materialistic—account of the creation (1.7.1–15). It is easily shown that the earliest Greek philosophers were equally ignorant of the first cause, and Plato himself bears witness that the first gods of the Greeks were the sun and moon (1.8.1–13; *Cratylus* 397d). And now to the calculated peroration of the whole exercise: the Greeks and Egyptians also worshipped anthropomorphic deities, and no less a figure than Porphyry, the Hellenized Phoenician who has made himself notorious by his abuse of the church, can be summoned to testify that these glorified hominids were initially human beings like ourselves, or a little worse.[23] Porphyry's source was his countryman Sanchuniathon,[24] who, according to his translator Philo of Byblos, wrote his *Phoenician History* long before Moses, and therefore long before the Trojan War (1.9.21). An atheist himself, he deserves a hearing from other atheists when he chronicles the intrigues and atrocities of the beings whom the Greeks know as Zeus and Cronos (1.7.9–29). If it be asked why the facts that he relates fell into oblivion, the answer is that they were purposely obscured by priestly allegories, which could be exploded only when the work of Sanchuniathon was retrieved from the temple in which it had been deposited (1.9.21). Thus it would appear that the deification of the elements is a younger error, if not a less nefarious one, than the cult of men as gods.

The second book quotes from Diodorus a long account of the human wars, inventions, and vicissitudes which gave rise to the mythology of the Egyptians (2.1).[25] In the course of his narrative, Diodorus reveals that Cadmus was the progenitor of the Greek gods (2.2.1–4), and thus corroborates the antiquity of Moses, who is proved by 'exact chronography' to have antedated Cadmus (2.1.56). Among the Greeks, the theory that all the gods had human prototypes was first elaborated by Euhemerus of Messene, whose patently fictitious

[22] See further Doergens (1915), 66–8.

[23] On the use of Porphyry against Porphyry see Kofsky (2002), 250–75.

[24] For commentary on the fragments of Philo of Byblos see Baumgarten (1981).

[25] Many excerpts, of which the longest is *Histories* 1.86.3. Diodorus is frequently abridged in the Eusebian transcription.

report of his travels is transcribed from Diodorus by Eusebius without a flicker of humour (2.2.53–62). The inscription which Euhemerus purports to have discovered preserves a tale of unrelieved folly and turpitude which cannot be redeemed by allegory.[26] The philosophers themselves are not united in their use of this expedient: Plato in his *Republic* protests that lewdness, even in allegorical narratives, will always corrupt an audience (377e–378d), and yet the same Plato declares in his *Timaeus* (40d–41e) that we cannot disbelieve the stories told about the gods by their descendants (2.7.1–7). Clement of Alexandria has already denounced the obscenities of myth and its re-enactments in the mysteries (2.3; *Protrepticus* 11.1–11); in contrast to Lactantius, however, Eusebius quotes with approval the assertion of Dionysius of Halicarnassus that no such blemishes disfigure the native religion or mythology of the Romans (2.7.9; *Antiquities* 11.182–21.1). In the third book the physiological interpretation of myth is exemplified by Plutarch, Diodorus, and Chaeremon (as quoted by Porphyry), each of whom fails to perceive that by personifying excess and defect in the strife of physical elements one can only encourage surfeit and dissipation in their human votaries. A younger generation of philosophers, led by Porphyry himself,[27] invites the same criticism when it justifies the manufacture of idols as cryptic intimation of sublime truths under the necessary limits of plastic art (3.7.1). The best that can be said of these manoeuvres is that their premisses are theological rather than physiological. There is no need to create a graven image at all, and no plausible rule that enables us to detect the attributes of an invisible deity in a crocodile or a lotus (3.11.48). The vulgar will see only what is visible, and go on with their fabling. The philosopher may deduce from the carnal image that God is a bodiless mind, but only because he knows this already; in an Orphic poem which Porphyry commends without reserve this mind is identical with the aether, and Zeus is represented by an incongruous medley of images which communicates the true nature of God less aptly than the chaste metaphors of scripture (3.9.1–2). Anthropomorphic language is inescapable, but the conversion of words into sculpture is prohibited because it tempts the multitude to honour the imperfect form and not the One of whom it is an image.[28]

Book 4 takes leave of the poets and philosophers and proceeds to the third, or political,[29] branch of counterfeit religion. This is treated as though it consisted wholly in the consultation of oracles, a practice which, according to Eusebius, is almost obsolete because the masses have become conscious of

[26] See further Brown (1946); Winiarczyk (2013).

[27] The fragments on the treatise on statues appear as an appendix to Bidez (1913), and in Porphyry's *Fragmenta*, ed. Smith (1993).

[28] *Preparation* 3.13.24; 4.1.6. Eusebius has been regarded, on uncertain evidence, as an opponent of images within the church: see Barnes (2010b).

[29] Eusebius seems to be following the taxonomy of Varro, though he never names the Roman polymath.

its futility, abandoning Delphi and Claros for a God who demands no sacrifice but a pure heart and upright conduct (4.2.8). Chrysippus the Stoic could adduce the success of oracles as evidence that all our affairs are controlled by fate, but his sophistries were exposed by another Greek, Diogenianus, who pointed out that the prophecies came true so rarely that chance alone would account for their verification (4.3). Any review of history will show that when the oracles gave unambiguous predictions they were generally erroneous, and that their acolytes did nothing to restore the inward or outward health of their petitioners. The most discerning philosophers have perceived that they are not merely unprofitable but pernicious because the beings who preside over them are not gods but the counterfeit deities whom every Christian knows to be fallen angels (4.4.4). Porphyry, not for the first time, is at once in the van of truth and the rearguard of error, for, although he unmasks the maleficence of the demons, he regards them as vassals to whom the governance of civil society has been entrusted by higher agents (4.6.2). Thus the 'ten thousand guardians' or shepherds of humankind remain unmoved when the bloodless offerings of old gave way to the slaughter of innocent beasts; Porphyry himself not only acquiesced in the popular devotions, but collected precepts for sacrifice to three different orders of gods from reluctant demons whom he knew to neither omniscient nor well disposed.[30] In the fifth book the tyranny of the demons is illustrated by further excerpts from Porphyry's treatise *On Abstinence*,[31] while the *Philosophy from Oracles* affords copious illustrations of his readiness to collude with their impostures.

The *Life of Constantine* leaves no doubt that Eusebius and his sovereign were united in their enmity to Apollo. It is this work that preserves the letters of Constantine alleging that the Great Persecution was instigated by Apollo's response to Diocletian, and Constantine himself passes censure on the god's amours in his *Oration to the Saints*, with a glancing allusion to his oracle at Daphne.[32] But while events may have concentrated zeal, we cannot deduce from the invectives of Eusebius that the *Philosophy from Oracles* was conceived in a spirit of enmity to the Church,[33] or that Porphyry was a willing catalyst to persecution. Both conjectures are reasonable, but either may be false. Eusebius may have singled out the *Philosophy from Oracles* because it

[30] Citations from *The Philosophy to be Derived from Oracles* are found at 3.14, 4.9, 4.20, 4.23.6–8, 5.7–16, and 6.1–3.

[31] *On Abstinence* 2.34 (p. 164 Nauck) at *Preparation* 4.13; 2.7 (p. 138 Nauck) at 4.14; 2.36 (p. 168 Nauck) at 4.15; 2.54–56 (pp. 179–81 Nauck) at 4.11.1–11.

[32] See *Oration to the Saints* 18 with Digeser (2004).

[33] Addey (2014), 110–17 warns us not to forget the polemical character of the work to which we owe most of our knowledge of the *Philosophy from Oracles*. Beatrice (1989) maintains that it was identical with the work *Against the Christians*, but *Preparation* 5.5. and 5.36.5 imply that the two were distinct.

gave him a serviceable handle against his pagan adversary,[34] and because the defence of oracles raised questions of some moment for all believers. In Book 6 the polemic against the oracles is reinforced by excerpts from philosophers who have defended the liberty of human will against fatalism. The voices of Plutarch,[35] the Cynic Oenomaus,[36] Diogenianus,[37] and Alexander the Peripatetic[38] are mingled with those of Origen and Bardesanes, the latter a Christian in his own mind, but of dubious orthodoxy. Origen, adducing a catena of testimonies to human freedom from the prophets, contends that the predictions of astrologers are uncertain, that even divine foreknowledge is not the cause of the thing foreknown, and that if all our actions were foreordained there would be no occasion for prayer and no occasion for the judgment of the dead.[39] Bardesanes argues that the stars under which we all live could not be responsible at the same time for the diversity of customs and for the unanimity with which each nation observes its own customs.[40] Thus the rigidity of ancestral traditions is found to be salutary, not insofar as it prevents conversion to the true faith, but insofar as it vindicates our freedom, and hence our freedom to choose our own religion.

Thus we come in Book 7 to that nation which has been favoured, not by coercion but by divine largesse, with the highest share of wisdom and the most equitable laws. The Hebrews understood (perhaps not only by revelation) that a cosmos so harmoniously ordered and populated by so many rational beings cannot have been the product of chance (7.3.1); rising above the worship of the tangible and visible which has enslaved the other nations, they also disenthralled themselves from their carnal appetites, dedicating themselves in body and soul to the knowledge and service of the Creator (7.4.1). By 'Hebrews' the Christian theologian means such men as Abel, Enoch, Noah, and Jacob, not the Jews who lived under the constitution of Moses (7.6; 7.8.5–18). His legislation taught them to honour God and spurn the devil, to shun idolatry and to cherish the image of God in the highest part of the soul. It taught that God was not light but the source of light (7.11.2; Genesis 1.3). To the Jewish philosophers Philo and Aristobulus it was evident that the scriptures testify to the existence of a second being,[41] the Wisdom or Word of God, through whom he exercises his powers of creation and governance, and after these to a third coadjutor, the Holy Spirit. Eusebius also relies primarily on Christian

[34] Edwards (2011), 231–2 suggests that Eusebius exaggerated the role of oracles in the persecution.

[35] *On the Decline of the Oracles* 414f–415b at *Preparation* 5.4

[36] Eusebius is the main source: *Preparation* 5.20–27; 5.32–36; 6.7.

[37] Cited again at 6.8. [38] *On Fate* 3–5 at *Preparation* 6.9.

[39] *Preparation* 6.11; cf. Origen, *Commentary on Genesis* 7.

[40] *Preparation* 6.10.1–48; cf. *Clementine Recognitions* 9.9–29.

[41] Philo, *Questions and Solutions* 1 at *Preparation* 7.13.1–2; Aristobulus at 7.14.1–2. Cf. 7.12.4 and 7.12.9.

exegetes—Dionysius of Alexandria,[42] Origen,[43] and Maximus[44]—to demonstrate that the matter from which the universe was fashioned is itself a creature of God, and that those who venerate idols are consequently denying the unity of the first cause.[45]

In the eighth book long excerpts from the letter of Aristeas bear witness both to the sanctity of the Hebrew scriptures and to the inspiration of the Greek version to which the Church has been wont to appeal since the time of the Evangelists (8.1.2–6). The superiority of the Jewish polity to every other is learnedly demonstrated by Josephus (8.8.1–55; *Against Apion* 2.163–228); since the Jews cling only to the husk of the Law, a spiritual reading of the dietary code, in which the status of foods is determined by symbolic rather than natural properties, is quoted from Aristeas (7.9.1–28). Philo is easily shown to have held that the purpose of the Law is to restrain the carnal appetites, not to encourage an addiction to outward forms; we cannot be sure, however, that he is the author of the passage which concludes this book, ostensibly from an otherwise unknown work of his *On Providence* which, in order to relieve God of the blame for adventitious evils, allows more to the play of chance than any prudent theist would concede.[46] The encomium of Moses and his people is completed in Book 9, where Porphyry bears witness to the frugality and fortitude of the Essenes,[47] Apollo (by way of Porphyry) to the purity of the Hebrew cult,[48] Hecataeus (by way of Josephus[49]) to their rejection of idolatry, Numenius to the antiquity of their teachings (9.6.9–8.3) and Aristobulus (through Clement) to the dependence of Plato on Moses (9.6.6–8). In excerpts from Artapanus, lifted bodily from the encyclopaedic work of Alexander Polyhistor, Joseph becomes the instructor of Egypt (9.23.23) and Moses the teacher of Orpheus (9.27.4); the same ensemble furnishes Eusebius with long passages from a dramatization of the life of Moses by Ezekiel the tragedian and a questionable exchange of letters between King Solomon and two eastern potentates (9.31.1–34.18).[50] In the tenth book Porphyry's testimony to the antiquity of the Jews is placed alongside those of Africanus, Clement, Josephus and Tatian;[51] another of his books, *On Plagiarism*, supports a more compendious charge of Greek

[42] Otherwise unknown excerpt from Dionysius, fl. 250, at *Preparation* 7.19.

[43] *Preparation* 7.20.

[44] *Preparation* 7.22. This text, attributed here to a second-century philosopher, is attributed to Origen at *Philokalia* 24, but also to Methodius.

[45] There is a dubious quotation from Philo to the same effect at 7.21.

[46] *Preparation* 8.53–56 acquits God of causing earthquakes.

[47] *On Abstinence* 2.26 (p. 155 Nauck) at *Preparation* 9.3.2–21.

[48] *Preparation* 7.10–25, again citing the *Philosophy from Oracles*.

[49] *Against Apion* 1.197–204 at *Preparation* 9.4.

[50] *Preparation* 9.28–29; cf. Jacobson (1983).

[51] Clement, *Stromateis* 6.4 at *Preparation* 10.10; Africanus at 10.10; Tatian, *Oration* 31 and 36–42 (modified) at 10.11.

indebtedness to the barbarians (10.3.1–25), which is further substantiated by the confessions of Plato, Democritus, and Diodorus Siculus. The arrogance of the Greeks will not survive a comparison of their alphabet with that of the Hebrews, which (as we have seen) was already in use before the Trojan War.

In accordance with the practice of Greek apologists since Justin, Eusebius proceeds in Book 11 to circumstantial proof of the agreement between the philosophies of Greece and that of Moses.[52] Plato is allowed to stand for all, and the choice is justified by pagan affidavits to his eminence;[53] yet even the division of philosophy into ethics, physics, and logic for which Atticus extols him was anticipated by Moses (11.4.4–5). In his ethical legislation Moses laid the foundation of virtue by his universal precepts, from which he advanced by reason to particular applications. His superiority to Plato in the science of logic is shown by his use of names to designate the essence of what they signify—a project of which Plato had merely dreamed in the *Cratylus*.[54] Thus the names of Adam and his progeny betoken our present weakness and the necessity of redemption (11.8.8–41); their Greek equivalents, according to Plato's etymology, convey an overweening sense of our closeness to the divine. Physics, the third division of philosophy, is encapsulated in the writings of Solomon which presuppose a more ancient and more authoritative cosmogony than that of the *Timaeus*.[55] This text draws a famous antithesis between that which is always in process of becoming and that of which we can only say that it is, not that it was or will be (11.9.4; *Timaeus* 27d–28a); for Moses, long before Plato, the eternity of God was expressed in his name, 'I am that I am' (11.9.3; Exodus 3.14). Plato's belief that that which truly is must be eternal and immutable is illustrated by extracts from Numenius (11.10) and Plutarch;[56] the heirs of Plato—Numenius and Plotinus among them[57]—were also aware that his letters had alluded to a second God after the first. David had spoken likewise of a second Lord, distinct from the first,[58] and Philo had identified this lieutenant as the Word, or supernal image, of the Father (11.15.2; *Confusion of Tongues* 24). The Platonist Amelius was acquainted with this Word and his incarnation (11.19.1–3); Porphyry, his contemporary, is a witness to Plato's doctrines on the immateriality of the true heaven (11.37) and the immortality of the human soul (11.33), both of which can be shown (with Philo's assistance) to have been

[52] Kalligas (2001) suggests that the materials for this book came from the library of Longinus the philosopher.

[53] Atticus at 11.2; Aristocles at 11.3: both extracts are known only from Eusebius.

[54] At *Preparation* 1.6.2–7 Eusebius cites *Cratylus* 353a, 390a, 396d-e, and 409 d-e.

[55] *Preparation* 11.7.4–6 cites Wisdom 7.17–21 and Ecclesiastes 1.2; 11.9.3 cites Ecclesiastes 1.9.

[56] *On the E at Delphi* 391f–393b at *Preparation* 11.11.

[57] Numenius at 11.18.22; Plotinus, *Enneads* 5.1.6 at *Preparation* 11.17.8, citing Plato, *Second Letter* 312e.

[58] Psalm 110.1 at *Preparation* 11.14.3; cf. Psalm 33.6 at 11.14.8.

prefigured in the Mosaic scriptures (11.24–27). It will also have been from Moses that Plato learned of the just and infallible tribunal which awaits the soul after death.

Further plagiarisms, documented in Book 12, include the tale of the birth of Eros in the garden of Aphrodite—clearly an echo of the Mosaic account of Paradise—the description of a primaeval state of innocence in the *Statesman* and the reference in the *Laws* to the destruction of humanity by the Flood.[59] Socrates purloins a biblical metaphor when he likens philosophy to midwifery in the *Theaetetus*;[60] the Stranger who recommends in the *Laws* that the ideal city should be far from the sea is clearly aware of the situation of Jerusalem (12.48; *Laws* 704b–705b). But Plato is an ally as well as a thief, for he equates righteousness with faith (or at lest with faithfulness), displays the same contempt for political office which was often regarded as a vice in Christians and proposes to replace the lewd songs of Homer with odes to virtue and the praises of just men (12.20; *Laws* 659a–660a).[61] This dream had already been realized in the psalms and canticles of the Old Testament, which were set to music as austere as any that Plato would have prescribed, without the theatrical accompaniments that he rightly deprecated. In Book 13 his satires on the popular theology of the Greeks are reproduced with approbation,[62] and Socrates, who voluntarily goes to his death in the *Crito* as a victim of superstition, is said to exemplify the scriptural truism that we ought to seek the glory of God and not the praise of mortals (13.6; Crito 46b–48a). Clement's demonstration of the harmony between Plato and the scriptures is juxtaposed with the claims of Aristobulus for the priority of Moses (13.120).[63] Yet Plato differs from Moses, and thus falls into error, when he enjoins the worship of the heavenly bodies,[64] countenances sodomy,[65] permits women to fight in wars and strip for exercise,[66] and teaches that the soul after death will inhabit another body (13.16).

Such aberration is typical of the Greeks, who, as Eusebius shows in his fourteenth book, made a point of betraying their teachers and of being at variance in their opinions. A whole treatise was devoted by Numenius to the wilful improvisations and apostasies of Plato's own disciples (14.4.16–14.9.3);

[59] *Symposium* 203b-c at preparation 12.11.2; *Statesman* 271e–272b at 12.13.2; *Laws* 677a–c at 12.15.32.

[60] *Preparation* 12.45, citing *Theaetetus* 151a and Isaiah 26.17.

[61] *Preparation* 1.9.3, citing *Republic* 346e–347a.

[62] *Timaeus* 40d–41a at *Preparation* 13.1 (but cf. 2.7.1–7); *Epinomis* 980c at 13.2; *Republic* 377c–383c at 13.3; *Euthyphro* 5e–6c at 13.4.

[63] Lilla (1971) remains the standard work on Clement and the Platonic Tradition, though he sometimes forgets that Clement was a Christian.

[64] *Epinomis* 977a and 984d-e at *Preparation* 13.8.2–3.

[65] *Phaedrus* 255b–d at *Preparation* 13.20.1.

[66] *Laws* 804c–e and 813b at 13.19.3–5.

the unanimity of the Hebrew scriptures is a mark of veracity, just as the discord of the Greek schools subverts their pretensions to knowledge. Plutarch records a cacophony of opinions on the origin of the universe and the nature of the gods.[67] According to an encyclopaedic diatribe by Aristocles, Parmenides teaches us to distrust the senses (14.17.10), Protagoras to trust nothing else (14.20.1), Aristippus to admit only the reality of feeling (14.19) and the Sceptics to admit no truth whatsoever (14.18). The dissolute Epicureans, making pleasure the test of the good life, hold that even the gods are idle (14.21). By contrast, the scriptures teach us that God is always working, though without the pain and fatigue that his creatures suffer.[68] The fifteenth recapitulates the errors of those philosophies which are opposed to Platonism. Atticus, a faithful student of Plato, shows that Aristotle contradicts not only Moses but his own master in banishing providence, in affirming the eternity of the world, in positing a fifth element, in denying the transcendence of the eternal forms and in holding the soul to be inseparable from the body (15.4–9; 15.13). The absurdity of Aristotle's notion of the soul as entelechy is demonstrated by Plotinus in a version of the *Enneads* which is not that of Porphyry.[69] The latter, however, joins forces with his master not only on this point, but against the Stoics, who falsely suppose that even God is a body and that properties which rightly pertain to the soul could have been engendered by a fortuitous concourse of atoms. (15.19–22) The other philosophers are represented by an inventory of conflicting propositions on the nature of soul, the origin of matter, the phases of the moon, the constitution of the stars, and other topics too abstruse (as Moses knew) for our comprehension. After a lesson from Xenophon on the humility of Socrates,[70] two epigrams by the satirist Timon concludes the whole work and ensures that a sense of dissonance will prevail (15.62.14–15).

CONCLUSION

Theologians and historians of dogma are apt to be disappointed by the *Preparation for the Gospel*. It was written, of course, for neither, though the author's other works prove that he was capable of fencing with the ablest theologians of his day. The *Preparation* is better read as an essay in

[67] Properly pseudo-Plutarch, *On the Tenets of the Philosophers* 875d–878a at *Preparation* 14.14.
[68] *Preparation* 14.27, again citing an otherwise unknown text by Dionysius of Alexandria.
[69] *Preparation* 15.10: see Chapter 3, this volume.
[70] *Memorabilia* 1.1.11–16 at *Preparation* 15.62.1–6.

comparative religion, half eirenic and half didactic in the style of the nineteenth century. Recently it has been studied as an essay in the ethnography of religion—aptly enough, since when the Greeks wrote accounts of other peoples they often commenced with a description of their gods. As Aaron Johnson has noted,[71] Eusebius differentiates *genos* and *ethnos*: the *genos*, or race, is defined by consanguinity, whereas the members of an *ethnos*, for which perhaps the best term is 'nation', may be united by shared speech and culture rather than bonds of kinship. For Eusebius the Jews are a *genos*; the *ethnê*, in biblical usage, are the rest of the world's population who are not of the chosen people. The plasticity of nomenclature is exemplified, however, by the term 'Hellene', which at its narrowest denotes those who are Greeks by descent and at its widest all who are Greek by culture. In Matthew's gospel Christ predicts that the patrimony of Israel will be given to a new ethnos, which is evidently the church; that Christians were a third race, *tertium genus*, was a commonplace—though maybe a pagan rather than a Christian one[72]—by the end of the second century. We observed above that certain apologists, mocking Greek pretensions to a monopoly of wisdom, had taken a pride in the name barbarian; on the other hand, pagans like Porphyry and Lucian could boast simultaneously of their Greek education and their barbarian ancestry. Eusebius has no desire to pass as a barbarian: he flaunts his erudition in the hope of convincing his readers, believers and unbelievers alike, that everyone can enjoy dual citizenship as a Greek by nurture and a Christian by faith.

The term 'citizenship' is apposite because Eusebius also follows Josephus, the Jewish historian, in representing Christianity as a *politeia*, a commonwealth of shared laws and values. All free-born subjects of the Roman Empire had been made citizens by the *Constitutio Antoniniana* of 215; many were also citizens of a local community by birth or purchase. In return for the questionable privileges of citizenship, the government required that the gods should be worshipped on demand according to Roman custom, but at the same time permitted, and even encouraged, the worship of other deities according to the custom of one's own fathers. Even the Jews were tolerated under this dispensation; toleration had not been extended to Christians during the period from Nero to Gallienus because they were deemed to have forsaken their ancestral cults for one which forbade compliance with the ordinances of Roman magistrates. Paul, a Roman citizen at a time when this was still a rare prerogative, had assured his disenfranchized readers that their *politeia* was in

[71] Johnson (2006), 46–50. By contrast, Johnson (2013a), 265–71 construes Porphyry's treatise *On Abstinence* as an exhortation to adopt every dietary restriction that is observed by the wise men of other nations, with the inevitable result that one will abstain from all eating of meat.

[72] Harnack (1908), 266–78.

heaven (Philippians 3.21); another had reminded them that they had no abiding city in this world (Hebrew 13.14). When the preparation was published, half of the Roman commonwealth at least was under the sway of a Christian ruler; the use of the term *politeia* in this work implies that Christians have a right to hope, not only for relief from judicial terrors but for the gathering of all nations under the temporal dominion of the church.

2

Latin Apologists and Roman Culture

Eusebius yields in eloquence, though not in scholarship, to his Latin contemporaries Arnobius and Lactantius. Both at some time made a profession of rhetoric though Arnobius, the teacher, wields his pen with a truculent vigour that often tempts him into bombast, whereas Lactantius, the pupil, seldom departs from the orotund style that earned him his reputation as the Christian Cicero. They wrote for a Latin world in which Euhemerism, the theory that the gods were deified men, had not only been canonized by Ennius but verified by the legends surrounding Romulus,[1] the founder of Rome, and by the posthumous elevation of a succession of emperors. The same audience had also learned from Virgil, Horace, and Ovid that an inexpiable sin had bedevilled Rome since her foundation, repeatedly driving her into civil war at home and ignominy abroad. Rome's magistrates professed to be upholding the way of the fathers to whom they traced both the prosperity of the city and its distempers; at the same time, the superior antiquity of Greek culture was offset by the boasts of one poet after another who proclaimed himself the first to translate some Greek form into Latin. The champions of Latin Christendom, thoroughgoing Euhemerists with regard to every religion but one, professed to see no virtue in patriotism or in fidelity to the customs of any human ancestor. Making no great show of their African origins, they are Romans only in their disdain for everything that is not Roman, and in their eyes Rome herself is guilty of all that she disdains. Against the civic idolatry of the dead they could set their own divine man; against the universal sin of the nations they could set the perfect righteousness exhibited by this man and his disciples; against the atavistic pride of Rome and the interminable wrangling of the Greek schools they could set a new pattern of thought and conduct, all the more cogent because it had not been shaped by some inveterate history of use and wont.

[1] See now Winiarczyk (2013), though at 119–21 he concludes that Lactantius did not make direct use of Ennius; translation. Cf. Canfora (1993), 319–21.

LACTANTIUS AND THE *DIVINE INSTITUTES*

The one source of biographical information about Lactantius apart from his writings is a lapidary notice in Jerome's treatise *On Famous Men*. This tells us only that he was an African and a pupil of Arnobius, that at Diocletian's summons he became a teacher of rhetoric in Nicomedia, and that for want of students (*penuria discipulorum*) writing became his principal occupation. Jerome lists a number of works, the majority of which are lost, and adds that in extreme old age Lactantius held the post of tutor to Constantine's son Crispus. Since Crispus was an adult by 323, we may infer that Lactantius had passed the average span of human life before 320, and must therefore have been born in the middle of the third century. In his own works he names neither his birthplace nor his tutor, but alludes to the exercise in pleading imaginary cases which was imposed on him as a student of rhetoric in his adolescence. He records that he witnessed the suffering of Christians in Bithynia after the publication of Diocletian's edicts against the church; confident assertions that he was converted to Christianity by this spectacle have no foundation in any ancient testimony.[2]

The date of his magnum opus, the *Divine Institutes*, is equally elusive. Constantine is saluted in the first book as the successor to his father, and as a Christian, but with no indication that he is yet sole emperor. It is widely held today that the *Divine Institutes* of Lactantius passed through two editions, the first of which was complete before the end of the Great Persecution in 311, while the second was begun, but not completed, after Constantine had defeated his last rival in 324.[3] Unfortunately, these conjectures rest upon a fragile chain of inferences. It is far from clear, for example, that the passages which are said to show that Galerius was still living do imply this;[4] on the other hand, a passage celebrating the overthrow of a tyrant is as likely to have been inspired by the death of Maximinus Daia in 313 as by that of Licinius in 324.[5] The only persecution to which clear reference is made in the *Divine Institutes* is the one initiated in 303 by Diocletian and Galerius, whose western colleague Maximian is portrayed as their willing accomplice in the treatise *On the Deaths of the Persecutors*. Maximian and Diocletian abdicated in 305, but Maximian returned to rule jointly, though unconstitutionally, with his son Maxentius, and subsequently with Constantine himself. The latter, on discovering in 310 that Maximian was plotting against his life, put him to death; within a year Diocletian and Galerius had expired of natural causes. From 311

[2] In his introduction to *Deaths of the Persecutors* (Bibliography A), 76–7 Städele wisely declines to imitate the speculations of Wlosok (1989), 378–80.

[3] Heck (1972) is the seminal study.

[4] Barnes (1981a), 291 n. 96 cites *Divine Institutes* 5.11.5 and 5.23.1.

[5] Moreau, in his edition of *Deaths of the Persecutors* (Bibliography A), 19–20 maintains that Maximinus was not remembered by the Christians as a tyrant; this argument presupposes Piganiol's dating of the *Oration to the Saints* to 323 (see Chapter 9, this volume).

onwards, it would therefore have been possible for a Christian to celebrate the deaths of all the original persecutors; after the conversion of Constantine in 312, it was obvious to any student of the ways of providence that his victories had been achieved with divine assistance in the interests of the church.

In the preface to the *Divine institutes* Lactantius introduces himself as an orator who, after many years of pleading imaginary cases, has resolved to put his talents at the service of philosophy, in order to impart to his readers the knowledge of God which multitudes seek in vain. In a manner that is typically Roman, he argues that the Greeks who have preceded him in this inquiry have achieved more renown in philosophy than in rhetoric; and yet there can be no better subject for eloquence than the nature of the gods and the world, for only such knowledge can teach us the ends of life. For readers who knew their Cicero and Quintilian, it will already have been a commonplace that the true orator unites the art of speaking well with the art of living well. In the preface to his fifth book Lactantius presents himself as a second Quintilian, whose aim is to produce not merely a Christian apology but a manual of good practice which will enable his successors to surpass the flawed though noble exercises of Tertullian, Minucius Felix, and Cyprian of Carthage (5.1). In this preface, as in that of the first book, Constantine is saluted as the first emperor to have renounced the absurdities of polytheism.

These errors are propagated by the poets and upheld in the pagan school. Orpheus divined that there was only one God, yet in contrast to the Hebrew prophets (1.4), neither he nor any of the philosophers dared to proclaim that the Creator of the world must be greater than any material element (1.5). The task of a Christian orator is to rekindle the light of reason which has been obscured by the customs of the state. It is obvious folly to worship things that can neither make nor preserve themselves, and it ought to be equally obvious to the citizens of an empire that no polity as vast and heterogeneous as the cosmos could remain at peace unless it were governed by a single will (1.3). The origins of the gods are revealed by myths which relate that Hercules and Aesculapius were sons of mortal women (1.10), while Jove himself (the putative father of Hercules) has a tomb in Crete and was hidden as an infant on the same island so that he might not be eaten by his father Saturn (1.11). The poets may have embroidered their traditions, but cannot have invented everything (1.11), and Christians are not the first to lift the veil that the priests hold up between us and the golden age when Saturn was king. We owe to Lactantius a number of our few surviving testimonies to the lost work of Euhemerus, a romancer of the fourth century BC, who pretended that on an imaginary island he had discovered a pillar dedicated to Zeus and preserving a catalogue of the births and deaths of many of those beings who passed for gods among the Greeks and other nations.[6] The Euhemeristic theory had already

[6] See Winiarczyk (2013).

coalesced in the works of Christian apologists with another account of the origins of false religion, derived from the Book of Enoch. This text, often treated as scriptural in the second century, recorded the fall to earth of certain angels who had been tempted by the beauty of mortal women. Determined to involve their seducers in their own ruin, these demons (as they now became) set about the invention of all the arts most pernicious to humanity. For Justin these included the erection of shrines to imaginary deities, and Athenagoras added that the demons concealed their role by naming the statues in these shrines after rulers and benefactors whom the world did indeed have a duty to honour. When he takes up this theory in his second book, Lactantius notes that the angels who fell had been appointed as guardians to the nations (2.15): the promotion of false religion is thus a breach of trust, no doubt to be compared with that of governors who exceeded the royal mandate in their harassment of the church.

Rather than mitigate the improbability of Christ's birth by likening it to that of Hercules, Lactantius protests that the services of Hercules to humanity cannot be ranked with those of Christ (1.9). Hercules was by common consent what Jupiter becomes in the Latin rendering of Euhemerus,[7] a mortal deified in the imagination of posterity. Elizabeth Digeser argues that in Jupiter the reader was intended to see Diocletian, who had taken the epithet Jovius, and in Hercules his western colleague Maximianus Herculius.[8] This is likely enough: Lactantius indicates by his frequent appeals to Constantine that, while he was avowedly writing for all times, he had not lost sight of his own. On the other hand, not every reader of the *Institutes* detects a particular animus against Hercules and Jupiter, who in any case were sure to figure prominently in a representative skit on the myths and institutions of the Roman world. Nor can it be proved that even the first book of the *Institutes* was composed before the voluntary abdication of Diocletian and Maximian in 305. What is certainly true in Digeser's thesis is that this was an age in which the theory that all gods had once been mortals would commend itself with unusual force to a Christian apologist. It is widely held that one object of Euhemerus was to justify the worship of living monarchs, a new phenomenon of the Hellenistic era.[9] This rationale was turned on its head when Christians were forced to sacrifice to imaginary deities by their living representatives: if it is plainly monstrous, they urged, to treat a living man as a god, it is heaping folly on sacrilege to raise altars to those who have shown themselves to be mortal. As emperors started to persecute the church in the mid-third century, this argument served as the

[7] Ogilvie (1978), 50–7 notes that all allusions to Euhemerus in Lactantius concern Jupiter and proposes that a commentary on Aratus is more likely to have been his source than the prose translation of Euhemerus by Ennius.

[8] Digeser (2000), 17–32, citing *Latin Panegyrics* 10.11.6, 8.4.1–2, and 11.3.4.

[9] Brown (1946).

cornerstone of Cyprian's tract *On the Vanity of Idols*. It was answered in kind by Porphyry, who professed to have learned from an oracle that Christ was worthy of all the honours due to a sage but was not, in any loftier sense, divine.[10] A demonstration of Christ's superiority to Hercules was the best rebuttal of Porphyry—all the more so as it was a Roman trope, with a famous model in Lucretius' panegyric on Epicurus at the beginning of the fifth book of his poem *On the Nature of Things*.[11] Nevertheless, the unmasking of paganism is not in itself a vindication of Christianity: when Epicurus is praised as a god by his Roman disciple Lucretius, the accolade is plainly hyperbolic, and lends no sanction to the cult of Mary's son as second person of the Trinity. Lactantius meets this objection elsewhere in the *Institutes* by attempting to show that Lucretius the poet is wiser than Lucretius the philosopher and testifies in spite of himself to the immortality of the human soul.[12]

Lactantius admits in the *Epitome* of his *Institutes* that temples have also been erected to Concord, Faith, and Peace.[13] Nevertheless, the true image of virtue, he contends, is to be found in the living adept, not in an anthropomorphic sculpture which profanes the image of God. The philosophers, had they but courage, are natural allies of the Christians, since the majority of them perceive that if the gods are to govern the world, they cannot be confined to one locality or limited by corporeal attributes. The Epicureans differ in believing that the gods inhabit a realm of their own, untroubled by the flux of the lower elements; but they are rightly abhorred by the other schools, since they alone have failed to deduce from the beauty and harmony of the cosmos that it must be the work of rational beings who have some care for its denizens. Once we have grasped that the word 'god' implies the exercise of providence, it will be clear that there can be only one such being, since anyone who reflects can see what anarchy would ensue if each god ruled one place or element as a private fief in constant enmity to all the rest.[14] The best of the philosophers are those who acknowledge, with Plato, that god is one and the world is his creation. Aristotelians go astray in teaching that the world has no beginning in time (2.10.17), and Stoics in denying the incorporeality of God (1.17; 2.5.28–42). All the schools are at fault in that they encourage us to squander our talents in barren feats of logic, or in useless investigation of the

[10] Augustine, *City of God* 19.23. Digeser (2000) maintains that the *Divine Institutes* was conceived as a refutation of Porphyry; Schott (2013a), 87 remarks neatly that while Lactantius had read the same works as the pagan controversialist, his books must have been arranged in a different order.

[11] Lucretius, *On the Nature of Things* 1.62–79; 5.22–54. At *Institutes* 3.14 Lactantius cites panegyrics on Epicurus from 5.6–8 and 5.30–31.

[12] *Institutes* 7.12, citing Lucretius 3.417–418 and 440–442 as testimonies to the separability and survival of the human soul after death.

[13] *Epitome* 11; cf. *Institutes* 1.20.24. F.

[14] *Institutes* 1.3, 1.5.23, 4.29.12, 5.14.13.

mysteries that God has hidden from us: as every Roman knew, and many Greeks under Roman tutelage, the only fruitful science that philosophers teach is ethics, since to understand the norms of conduct and the ends of life is to understand all that is necessary to our salvation.[15]

Cicero had boasted that, whereas the Greeks could only dream of governing better than they were governed, the founder of Rome had established the closest approximation to an ideal commonwealth that can be sustained on earth.[16] Polybius, the Greek historian, had attributed the longevity of Roman institutions to a shrewd combination of magisterial and religious offices.[17] Lactantius, judging Christianity by the same criteria, maintains that the pretensions of Rome, which were mere pretensions before the advent of Christ, have now been realized in the church. Only in this new polity does religion acquire the wisdom of philosophy and philosophy the strength of true religion. Among the Greeks strict morality and practical conduct were never reconciled. Carneades (an infamous casuist, driven from Rome because of his facile tongue) had argued that a man who is just in Plato's eyes will prove himself a fool in worldly affairs by shirking legitimate chances to overreach his neighbour (5.17); his criticism is salutary, Lactantius tells us, not because it is sound, but because it shows that the higher principles of rectitude will always remain theoretical while they lack the support of religion. Cicero, an abler and more honourable philosopher than most Greeks, had upheld the most stringent precepts in his ethical works, but his religious scepticism left him stumbling to a wretched death after years of tergiversation (6.18). The Ciceronian view of the gods (personified by the pagan speaker in the *Octavius* of Minucius Felix[18]) was that, since we know nothing of them, we must worship them in the way prescribed by our ancestors, to whom the state owes its greatness. To this Lactantius rejoins that there is more to greatness than the spoliation of peaceful territories and the unjust subjugation of their inhabitants. As for the way of the fathers, it is not so old, as even the earliest Roman institutions date from no more than three centuries before the Trojan War (1.23; *Epitome* 37). In any case, customs held without reason and maintained by torture have no claim on our reverence. The oppression of Christians cannot tame the conscience though it may induce compliance in behaviour; it cannot even thin the ranks of the church, since she provides measures for the reconciliation of the lapsed in the aftermath of persecution. If the defence of piety is the goal, why does the rigour of the law not fall on the superstitious Egyptians or the atheistic Epicureans, Lactantius asks with his usual trick of naming groups whom Rome's best writers have taught her to despise (5.12–15).

[15] See especially *Institutes* 6.18.
[16] *On the Commonwealth* 1.21.
[17] Polybius, *Histories* 6.56.
[18] *Octavius* 6.

In early Christian literature it was a commonplace that two paths are set before us, one leading to life and the other to death.[19] Pagans, as Lactantius reminds them, had frequently encountered the same motif in the works of poets and philosophers (6.3.1). Here he is alluding on the one hand to Homeric and Orphic descriptions of the underworld, and on the other to Prodicus' fable of the choice of Heracles, the Pythagorean tablet of Cebes and the peroration to Plato's *Gorgias*.[20] The philosophers, in his view, fall short of the poets, because for them the two ways represent conditions that can be realized in the present world, such as vice and virtue, unease and happiness, lassitude and labour (6.3.2–5). Those who deny the immortality of the soul have no expectation of rewards and punishments in a future life as an incentive to righteous conduct in the present one; those who, like Plato, ascribe the immortality of the soul to its natural properties rather than to the will of God, will not believe, as readers of the scriptures do, in an everlasting heaven and hell, but only in a ceaseless alternation of woe and felicity as the soul migrates from one temporary domicile to another (7.8). That there will none the less be a final judgment of all, assigning each soul to its unchangeable abode, is the witness not only of the scriptures but of the Sibyl[21]—or rather of numerous Sibyls, whose names have been made familiar to the Roman world by Varro, its greatest antiquarian (1.6.6–10). Some of the poets have erred on this matter, but even Lucretius, the eloquent mouthpiece of Epicurus, betrays a sounder knowledge of the divine in occasional utterances.[22] When, on the other hand, Virgil's *Fourth Eclogue* celebrates the birth of a miraculous child who will usher in the new age foretold by the Sibyl, he had evidently received some inspiration, since there is only one child of whom he can be speaking (7.24.11–15). The sinless example of the incarnate Word, combined with his infallible assurances of a future life, enables Christians to take the strait path that has eluded the philosophers. By this faith one abstains not merely from sin but from the contemplation of it, not only from murder as the Roman law defines it but from abortion and infanticide, not only from fraud but from all forms of mendacity, not only from the invasion of another man's conjugal property but from all violations of the marital bond. Virtue in a philosopher is personal integrity; in the elect it is self-abandonment and universal benevolence. They will succour the weak, protect the innocent, and redeem the captive at the cost of any sacrifice; they will not be pious only by permission, but will readily give their lives for the glory of God.[23]

[19] Aldridge (1999).
[20] Xenophon, *Memorabilia* 2.1; Trapp (1997); Plato, *Gorgias* 527e.
[21] *Institutes* 7.8–20, 23.4, and 24.1–6.
[22] Institutes 7.12.26, citing Lucretius 3.612–614.
[23] Paraphrasing *Institutes* 6.20 and 7.27.

For Lactantius Christianity is *vera religio*, 'true religion', and indeed God's own religion, *religio dei* or *religio divina*. Rival practice is *religio falsa*, all the more so when it sets up shrines to many gods and pollutes them with innocent blood. In his deservedly famous book, *The Meaning and End of Religion*,[24] Wilfred Cantwell Smith maintains that in classical usage *religio* had no plural because it denoted not a particular way of worship but propriety in worship, to be contrasted with the aberrant practices which fell under the name of *superstitio*. *Religio* thus has a normative force like that which English once accorded to the noun 'religion' and still accords to 'piety', 'godliness', or 'morality'. A cult that was not Roman might be denounced as a superstition or commended as another form of *religio*, but would not be characterized as a second *religio* beside that of the Roman people. When 'religion' has this sense, the addition of the word true is at worst redundant, at best emphatic, but never descriptive. When Lactantius sets true religion against false religion, according to Smith, we see the germ of the modern, and purportedly scientific, notion that each society has its own religion, so that Islam is for the Arabs what Christianity is in Europe or Hinduism in India. Since Lactantius makes no pretence to impartiality, and never doubts the uniquely prescriptive character of his own religion, his direct heirs today are the 'exclusivists', who assert that their own religion is superior to all others; perhaps he also stands in an avuncular relation to the deists, who believed that they could winnow the false from the true in all the religions of the world.

As a thesis about the use of the Latin plural, this is easily refuted from a writing by Lactantius himself, of which Smith takes no account. In the treatise *On the Deaths of the Persecutors*, he republishes a number of edicts in which the pagan emperors protest their solicitude for the 'public religions' (11.6: *religionum publicarum*) and their desire to render what is due to 'each religion' (48. 6: *cuiquam religioni*) as a reason for their measures against 'that religion' (11.3: *ea religio*) which is disturbing the peace of the Empire. Lactantius, for his part, never admits a plurality of religions, and does not even credit his persecutors with a 'false religion';[25] the only creed to which he extends the term is Christianity, the 'divine religion' or the 'religion of God'. It may be that the use of the noun *religio* in the plural was an innovation of the Tetrarchic era, and that Lactantius characteristically adheres to the older custom of using it only in the singular, in order to demonstrate that Christianity is more Roman in spirit than the laws which are passed for its extirpation.[26]

[24] Smith (1978). See further Hughes (1986).

[25] As Smith (1978), 27–8 observes. When Lactantius speaks of 'false religion', he means a false show of religion, not a system of false belief.

[26] Schott (2013a), 79–109 regards Lactantius as the architect of a new and tendentious history of religions, which he bequeathed to Constantine.

Smith's argument would hold good for the earlier period if the absence of the plural *religiones*—and of any Greek equivalent to *religio,* whether singular or plural—had prevented ancient authors from acknowledging a plurality of religions in the modern sense; in fact, however, both pagan and Christian authors, for centuries before Lactantius, had been conscious of the diversity of beliefs and customs regarding the gods among the *ethnê* or races of the world. What they may have lacked before the rise of Christianity is the notion of religion as a portable system of beliefs and practices, not bound to any larger ensemble of values and allegiances, and therefore not hereditary or peculiar to one people, but open to neophytes from every people within or outside the empire. Or rather, we should say not that were ignorant of such systems, but that they knew them as philosophies rather than cults. While the noun *philosophia* also has no plural, anyone who donned the philosopher's cloak was bound to choose one from a number of schools, without denying that those who made a different choice had a right to wear this garment.[27] In the second century, as Christians began to eschew the term *ethnos* in favour of *philosophia*, they argued not that theirs was the sole philosophy, but that theirs was the truest, the first, the most comprehensive and the one from which the others had surreptitiously imbibed what they knew of God.

Philosophy in the ancient world was licensed nonconformity, a mandate to live and think as others did not. Thus a Pythagorean like Apollonius of Tyana could go about denouncing animal sacrifices; philosophers could find half a dozen reasons not to marry without being treated as enemies of society; within limits that they often chose to exceed, they were permitted to speak more frankly than others in the presence of the emperor. Christians, on the other hand, were put to death for refusing to scatter incense, for breaking up marriages and for slighting the cult of the emperor. Pagan critics retorted that it was not enough to die like a philosopher unless one had lived and thought as a philosopher: by conceiving his work as an 'institution', of educative manual, rather than a mere apology, Lactantius undertook to meet this charge more comprehensively than any of his Latin predecessors. One stratagem, embraced by Greek apologists long before him, is to argue that the schools are irremediably divided, and that only a voice from above can put an end to their logomachies. He points out—in a manner calculated to touch the Romans whom he is belabouring with quotations from their own libraries—that Cicero would have been a greater man had his conduct been of a piece with the moral principles that he endorses in his writings (6.18.27). Cicero's frailties are almost pardonable because he had no example to follow:[28] now,

[27] Snyder (2000).

[28] Lactantius is inverting the quip of Juvenal, *Satires* 10.110–112 that if Cicero's prose had been as bad as his verse he would not have suffered proscription.

however, Christ has shown the world that it is possible not only to preach perfection but to make it a rule of life (*Institutes* 5.24).

We should not infer from his lack of dogmatic rigour in apologetic writing that Lactantius was either a novice in theology or a latitudinarian in spirit. Eusebius as a historian and biographer extols the unanimity of the bishops in the castigation of heresy; in his *Preparation for the Gospel* and *Demonstration of the Gospel* he proves the Trinity from scripture, but it is only in his writings against Marcellus of Ancyra that he contests the nicer points of exegesis. Even the work of Athanasius *On the Incarnation*, of which more will be said in the final chapter, offers only an oblique reply to the Arians whom he refutes at length in his controversial writings. If we cannot expect Lactantius to surpass the two most eminent theologians of his day in the precision of his teaching, we should also hesitate before claiming him as an early proponent of religious toleration. Writing as one who had shared the fears of an imperilled minority, he of course takes up the argument of Justin and Tertullian that no government should persecute loyal subjects merely because they differ in creed. It is also true, as Elizabeth Digeser argues, that he thought it impossible for a rational intellect to resist the light of the gospel, and thus could have held that other religions would die for want of fodder once the church was free to preach.[29] We must remember, however, that when a sect acquires the power to avenge itself on its former persecutors it often ceases to regard tolerance as a virtue. The recorded measures of Constantine against pagan cults were desultory, and the *Oration to the Saints* offers plentiful evidence of his familiarity with the writings of Lactantius. Nevertheless, we shall see in Chapter 9 that this speech is a belligerent vindication of Christianity, in which the legality of other cults is only satirically acknowledged. The scanty information at our disposal does not permit us to say that Constantine ever spared a cult that he might have suppressed with impunity; if we can be almost certain that he did not set out to extinguish paganism, we can be absolutely certain that he could not have extinguished it had he set out to do so. In fact, when we bring his own words under scrutiny, it will be clear that he was not so much unwilling as unable to establish the monopoly to which the more ardent of his co-religionists aspired.

THE DEATHS OF THE PERSECUTORS

The treatise *On the Deaths of the Persecutors* is the most detailed narrative by a contemporary of the policy of the Tetrarchs and the series of wars and

[29] Digeser (2000), 111, citing *Institutes* 5.4.8.

accidents which eliminated every western rival to Constantine.[30] Historians have no choice but to make use of it, but to suppose that any dispute could be finally settled by appeal to its testimony is to overlook the difference between historiography and propaganda. Even the most objective writers of history in the ancient world are rhetoricians, for whom events are interesting as illustrations of some general law and written sources are no more to be retained in the final draft than a sculptor's chisel in the statue. Lactantius, for his part, writes with an avowed theological motive that precludes even the most cosmetic pretence of objectivity: no transaction has a place in his scheme unless it proves that a wretched death is the inevitable reward of the persecutor or reveals the hand of God behind some intrigue which brought Constantine a step nearer to the throne. Thus Constantine's assumption of the purple in 306, an act of dubious legality,[31] is treated as the assertion of a right (18–19), and is said to have been succeeded at once by measures in favour of Christians which are not recorded by any other witness. An alliance with Maximian, former Augustus of the west, is dissolved, according to Lactantius, when Maximian conspires against Constantine, is outwitted, and suffers the capital penalties that his actions clearly merited (29–30); even as his encomiast tells the story, Constantine is guilty of causing the death of a slave by substituting the slave for himself in his bedroom. Maxentius, son of Maximian and de facto ruler of Rome from 306 to 312, is caricatured as arrogant despot, who showed no reverence even to his father Maximian, let alone to Constantine, his father-in-law (26); the slaughter of Maxentius with his 30,000 troops, which tested the eloquence of Constantine's panegyrists at the time, is here depicted as a condign visitation of wrath on a usurper who had read his doom in the sacred books of Rome (44.7–9).

Licinius, who was still an ally of Constantine when the work was written, is also painted in favourable colours. Although he was installed in 308 as the successor to Severus, and hence Augustus of the west (29.3), his struggle with Maximinus is represented as the result of the latter's aggression, notwithstanding the plausible claim of Maximinus to be the one legitimate heir of Galerius in the eastern provinces (43; 45.1). The repeal of persecution by Galerius, which ends with a perfunctory command that prayers should be said for his health by Christians,[32] is construed as an admission of guilt, occasioned by a wasting disease that proved to be fatal and hence (by Christian logic) providential (34). In compensation for Diocletian's failure to die as

[30] For a defence of his veracity see Barnes (1973b), 44–6. Barnes argues for a date before 315 on the grounds that Lactantius makes no reference to the rupture between Licinius and Constantine in 316 (p. 38) and that an author writing later would have been more severe to Maxentius but kinder to Maximian.

[31] See Humphries (2008), but cf. Barnes (2011), 89.

[32] *Deaths of the Persecutors* 33.11–35.1; cf. Eusebius, *Church History* 8.17, with Barnes (1976c), 189–90.

horribly as he ought to have done, Lactantius emphasizes, and perhaps exaggerates, the role of Galerius as instigator of the persecution;[33] as evidence of God's continuing enmity to the man whose name stood first in the edicts of 303, he can find no more to say than that Diocletian lived to witness the disfigurement of his own statues (42). On the principle that those who do not die well must be persecutors, he counts Aurelian as the third oppressor of the church, though in intention rather than act, as he was aware that Aurelian never issued edicts comparable to those of Decius and Valerian (6). We cannot say with confidence that he misrepresents Licinius, Galerius, Diocletian, or Aurelian, but we can say that his narrative is constructed as a drama—a Terentian comedy rather than a Sophoclean tragedy—in which the gods ensure that every character receives his true deserts.

MINOR WORKS OF LACTANTIUS

The short text *On the Workmanship of God* (*De Opificio Dei*) is perhaps the first Christian essay on protology—the doctrine of the first things—which does not take the form of a commentary on Genesis. It courts the attention of pagan, and of Christians with a liberal education, by assembling testimonies from classical authors to the godlike status of man among the animals. Others had adduced our upright stature as a token that we are formed to look up at the heavens,[34] but Lactantius may be the first to have drawn the whimsical corollary that man is the only creature who is able to lie on his back (9). In his character as a Christian, he adds that the human mind directs the body from the cranium as God directs the universe from heaven (16). The undivided presence of the mind in all our members, along with its unquenchable rapidity of motion which is not suspended even in sleep, suffice to prove its incorporeality; that it is a thing in itself, not merely the harmony of our members and bodily functions, is apparent from the fact that it is the author of its own motions, whereas the harmony of an instrument must be awoken by the musician (16). The senses, appointed as servants to the mind, never lie (9)—so far Lactantius goes with the Epicureans—and, so long as the mind itself remains incorrupt, will not mislead us. If the essence of the mind and its relation to the body are still unfathomed, how much more wonderful, says the Christian apologist, must be the nature of the God who creates the mind. The same God gave us sexual organs so that we might form chaste unions for the purpose of procreation; so long as this is granted, we may defer to the physiologists who tell us that feminine traits accrue to the masculine seed that

[33] Davies (1989). [34] Cicero, *On Laws* 1.26; Ovid, *Metamorphoses* 1.85.

is planted on the left side of the mother's womb and male traits to the feminine seed that is planted on the right (12). Again, the Christian does not need to ascertain whether soul and intellect (*anima* and *animus*) are one subject or two, so long as, in the spirit of Proverbs 30.19, he contemplate the work of God with reverence (17). The subtle adaptation of the parts to the whole in every creature refutes the Epicurean who holds that the world and its contents came into being by chance (6); philosophers of the opposite persuasion, on the other hand, may not be wrong in attributing the accidents of birth to the stars so long as they remember that the stars too have a Creator. Oneiromancy, or dream-divination, is tacitly excluded by Lactantius' observation (1500 years before Freud) that the function of nocturnal visions is to protect sleep (18). At the beginning of his peroration the 'Christian Cicero' acknowledges his master (20); he concludes none the less in a vein more Christian than Ciceronian, exclaiming that, void of eloquence as he is, he will not have lived in vain if he weans some fellow-mortals from their errors and sets them on the path to heaven.

Thus the Christian gilds the commonplaces of philosophy. The fall, unpalatable to all the schools, is ignored in this work; and yet Lactantius is not afraid to uphold a more unpalatable thesis in his essay *On the Wrath of God*. Wrath, for the philosophers, was an inward perturbation that the wise man would feel, if at all, only temporarily and in proportion to the offence. No perturbation is logically consistent with the necessary goodness and impassibility of an eternal being, as Celsus the pagan rhetorician had scoffed in his inventive against Christianity more than a century before.[35] Origen had replied that wrath is predicated of God by accommodation to our understanding; Lactantius prefers to argue that it is ascribed to him as properly as love. God's wrath, like his love, it is not a passion, in the sense of a commotion excited by external factors, but a disposition inalienably grounded in his omnipotence and foreknowledge. The argument is addressed, we are told at the outset, not to infidels of the first degree, who worship the elements and the effigies that their own hands carve from them, but to those of the second degree, who acknowledge one God but presume to know more of his nature than his own prophets. Of these the most commendable are the Stoics, who celebrate the benevolence of God but fail to perceive that he could not exhibit *gratia*, or mercy, unless there were some who had reason to fear his severity (5). It is in the nature of God to reward the good, but this would be no reward at all if the wicked were treated with equal lenity. To spare them is to remove the incentive to virtue, and thus to curtail the exercise of providence—in short, to make common cause with Epicurus, whose doctrine of divine impassibility was seen by the Greeks themselves to be atheism in disguise.[36]

[35] Origen, *Against Celsus* 71. [36] *Wrath* 4.7, 13, 17.1.

Lactantius characteristically cites Lucretius as the mouthpiece of Epicurus.[37] It is equally characteristic of him to borrow an anecdote from Cicero to illustrate the necessity of punishment: suppose that the head of a household were to overlook every iniquity committed by his slaves, even when they robbed him and murdered his family, he would not be admired for his clemency but censured for his negligence.[38] The philosophers say justly enough that he will not feel anger as an inward commotion, as we do: Cicero is again his unnamed source when he recollects that the Pythagorean Archytas once refrained from beating a slave because he knew that his anger would compromise the justice of his action.[39] Scripture too, Lactantius observes forbids us to let the sun go down on our anger; it follows, not that God feels no indignation when we sin, but that his indignation will not exceed the sin or linger after our repentance. The cause of sin is the frailty of our animal nature,[40] which binds us to the transient goods of this world while our souls aspire to heaven: this is Platonic, rather than biblical reasoning, and no allusion is made to the fall of Adam. In its account of the human condition, the treatise recapitulates much that is said in *On the Workmanship of God*, and, as in the *Divine Institutes*, the supposedly pagan Sibyl is adduced as a corroborative witness to Christian prophecies that God will judge the reprobate (22.5–23.9). That all are not punished, when all deserve punishment, is itself a proof of God's benignity (21.5–9); the duty of the apologist is to soften the obdurate heart and refute the sophistries which 'undo all religion'.[41] Here, perversely yet typically, he compares himself to Cicero, whose *Tusculan Disputations* were written in fact to extinguish the fear of death without invoking the expectation of a future life.

The principles laid down in the *Divine Institutes* thus hold good for these minor essays by Lactantius. He does not create his own style, like Tertullian, in defiance of the classical norms of eloquence; he quotes from pagan authorities with more freedom and more reverence than any previous Christian writer in Latin; he does not oppose philosophy but disarms his opponents with their own philosophy. Of the three precursors whom he names he most resembles Minucius Felix (*Institutes* 5.1.22), who had taken up his pen in response to a pagan ebullition against the Christians, deploying Ciceronian tropes against a Ciceronian appeal to the way of the fathers. Neither Minucius Felix nor Lactantius is simply conforming to the ambient culture: philosophy was licensed non-conformity, and had they not asserted the philosopher's right to differ, Christians would not have given such offence to pagan intellectuals.

[37] *On the Nature of Things* 1.159–160 and 205–207 at Wrath 10.16.

[38] *Wrath* 17.9, citing *Catilinarian Oration* 4.6.12.

[39] *Wrath* 18.4.7, citing *Tusculan Disputations* 18.4.2.

[40] Though *Wrath* 13.10–18 implies that it the possibility of sin is a necessary condition of doing good.

[41] *Wrath* 22.2, citing *Tusculan Disputations* 1.47.112.

When they were Greeks these were the same intellectuals who discovered fearless probity in the Cynics and profundity in the decorations of Mithraic caves; Latin-speaking Christians, who at this time were always Africans like many of their pagan interlocutors, had all the more reason to urge that it was they, not their Greek detractors, who were the sole friends of the emperor, the true physicians of the body politic so long as it had no Christian for its head.

ARNOBIUS OF SICCA

An apology in seven books, under the title *Adversus Gentes* or *Adversus Nationes*, is the one extant work of Arnobius, the tutor of Lactantius.[42] Ostensibly a response to pagan calumnies, embittered by persecution or the recollection of it, it contains no allusion to any recent episode, or to any living magistrate, that might serve as a clue to the date and circumstances of its composition. The first book rebuts the charge that Christianity has brought the wrath of the gods upon the Roman world by propagating the superstitious worship of a man. Most of the second consists of a harsh and tantalizing commentary on the teaching of certain 'new men' (*novi viri*), which is represented here as a hybrid of Platonism and more arcane traditions. The third, deriding the notion that a god can be subject to passions or be fathered by the passion of some other god, applies this canon in turn to each member of the Roman pantheon. This catalogue of false deities is completed in the fourth book, where frank expressions of incredulity punctuate the sniping. In the fifth, the diabolical origins of sacrifice are exposed, and Rome is admonished that if she absorbs the religion of a conquered race, she must answer for all its atrocities. Book 6 is a jeremiad against the pagan use of images, Book 7 a rather prolix demonstration that no god who deserves the name could be pleased or honoured by an animal sacrifice.

Jerome records that Arnobius 'taught rhetoric with great renown at Sicca in Africa during the reign of Diocletian, and wrote (*scripsitque*) books *Against the Nations*, which are in general circulation' (*On Famous Men* 79). Although the use of the suffix *que* would normally imply that he not only lived but wrote under Diocletian, this is not an inescapable deduction, as Oliver Nicholson has observed.[43] In Jerome's earlier *Chronicle*, where a short account of the writing of the treatise *Against the Nations* is set against the year AD 326, we learn that this exercise was imposed on Arnobius as a neophyte seeking admission to the church 'which he had constantly impugned'.[44] This date is corroborated by his

[42] Jerome, *On Famous Men* 80: *Firmianus, qui et Lactantius, Arnobii discipulus.*

[43] Nicholson (1984).

[44] *Chronik des Hieronymus*, 231 helm.

own estimate that Christianity has been in the world for three centuries 'more or less',[45] and by his allusion to the spread of Christianity among the Alemanni, which, as one distinguished authority has observed, we can scarcely assign to an earlier period.[46] At the same time evidence can be found within the treatise *Against the Nations* to support the date implied by the natural reading of Jerome's later work, which ought to be have been composed with superior knowledge. Arnobius not only speaks repeatedly of persecution as a present fact, but states at one point that the city of Rome has existed for 1050 years (*Against the Nations* 2.71). Reckoning from 753 BC, the year fixed by Varro for the origin of Rome, we arrive at AD 297, which is generally agreed to be too early, since Diocletian's measures against the church commenced in 303. Although it requires us to postulate either an error in calculation or the use of a less familiar chronology,[47] this is the date to which the inception of the treatise is most commonly assigned.

Yet this is a fragile argument, not least because it imputes a mistake to Jerome when he is at his most circumstantial. It also fails to explain how Arnobius could have thought—or rather heard, by his own report—that the Christian faith had taken root among the Alemanni by 303. The case rests heavily on the assumption that he would not have said 'you persecute us' unless he meant 'you persecute us now', and that he would not have denounced the invention of 'new tortures' against the Christians if they were not still new at the time when he was writing.[48] If that is so, and the edicts of Diocletian were still in force, we can only marvel at the timing of his conversion, at the doubts that were cast upon it, at the prolixity of his treatise and at the intrepidity of its publication. It ought to be obvious, even if we did not have the example of Lactantius, that the aftermath of the storm is the most propitious time for such labours. Lactantius himself was a pupil of Arnobius, but omits him from the list of his predecessors in the *Divine Institutes*; it is hardly 'perverse' to infer that he ignored the treatise *Against the Nations* because it had not yet appeared.[49]

[45] *Against the Nations* 1.13.2; McCracken (1949), 275 suggests that the era is reckoned from the birth of Christ rather than from his death c.AD 30.

[46] *Against the Nations* 1.16.1. See Edwards (2004), 269 citing Thompson (1963), 58. He also alludes to a recent victory over the Scythians, i.e. Goths, but it was only in 315, according to Barnes (1976c), 192 that this title was accorded to one of the Augusti, in this case Constantine.

[47] Simmons (1995), 54–62 points out that Arnobius does not always embrace the Varronian chronology, which would fix the year 1050 *ab urbe condita* in 297 (see *Against the Nations* 3.39.3) and that Fabius Pictor's date of 747 rather than 753 for the founding of Rome is consistent with a dating of Arnobius to 303.

[48] Simmons (2009), 169 dismisses my contention that the present tense refers to habitual rather than contemporaneous actions. He might not be so peremptory had he noted that the expression 'new tortures' (*novae poenae*) is borrowed, with much else, from Cyprian, *To Demetrianus* 12.

[49] Barnes (2001a).

Scholars have detected signs of incomplete redaction in the treatise, above all in the last twenty chapters, which are extrinsic to the argument of the seventh book, and therefore may not have been designed to stand where the scribe has placed them.[50] One likely reason for this would be that the author died before he completed his task; and one hypothesis to explain the position of Jerome's comment on Arnobius in his *Chronicle* is that 326 was in fact the year of his death, not the year in which he composed his treatise. If the tutor of Lactantius was still alive in 326 he cannot have lived much longer,[51] and surely it is more probable that death forestalled the completion of his work than that he chose to leave it unfinished for fifteen years. Perhaps we are not obliged to choose between mutually exclusive possibilities: all the evidence can be accommodated if we suppose that Arnobius became a convert when the church had nothing to fear from Diocletian, that he wrote his own testimonial around the year 297 in the form of a short apology which did not deserve the notice of Lactantius, and that in his later years he undertook a vast elaboration of the original text, which has come down to us bearing all the usual marks of imperfect revision.[52] This theory will mitigate, though it cannot remove, the chronological inconsistencies; at the same time, it should be said that jarring indices of the date are not the only anomalous features of the work, and that even if every seam in the final draft had been sewn to the author's satisfaction, the resulting pattern would have been one that no other Christian cared to imitate.

CONTENT OF *AGAINST THE NATIONS*

Arnobius' stated motive for writing is conventional enough: he has heard it widely alleged that, since Christianity entered the world, the shrines of the gods have been neglected, and they have avenged themselves by visiting new calamities upon their rebellious subjects. Much in his reply is also conventional: that recent times have not seen greater calamities than those recorded in myth, that if the gods are such as their worshippers think them to be they do not deserve our worship, that the Christians who revere one God are more pious than the multitude and more honest than the philosophers who continue to throw themselves at the feet of idols. Yet even in his first rebuttal he

[50] Fragu (2010), xiv–xvi; Monceaux (1905), 252.

[51] Fragu (2010), xxii surmises that death cut short the work around 303, but we need not endorse his argument that because Arnobius taught Lactantius he must have been his senior.

[52] This theory is analogous to the one that has bene advanced to explain why Jerome knew only six books of the treatise of Optatus, *Against the Donatists*, which now exists in seven. See Edwards (1997), xvi–xviii.

strikes a new note, choosing as evidence of continuity the perennial phenomenon of change in the natural world:

> 'We are oppressed by dearth of crops and meagre harvests', says [the pagan]: so then, has any age, from time immemorial, been free from such exigencies? Do not the very names by which these ills are designated bear loud witness that no one of mortal race has hitherto been immune to them? But even if this were a hard thing to believe, we would be able to show by the testimony of authors what nations they are—so many and such great nations—who have suffered dreadful famine and perished as a result of widespread desolation. Frequently great falls of hail occur and destroy all things. Do we not find it contained and written in ancient texts that whole regions have been wasted by showers of stones? Harsh rains kill the crops and bring infertility on the land. So was antiquity immune to these evils, when we know that even great rivers have dried up because of the desiccation of their mud? (*Against the Nations* 1.3)

This exordium prepares us for the most original argument of his treatise[53]—that the Christian is under no obligation to prove the antiquity of his religion, since the practices that pass for ancestral cults in Rome itself are the products of one innovation after another in the course of the millennium that has passed since the foundation of the city. To the Roman mind it was creditable for a poet to boast of his novelty in the imitation of models, and a philosopher like Cicero might cite the adage that new things are better than old to justify a change of allegiance from the Old to the New Academy. Yet neither a philosopher nor a poet would profess to create from nothing, and in religion, as Cicero himself declares through the mouth of a privileged speaker in his dialogue *On the Nature of the Gods*, we can make no pretence to be wiser than our fathers. If the way of the fathers, the *mos maiorum*, proves after all to have been erratic and unfilial, the case for worship in the traditional manner must be given up, and the Romans are at the mercy of the philosopher who can demonstrate, with Arnobius, that a god who is truly god will be omnipotent, that therefore there will be one god and not many, that being captive to no form he will not inhabit a graven image, and that since he is free from passion and need he will not live on a diet of animal, let alone human, blood.[54]

This argument, we must remember, is strictly apologetic. Its purpose is to show that the Romans, being perpetual innovators, have no right to despise a new teaching simply because it is new; on the other hand, it is not an axiom for Arnobius, any more than for his pagan audience, that the new is always better.

[53] See further Kinzig (1994), 329–41. As Petropoulou (2008), 54 observes, the ancients were not wholly unaware that cults were subject to innovation. The frequency with which they note the antiquity of certain cults suggests to me (though not to Petropoulou) that they regarded some degree of change as normal.

[54] *Against the Nations* 1.17–33 may be regarded as a programmatic epitome of the whole treatise.

He is happy enough to play on the common prejudice when he accuses the persecutors of devising new expedients of torture (*novas artes*), and he flaunts his erudition by recounting the recent origin of various cults with wearisome jocularity. The great poet Horace, for whom originality consisted in out-Greeking the Greeks, had coined the aphorism *Graecia capta ferum victorem cepit*, 'Greece when captured took the fierce victor captive' (*Epistles* 2.1.155). Arnobius turns the jest into a jibe, upbraiding Rome for her ready acquiescence in the superstitions not only of the conquered Greeks, but of the effeminate Phrygians. His paraphrase of the myth that was re-enacted in the mysteries of Attis is taken from the Greek poet Timotheus, who had arrogantly proclaimed the superiority of latter-day songs to those of the classical era.[55] The longest of Arnobius' polemics is addressed to certain 'new men' (*novi viri),* philosophers in their own eyes at least, who had married the errors of Plato with absurdities for which they could adduce no precedent.

Inasmuch as these men believed the soul to have been sent down into the body from a higher world, they were merely Platonists; one of their unprecedented conceits, however, was the postulation of a supernal triad consisting of two minds (the *geminae mentes*) and the soul.[56] Numenius, the second-century Platonist (a favourite, as we hear, of the *novi viri*), had distinguished the demiurgic mind from a mind at rest, corresponding to Plato's form, of the Good, and may have regarded the world-soul as a third mind produced by a schism in the second.[57] His Latin heirs include Chalcidius, the translator of Plato, and the obscure Cornelius Labeo, though neither of these men can be dated confidently to the epoch between Numenius and Arnobius.[58] Since he read Greek, Arnobius may have known Porphyry's treatise *On the Return of the Soul*, in which he had spoken of a paternal intellect, a filial intellect, and a third principle which Augustine calls the *medium*, though he implies that it was not so much an intermediary as the joint offspring of the two, and therefore comparable to the Holy Spirit in his own doctrine of the Trinity. Pierre Courcelle's identification of the *novi viri* as Porphyrians remains the most seductive of current theories.[59] Porphyry's *On the Return of the Soul*, known only from Augustine, had much in common with the *Philosophy from Oracles*, and is indeed thought by one distinguished scholar to be the same work. Michael Simmons, who holds that the *Philosophy from Oracles* is a part of, if not coterminous with, Porphyry's effusion against the Christians, has suggested that all seven books of *Against the Nations* are conceived as a rejoinder to his attack.[60] It is difficult to cite evidence that would either confirm

[55] *Against the Nations* 5.5–7.

[56] *Against the Nations* 2.25. On Porphyry's adoption of this tenet see Dillon (1973).

[57] Arnobius, *Against the Nations* 2.11; Numenius, Fr. 11 Des Places.

[58] Smith (1987), 766–8; Mastandrea (1979), 127–9.

[59] Courcelle (1953).

[60] Simmons (1995), esp. 278–91 and 304–27.

or weaken such a thesis. Porphyry accepts instruction from oracles, Arnobius denounces them; Porphyry defends images, Arnobius thinks them sacrilegious; the daemons whom Porphyry thinks it right to honour are equated by Arnobius with the demons of the New Testament; Arnobius condemns the sacrifices for which Porphyry offers a limited apology; he mocks those who, like Porphyry, allot a different victim to every altar; and he vindicates the divinity of Jesus, whom Porphyry regards as a great man ignorantly deified by his admirers.[61] But for the last, however, Arnobius could have found a foil to any of these arguments in Varro, in Ovid, and in a host of writers whose names are lost to us. The polymathic and eclectic character of Porphyry's writings, whether or not they were all aimed at the Christians, ensured that he would seldom say anything that would not be gainsaid by a Christian of the next generation.

Whoever the *novi viri* were,[62] there is no doubt that Arnobius was well versed in the philosophy and literature of his pagan interlocutors. As a Christian apologist, on the other hand, he scarcely seems to know when he is on the verge of heresy. He might be Gnostic rather than a catholic when he protests that no benign deity would have caused our souls to descend, as the *novi viri* imagine, into this crepuscular realm of vice and tribulation. Again, he seems to forget, or at least suspend, the first principle of his religion when in his sixth book he repeatedly shows himself willing to grant the existence of the gods so long as they are agreed to be free of the passions and infirmities that are ascribed to them in popular devotions. It is true, and was admitted by Clement and Origen, that the Old Testament finds occasional use for the plural of the term *theos*,[63] but evidence that Arnobius was acquainted with the Old Testament is not easily supplied. It may be that his concessions to polytheism are merely provisional, that his object is at this point merely to illustrate the superior purity of Christian worship. Even if this is so, we cannot deny that he has hit the tone of a philosophical oration rather than a Christian homily. It would not be wholly fanciful to surmise that he had such an oration before him, the work of a Neoplatonist, perhaps, or even a lucubration of his own pagan youth.

The burden of the seventh and final book is the futility of sacrifice, a topic on which Christians could make common cause with otherwise antipathetic figures—Porphyry for one, in his treatise *On Abstinence* though not in the *Philosophy from Oracles*, and the wandering sage Apollonius of Tyana, who had become a rival to Christ in the work of the sophist Hierocles.[64] In the sixth book it had been the Christian's role to decry, and the pagan's to defend, the

[61] Simmons (1995), 224–6, commenting on Arnobius 1.34–37. Cf. Augustine, *City of God* 19.23.107.

[62] Edwards (2007), 125 observes that Iamblichus displays more interest than Porphyry in Hermes Trismegistus (2.13) and that Amelius, as a Tuscan, was more likely to consult the lore of Etruria (2.62). Festugière (1940) suspects that the new men are a composite.

[63] See Exodus 15.1; Psalm 82.6.

[64] See Chapter 4, this volume.

use of images: the question was not 'Why do you, the iconoclasts, break our images?', but 'Why should we, the iconophiles, be suspected of impiety?' Similarly, in the seventh book there is no command to sacrifice, no inquisitorial 'Why will you not sacrifice?', but a protracted Christian diatribe against the pagan usage, punctuated by the effete remonstrance, 'Why should we not sacrifice?' The rejoinder is a series of philosophical objections to the practice, none of which would be new to a reader of Porphyry. If the gods are incorporeal, how can they require material sustenance? Why should each god be capable of consuming only one species of victim? If it were conceivable that an impassible being should be moved to anger, why should an effusion of blood be required to appease that anger? How can such barbarities, which any benevolent ruler would despise, do honour to a celestial being? If the gods are free to bestow their bounties—if, that is, they are not governed by an implacable fate, as some believe—why do we see that the pious everywhere suffer the same afflictions as the impious? As I shall argue in chapter 10, the implied scenario is not one in which Christians are being compelled to sacrifice under pain of death, but one in which pagans feel obliged to make an intellectual case against zealots who contend that there should be 'no sacrifice at all'.

Arnobius is not a Christian Cicero: his style is often bombastic and jarring, his periods poorly rounded, his authorities strange to those who were nurtured on the Latin classics. In making a virtue of novelty, he is mocking that specious reverence for the past which was endemic in Roman literature and oratory, and even in the rhetoric of legislation under pagan emperors. For all that he is a Roman,[65] steeped in the history of a people who have assiduously welcomed the foreign customs that they affect to despise, and have followed the purported way of the fathers with no conviction that this way leads to the gods. Where Lactantius undertakes to refute his persecutors from their own books, Arnobius casts in their teeth a long history of pragmatic subterfuge and concealed apostasy, claiming for Christianity alone that perfect consonance of practice and belief which is the agreed foundation of virtue.

AFTERWORD

Neither Greek philosophy nor its barbarian antecedents are of more than occasional interest to the Latin rhetoricians whose works are examined in this

[65] Edwards (1999) remarks that, while Arnobius is an African, his Saturn is always a figure in Roman mythology. If Barnes (2001a) were correct in identifying Frugifer at 6.10.7 as the African Saturn under another name, this would be a proof of the converse proposition (i.e. that when he is not speaking of the Roman Saturn, he does not use that name for him). Thus my argument would be confirmed, not (as Barnes contends) refuted: see, however, Fragu (2010), 123–6.

chapter. Their chief concern is to show that only the church can restore the aboriginal virtue that Rome claims as its patrimony. Lactantius sets the gospel against the sterile casuistry of the dialecticians, Arnobius against the sanguine excesses of myth and ritual which are the Romans can no longer disavow as alien customs. One writes as a pedagogue, one as an antiquarian; neither thinks it profitable to represent Christianity as the philosophy of barbarians even to prove that the Latin-speaking church is the heir to prophecies delivered long before to Israel in a foreign tongue. Each can be said to offer his own Latin version of an argument first advanced by Justin in the second century but developed in the third century by Clement and Hippolytus: according to this indictment, the Greeks are not only deaf to the scriptures, but have fallen away from the loftier and more accurate knowledge of God that was put abroad by their first earliest teachers. It is possible that Hermes represents this pristine theology for Lactantius, though Arnobius lists him among the preceptors of the *novi viri*. Neither, however, bases his appeal to the Roman world on a reconstruction of the history of philosophy: the 'true religion', as they conceive it, is not so much an intellectual system as an antidote to the unacknowledged malady of the soul.

3

The Metamorphoses of Platonism

To some it will appear strange, and to others banal, that this book should include a chapter on Platonism. Everyone will agree that it belongs to the cultural milieu of Christianity, and perhaps of other religions, in the Constantinian era; but does it follow that Platonism itself ought to be counted among the religions of antiquity? In our academic discourse it has the more respectable status of a philosophy, though we speak not uncommonly of the religion of Plato. If this term implies that one not only holds a metaphysical system but engages in cultic practice, one could argue that Plotinus, the founder of Neoplatonism, had no religion, as he was barely a theist and said, to the consternation of his disciples, 'the gods should come to me, not I to them'. But Porphyry, who recorded this aphorism in the reign of Diocletian, was a man of eclectic piety, who did not hesitate to give the name *theos* or God to the summit and fountainhead of being. His writings include a treatise on iconography, a compendium of the philosophy to be derived from oracles and a tract against eating meat which recommends that the gods should be honoured but without the slaughter of beasts. A number of practices that he could not defend were vindicated by Iamblichus, under whose influence a succession of Platonists strove to protect the ancient cults from obsolescence. Yet Platonism remained what it had always been, a philosophy which never demanded that reason should submit to revelation or that the individual should entrust his faith to a hierarchical consensus. For that reason the Academy and the church were antipathetic as institutions: yet since it taught (or was thought to teach) the unity of God and his creation, the benign direction of human affairs by providence and the survival of the soul for reward and punishment after death, Platonism was often the philosophy of choice when Christians sought to give more intellectual clarity to the dogmas that they believed on the authority of the church. When competent theologians were also bishops they took care not to adopt philosophic tenets for which they could not find scriptural precedents; others, less watchful of their orthodoxy, constructed systems that, as we shall see in the case of Chalcidius, are not easily labelled 'Christian' or 'Platonic'. Hybridity of another kind arises when

Platonism in Christian sources is subject either to assimilative revision or to malignant caricature.

WHAT IS NEOPLATONISM?

Plotinus, the founder of Neoplatonism, once declined to attend a sacrifice, saying 'the gods should come to me, not I to them'.[1] In his *Enneads* (that is, Porphyry's redaction and arrangement of his unpolished writings) references to the gods, and even to 'God', are not infrequent, but in contrast to Socrates in Plato's dialogues, he never apostrophizes a higher being when he is on the point of disclosing some great mystery. Demiurgic activity is more commonly attributed to Nous, the supernal intellect which is coextensive with the forms and therefore with the purity and plenitude of being. That which we call the One—so named because it is the cause of unity, not because it participates in unity—is superior to being and thought, and even to say that it 'is' would be a pragmatic solecism. If willing or loving are predicated of it, these are only imperfect characterizations of the energy (*energeia*) which precedes essence in a mode inscrutable even to the purified intellect.[2] Insofar as this energy has an object, it is the One itself, not anything in the lower tiers of existence. Whatever the One can be said to do, it does by logical necessity, contingency being the enemy of freedom: nothing could be more alien to the thought of Plotinus than the Christian notion of a God who arbitrarily creates a world, permits it to fall and redeems it by his love.

Porphyry of Tyre, who was born in 232 and commenced his studies with Plotinus in 262, belongs to our period only by virtue of his *Life of Plotinus* and his *Letter to Marcella*, both of which appear to have been written in the first years of the fourth century. We may add that his philippics against Christianity, whatever their date and content, many have done something to reinforce the zeal of Diocletian and his fellow-persecutors, and certainly did much to shape the Christian memory of the persecution. Moreover he left two legacies to the Platonists of the fourth century, one by publishing the *Enneads* of Plotinus, the other by reminding the world that Platonists before Plotinus had not regarded wisdom as a monopoly of the Greeks. A Phoenician proud of his ancestry, he numbers his compatriots with Hebrews and Arabs among the early teachers of Pythagoras; in his book *On the Styx* he describes a floating statue of the Buddha on the authority of the much-travelled Apollonius of Tyana; in his treatise *On Abstinence* he exhorts a truant disciple of Plotinus to take a lesson in abstinence from the Indian sages and the Essenes of Palestine.

[1] Porphyry, *Life of Plotinus* 10.45.

[2] See especially *Enneads* 6.8 with Edwards (2013a).

To the utterances that he gathered from Greek shrines he added a new collection of *Chaldean Oracles*, which were held in as much regard as the works of Plato by at least one his successors; in this work he denied that there was one universal way to liberation, as the Christians imagined, yet he quoted verses extolling the sagacity of the Hebrews and reckoned Christ himself among the seers who have trodden their own path to communion with the gods.

By comparison with his master, Porphyry is a model of conventional godliness. In his letter to his wife Marcella he enjoins prayer, not as an occasional means to illumination, but as an attitude of reverence which should be sustained in all one's daily business. When he distils the philosophy of the *Enneads* into apophthegms or *Sententiae*, one of the longest of these is a sketch of progress in the virtues, the penultimate stage of which will make the philosopher a god and the final stage *patêr theôn*, a father of gods.[3] Precedents for every stage in this itinerary can be found in Plotinus, but it is Porphyry who gives this linear form to his *obiter dicta*. In the *Life of Plotinus* he describes the evocation of the philosopher's guardian spirit by an Egyptian priest, who was terrified to discover that this spirit was no daemon but a god. Porphyry states that this episode prompted the writing of a treatise 'On our Tutelary Daemon', but there is nothing in this text to suggest that our daemon, who inhabits the plane being and thought superior to the one that we currently occupy, could ever be drawn into the physical realm.[4] In the same work, Porphyry finds a divine corroboration of his own eulogies on Plotinus in an oracle which his fellow-disciple Amelius professed to have received at a shrine of Apollo;[5] Plotinus never quotes such vaticinations in his *Enneads*, though Porphyry spent many years assembling a 'philosophy from oracles'. In this work he distinguishes three orders of divinity—heavenly, earthly, and subterranean—and professes to have learned on divine authority what victims and what rites of immolation are pleasing to each. It is hard to reconcile the minute prescriptions of this treatise with the austere theology of his four books *On Abstinence*, certainly written after the death of Plotinus, which not only declare the sacrifice of animals incompatible with philosophy but denounce the civic cult as a bloody system of imposture, whose beneficiaries are not true gods but daemons who have usurped their titles and prerogatives. It is equally difficult, and may not be necessary, to discover any trace of the *Philosophy from Oracles* in the *Letter to Anebo*, which appears to discountenance both the coercion of gods and the propitiation of daemons. More will be said on the theory of sacrifice in Chapter 11; here it will suffice to observe that in our attempts to reconstruct the *Philosophy from Oracles* we are the mercy of

[3] *Sententiae* 32. [4] See Porphyry, *Life of Plotinus* 10; Plotinus, *Enneads* 3.4.
[5] *Life of Plotinus* 22.

Christian informants, who were only too happy to catch their enemy in a contradiction.

This animosity is all the more striking when we observe that his philosophy is sometimes couched in terms that have a Christian rather than a Platonic timbre. Four times in the course of his acquaintance with Plotinus, he tells us, the latter enjoyed communion with the 'god over all':[6] there are precedents for this locution in Origen and parallels in Eusebius, but it was not his master's way of recollecting the ascent 'above all that is lower than the highest' or the 'flight of the alone to the alone'.[7] Again it was Porphyry who gave the title *Against the Gnostics* to a treatise in which Plotinus had described his interlocutors as erstwhile friends, that is as fellow-students in the Alexandrian school of Ammonius Saccas. He may have known more of the Gnostic than he cares to disclose, for his *Letter to Marcella* reproduces a tetrad of cardinal virtues—faith, hope, love, and truth—which is also found in the Valentinian *Gospel of Philip*.[8] The famous superscription to another treatise, *On the Three Hypostases*, is not warranted by the usage of Plotinus in this text or in the other fifty-three which make up Porphyry's edition of the *Enneads*; on the other hand, it had been a conventional formula among Christians since the beginning of the third century.[9] The tradition that he was himself an apostate from the Christians becomes a little more plausible when we add this familiarity with ecclesiastical idiom to the undeniable evidence of his knowledgeable but invidious handling of the texts that Christians knew as scripture.

IAMBLICHUS OF CHALCIS

A notable school was set up in the reign of Galerius by another Platonist, Iamblichus of Chalcis.[10] From his Semitic name it can be surmised that his birthplace was the Syrian, not the Euboean, Chalcis.[11] If we accept the modern consensus that he was born around AD 245 he was Porphyry's junior by a dozen years, and therefore young enough to have been his pupil,[12] as Eunapius records.[13] While he did not inherit his teacher's fame as an instigator of

[6] *Life of Plotinus* 23. [7] Plotinus, *Enneads* 4.8.1 and 6.9.9.

[8] *Nag Hammadi Codices* II.78.24–25; Porphyry, *Letter to Marcella* 24, p. 289.18 Nauck.

[9] Cf. Chitchaline (1992).

[10] See further Bidez (1919). Malalas states that Galerius was also called Maxentius, but we must take him to mean 'Maximian'.

[11] See the edition by Dillon (Bibliography A), 5.

[12] Cameron (1968); Dillon (1987), 865–6. I suspect, however, that Cameron and others have been too quick to identify the philosopher of Chalcis with the Iamblichus who appears as a contemporary (perhaps a younger contemporary) of Plotinus in Porphyry, *Life of Plotinus* 9.

[13] Text at Bidez (1913), appendix 3, 51*.

persecution, posterity has not been very much kinder to his writings. The chief surviving works are a *Protreptic* to philosophy, the treatises *On the Pythagorean Life* and *On the Common Science of Mathematics*, an *Introduction to the Arithmetical Theology of Nicomachus of Gerasa*, and (most famous of all) the pseudonymous diatribe *On the Mysteries*. A handful of texts, more useful to the historian than instructive to the philosopher, can be reconstructed from Christian florilegia; the leading principles of his own philosophy must be gleaned from later commentaries on Plato, whose authors cite him either to prove him wrong or to gain an ally.

A philosophical scholar where Plotinus had been a scholarly philosopher, Iamblichus postulates as many principles anterior to being as was necessary to harmonize Plato's tentative and dissonant speculations. The first antinomy of Plato's *Parmenides* contends that if the One exists we cannot predicate anything of it without compromising its unity. The second contends that if we are not to negate the very existence of the One it must be patient of an infinity of predicates. In the third it appears that we cannot even affirm that the One is other than everything else, since otherness would then become a shared predicate. From these paradoxes flowed the vertiginous speculations that distinguish the Neoplatonic school of Plotinus from those whom we have now learned to call middle Platonists. The Parmenides, however, is not Plato's only dialogue, and the One does not appear in the *Philebus*, where all existence is derived from limit and the unlimited. The eponymous speaker in the *Timaeus* reasons that the world must be one because it is a copy of the one paradigm; this paradigm is the realm of archetypal forms, and what (if anything) is superior to it we are not told. From this cocktail (stirring in perhaps what he knew of Plato's oral teaching on the good) Iamblichus derives a strange and populous monadology. Above the noetic or intellectual plane (Damascius tells us[14]), he posited an ineffable first principle, and below this a second, unrelated to anything that exists. The latter—the 'simply one'—holds the middle place between the ineffable One and the dyad of limit and unlimited.[15] Then follows the 'One that is', the first of these four transcendent principles that we are capable of knowing by intellection.[16] It owes its knowability, as all things knowable do, to the determinative action of the limited on the unlimited; absolute unity being incompatible with this double provenance, every Platonist would concur in positing a One above the dyad and in stripping it of the properties that appertain to the One in the realm of essence. If a scholastic desire to accommodate two of the Parmenidean antinomies will not suffice to explain why there are two ineffable principles above the dyad, Iamblichus could advance the philosophic plea that the oneness which the

[14] *Doubts and Solutions* 43, cited by Dillon (1973), 29.
[15] Damascius, *Doubts* 50–1; Dillon (1973), 31. [16] Dillon (1973), 32.

noetic One and the supranoetic One have in common must be a unity of a higher order.

As there is a One before the One in Iamblichus, so there is time before time. His argument seems to be that that the world would not be a single entity which endures through time if time itself were no more than a succession of vanishing instants (Fr. 63 Dillon). We experience time diachronically, as a series which does not contain its own principle of unity; that principle must be sought in the primordial time, the bare temporality, which precedes the series but is present like a transcendent form in every interval or instant of it. By parity of reasoning, we must posit an unextended space, or potential spatiality, behind the seamless manifold of our experience; otherwise we would not experience a seamless manifold but an infinity of discrete extensions (Fr. 64). Time and space as we know them are measured quantities, finite determinations of the temporality and spatiality which in themselves admit no measure or determination. In homelier terms, Iamblichus distinguishes time and space in the world from the time and space in which the world comes to be. This 'coming to be' does not imply a temporal beginning: Iamblichus believed, with the majority of Platonists in his day, that the world is 'generated' only in the sense that it is the sphere of generation and corruption, and therefore sempiternal or everlasting rather than eternal.[17] Once again, it does not contain in itself the principle of its own unity and wholeness; these are furnished by the immutable paradigm, which occupies neither space nor time and suffers no generation or corruption. Just as the world is an image of this paradigm, so time—or rather its logical antecedent, temporality—is styled by Plato the 'moving image of eternity'.[18] The Greek word for eternity, *aiôn*, is also the name of a deity who was honoured in inscriptions of the period and worshipped at an Alexandrian festival. Some have detected an echo of this popular devotion in the eulogistic language of Iamblichus; be that as it may, it is by strict metaphysical reasoning that he identifies *aiôn* with the 'One that is' and sets it at the apex of the noetic realm.

He is generally supposed to have conceived this realm as a triad of being, life and intellect. Being in this scheme represents the object of cognition and intellect the cognitive subject.[19] According to Plotinus and all who follow him, the intellect of the Demiurge must contain the Forms in order to know them perfectly, while the forms have no other substrate than the demiurgic intellect which contains them. This doctrine that 'the intelligibles are not outside the intellect' entails on the one hand that the knower and the known are coextensive in the realm of being or essence, and on the other hand that this is not the realm of pure identity, because knowing and being known remain conceptually distinct. Intellect is therefore a duality in unity, and the

[17] See Fr. 37 Dillon, and pp. 311–12 in this commentary.
[18] Plato, *Timaeus* 37c at Fr. 64 Dillon. [19] See especially Fr. 65 Dillon.

source of its unity must be higher than being, and hence beyond thought or expression. It seems, however, that as the ontological hiatus between the One and the demiurgic intellect widened in Platonic speculation, it was felt that the opposition between the knower and the known would remain intractable unless a intermediate term were added to reduce the polarity to a dynamic tension. The term 'life' was suggested by Plato's dictum in the *Sophist* (248d) that we rob the forms of dignity if we imagine them to be destitute of life or intellect. Proclus at least allows no other ordering of the three terms, because the category of things that exist subsumes all living creatures and the category of living creatures subsumes all those endowed with intellect. The history of the triad before him remains elusive: is it, for example, a variation on the triad of being, power and life which Porphyry derived from the *Chaldaean Oracles*? If so, and if the *Oracles* date (as the ancients believed) from the reign of Marcus Aurelius,[20] it would follow that the origins of the triad must be sought neither in the *Sophist* nor in the doctrine that 'the intelligibles are not outside the intellect'. Later in this chapter, we shall take note of its Gnostic antecedents and of the different permutation of the three terms in Theodorus of Asine. Iamblichus undoubtedly employs the three terms in the order approved by Proclus when he writes that time participates in being, life, and intellect; yet we also find him asking polemically where Plato himself had used them to designate three stages in a planetary ascent. He does not name his interlocutors, but in anticipation of what is said below, we may observe here that he must have had some knowledge of the Gnostics, since he mentions them at one point, without obvious rancour, in his treatise *On the Soul*.[21]

THEURGY IN IAMBLICHUS

This work is largely a digest of opinions held by others. When writing in his own person, as we shall see in Chapter 4, Iamblichus holds that fate is not the jailer but the guardian of the body; on the other hand it has no place in the realm of the gods, and the soul must escape its tutelage if she is to realize her own divinity. Whether fate is a guardian or a jailer to the soul in the lower world is for the soul itself to determine: if we forget our higher abode we become enthralled to the instruments which are given to us as the means of liberation. Iamblichus holds that our souls did not fall blindly but with one of two objects: the 'salvation, purification and

[20] See further Saffrey (1988), 19–20, who argues that the first Platonist who can be shown to have made use of these apocrypha was Antoninus, a pupil of Ammonius Saccas. On the importance of the *Oracles* to Iamblichus see Cremer (1969).

[21] *On the Soul* 23, 49 Finamore and Dillon.

consummation of things below' or the 'disciplined correction of their own characters' (*On the Soul* 29). To the soul that weathers this ordeal and does not fall into delusion and multiplicity, the primordial state of unity to which it returns is more secure for having once been lost. These doctrines are not entirely new: it can be argued that Plato himself regards embodiment as a prerequisite for the vision of the Good which the soul pursues in vain so long as dwells only in the 'supercelestial place'. Plotinus, too, opined that souls descend for the sake of the bodies that they animate, while Porphyry observed that the lower world provides a theatre for the exercise of virtue. Iamblichus departs from Plotinus, however, on two important counts: he holds that there is no part of the soul that remains undescended,[22] and he believes that the matter into which it descends is not a bare potentiality or a spontaneous emanation, but the product of a divine will that is superior even to the Demiurge. In the second of these tenets he is almost at one with Porphyry, but the consequence which he draws from it—that the favour of the gods can be won by the use of material instruments—is formulated in answer to the sceptical inquiries of the *Letter to Anebo*, which is commonly attributed to his teacher.

In his treatise *On the Mysteries* Iamblichus upholds the salvific efficacy of incantation and sacrifice; he defends both the propitiation and the coercion of daemons, while enjoining obedience to the natal daemon who unites the soul with a body under its regnant constellation. On these grounds he has often been accused of deserting philosophy for magic;[23] he is far, however, from holding that the powers which he ascribes to rites and objects proceed from virtues which are naturally inherent to them, or even the cosmic sympathy which Plotinus assumed to be the sorcerer's reservoir of power (*Enneads* 4.4.40). The soul being wholly below and the gods above, it is by their favour that it traverses the gulf; the means at our disposal belong to this world, since we inhabit no other at present, and for that reason they can have only as much utility as the gods confer upon them. The gods fall into three types—the hypercosmic, the liberated, and the encosmic—and the ladder between the lowest of these and the human soul is occupied successively by archangels, angels, daemons, heroes, sublunar archons, and material archons.[24] A lower manifestation of divinity is more subject to compulsion or cajolery: the practitioner who is capable of no higher arts must be conscious when he summons them that they are limited in knowledge, subject to passion, and liable to deceive. *Theourgia*—a compound of *theos*, 'god' and *ergon*, 'work'—is a work appointed

[22] Compare *Commentary on Timaeus*, Fr. 87 Dillon with *Enneads* 4.8.8. On Plotinus see further Rist (1967).

[23] E. G. Dodds (1960), 7.

[24] See further Shaw (1995), esp. 79 and 138.

by gods and not, as has been too often assumed, the art of working on the gods against their will.[25]

In his treatise *On the Pythagorean Life* Iamblichus hints that there is a mathematical way to the apprehension of truths that exceed discursive knowledge.[26] The work *On the Common Science of Mathematics* is a propaedeutic to this higher discipline, but even this is commended as an adumbration of truths that would otherwise be inexpressible.[27] Plato and all who followed him agreed that mathematics stands to dialectic as images and shadows stand to the objects of the phenomenal world, which most of us take for the real one. In contrast, however, to Porphyry, who deplored the failure of 'unlettered' critics to construe the symbolic language of cultic statues,[28] Iamblichus does not extend the same indulgence to three-dimensional images. In language reminiscent of Plotinus (who had belittled his own corporeal frame as *eidôlon eidôlou*, the shade of a shade[29]), he asks why one would prefer the phantasmal replica to the truly existent thing that it purports to copy: he even goes so far as to say, 'What good can come of matter?' (*Mysteries* 3.28). We may feel that this question sits uneasily with more than one passage elsewhere in the treatise, where he asserts that divine power can inhabit even the inanimate objects of the natural world.[30] His objection is not so much to the commerce of the divine with matter as with to the failure of certain practitioners to see that matter is always a datum, always the first stepping-stone to the invisible. It is one thing, then, to make use of the material in our practice or our reasoning, another to make it the object of a deliberative process. True images of the supernal are found not made, and the error of those who imagine that the gods will impart their powers to a man-made effigy is analogous to the error of those who sacrifice in the belief that the daemons are literally sustained by our gifts of food.

No reference to Christians is found in the extant writings of Iamblichus, but we can sure that he disapproved of their anthropomorphic theism, their worship of a crucified man, and their bellicose contempt for polytheism with all its practices of devotion. On the other hand, a Christian reading Iamblichus would discover an iconoclast,[31] an antagonist of Porphyry, a Platonist who did not subscribe to the heresy that matter is uncreated, and a monotheist who understood that humans have no claim upon divinity except through appointed instruments of grace.

[25] Cf. Shaw (1995), 69: 'Theurgy transformed the soul's *prohairesis* by conforming it to the divine *actions* communicated in theurgic symbols.'

[26] See further Sheppard (1982).

[27] See *Common Science of Mathematics*, pp. 19–20, 39, and 67–8 Festa.

[28] See Chapter 1, with Bidez (1913), appendix 1, p. 3* (Eusebius, *Preparation* 3.7.1).

[29] Porphyry, *Life of Plotinus* 1; cf. Enneads 2.9.10.

[30] See further Addey (2014), 215–38.

[31] Yet one of his admirers, the sorcerer Maximus, is said to have won the confidence of Julian the Apostate by causing a statue to smile: Eunapius, *Lives of the Philosophers* 7.2.7–12.

THEODORUS OF ASINE

The most celebrated pupil of Iamblichus, Theodorus of Asine, was also an admirer of Numenius and Porphyry, and in his turn the recipient of an unctuous letter of admiration from the Antiochene orator Libanius.[32] Almost all that remains of his cosmology and theology, however, we owe to the commentary of Proclus on the *Timaeus*. Here we learn that Theodorus followed his master Iamblichus in positing three triads, the first noetic, the second noeric, the third demiurgic.[33] The adjective 'noetic' implies an instantaneous unity of knowledge, and 'noeric' a mode of knowing which is more discursive though equally independent of the senses. The three terms in the demiurgic triad are intellects, the first 'essential' (*ousiôdês*), the second subtending wholes, and third discrete particulars.[34] The second possesses a higher degree of unity than the third because it contemplates only a logical, not a spatial or temporal multiplicity. The noeric triad consists of the being prior to being, the intellect prior to intellect, and the life prior to life; the first term in the demurgic triad is the seat of being, the second of intellect, the third of the source of souls.[35] Moreover, each member of this triad is threefold, and in each third term corresponds to the *autozôon*, or living creature, which appears to be synonymous with the paradigm in the *Timaeus*.[36]

The third demiurgic intellect, as we have said, is the 'fount of souls'. Yet souls too form a triad, each member of which has its counterpart in the demiurgic triad.[37] The first is soul as Plato first defines it in the *Timaeus*, the *meson* or medium (in fact, the hybrid offspring) of the divisible and the indivisible.[38] Most scholars would now construe this an allegorical way of saying that if we had no timeless seat of consciousness we would not be conscious even of what passes in time; to Theodorus, however, there is no such thing as a mere conceit in Plato. In his mingling of the contrary essences, Plato's demiurge applies the ratios which define the notes in a musical scale; Theodorus therefore posits a second soul, corresponding to the generic intellect, which is called harmonic because it creates multiplicity then reduces it to order. The third, corresponding to the particular intellect, is the soul that Plato envisaged as a coupling of the straight and the curved, in the shape of the letter χ, to form the ecliptic and the sidereal equator. Both the demiurgic and

[32] Epistle 487 = Fr. 5 Deuse, p. 31. Theodorus may have been associated with Rhodes: Saffrey (1984).

[33] Fr. 6 Deuse, p. 32 = Proclus, *Commentary on Timaeus* II.274 Diehl.

[34] Fr. 11 Deuse = Proclus, *Commentary on Timaeus* I.425.19–22 Diehl.

[35] Fr. 6 Deuse, p. 32.

[36] Fr. 14 Deuse.

[37] I summarize Fr. 6 Deuse, p. 33, passing over many obscurities.

[38] Also, in Fr. 19 Deuse, of the intellect which contains the forms or ideas of wholes and that which contains the forms or ideas of particulars. As Deuse, p. 119 shows, these are alternative designations for the 'first god according to being' and 'the second god according to intellect'.

the psychological triads can be aligned with another series, in which being is followed by intellect and life. The order is philosophically determined, as is that of the cardinal triad in the system of Iamblichus, where intellect is the final term and life or power the intermediary. These are not congruent hierarchies: in that of Theodore, intellect takes precedence over life as the nobler quality, whereas in Iamblichus life precedes intellect because intelligent beings form a class within the larger class of beings who are endowed with life.

This discrepancy argues against the ascription to Theodorus of an anonymous commentary on the *Parmenides* of Plato, in which a triad of 'being, life and intellect' is adopted as a hermeneutic key.[39] Since this triad, though derivable from the *Sophist* of Plato, is not expressly attested in Plotinus, it has commonly been assumed that the author of the *Commentary* must be Porphyry or a later author.[40] Our evidence suggests that Porphyry followed the usage of the *Chaldaean Oracles* in designating the middle term in the triad as power (*dunamis*) rather than life; furthermore, the *Commentary* cannot be accused, as Porphyry was accused by later Platonists, of underestimating the transcendence of the first principle. To Neoplatonists of the Constantinian era the triad was familiar enough, as we have seen; but this is also the era to which we must date the surviving redactions of two Gnostic texts, the *Zostrianus* and the *Allogenes*, in which the soul ascends from Mentality to Vitality and thence to 'That which is'. Versions of both writings had been cited against Plotinus by the 'friends'—that is, fellow-pupils from his days in Alexandria—whom Plotinus upbraids in the treatise to which Porphyry gave the title *Against the Gnostics*. Porphyry describes them as Christian heretics, concurring in his nomenclature with ecclesiastical writers of this period. Those who were then called Gnostic are now called Sethians, and it is generally agreed that their founding scripture was a document of the early second century, the *Apocryphon of John*. This text ascribes the origin of the cosmos to a schism in the Godhead, as did a younger contemporary of its author, the philosopher Numenius of Apamea; in the second century neither Apamea not Alexandria would have had a bishop strong enough to prevent the miscegenation of Platonism and Christianity. Plotinus and the Christian Origen laboured to purify their own traditions; Porphyry as a disciple of Plotinus and Theodorus as an admirer of Porphyry both had reason to eschew that form of the triad which had found its way into Gnostic speculation. Iamblichus, who had no such qualms, is also the only writer of antiquity who mentions the Gnostics as one sect of philosophers among many, with no disparagement and no allusion to their profession of Christianity.

[39] Edwards (1990), 17–19.

[40] Hadot (1968); Bechtle (1990) argues, however, for a second-century date.

The one thought that can be ascribed uniquely to Theodorus appears barely worthy of a philosopher's attention, since it implies that one could elicit metaphysical truths from the mere analysis of the letters making up a Greek word:[41]

> The first of the things that emanate from [the One] is represented by the rough breathing with which we utter *hen*. Itself, it is unnameable, just as the breathing is by itself silent. The second is represented by the unutterable vowel which now becomes utterable with the breathing, and it itself becomes both utterable and unutterable, speakable and unspeakable; for the procession of the second order of essence has to be mediated. Third comes *hen*, which contains the unutterable breathing and the soundable force of the *e*, and the letter that goes with this, the consonant *n*, which represents in a converse way the same thing as the breathing. (Proclus, *On the Parmenides* VII, pp. 52.19ff. Klibansky, trans. Morrow and Dillon)

As Stephen Gersh observes,[42] the mysticism of letters was not entirely foreign to the Greek tradition. At *Enneads* 5.5.5 Plotinus argues that as the participle *on*, which signifies being, differs only by the pressure of an aspirate from the word *hen*, which signifies unity, those who use the Greek tongue are constantly bearing witness to the dependence of all being on the one. The signs representing letters were also numerals, and the Pythagoreans, to whom a disciple of Porphyry would never refuse a hearing, had made a science since ancient times of drawing out the significance of numbers. Their teachings are preserved and elaborated in the *Theology of Arithmetic*, attributed to Iamblichus but derived perhaps from a lost work by Nicomachus of Gerasa, and in a treatise which is certainly by Iamblichus *On the Common Science of Mathematicals*: both will have been current in the time of Theodorus. Furthermore, the Pythagoreans known to Aristotle appear to have held that the space between the elementary bodies which make up the physical world was filled by a boundless breath, inhaled from a place or plane beyond the heavens.[43] Nicomachus says, in an extant work, that the vowels derive their sounds, and hence their names, from the tones emitted by the seven planetary spheres;[44] in similar vein, a magical papyrus invokes a deity whose name contains seven letters corresponding to the seven planetary tones,[45] while Alexander of Tralles reports that certain astrologers claimed to be able to fetter the sun by the recitation of twelve apparently senseless monosyllables.[46] We know of

[41] See also Proclus, *Commentary on the Timaeus*, vol. 2, 274.10–277.20.

[42] See his excursus in *From Iamblichus to Eriugena* (Leiden: Brill, 1978), 289–304.

[43] Aristotle, *Physics* 213b22.

[44] *Musici Scriptores Graeci* (ed. K. Von Jan, Leipzig: Teubner, 1895), 276.8ff., cited by Dornsieff (1922), 52.

[45] Gersh (1978), 294–5, citing Dornsieff (1922), 37.

[46] *On Medicine*, book 2, cited by Taylor (1821), 289–90.

three philosophers at least who found significance in the physical shape of a letter. Plato, as Theodorus himself recalled, says in the *Timaeus* that the Demiurge formed the soul of the world by weaving the Same and the Other into the figure of a khi (X).[47] In *On the E at Delphi*, Plutarch deduced the hidden import of the E at Delphi from its shape, its place in the alphabet, and its phonetic resemblance to the second person (*ei*) of the verb *einai* 'to be'. The *Theology of Arithmetic*, wrongly attributed to Iamblichus, contends that a numerical relation between the letters ϵ and θ may be inferred from the fact that in writing we can produce one by the bisection of the other.[48]

Furthermore, it was widely believed that hieroglyphs (at that time indecipherable to the Greeks) were distillations of Egyptian theology in a pictorial form that none but the priests were able to construe. Plotinus of Alexandria, alleged by some to have been by race an Egyptian,[49] proves himself a thoroughbred Greek when he speaks of the Egyptians as foreign people who, rather than using 'characters that represent sounds and communicate rational propositions', engraved in their temples 'a distinct icon for every distinct particular' (*Enneads* 5.8.6). Writing in the persona of an Egyptian priest, Iamblichus explains the phrase 'sitting above the lotus' as an emblem of the sovereign transcendence of the deity.[50] We shall note in a later chapter that Pachomius, the abbot of the earliest Christian monastery in Egypt, was similarly predisposed by his ignorance of the Greek language to detect an arcane significance in its letters; both the shapes of letters and their positions in the alphabet become replete with meaning in an anonymous Christian treatise of the fourth century, whose author also exhibits some knowledge of Hebrew. His prototype may have been a Jewish reverie, the Sefer Yetzirah, which (as we shall see) derives an entire theology from the twenty-two characters of the Hebrew alphabet. If Theodorus goes beyond the examples of Plotinus and Iamblichus, he proves himself not so much a truant Platonist as a child of the ambient culture.[51]

[47] Proclus, *Commentary on the Timaeus*, 277.20 Diehl, citing *Timaeus* 36b.

[48] *Theology of Arithmetic* 2.4, cited by Gersh (1978), 291.

[49] Eunapius, *Lives of the Philosophers*, p. 4.55.33–35 Boissonade.

[50] *On the Mysteries* 7.2. See further the translation by J. Dillon, J. Hershbell, and E. Clarke (Atlanta: Society of Biblical Literature, 2003), xli.

[51] An even closer parallel can be found at *Mundakya Upanishad* 9–12, pp. 700–1 Radhakrishnan: '*Vaisvanara*, whose sphere (of activity) is the waking state, is the letter a, the first element. *Taijasa*, whose sphere (of activity) is the dream state, is the letter u, the second element, from exaltation or intermediateness... *Prajna*, whose state (of activity) is the state of deep sleep, is the letter m, the third element... The fourth is that which has no elements, which cannot be spoken of, into which the world is resolved, benign, non-dual. Thus the syllable *aum* is the very self.' Nevertheless, remembering, as Armstrong (1936), 28 observed, that 'Plotinus never reached India', it is hard to pursue an argument for the direct influence of Indian thought on the Neoplatonists of the fourth century.

CHALCIDIUS AND HYBRIDITY

The first known Latin translation of the *Timaeus* was that of Cicero; the first to survive entire is that of Chalcidius, which is accompanied by a commentary on select passages of the text. To say that it is the earliest is not to say that we can determine the century, let alone the year, of its composition with any confidence; nevertheless, as the drowning swimmer grasps at every plank, so the majority of scholars have agreed to take the dedication to a certain Osius as evidence that the author was a contemporary of the celebrated Hosius of Cordova.[52] The fact that he cites no author later than Origen lends some weight to this conjecture;[53] a dating later than about 300 is precluded, in the opinion of the scholars who have devoted most attention to his philosophy, by the middle Platonic rather than Neoplatonic tenor of his commentary. Neither of these arguments is strong, since the publication of the *Enneads* was only the death-knell, not the death, of Middle Platonism, and Chalcidius' citations from earlier writers are too sparse to admit of our building any hypotheses on his silence. On the other hand, there is no evidence for a later date to be set against the dedication to Osius, unless it be the caveat that a Platonist of any stamp was unlikely to be the friend of an orthodox bishop. To this we may answer—trivially—that Hosius may not yet have been a bishop, and—more profitably—that if we look for indices of the author's Christianity in this commentary we shall find enough to satisfy an indulgent prelate, though not enough evidence of orthodoxy to escape the reproof of an oecumenical synod. More prudent than most heretics, Chalcidius chose as his medium not theology but the exegesis of Plato, which has never been the subject of a conciliar decree.

While Chalcidius never declares himself to be a Christian, he makes use of expressions that would fall most naturally from a Christian pen. Thus, while it was usual for pagans of this period to identify the 'receptacle' of the *Timaeus* with the indeterminate substrate that Aristotle called *hulê* or matter, the assertion that God is the *opifex* or artificer of matter (ch. 311) is more redolent of Christian apologetic than of pagan commentary. Iamblichus had indeed affirmed, in his treatise *On the Mysteries*, that matter was produced by God from *ousiotês* or essentiality, either by derivation or by division; in this passage, however, God is distinguished from the demiurge, who does not create but receives the matter which he distributes to the lower planes of being. Porphyry, who is always more likely than his coreligionists to employ a

[52] See now Reydams-Schils (2010), 498. Here and at Reydams-Schils (2002), it is argued that Christian elements in Chalcidius may be concessions to the faith of his addressee, which is also attested at *Commentary* 126 and 133.

[53] On his knowledge of Origen see Van Winden (1959), 54–66; on p. 162 his allusions are taken as evidence of his middle Platonism rather than his Christianity.

Christian formulation, may have spoken of matter as the first product of the Demiurge, but it is possible that he is speaking of the intellectual matter which sustains the multiplicity-in-unity of the Forms. Chalcidius too is willing to postulate this as the necessary substrate of an 'intellectual heaven', but his choice of that locution (rather than *kosmos noêtos*, 'intellectual cosmos') suggests once again that his interlocutors were Christian rather than pagan (278). Again, the Platonists granted that the matter in which the Forms reside is devoid of qualities, they denied for this very reason that it is the true stuff of creation and did not speak, as Chalcidius does, of the origin of the world from 'that which is not' (31).

Chalcidius appears to hold, with the Platonists of his day and in defiance of all his Christian predecessors, that even the corporeal world is eternal in the sense that it has no temporal beginning (27), though he rests this belief on the axiom that whatever God does he does eternally, rather than (as a Platonist might) on the argument that, since there is nothing other than soul that could cause the soul to move or arrest its motion, there can be neither beginning nor end to the motion of the world-soul. The eternal stands in a causative, not a temporal relation, to the temporal; our world exists *per omne tempus* ('throughout all time'), while the intelligible universe, like God himself, exists *per aevum*, or in Greek *eis aiôna* (105)—not so much 'eternally' as 'from age to age', a locution which has more biblical authority than the Platonic term *aidios*. Platonists and Christians agreed that the inescapable division of our lives into months and days does not entail that we are mere puppets of the stars. Whereas, however, a Platonist might be content to uphold the hegemony of reason, the clear signs of a providential ordering of the cosmos, and the necessity of our being justly amenable to punishment and reward after death, Chalcidius makes the typically Christian protest that the teaching of the astrologers curtails the foreknowledge of God (162). Platonists, following Aristotle, held that the eternal contemplates only the eternal; Chalcidius attributes to God a particular knowledge of, and solicitude for, his human creatures (55), notwithstanding the clear assertion of Plato that the Demiurge has entrusted the tutelage of these lesser beings to lesser gods.

To these echoes of biblical diction we may add explicit quotations from the opening chapters of Genesis, which are all the more revealing in the absence of any appeals to other nations who seemed equally wise to Porphyry and Iamblichus. Urging that it would be absurd to deny souls to the imperishable stars, who (in contrast to us) have committed no sin in the course of their eternal revolutions, he adds that the Hebrews prove themselves to be of the same opinion when they represent God as giving the charge of the day to the sun and that of the night to the moon (130). The very perversity of this allusion to Genesis 1.18 is surely a measure of the importance that Chalcidius attached to the suffrage of Moses on a point that would have been contested by his fellow-Christians. A few lines later he states that the Hebrews were also at one with Plato in their recognition of a class of beings who, though they share the immortality of the gods, resemble us in their liability to passion; he thus transforms the daemons into angels at a time when for other Christians the word *daimon* always signified a false god of the race of Satan and Beelzebub.[54] In his defence of freewill Chalcidius cites the famous aphorism 'the blame lies with the doer; God is blameless'; without accusing the Greek of plagiarism, as Justin Martyr had done, he finds a corroborative parallel in the story of the first humans who, 'according to Moses', wilfully transgressed the divine prohibition which had the power to obey (154). When later he wishes to vindicate Plato's teaching that the heart is the seat of judgment, in opposition to those who would locate it in the head, Chalcidius begins by quoting the dictum of Empedocles that 'the blood of the heart is the intellect' (218), then crowns the argument with two biblical verses, one forbidding the consumption of blood on the grounds that 'the blood is the life', while the other—'the blood of thy brother crieth unto me' (Genesis 4.9)—implies that this life is not quenched by its severance from the body (219). Nevertheless, it is not the life of the rational soul, which, according to Chalcidius, we receive by divine insufflation (219). This tendentious reference to Genesis 2.7 is another specimen of his unwillingness to maintain a contestable view without scriptural warrant.

In chapter 256 we are told 'Hebraic philosophy', like Plato in the *Timaeus*, acknowledges more than one variety of dream. It is probable that Philo's treatise on dreams is the true authority for a statement which Chalcidius barely attempts to justify by direct quotation from the scriptures. Certainly Philo is cited in chapter 276 as a witness to the presence in the divine mind of an incorporeal heaven and earth, which are logically anterior to the world below the firmament and metaphorically represented at Genesis 1.1 as the first creation. The intellectual matter presupposed by this conjecture is equated by Chalcidius with the inchoate state described in Genesis 1.2, the Hebrew words for which are evidently unknown to him, since he juxtaposes the rendering in the Septuagint with those of Aquila and Symmachus, concluding with a fourth which Origen claims to have derived from the soundest copies. In the manner of Origen he proceeds to ask what was the beginning in which the first heaven and earth were created; having already established that this cannot have been a temporal beginning, he goes halfway with Origen, endorsing the latter's inference that all things have their cradle in the Wisdom who says of herself 'the Lord created me in the beginning' (Proverbs 8.22), but avoiding the invidious equation of this Wisdom with Christ, the Second Person of the Trinity. We may take it as evidence of the Constantinian date of the commentary that the alternative reading 'possessed' is not considered; on the other hand, Chalcidius has no reason to entertain so long as Wisdom is for him

[54] See further Den Boeft (1977).

simply a creature with no claim on our reverence. In short, this passage lends no colour to any attempt to make either an Arian or an anti-Arian of Chalcidius, who, if he ever adumbrated a doctrine of the Trinity, had the good sense to choose some other medium for it than a commentary on Plato.

No doubt his citation of Origen affords the best proof of his being a Christian rather than a Jew.[55] As evidence that he was touched by the theology of Origen and not only by his scholarship, we may note a laconic allusion to the individual form of Socrates (349) and a wordy denial that Plato literally taught the transmigration of rational souls into animal bodies (197–198). Plotinus devotes a short treatise (*Enneads* 5.7) to the possibility of a form of Socrates, but it is Origen who maintains that no named person has ever been a different person, and that God's foreknowledge of such an individual is of a piece with his knowledge of all genera and species.[56] It was a natural consequence of Origen's doctrine that, although a soul could sink incorrigibly into bestial habits, it could never pass from a human body into that of a beast. Since however, Chalcidius purports to be expounding another author's philosophy rather than his own, it may be thought more probably that he is following Porphyry's interpretation of the Platonic doctrine as a moral fable.[57] His teaching on time is not entirely congruent with Origen's, for when the latter maintained that time is coeval with the world, he drew the inference that both have a finite history. And, while Origen agreed that the heavenly bodies are ensouled and that their servitude in this world is not the penalty for some previous sin, he would have admonished Chalcidius that, according to Job, the stars are not clean in the sight of God.

Chalcidius upholds the Christian norm when he attributes to the highest God a peculiar concern for the welfare of humans. He departs from it, however, when he embraces the Platonic view that providence is exercised not directly but at one remove through the soul of the world—or rather at two removes, for as providence is the minister of God so fate is the minister of providence, and the legislator to all things in the lower realm 'according to their own nature' (177). The activity of the three is so distinct that one can speak not only of providence as a 'second mind' (188), but of a descending triad, in which the second god disposes and third applies what the highest has commanded (189). The human soul, as Chalcidius conceives it after Plato, is also a hierarchy of three elements, each of which has its natural overlord. God is the pilot of the contemplative intellect, fate the tyrant of the appetites;[58] who then could be unaware, Chalcidius wonders, that so long as the soul is in thrall to the body 'something belongs to fate and is not subject to our control?' (190).

[55] If he believed that 'Origen the Christian' and 'Origen the Platonist' were the same man, he was in agreement with some modern historians, on whom see Zambon (2011), 160–4.

[56] Origen, *First Principles* 1.5.4.

[57] See further Waszink (1974).

[58] See further Den Boeft (1970).

Origen might have answered, 'Who but a heretic would think so?' Chalcidius is what Origen is not, a Christian Platonist for whom the *Timaeus* is a sovereign text and scripture a malleable foil.

THE CHRISTIAN *SYMPOSIUM* OF METHODIUS

Chalcidius is a Platonist who, like his pagan contemporaries, makes no effort to write like Plato. The one author of this period who has Plato not so much at his finger's ends as in his veins is a Christian bishop, Methodius of Olympia, who died around 312.[59] As he himself intimates, the fine pastiche of Plato's style in his *Symposium* throws into relief the novelty of its content, for neither the great Athenian nor his fellow-Greeks would had given a patient ear to ten virgins speaking in honour of their own vocation. The speakers in the original *Symposium* are all men of note in Athens, each of whom, as his tongue is loosed by wine, finds his own way of sublimating the pleasures of homoerotic intercourse.[60] Aristophanes, less comically perhaps than he intended, laments the primitive wholeness which was lost when Zeus was obliged to bisect our ancestors, and which now can be restored only when the sundered hemispheres are brought together again by love. Socrates, purporting to quote the priestess Diotima of Mantinea, declares that the proper work of love is to apprehend the eternal form of beauty and thus beget immortal offspring, leaving the multitude to enjoy the more ephemeral fruits of sexual reproduction. At the end all is thrown into confusion by the irruption of a tipsy Alcibiades with his picaresque account of an ill-judged attempt on the chastity of Socrates. In the Christian *Symposium* all the characters, with the exception of Paul's friend Thecla, are imaginary; wine has only a spiritual significance, and the bridal which awaits them in heaven is one that is not even prefigured by ordinary marriage. The expulsion from paradise to which they repeatedly look back is not a parable, and the virgin's consecration of her body to God is the only means vouchsafed to us of reversing the consequences of the fall.[61]

The setting for the dialogue is a flower-studded meadow (proem 7–9), reminiscent both of paradise and of the 'closed garden' which was thought to symbolize virginity at Song of Songs (4.12). It also suggests the 'supercelestial place' from which, according to Plato's *Phaedrus*, the soul descends when she loses her wings, and to which she will rise once more when the memory of supernal beauty is quickened by the sight of a beautiful body. The first speaker,

[59] Jerome, *Famous Men* 83 says that he died soon after the end of the persecution; see further Barnes (1979).

[60] See further Bril (2006).

[61] Methodius introduced the word *ptosis* to the Greek Christian vocabulary:

Marcella, urges that the human race is now in no further need of multiplication, and that the time has come to restore the flesh to its aboriginal purity, thus perfecting the 'likeness of God' which is sought by philosophy and promised in the scriptures.[62] Marcella's successor Theophila is bold enough to maintain that, while it is better to aspire to the state of the angels, God has also given his blessing to procreation; in the third speech, however, Thalia replies that when Paul likens the relation of Christ and the church to that between man and wife, he has in mind not the union of a common human couple but the creation of Eve from Adam's rib as his helpmeet (3.54–61). The incarnation of Christ is a *kenosis* or self-emptying of God in order that through his death and return to life he may effect a 'recapitulation' (*anakephalaiosis*) of Adam's fall from life to death (3.71).[63] Through the Word's manhood the whole race achieves a victory over the devil, which the fourth speaker, Theopatra, represents as a subjection of the feminine to the masculine in our own nature.[64] Thallousa next exhorts her fellow-virgins to drink only from Christ, the true vine, eschewing the blood of the common grape,[65] while in the sixth speech Agathe construes the five wise virgins of Christ's parable as the five spiritual senses, to which she opposes the carnal sense typified by the foolish virgins.[66] Speaking seventh, Procilla interprets Solomon's one bride (Song of Songs 6.7) as the flesh, while his sixty queens are the righteous Seth and his progeny up to Noah, the eighty concubines are those who were pleasing to God between the flood and the incarnation, and the countless host of maidens the virgin disciples of Christ from whom he has now opened the way to heaven (7.157–164).

The eighth and longest speech is assigned to Thecla, who describes the soul's return to God in language rich in echoes of the *Phaedrus*.[67] She goes on to interpret the figure of the woman clothed with sun in revelation, who gives birth to a male child after she is driven into the wilderness by the serpent (Revelation 12.1–6). The serpent is our destroyer Satan, the flight to the wilderness is the escape of the soul from sin and passion (8.193–194). The woman is an emblem not only of Mary but of the church, which brings forth a new Christ whenever the flesh recovers its masculinity by vowing itself to sexual abstinence (8.189–190). The ninth speaker Tysiane expounds the feast of booths as proleptic celebration of Christ's advent, the meaning of which is still invisible to the Jews. Finally Domnina interprets the parable of Jotham

[62] Methodius, *Symposium* 1.23 and 1.25; Genesis 1.26–28; Plato, *Theaetetus* 176c.

[63] Cf. Philippians 2.6; Ephesians 1.10: Irenaeus, *Against Heresies, passim.* Methodius at *Symposium* 1.23 echoes the statement at AH 3.48.1 that humans were not yet perfect when created.

[64] *Symposium* 4.97; cf. 1.41, 1.56, and Irenaeus, *Against Heresies* 5.21.3.

[65] *Symposium* 5.121–122; John 15.1.

[66] *Symposium* 6.138–139; Matthew 25.1.

[67] Compare 8.171–173 with *Phaedrus* 246–248; 8.176 with 250b.

(Judges 9.8–15), in which successive trees refuse an offer of sovereignty, as an adumbration of four successive epochs in human history. The fig, she says, stands for God's commandment to Adam, the vine for the laws of Noah, the olive for those of Moses and the for the precepts of the Saviour, which cannot be abused in the way that our ancestors, at Satan's prompting, abused the fig and the vine (10.263–275). Arete or Virtue, who presides over the gathering, awards the palm to Thecla (11. 284), and the whole company intones a hymn to virginity in 24 strophes, each commencing with a different letter of the Greek alphabet. No Alcibiades breaks in upon the proceedings, but the epilogue is a Socratic elenchus or cross-examination, which purports to show that the merit of virginity is greater in those who remain who remain susceptible to temptation (epilogue 293–302). The elenchus is not a tool employed by Platonists of this era, and the conclusion is not one to which Plato would have subscribed.

THE SECOND GOD

The index to the standard edition of the *Preparation* shows that the works of Plato which are most often cited by Eusebius are the *Timaeus*, the *Republic* and (more common than both) the *Laws*.[68] Cosmogony being a topic of perennial debate among both Platonists and Christians, the first of these had never been out of fashion; the *Laws*, on the other hand, was barely more popular then than now, and even Plotinus, who thought that it would serve him as a charter for a city of philosophers,[69] makes less use of this text than of the *Parmenides, Phaedo, Phaedrus, Philebus*, and *Symposium*. These texts, which (with the *Timaeus* and the *Republic*) contained in embryo the entire metaphysical system of Iamblichus,[70] were of scant interest to his ecclesiastical contemporary, since they could not be set line by line against the Pentateuch and found wanting, like the *Laws*, and contained no paragraph that even a skilled apologist could construe as an adumbration of the Trinity. Iamblichus never appears in the fifteen books of the preparation;[71] the abundant quotations from Porphyry are invariably malicious; the longest of seven excerpts

[68] Mras's index records in total 1 reference to the first *Alcibiades*, 3 to the *Apology*, 1 to the *Axiochus*, 19 to the *Cratylus*, 4 to the *Crito*, 7 to the *Epinomis*, 1 to the *Euthydemus*, 6 to the *Gorgias*, 1 to the *Lesser Hippias*, 77 to the *Laws*, 1 to the *Lysis*, 2 to the *Parmenides*, 14 to the *Phaedo*, 17 to the *Phaedrus*, 3 to the *Philebus*, 54 to the *Republic*, 4 to the *Sophist*, 7 to the *Statesman*, 3 to the *Symposium*, 7 to the *Theaetetus*, and 44 to the *Timaeus*.

[69] Porphyry, *Life of Plotinus* 12; cf. Firmicus Maternus, *Mathesis* 1.14.1–7.

[70] See his syllabus of twelve dialogues at *Prolegomena to Plato* 26.

[71] He is more likely to have been acquainted with Iamblichus if the latter's teacher was Bishop Anatolius of Laodicea, as Dillon (1987), 866–8 surmises.

from Plotinus, a polemic against the Aristotelian concept of the soul as entelechy, does not agree in all respects with the corresponding portion of the *Enneads*, a recent compilation in which Porphyry had corrected his master's drafts and arranged them in six groups of nine.[72]

It is probably true that no Christian theologian in the Roman world was wholly untouched by Plato; it is certainly true that none was strictly a Platonist, if that is the term for one who accords to Plato an authority resembling that which Christians accorded to the scriptures. Both statements are eminently true of Origen, whose language is often more redolent of Plato than his thinking, and whose frequent praise is outweighed by his criticisms in the eight books *Against Celsus*. Of Origen in turn we can say as truly as of Plato that no Christian was wholly immune to his influence or quite faithful to his teaching. Historians none the less devise taxonomies in which some theologians are more Platonic than others, and in which the term 'Origenist' denotes a member of a particular group, perhaps most commonly the group that signed the Creed with greater reluctance at the Council of Nicaea in 325. Eusebius of Caesarea is often regarded both as the arch-Origenist of his day and as a tardy, if not disingenuous, signatory to the Nicene formula. Since the same taxonomies are apt to cite the Platonism of Origen as the cause of his holding opinions that were later deemed heretical, it is readily assumed that when Eusebius entertains the same opinions (or even when he employs the same locutions) he is a Platonist by proxy. A writer of the fourth century observed that the phrase 'second god', which was applied to Christ by Origen and Eusebius, but not by other Christian theologians, has its origin in traditions of thought that may loosely be called Platonic:[73]

> Hence [i.e. from Plato and Hermes] comes their conceit of a 'second god' (*deuteros theos*) before the ages, as their esteemed Asterius says, having learned this from Hermes who us surnamed Trismegistus . . . In this their notion of a first and second has its origin, and this is why the term 'unbegotten' appears in the writings of Eusebius of Caesarea. (Pseudo-Anthimus, *On the Holy Church* 10 and 12)

Marcellus—the presumed author who was also (as we shall see) an inveterate enemy of Eusebius—proceeds to cite a passage from *Timaeus* 52a as the source of his rival's vocabulary (15) and to accuse him of following other notorious heretics who had styled Christ a 'second cause' (17). In his view the proponents of this 'second god' cannot escape polytheism unless they subordinate the 'second' to the first in a manner that robs the term 'god' of its literal

[72] A collection of scholia by Eustochius, the physician of Plotinus, is attested, according to Henry (1948), 135, 157, 183, and 207 in scholia to *Enneads* IV.4.19 in four MSS: Laurentianus 87,3, Parisinus Graecus, Urbinus Graecus, and Monacensis Gracecus. At 325–40, however, Henry contends that manuscripts which been have taken for 'missing links' were in fact produced by contamination of Porphyry's version with the matter peculiar to Eusebius.

[73] Text from Mercati (1901), 89–98, partially reproduced in Scott (1936), 155–61.

signification. Origen (whom Marcellus refrains from naming) would not have taken either horn of this dilemma: he speaks of a 'second god' only as a concession to pagan usage, and, while he may accept the subordination that it implies, it is evident from his other works that he believed the Son to be of the same nature as the Father. Conscious that some Greeks went so far as to posit not only a second god but a third, he refrains from naming them (*Against Celsus* 5.7); Eusebius, on the other hand, is our chief source of information on the cosmogony of Numenius, a Pythagorean of the second century who was much admired in the circle of Plotinus. But for Eusebius, we should not know that the first god of Numenius represents Plato's form of the Good and the second the demiurgic intellect of the *Timaeus*. We should not know that the first god remains at rest while the second governs the material realm which came into being as a tragic result of his inadvertence:[74]

> Now the second god and the third are one; but as this is brought near to matter, which is a dyad, it unifies the matter but is itself divided by it because it is fluid and concupiscible in nature. Because it looks toward matter it is not turned toward the noetic—which would mean being turned toward itself—and thus it becomes forgetful of itself in its preoccupation with matter. Entering into contact with the sensible, it honours it and draws it toward its own nature as it reaches out for matter.

Yet even if one reads this text without an intimate knowledge of Christian doctrine, it will be obvious that the relation of Numenius to Eusebius is not that of master to pupil.[75] The apologist hopes to show through a philosopher's testimony that the doctrine of the Trinity is not absurd; he does not fall, here or elsewhere, into the heresy of teaching became a Trinity because of a schism in the second person. Eusebius is in fact a 'theological conservative', who reserves his use of the formula 'second god' for his propaedeutic and apologetic essays, and never falls into polytheism by speaking at the same time of a first and a second deity. When he refers to a 'second lord and god' or to a 'second god' after the first, he is affirming two things—the divinity of Christ and the causal priority of the Father—which were axiomatic to the thought of every good churchman before and after the Council of Nicaea. That he does indeed place the Son 'second' to the father (without the addition of the noun 'god') in writings addressed to his fellow-Christians is undeniable and of little import: we shall find, when we come to examine the Origenist controversy at great length, that in this age the suspicion of heresy was most likely to fall on those who declared the Son to be coeternal or consubstantial with the Father.

[74] Fr. 11 Des Places, from Eusebius, *Preparation* 11.18.

[75] Strutwolf (1999), 187–94 observes that for Eusebius the Second Person of the Trinity has the functions of both an intellect and a world soul—i.e. of both the second and the third god in Numenius. The rupture in the second god which Numenius imagines, however, finds no parallel in Eusebius but rather in the contrast drawn by his adversary Marcellus between the immanent and the projected Logos.

To theologians of the early fourth century it was obvious that if the Son were not in some sense inferior to the father he would not have said 'The Father is greater than I' (John 14.28).

CONCLUSION: THE VARIETIES OF LOGOS

One of the oldest tenets of Christianity is that Christ is the Logos, or Word of God, 'through whom all things came into being' (John 1.3). Behind this dictum stand the magisterial words 'And God said, *let there be light*' (Genesis 1.3) and the Psalmist's assurance, 'By the word of God were the heavens made' (Psalm 33.6). To Ignatius of Antioch Christ was the Word whose birth revealed the secret design of God (*Magnesians* 8.3); to Justin he was the word through whom God made himself known not only to the prophets but to all peoples; to Origen the title Logos signifies that every *logikos*, every creature endowed with reason, derives its rationality from him. Despite its biblical pedigree, the doctrine of the Logos is frequently reckoned among the plagiarisms of early Christian thought from Platonism, notwithstanding the absence of any such doctrine in the writings of the Greek exegetes of Plato. If we define the Logos as a 'transcendent intermediary'—that is, as one superior to the world but in some way subordinate to the Father—his counterpart in Platonism can only be the 'second god' of Numenius or *nous*, the second hypostasis of Plotinus; neither of these was ever styled 'the Logos', and indeed we never meet Logos as the unique appellation of any transcendent being in these authors. Plutarch, in expounding the myth of Isis and Osiris, used the term Logos to denote the immanent working of the demiurgic intellect in the lower world, but here there is obviously no connotation of transcendence. Philo of Alexandria is the one 'middle Platonist' for whom the Logos is the archetypal form of the world in God's mind and the instrument of divine creation and governance; but his very singularity is sufficient proof that his speculations are grounded in his native scriptures, not in the works of Plato. Porphyry was so unconscious of any Platonic ancestry for the notion of Christ as Logos that he lampooned it in one of his most notorious sallies against the church:[76]

> If this were the occasion for resolving difficulties, I would also have cited Porphyry's antithesis, which he introduces in his ravings against the Son himself. 'He is either', says he, '*prophorikos* or *endiathetos*. Now if he is *prophorikos*, he ceases to be as soon as he is uttered; if he is *endiathetos* to the Father, how is he separated from him?' (Michael Psellus, *Opuscula Theologica* 97.18–21)

[76] For a longer version of this objection, preserved by Theophylact of Ochrid, see Goulet (2010).

Perhaps we can deduce from this passage how Arius came to be branded a 'Porphyrian' in an edict which affords our only evidence for the burning of that philosopher's books in the reign of Constantine:[77]

> Just as Porphyry, the foe of piety, having composed certain lawless writings against the faith, has received his due reward, so as to have become a crying scandal for future times, and replete with the greatest infamy, while his impious writings have perished: so now it seems goods that Arius and the sympathizers of Arius should be called Porphyrians, so that they may bear the name of those whose ways they imitate.

Porphyry's ill fame might account sufficiently for the choice of his name as an epithet, were it not that Constantine also accuses Arius of putting a false construction on the term Logos. Having ratified the condemnation of Arius at Nicaea in 325, Constantine pronounced himself satisfied a few years later with a creed in which Arius failed to state that the Son is consubstantial with the Father, but described him as the Logos through whom all things have been created.[78] It is impossible now to trace the causes of a subsequent eructation in which Constantine pretends to congratulate Arius on teaching that the *logos* of God's essence is 'without beginning or terminus' and that 'the spirit of eternity was in the supernal logos', then goes on to denounce him for having subordinated a foreign hypostasis to the Father thereby denying that the Father and the Son share a single essence.[79] Beneath the bombast Constantine's argument seems to be that if the Son is not of the Father's essence he does not have a share in the eternal logos—or, to borrow the terms of Porphyry's dilemma, the *logos endiathetos* will remain with the Father, rather than coming forth as *logos prophorikos* in the Son.

Arius would certainly have rejected the position held by a number of second-century apologists, and perhaps also by Marcellus of Ancyra, that the Son enjoyed a latent existence as the Father's reason or wisdom before he was projected as word for the purpose of creation. He was later accused of juggling with two senses of the word *logos*, so that it meant one thing in relation to the Father and another in relation to the Son.[80] Whether or not this charge is just, the invective of Constantine shows clearly enough that in this era it was those who denied, not those who affirmed, that Christ was the Word of God who were more likely to be accused of Platonism.

[77] Athanasius, *Decrees of Nicaea* 38; Opitz (1934), item 33. The authenticity of the decree is doubted by Kraft (1955), but for other scholars only the date is a matter of controversy: Barnes (2009) upholds a date of 327 against Brennecke et al. in their introduction to Athanasius: *Werke* 3.1, xxxvi–xxxvii.

[78] Opitz (1934), item 30.

[79] Athanasius, *Decrees* 40.13–14; Opitz (1934), item 34. See further Edwards (2013b).

[80] See Chapter 13, this volume.

4

Pagan Holiness?

It has been alleged that Christianity is the one religion founded on miracles. It is also said that it rests on one great miracle, the resurrection, or even only on one continuing miracle, the internal witness of the Holy Spirit. In the Roman world no Christian denied the historicity of the 'mighty works' ascribed to Christ in the gospels; pagans, on the other hand, were free to doubt either that such things had occurred or that they signified all that the Christians read into them. In his first book *Against the Nations*, Arnobius retorts that if Christ's miracles were illusory so were those of his pagan rivals:

> You do not believe our writings; then we do not believe your writings. We make up false things about Christ; then you make false and empty boasts about your gods. For neither has any god dropped from heaven or commented with his own hand on your affairs, or by the same token disparaged our affairs and religious beliefs. These are written by human beings; those too are written by human beings and set forth in mortal speech. Whatever you have in mind to say of our authors, you must accept and judge that these things are said with equal weight of your own. (*Against the Nations* 1.57)

Who are the wonder-workers whom Arnobius derides here? A *theios anêr* in Greek was commonly not a thaumaturge but a sage of godlike intellect (*Meno* 99b–d), who won his followers not by meddling with the natural order but by strictness of life and the sober profundity of his conversation. Miracles of healing, exorcism, and abundance are far more common in the gospels than in pagan hagiography; no life of Pythagoras, so far is known, was such a catena of marvels as the first eight chapters of Mark. The life of Apollonius of Tyana by Philostratus (properly, *Things in Honour of Apollonius*) reads at certain points like a burlesque of the Christian narratives, though we often see it cited as though it might be a pagan model. In fact it is chary in the ascription of preternatural acts to its hero, recounting some of the taller stories only to disavow them; its leitmotif is that miracles are only for the vulgar and that this is a portrait not of a mountebank but of a magician.[1] Neither the magician's

[1] See Kee (1988), 84–6.

powers of illusion nor his authority over matter, even if granted, will afford evidence of his closeness to the gods.

In this chapter we shall consider three embodied paradigms of the godly life: Pythagoras, incomparable yet a beacon to many disciples; the astrologer, as apattern for universal imitation;[2] and finally Apollonius, or rather his antitype, not the Pythagorean apostle of purity but the popinjay and arch-deceiver of Christian polemic. By way of conclusion we shall note two Christian rejoinders to the inevitable charge that their redeemer was a Greekless charlatan.

IAMBLICHUS AND THE PYTHAGOREAN WAY

The treatise *On the Pythagorean Life* is not a biography (or not merely so), but the first of ten instalments in an encyclopaedic project which, as Dominic O'Meara says, was intended to lead the student from the more generic truths to those that are 'higher, more difficult and specifically Pythagorean'.[3] Thus, although the historical matter is of course 'specifically Pythagorean', the philosophic content does not take us beyond the foothills of the ascent which is continued in the *Protrepticus*, the work *On the Common Science of Mathematics*, the *Introduction to Nicomachus* and half a dozen other books now known only by their titles. It is the gospel of a sect to which Iamblichus acted simultaneously as evangelist and theologian. Such terms may seem incongruous, as Iamblichus never mentions Christianity;[4] it should be apparent from the following summary, however, that it would not be fanciful to read this work as a pagan gospel, designed to surpass its models without the homage of quotation or patent allusion. We shall see at the end of the chapter that another Pythagorean hagiography, the *Life of Apollonius* by Philostratus, was held up as a foil to the gospels by both pagan and Christian writers of this age.

Just as Christians held that they had freedom of access to God and that he ordains all things for the good of the saints, so Iamblichus tells us that the Pythagoreans thought it absurd to address their petitions to any being but the highest god (50.21–23 Deubner), and denied that anything came to pass without his consent (80.10). They did not contemn the lesser gods, however, and did not believe that divinity achieves its ends by a violation of the natural order. It is the task of the truly divine man to cement the ties of family, not to sever them, to establish justice in the earthly city, not to postpone the tribunal

[2] See also Addey (2014), 117–24.

[3] O'Meara (1989), 33. See p. 32 on variations in the titles of relevant works.

[4] Crystal Addey has suggested to me that Christians are the 'atheists' who attribute all oracles to the evil demon at *On the Mysteries* 3.38.

to another world. The mother of Pythagoras was called Parthenis, the virginal one, before she took the name Pythais (7.19 Deubner); nevertheless, she was always a married woman, and, although there is a tale of Apollo's mating with her (7.24), Iamblichus appends this to the story which he evidently favours, in which Apollo merely prophesies the birth through the mouth of the Pythia (7.8–22). Pythagoras does more to verify than to disarm the suspicion that he is Apollo in human form (75.12–19; 76.16–24), yet he does not make the claim spontaneously and his recollections of his previous lives might seem to gainsay it.[5] As a child he grows rapidly in wisdom, like the Jesus of Luke (2.52), and his even in youth his sagacity astonishes his elders (8.15–17); for all that, it is not given to any man to acquire all knowledge without instruction, and his numerous journeys, in which he is at once apprentice and master, are the pilgrimages of a man who never pretended to be more than a lover of wisdom (*philosophos*).[6] While Jesus that a prophet has no honour in his own country, Pythagoras did not 'despise Sidon because it is his fatherland, but wished the folk of that country to taste the beauty of his teachings to the utmost' (14.6–8). Christ said 'My mother and my brethren are those who hear the word of God and do it' (Luke 8.21; cf. Matthew 12.50 and Mark 3. 35); for Pythagoras in this narrative the command to honour one's parents is the plainest and most binding of all.

John had exclaimed that if all the words and deeds of Christ were written down the world would not contain them (John 21.25); Iamblichus says, more modestly, that a recitation of all the fraternal offices that Pythagoreans had rendered to one another would exceed the bounds of his treatise (73.9–12). Only passing reference is made to any actions of Pythagoras that were unequivocally miraculous.[7] Of him no less than of Jesus at John 2.25, it could be said that he 'knew what is in' every one of his neophytes (45.20–46.2), but he learns it by interrogation, not by divine clairvoyance. Spectators may admire his 'more than human' mien when he comes down from Mount Carmel (11.19–21), but there is no cloud, no proclamation from above and no superfluous albescence of his white linen.[8] Taken aboard a vessel, as so often in the gospels, he directs its course infallibly (12.1–3), but not by abridging the voyage as he appears to do at John 6.21. He can cure a lovesick maniac, but since the cause of the infatuation is an air played on a flute and not a demon, no exorcism is required except a more emollient strain of music.[9] John 21.11 describes the numbering of a miraculous draught of fish;

[5] *Pythagoraean Life* 14, 34.9–35.15 Deubner. At *Life* 8 (7.27–8.5) the question is left open. For the term *anthrôpomorphos* see 54.14.

[6] See esp. *Pythagorean Life* 11–12 (8.29–10.9 Deubner). For the term *philosophos* see 30.20 and 89.23.

[7] See *Pythagorean Life* 135 (76. 19–24).

[8] Cf. Matthew 17.1–8; Mark 9.2–5; Luke 9.28–35. For the wearing of white linen see 58.5.

[9] *Pythagorean Life* 112, 64.16–65.5 Deubner. At 65.4–5 the former lunatic becomes a disciple, as the cured demoniac wished to do at Mark 5.18.

in the anecdote related by Iamblichus (21.5–10), Pythagoras correctly predicts the result of another count before the net is brought to shore. His purpose, unlike that of Christ, is to save the fish by winning his wager, and the one preternatural feature of the episode is that, while they are being counted, the fish survive a long exposure on dry land (21.11–14).

Pythagoras speaks 'as *logos*' (53.21), but is not styled the Word of God (John 1.1; Revelation 19.13). Once he surpasses Christ, for where the latter had appeared to two disciples without being known (Luke 24.13–33), Pythagoras is recognized by different disciples on the same day (76.10–11; 77.8–9) in two localities. Even in this case it is the Christian narrative that contains the more fantastic conceit of a posthumous apparition. Too many biblical scholars, for whom the supernatural element in the gospels is an impediment to rational faith, have argued that its presence is dictated by some Hellenistic model. Apollonius of Tyana and Pythagoras have been cited as examples of the ubiquitous *theios anêr*, or divine man, of pagan hagiography, who does nothing without a miracle. Yet our only remaining specimens of this literature (which are Roman, not Hellenistic) distinguish clearly enough between the man who is truly divine and the *goês*, or thaumaturge, who plays on the credulity of the masses by perverting the course of nature. The Pythagoras of Iamblichus, selecting his disciples for their philosophical aptitude, teaches them that the gods bestow their favour on the same principle, reserving a place of honour after death for those who meditate 'on the soul, on its essence and on the primal origin of all' (100.14–15).

The Pythagorean philosophy, as Iamblichus expounds it, awards no praise to virginity in common life: it is better to rear up children to serve the gods. The members of a Pythagorean lodge are bound to uncommon rules of abstinence, forgoing not only meat but the eating of beans. For this last taboo they will die, though they are not permitted to divulge the reason to an outsider. This and other precepts they receive without contention from 'the man', as they call Pythagoras, much as Jesus is styled both 'man' and 'son of man' in certain passages of the New Testament. The purpose of their long initiation, which entails five years of silence, is to impart an understanding of these precepts and to inculcate a fixed habit of obedience. During this sequestration, all the individual's goods are held in common with the rest, but those who prove unworthy are dismissed with twice the portion that they gave. No one suffers a punishment comparable to that of the Christians Ananias and Sapphira, who were struck down instantaneously by God when their avarice marred the one experiment in the community of goods that is attested in the earliest Christian writings (Acts 5.1–11). The 'common life' (*koinos bios*) of these disciples bears a closer resemblance to that of the Essenes, who were also characterized by strictness of diet and simplicity of vesture. The Essenes and Christ are at one with Pythagoras in demanding that the truth should be told at all times without the specious confirmation of an oath; for Pythagoras, however, this is one of many injunctions which are designed to promote the exercise of civic benevolence, not to create a self-sufficient coterie of the pure. The virtues cultivated under the seal of friendship are wisdom, temperance, justice and courage, the four that Plato held to be indispensable to the integrity of a commonwealth. Political duress or the desire to evangelize others may force an adept into temporary solitude, but there is no such thing as a monk, no celebration of the eremitic life, not even Porphyry's aspiration to be alone with the alone.

THE FREEDOM OF AN ASTROLOGER

The treatise *On the Pythagorean Life*, as was noted above, is the first of ten books in an encyclopaedic project. A Pythagorean relish is imparted to the second, the *Exhortation to Philosophy* or *Protrepticus*, by long quotations from works in the Doric dialect attributed to Archytas and by an epilogue which translates the master's cryptic sayings into clear rules of conduct (133–151 Des Places).[10] It also draws, however, on the lost work of the same name by Aristotle, and for the most part it is a general manifesto, addressed to educated worldlings who regard philosophy as a useless science. Iamblichus replies that in the present world whatever is not the product of chance is the product of skill or nature (79.9–13). Every skill is directed to an end, and we divide ends into those that are chosen for the sake of others and those that are chosen for themselves. Ends of the latter kind are prescribed by nature, whose workings are as infallible and perfect as ours are fallible and imperfect (80.5–7); the skills that we exercise are at best supplementary to her operations and dependent on them (80.8–25). Now nature, in denying us the speed and strength of other creatures, endows us with a vast superiority in intellect (67.1–19; 81.5–15); to realize the end proper to us as humans, we must cultivate this divine element in the self, which in fact is what the self truly is (59.26; 60.19–23). The native activity of the intellect is contemplation (52.20–25), and when set at large it is able to comprehend the whole universe of forms or ideas (51.15–27). In the present world, however, it is encumbered, or rather imprisoned, by a body of which there is nothing but ill to be said. The body is a crucible of illusion and base desire, an insuperable bar (before death) to the consummation of virtue; it is the nether world imagined in the mysteries, where the soul receives the penalty of past sins (96.3–21). The liberated intellect is not identical with the self as we know it here, where even the best of us is an unstable commonwealth

[10] See 14.10–220 Des Places; 48.27–49.8; 51.1–14; 52.15–18; 53.12–19; 85.2–9. All are commonly regarded as pseudepigraphic.

of reason, spirit and body; of this empirical and eclectic self we may say that the intellect is its god (78.19).[11]

Yet the intellect, according to Iamblichus, has fallen with the soul. So long as it is trapped in its house of clay it is second in honour to the gods who remain above (60.19–23), and indeed relies on their assistance to reach the state which they (or perhaps the one God, as at 81.12) have appointed for it. Although the logic of the *Protrepticus* is universal, Iamblichus warns his readers at the outset that the philosophic life cannot be pursued with success unless a certain tutelary daemon has been assigned to us on our entry into this world.[12] Under its guidance the soul of the philosopher ascends to the star ordained for it. Here Iamblichus takes up the enigmatic statement of Plato in the *Timaeus* (41e–42e) that every soul before its first embodiment is assigned to a star, is shown the pattern of life that has been vouchsafed to it, and receives as its pilot a lesser god who will make up what is lacking in its capacities. Later in the same dialogue we hear that the rational faculty is implanted in the soul as its daemon (*Timaeus* 90a); tacitly collating this with the teaching of other philosophers that our daemon, or fortune, is chosen for us by our characters, Iamblichus concludes that our path is determined by the innate predisposition of the intellect at the inception of each new life.

Plotinus had offered a somewhat different gloss on Plato's doctrine in his treatise 'On our Tutelary Daemon', concluding that within each soul there is a graduates series of powers, each corresponding to one of the spheres in the physical cosmos (*Enneads* 3.4). As the soul disenthralls itself from the body in successive lives, it realizes successively higher powers, and this receives as its pilot the star which corresponds to this. The daemon who personifies that star is neither wholly within nor wholly extrinsic to us. While he accords more freedom to the soul in its current embodiment than Iamblichus, Plotinus admits that our freedom is in some degree bounded by the conditions under which we enter the present world. In another treatise Plotinus grants that even the philosopher's body is not immune to the sorcery of nature, which acts upon it by cosmic sympathy, though the good man will ensure that his soul is drawn only towards the good (*Enneads* 4.4.45). Porphyry asserts that, having studied the casing of horoscopes, he found it to be a wholly chimerical practice; yet he also records that a rival was able to cause Plotinus acute discomfort through the power of the stars.[13] In his *Letter to Marcella* and his *Cave of the Nymphs* he intimates that the philosopher must undergo certain trials to propitiate his natal daemon.[14] Nevertheless, in his letter to

[11] Cf. 64.24 on the divine in humanity and 104.10–11 for the equation of likeness to god (*Theaetetus* 176c) with flight from the body.

[12] At 45.1315 we are told that we choose our own daemon, being the authors of our own fortune and the agents of our own happiness.

[13] *Life of Plotinus* 14 and 10.

[14] *Cave of the Nymphs* 80.8–81.21 Nauck.

Anebo, if he is indeed the author, he accuses the Egyptians of ascribing so much authority to the daemon who presides at our birth as to leave the soul no freedom in its endeavours. Who sends the natal daemon, he enquires? Is he set over one of our members or all? Is he in fact a being distinct from ourselves or a part of the soul (Iamblichus, *De Mysteriis* 9.1)?

Anebo is an imaginary figure and the aim of the letter may be to elicit an answer rather than to disparage a people whom Porphyry elsewhere describes as outstanding in sagacity (*logiôtatoi*). The answer of Iamblichus, in the ninth book of his treatise *On the Mysteries*, presupposes what he has shown repeatedly in the previous eight, that a daemon is not a portion or aspect of the soul but an imperfect apparition of divinity. He is not to be equated with the paradigm which affords an ideal pattern to the soul, nor with his *oikodespotês*, or 'master of the house' (9.2 and 5). The latter is the planet dominating the sign of the zodiac which the sun occupies at the time of birth, and functions here as a counterpart to the lesser gods of the *Timaeus*, who determine when and in what form the soul will commence a new life in the sublunar realm. Although no part of the soul remains above as in Plotinus, it does not follow that the embodied soul is in fetters. His Egyptian mouthpiece says that we have two souls, only one of which is piloted by the daemon, while the other is free and cognizant of eternal principles (*On the Mysteries* 8.6). Knowledge of the future may be included in this vision, but is never oppressive (as Porphyry imagines) because the objects of divine prescience are always 'boniform' (9.4). When the gods have led the soul to an understanding of totality, it is entrusted to the 'whole Demiurge' in the first stage of liberation. The details of this hybrid speculation remain obscure, but it is evident that, whatever was taught in Egypt, this philosopher is a Platonist, for whom virtue is the only measure of freedom but our freedom to be virtuous is constrained by circumstances that we have little power to mend in the present life.

Iamblichus, when writing in his own person, held that no part of the soul in the present world remains unfallen;[15] at the same time, he shared with other Platonists the conviction that the soul is not a slave to its environment, and his letters insist that a locus of absolute freedom can be preserved amid the play of fate or mechanical causation. Fate is not an enemy: it is the algorithm of providence in the lower realm, a regulated principle of change which, being rooted in the changelessness of the One, counteracts the centrifugal tendencies of matter (pp. 282–5 Taormina and Piccione). Encompassing every *taxis* or ordered process in the natural realm (284–5), it sustains the concordant motion

[15] See references in Finamore (1985), 35, 55 n. 11. At pp. 103–5 Finamore distinguishes three categories of soul, the first of which descends by choice to perform the task of administering the cosmos, the second for the same purpose but under compulsion, and the third to undergo punishment for wrongs committed in the upper realm. The rational element remains superior to the irrational, but the vehicle which sustains the fallen soul on earth will never be dissolved.

of the heavens, the alternation of birth and death in the sublunar realm and the temporary fabric of our own bodies. In each of us the lower, corporeal element is gratefully subject to the rule of fate, while the higher element, the incorporeal soul, remains free of suffering insofar as it freely elects to suffer. Nothing that occurs in the course of nature will seem evil to one who dwells habitually in the eternal realm of forms (292–3). Since the sphere of fate is administered not by gods but by intermediate beings, it can be said that the *tukhê* or fortune of the vulgar is daemonic, whereas that of the philosopher is divine (295–6). The god-given art of dialectic enables us to cross-examine, and thus dispel, our work-aday perception of goods and evils (286–7); it can be acquired only by gradual instruction, the teacher accommodating his lesson at each stage to the capacities of the pupil (288–9). The foundation of virtue is courage which teaches us, by estimating danger at its true magnitude, to decide whether to act or refrain from action (314–17). The virtuous soul is unified by wisdom, the eye by which we contemplate the unity of the first principle (310–11); temperance maintains the equilibrium of the virtues by communicating to them the beauty and symmetry which are the first expressions of unity in the cosmos (312–13). When courage, wisdom, and temperance act in concert, the sum is justice, which, as Plato says, allots to each its due (327–8). Thus justice implies discernment, and, since like is known by like, the soul that infallibly discerns truth from its counterfeits will be one that (quoting Plato again) has attained the goal of philosophy, 'likeness to god' (330–1; *Theaetetus* 176c).

CHRISTIAN ASTROLOGY?

Among Christians Chalcidius is alone in granting even a subordinate role to fate in the direction of human affairs.[16] All theologians of the episcopal church before Constantine maintained that if there is to be faith there must be freedom of will,[17] and this argument is turned against the astrologers by Methodius in a series of propositions attached to the longest of the speeches in his *Symposium*. Elliptical in construction and perhaps textually corrupt, it sits uneasily in the dialogue, and may have been inserted by a scribe who, having found it in some other work by Methodius thought it worthy of preservation.[18] It commences, in Plato's manner, with a sally against the

[16] See Chapter 3, this volume. For a full review of early Christian attitudes to astrology see Hegedus (2007).

[17] See Tatian, *Oration* 9; Hippolytus, *Refutation* 4.16–27 and 4.46–49; Origen, *Commentary on Genesis* 7; Barton (1994), 63–7.

[18] Might it once have formed part of the dialogue *On Free Will* ascribed to Methodius, the textual history of which is partly elucidated by Barnes (1979)?

poets: if it is good that the stars should rule us, they ought to have existed from the beginning, yet the majority of our constellations are said to have appeared only when some human had been translated to the heavens as the reward of sin or virtue (*Symposium* 8.7). Next, taking up two philosophical premises that were axiomatic to Porphyry, Methodius urges firstly that if the stars are exempt from wants or needs they will take no pleasure in causing us to do evil, and secondly that if God is perfectly good he will not permit us to do any evil except of our own free will. He concludes with a variation on the Peripatetic commonplace that our errors cannot be subject to praise or blame unless we have freedom not to err. Even to forbid a crime, he says, will be a futile measure if destiny rules that the crime must be committed; punishment will be not only unjust but otiose, and every law that we pass will be a dead letter, if the acts that we hope to deter are already written in the stars (8.8).

Perhaps we ought to make an exception for the *Mathesis* of Firmicus Maternus. Boasting itself the first manual of astrology in Latin, it is generally agreed to be inferior in technical accomplishment to the Greek works that it emulates, though it greatly exceeds them in vigour and rotundity of style. It is dedicated to Lollianus Mavortius, who, after holding a number of distinguished offices from 324 to 337, was raised to the consulship in 355. Since Constantine is addressed by name in the work, any date after 337 must be excluded; some maintain that a reference to an eclipse yields a secure date of 334.[19] Firmicus addresses the Christian Emperor with reverence and apparently with no fear of his laws against divination;[20] a few years later, his tract *On the Error of Profane Religions* urged the sons of Constantine to root out pagan cults with the zeal enjoined by the scriptures. Since he does not profess to be a convert, and does not include astrology in his catalogue of abuses,[21] it is possible that he regarded Constantine as his co-religionist even when writing the *Mathesis*. That is to say, he may be a Janus-figure who, like Chalcidius, did not believe that the paths which others shunned were forbidden to him.

Near the beginning of the *Mathesis* Firmicus apostrophizes Constantine and his 'ever-unvanquished sons' with the unctuous flattery that we otherwise look for only in Christian authors (1.10). His grovelling throws into relief the temerity of his project, for he was writing in the last years of the Emperor Constantine, who had imitated his predecessors in passing laws against the

[19] *Mathesis* 1.4.10. These arguments of Mommsen (1894) are more widely accepted today than his attempt to fix the date at 335 by identifying the subject of the horoscope at *Mathesis* 2.29.10.

[20] At *Mathesis* 2.30.5 he protests that no one can cast the horoscope of the sovereign, who is superior to fate. Zosimus, *New History* 2.29 records the suppression of private divination, though Constantine was willing to consult the public augurs as late as 320 (*Theodosian Code* 16.10.1).

[21] See Hegedus (2007), 21 n. 98 for a list of scholars who have been struck by his failure to denounce astrology in his assault on pagan religions.

private use of divination. Even had Constantine not feared conspiracy as much as any pagan, his own theology taught him that such practices were sacrilegious, even when not seditious, if they presupposed the subjection of the elements to mechanical laws and this belied the universal providence of God. If there is such a fatal ordinance, he declares in his *Oration to the Saints*, it implies the existence of a lawgiver; otherwise 'fate' is an arbitrary term that disguises our impotence and lack of understanding (*Oration* 6). The tacit corollary of this imperial logic is that fate, not chance, has brought the present occupant to the throne, just as it is a corollary of his argument for the oneness of God that the Roman state cannot prosper so long as its government is divided. Firmicus, for his part, holds that humans owe their capacity for knowledge to the presence of a spirit infused by the deity who has fashioned them from the elements; at the same time, we have also seen that he commends his Christian overlord not only to the hegemonic God but to his deputies in the cosmos. He is justified by Constantine's adoption of his sons as heirs and Caesars, in the light of which his own prayer for the eternal perpetuation of Roman rule will have seemed more timely than Lactantius' remonstration against the pagan abuse of military power.

Lactantius, rolling a blear eye over previous apologies in Latin, had commended his own *Divine Institutes* as a work that aimed, not merely to vindicate his faith against calumny, but to lay out a comprehensive system of conduct and belief. Firmicus too undertakes to produce a treatise that will be not merely a vindication of astrology but the first Latin work to supersede the Greek manuals of instruction.[22] Among the other writings of Lactantius is a short treatise on the divine creation of humanity. Firmicus might almost be quoting this when he writes that 'God in creating humanity, having composed this animal with divine and extraordinary craftsmanship, restrained the divinity of the immortal mind in the bonds of a mortal and earthly body, so that the mind, spread forth without and within, restrained by the behest of some great necessity, might govern the body, its frail and perishable servant, by permission of the divine power.'[23] Again, he yields to no Christian apologist, not even to the emperor himself, in his antipathy to Porphyry, whose *Life of Plotinus* records that Plotinus, having examined the writings of the astrologers, had pronounced them full of nonsense. If the lucubrations of his Christian contemporaries were familiar to him, he may have hoped that his readers, on perceiving these similarities, would deduce that the astrologer is as pious a subject and as sound a theist as the Christian, who is flaunting ignorance under the guise of piety when he reproduces sceptical, and sometimes godless, libels on the science of reading the future from the stars.

[22] Among those to be superseded is 'Fronto noster' (*Mathesis* 2, proem); did Firmicus know that Minucius Felix had styled Fronto *Cirtensis noster* at *Octavius* 9.6?

[23] *Mathesis* 4.1; cf. 2.13.6 and Book 3, proem.

Could Firmicus have imagined himself to be already a Christian,[24] as he obviously did a decade later in his jeremiad against *The Errors of the Profane Religions*? We might say that he puts himself outside the fold by acknowledging lesser gods, but the worship of angels and divine lieutenants is an aberration commonly attributed to heretics; at the same time, he firmly acknowledges on God and attributes the power of divination to the 'deathless incandescence of divinity' (1.41), to whom he prays on Constantine's behalf (1.10). In his encomium of the true astrologer, he assures his readers that, just as Cicero's orator is a good man and not merely an adroit one, so the man who studies the revolutions of the cosmos must himself be a microcosm of all the virtues:

> For he who speaks every day about the gods or with the gods is under a duty to form and instruct his mind so that it achieves the imitation of divinity at all times. Be shamefast, upright, content with a slender diet and slender means, lest a craving for base emoluments should sully the glory of that divine science. Take pains to surpass the discipline and resolve of excellent priests by your own discipline and resolve; for if a man is a minister of the sun, the moon and other gods, through whom all things on earth are governed, it behoves him always to cultivate that discipline of mind which will be deemed worthy of such offices by the universal suffrage of humanity. (*Mathesis* 2.30)

At the same time, such a paragon will be no patron of nocturnal cults:

> You may have a wife, a home, an abundance of honourable friends, and be accessible at all times to the public: but hold aloof from all contention, undertake no harmful transaction, and let no financial enrichment ever seduce you . . . never be present at any nocturnal sacrifice, whether these be deemed public or private.

Gatherings by night could be forbidden by any magistrate who feared that they might be used to disguise conspiracy. Foreign cults were assumed to be peculiarly apt to harbour enemies of the public weal,[25] and Pliny, in his interrogation of Bithynian Christians, found it necessary to ascertain the content of the oath that they took before sunrise. Innocuous as this proved to be, his strictures on their 'depraved superstition' echo Livy's report of a much earlier senatorial proceeding against the Bacchanals, which purported to have found evidence of licentious sexual congress and homicide under cover of darkness.[26] Under Christian rule the charge of treasonable assembly was more plausibly urged against a pagan sect, perhaps most plausibly of all against those whom Firmicus would soon commend to the vigilance of the heirs of Constantine.

It is clear from what has been quoted above that Firmicus is no ascetic even in principle, since the astrologer's creed requires him to accept with

[24] The question could be answered in the affirmative by those Christians, whose epitaphs, according to Pietri (1980), 44, 'évoquent parfois des croyances astrologiques'.

[25] Rives (1995b). [26] Pliny, *Letter* 96; Grant (1948).

equanimity the office or the household that are decreed for him by the stars. For Platonists, or at least for Plotinus, inward freedom could be achieved only by the renunciation of outward ties. To Firmicus, Plotinus is the type of the boastful philosopher, whose faith in the soul's capacity to overcome the infirmities of the body had been rudely contradicted by the stars:

> It is said that, in order to arm himself against all fortune's menaces with the solid and incorruptible shield of virtue, he choose a site for a city in Campania to serve him as an idyllic seat, where the quiet and gentle air unfailingly nourishes the inhabitants with wholesome vegetation . . . But lo! while he was secure in his overweening confidence, all the power of the fates descended upon him. First his limbs grew stiff with a torpid freezing of the blood and his eyes lost sight of the splendour of light as it slowly thinned; next a pestilence, fed by evil humours, spread through the whole of his skin, so that as his limbs ailed his putrid body was wasted by the deadly corruption of his blood. Daily and hourly small parts of his entrails melted away under the insidious malaise, and whatever you had seen to be solid a short while before was disfigured in an instant by the terminal ulceration of his body. (*Mathesis* 1.14–17)

There is no Christian theology here and still less Christian charity, comparison of this passage with its probable source, the *Life of Plotinus* by Porphyry, reveals it to be erroneous in almost all historical particulars. Nor does it offer a logical refutation of Plotinus, who never contended that the philosopher ought to be invulnerable, but only that he was capable of bearing all affliction with equanimity. Firmicus seems tacitly to assume that this is untrue or that if true it is of no consequence. His purpose is to demonstrate that astrologers have the better of philosophers because they do not try to escape the lot that the stars ordain for them. Astral determinism does not impair our inward freedom: indeed the soul is most divine when she contemplates the celestial writ. To know and accept the place that has been assigned to us is the only path to virtue, because it is only when we know what we cannot change that we can exercise the true liberty of seeking only what lies within our power.

CHRIST OR APOLLONIUS?

Among the works attributed to Eusebius is a ferocious retort to a pagan denunciation of the Christians, entitled *The Lover of Truth*. Its author, Sossianus Hierocles, had held a number of distinguished offices before being appointed governor of Bithynia.[27] It was after the outbreak of the Great

[27] Barnes (1976a). Digeser's suggestion (2002) that Hierocles may be the source of arguments ascribed to the Hellene in the *Apocriticus* of Macarius Magnes has recently been challenged by Borzì (2013).

Persecution in this province that, according to Lactantius, he wrote his satire in two books with no other aim than to exacerbate popular enmity to the Christians. To reciprocate obloquy was at this time considered a Christian duty, though the exultant tone of the one surviving answer, commonly known as *Contra Hieroclem* or *Against Hierocles*, suggests that the persecution must have been repealed before it was written. Eusebius would have undertaken such a task with zeal, yet Tomas Hägg, with the warm support of Timothy Barnes,[28] has argued that the true author of this declamation is not 'Eusebius, the disciple of Pamphilus', as in the superscription, but a sophist of the same name. The invention of 'Eusebius the sophist' merely weakens his conclusion, since the Eusebius to whom the work is assigned in extant manuscripts is certainly the historian, who was famous enough to be credited with the authorship of a piece of apologetic writing even when the true author was not his namesake. But of course it might be possible to show that the author is some other person without being able to identify him. Comparison with the voluminous body of uncontested writings by Eusebius will show that the tract against Hierocles, if he wrote it, was an exercise that was never to be repeated. For one thing, while it is not the only work in the corpus ostensibly designed for a pagan audience, it is the only one in which neither the Old Testament nor the New Testament is quoted at any point. Perhaps this counts for little, as the tract is a sustained lampoon on a work that is equally destitute of such references; if we ask why the prolific Eusebius never wrote in this vein again, a sufficient reply would be that Philostratus' *Life of Apollonius* was the one book that had shaken the faith of Christians without engaging in overt polemic against the Bible or the church.

It might be thought that no more needs to be said in rebuttal of Hägg's more telling argument from the disparity in style between this text and the remainder of the corpus.[29] Elsewhere, we may grant, Eusebius is sluggish and verbose with a chronic tendency to bombast; the antagonist of Hierocles constructs and adorns his sentences with a fluent virtuosity not unworthy of the Atticizing sophists whom he has taken as his model. If Hierocles affected such a style, we may argue, the best rhetorical strategy was to pay him in his own coin, and all the more so if this was not a coin that one could tender in a serious work of apologetic, exegesis, or historiography. This would indeed be an adequate response if we were certain that Eusebius had the skill to devise such a calculated anomaly. No one doubts the authorship of the *Symposium* on the grounds that it contains exquisite specimens of the Gorgianic style which Plato eschews elsewhere in his writings; on the contrary, Plato exhibits such a perfect mastery of so many different idioms in the rest of his works that we can scarcely imagine who but Plato could have produced the speech of

[28] Hägg (1992); Barnes (2001).

[29] For further discussion see Borzì (2003) and the rejoinder of Johnson (2013b).

Agathon in this dialogue. The other compositions of Eusebius, by contrast, give so little sign of literary aptitude that we cannot but wonder why, if he wrote so well on one occasion, he did not do so again. If Hägg's objections to the Eusebian authorship of this text are not decisive, they cannot be dismissed so easily as some of his critics assume.[30] Here we may leave the question, which is of more concern to biographers of Eusebius than to historians of the Constantinian era, since it has not yet been denied that this eloquent salvo is most likely to have been discharged, like the first rejoinders to Porphyry, within thirty years of the ambush that provoked it.

Whoever he was, the author measures his wit, not against the 'lover of truth' himself but against Philostratus, whose coruscating narrative of the life of Apollonius had served Hierocles as a gospel. After deploring the insults that Hierocles pours on the gullibility of Christians (*Hierocles* 2.1–2), he declares it blasphemous even to think of likening this Greek impostor to the Lord from heaven, whose condescension to human form (resembling that of a doctor to his patients[31]) has put the whole race in possession of a sovereign antidote to its moral ailments and the trumpery of demons (*Hierocles* 4.1–2). By contrast the miraculous birth of the Greek sage is a palpable fabrication;[32] his claim to know all tongues without having learned them is refuted by his use of an interpreter in India, and the first book of the *Life* describes the teaching that he received from a dissolute Pythagorean, and from the birds by way of the Arabs.[33] With all the incredulity of a Lucian, the author enumerates one meretricious wonder after another that Apollonius is supposed to have witnessed in foreign parts: pygmies and manticores, levitating brahmins, bronze automata, women of unnatural pigmentation.[34] He admits the celibacy of Apollonius, and his fidelity to a five-year vow of silence (12.3) but finds it inexplicable that he should not require his pupils to join him in abstaining from meat.[35] He allows that he is capable of astute speech when confronting obvious charlatans (12.2), but accuses him of a grovelling partiality for the rich when he judges a suit concerning the ownership of a field.[36] Any miracles resembling those of Christ are recounted with an emphasis on the more ludicrous features: is there no way of curing a lame man but by stroking his buttock?[37] As the fourth evangelist numbered the miracles of Jesus, so this Christian numbers the 'tricks' performed by Apollonius in the fourth book of the *Life*. First he interprets the speech of a sparrow, not doubt using the meretricious arts that the Arabs taught him.[38] Next comes the foretelling of

[30] See e.g. the introduction to Jones's Loeb edition of *Against Hierocles* (Bibliography A).
[31] *Hierocles* 6.3.
[32] *Hierocles* 8.1 and 12.1; Philostratus, *Apollonius* 1.4.
[33] *Hierocles* 8.2, 10.1, and 14; *Apollonius* 1.19.1–2, 1.20.3, 2.29.1.
[34] *Hierocles* 22, 18.1, 19.1, 19.2; *Apollonius* 3.19, 3.3.1, 3.17.1–2, 3.27.2.
[35] *Hierocles* 12.3 and 13; *Apollonius* 2.7.3.
[36] *Hierocles* 16; *Apollonius* 2.39.3.
[37] *Hierocles* 23; *Apollonius* 3.15.38.
[38] *Hierocles* 27.1; *Apollonius* 4.3.

a plague, which he strangely attributes to the lightness of his diet.[39] Thirdly he puts an end to a plague at Ephesus by unmasking, in his canine form, the demon who had caused it.[40] If this is absurd its sequel, the evocation of Achilles' ghost, was not only a sacrilegious act but a needless one had Apollonius been truly omniscient.[41] The fifth trick is the expulsion of a demon from a profligate youth, the sixth the liberations of another youth from a succubus—two instances (to twist Christ's words a little) of Satan exorcising Satan.[42] One can only wonder why his crowning feat, the resurrection of a dead girl, left so little trace in the public memory.[43]

If Apollonius did perform any miracles, it was with the intermittent help of demons. Why else would he be turned away from Eleusis as a sorcerer?[44] Why would he accept gifts from the Indians whose machinations he himself denounces as sorceries after he has left them?[45] Why did Damis fail to perceive his divinity until, by withdrawing his leg from the irons in which Domitian's jailers had bound him, he proved that he could escape the constraints of natural law 'without prayer or sacrifice'?[46] If his prescience was natural, why did he speak so highly of Euphrates to Vespasian, only to tell Domitian twenty years later that he was a charlatan and a toady?[47] It is not worthy of a philosopher to boast, as Apollonius does, of having created two emperors,[48] or to take such meretricious care in the drafting of his speech when one of these emperors puts him on trial. In this apology Apollonius not only flatters the tyrant whom he despises, contradicting his previous animadversions,[49] but maintains that all human affairs are ruled by fate.[50] If this were so (as Plato discerned[51]), the philosopher would not be free to pursue his own way of life or to upbraid the mistakes of others (*Hierocles* 45). After sneering at the unsubstantiated tales of bilocation and ascension at the end of the life,[52] the author proceeds to a diatribe in the Cynic (or we might say, hermetic) manner on the necessity of freedom as a criterion of merit (47.1–48.1). His final word, resembling Porphyry's judgement on the character of Jesus, is that Apollonius may have been a good man and worthy of honour, so long as we acquit him of all the humbug that has been imputed to him by the misnamed 'lover of truth' (48.2).

[39] *Hierocles* 27.1; *Apollonius* 4.4 and 8.5.1.
[40] *Hierocles* 27.2; *Apollonius* 4.10.
[41] *Hierocles* 28; *Apollonius* 4.16.
[42] *Hierocles* 30.1; *Apollonius* 4.20 and 4.25; Matthew 12.25–27.
[43] *Hierocles* 30.2; *Apollonius* 4.45.
[44] *Hierocles* 30.3; *Apollonius* 4.18.
[45] *Hierocles* 31.1–2, tendentiously contrasting *Apollonius* 5.12 with 6.11.12, 6.11.17, and 7.32.3.
[46] *Hierocles* 39.1; *Apollonius* 7.28.
[47] *Hierocles* 33.1–2; *Apollonius* 5.28.2 and 7.3435.
[48] *Hierocles* 32 and 42.1; *Apollonius* 5.21 and 78.7.10.
[49] *Hierocles* 43.3, citing three passages from *Apollonius* 7.8.1–7.9.1.
[50] *Hierocles* 43.1–43.2; *Apollonius* 8.7.47–48.
[51] *Republic* 617e is cited at *Hierocles* 45.1.
[52] *Hierocles* 44.3, burlesquing *Apollonius* 8.30.

CONCLUSION: CHRIST AS THAUMATURGE

In Book 3 of the *Demonstration*—the inception, as he says, of his 'proper task'—Eusebius undertakes to show that neither the historicity nor the probative value of Christ's miracles can be denied. At the same time, being conscious that to establish the factual truth of the gospel is not a sufficient answer to those who regard Christ as a charlatan, he continues the argument from biblical prophecy that he had pressed against the Jews in the first two books. The first stories that he rehearses are those that fulfil Isaiah's prophecy beginning 'Who hath received our report?' (Isaiah 53.1)—a hint to the Jews that if they deny the gospel they declare their own scriptures unworthy of belief. He then goes on to contrast the teaching of Christ with that of Moses, urging that while the ordinances of the latter are superior to those of any pagan legislator, including Plato, they fail to inculcate the cleanness of heart and probity in everyday life that Christ enjoined on his disciples. Moses said 'Thou shalt not kill', but Christ 'Thou shalt not be angry'; Moses laid down penalties for adultery but it was Christ who forbade divorce. Thus he displayed the sublimity of his intellect—the hallmark of godliness in pagan eyes, as we have seen—and demonstrated at the same time that he was the 'prophet greater than I' whose coming was foretold by Moses. His identity being now manifest, he is easily shown to be also the suffering servant of whom Isaiah foretold that the kings of the nations would conspire against him and that our sins would be laid upon him. That Christ had been crucified under Pontius Pilate with the consent of Herod Antipas was not a fact in dispute, as it appeared to be miracle; Eusebius wishes us to conclude, however, that when a prophecy comes true—and this one is true of Christ alone—God vindicates the miraculous character both of the prophecy and of the event that it portends.

Only now is it profitable to argue for the verisimilitude of the biblical narratives. First their number and character must be considered: to heal a paralytic, to cleanse a leper, to open the eyes of the blind, to staunch an issue of blood by silent fiat, to raise a girl from the dead, to feed five thousand at once with a morsel are all unprecedented feats—and so is the fortitude with which he endured the unmerited ignominy of the Cross. Here the interlocutor may object that if such miracles prove Christ to be the Messiah, they are all the more likely to have been invented for this purpose. To hold this, Eusebius answers, we must hold that illiterate men could trump up fables which have deceived intelligent readers throughout the world for centuries. And if we ask for a motive, we find none, because they suffered affliction and death in every land for the sake of a tale which, on this hypothesis, they knew to be an imposture. They cannot be suspected of venality, for they honoured their master more when he was dead than when he was still alive to tempt them with idle hopes. Let us suppose, then, that the pagan critic holds the miracles to have been real, but products of sorcery. A sorcerer is always out for gain, whereas Christ taught his emissaries to carry with them no gold and silver, not even a staff or a wallet. Sorcerers are notoriously libidinous, but Christ rebuked adultery and commended those who had made themselves eunuchs for the kingdom of heaven. He not only demanded nothing for himself, but even preached against idolatry, thus depriving himself of the posthumous memorial that every sorcerer craves. The purpose of every miracle that he wrought was to not to win glory for himself in the present world but to excite a yearning for the invisible kingdom, of which many heard for the first time in his preaching. The pagan who is not convinced will show himself to be more a scoffer than Porphyry, whose counterfeit gods cannot refrain from praising Christ and denouncing his assassins. Eusebius, however, gives the last word not to this feeble testimony but to the apostles, whose artless proclamation of incredible truths would never have won a convert if the spirit of Christ were not at work within them. Thus (we are left to infer), Christ is not dead and is something greater than the heroic sage of Porphyry's confession.

Arnobius, who may not have been so familiar with the Old Testament, does not invoke any prophecies; instead, conceding that true stories are told of pagan healers, he protests that none of them displayed the power that we see in the miracles of Christ (*Against the Nations* 1.44–49). He admits that there are men who predict the future, who enter locked rooms without a key, who kindle flames of unquenchable love with illicit potions; all this (he says), if they do it all, they do with the assistance of their gods, who in fact are demons (1.50). Again there are crowds of the sick in every temple of Aesculapius, who effects no cures directly but may sometime prescribe a curative regimen after incubation. He adds that there are also multitudes at the temple door who remained uncured (1.49). If it be alleged that they were not worthy of succour, the Christian has a saviour who heals without respect of persons, the good and the wicked alike, and not by prayer, prescription or any physical instrumentality but simply by his word. When he said 'Be whole' the lame walked, the tongue of the dumb was loosed, the eyes of the blind were opened; by his word he fed thousands with a handful of loaves and brought the dead to life (1.48, 1.50). If this is to be stigmatized as magic, exclaims Arnobius, let all the most famous magicians come together from every quarter of the world, bringing with them their herbal preparations: they will never compete with the miracles of Christ, not even if they are spared the challenge of raising the dead (1.52).

What if one doubts the veracity of the gospels? Arnobius replies that if these texts were our only records we might suspect interpolation; the credulity of whole nations, however, shows that reports had spread to lands in which the apostles, and even the art of writing were unknown (1.54–55). If pagans plead the superior antiquity of their records, Arnobius can advance the unusual argument that the more ancient they are, the more likely they are to have suffered falsification (1.57). Again it is not in doubt that the apostles were simple men and their prose unpolished (1.58); but that is all the more reason to believe them, for it requires more art to lie than to speak the truth (1.59).

There is some originality in this reasoning, but it would not have moved the philosophers who denied that knowledge of God can be communicated without intellectual discipline. Still less would they have been moved by the apologist's plea that we ought to believe in the miracles of Christ because the power to perform such works in his name has been imparted to legions of his followers. Arnobius is writing in the tradition of Tertullian, who had boasted that Christians everywhere were confirming the truth of the gospel by their miracles of healing, while demons everywhere were bearing witness to it at the command of Christian exorcists. Eusebius, more reluctant to test the incredulity of his pagan readers, may be more typical of eastern Christendom. The subject of the next chapter will be Christian asceticism, and in particular two paragons of holiness, both Egyptian, who were distinguished not so much by their power over nature as by the unprecedented severity of the regimen that they imposed on body and soul.

5

New Forms of Christian Holiness

The pagan holy man of late antiquity, if we may call him such, is a social being, a citizen of the world (as the Stoics averred) but also of the Roman Empire and of the urban communities. The Pythagorean ideal was not to shun political life but to reform it; the astrologer was a paragon of the domestic and civic virtues; even the nomadic Apollonius of Tyana had no quarrel with the *polis*, or with its gods so long as they were revered without bloodshed. By contrast Christianity is in origin an anti-social religion, which taught its adepts to renounce the ties of family, to abstain from marriage, to take no thought for the morrow and to regard themselves as dead until they were born again of water and the spirit. Magistrates were to be obeyed, but only as the unwitting tools of God, and not when they forbade the worship due to him. Since procreation was no longer a duty, no rules were laid down for worship within the household, and the one mandatory rite, the Eucharist, took place outside the home for the majority of participants. Although Paul hints that this severance from the world exempted Christians from the harsher requirements of the Mosaic Law, the common view appears to have been that they ought to fast, so long as they took care not to ape the practice of the Jews. Some of these precepts of renunciation were unenforceable if the church was to survive; others, though constantly reiterated, were more honoured in the imperative than the indicative during the centuries that separate Christ from Constantine. The age of Constantine, however, was also that of the desert fathers, who went far beyond the edicts of any ecclesiastical council in their efforts to live the angelic life that Christ enjoined upon his first disciples.

THE CHRISTIAN MILIEU OF MONASTICISM

According to an early, if not primitive, witness, Christ sent his disciples out to preach without staff or wallet, thus surpassing the austerity of the Cynics.[1]

[1] On the perceived resemblance between Christians and Cynics see Lucian, Peregrinus, and Downing (1992).

In our canonical narratives he endures forty days of fasting in the wilderness, then commences a roving ministry, without a wife or a place to lay his head, and enjoining those who follow him to renounce not only wealth and ease but their filial and domestic obligations. In the Sermon on the Mount believers are urged not to hoard their resources, but to live from day to day on the bounty of God. Paul, addressing sedentary communities, is more lenient, exhorting them only to give as much as they can spare without becoming paupers. He himself, however, is a perpetual itinerant, commending and practising celibacy, boasting of his shipwrecks and his public flagellations, keeping his body in subjection and proudly bearing his thorn in the flesh. While he does not condemn the eating of meat, his advice that one ought to abstain from foods that offend more tender consciences may have proved severely restrictive, since for more than a century after him there were consciences that took offence at the eating of bloody meat or the remnants of pagan sacrifice. In the letters ascribed to him, both forbidding to marry and refusing table-fellowship with Gentiles are acts of hypocrisy (Galatians 2.13; 1Timothy 4.2); nevertheless, he lives as a Jew among Jews and prescribes that those who are married should live as though they were not. Virgins receive a special place in heaven alongside martyrs at Revelation 14.1–14; the term *parthenoi* is here applied for the first time in Greek to men, and whatever else it may imply by way of metaphor, we have no reason to doubt that it also retains its literal sense.[2]

For all that, we never read in the New Testament that there is any merit in poverty or suffering when they have no other purpose. Paul's privations are always instrumental to his ministry, and at other times he 'knows when to abound'. The same can be said of the regimen that Christ imposed (temporarily) on his disciples, and the admonitions to 'take no thought for the morrow' and to live as though one had no domestic ties are grounded, not in contempt for the body and its needs, but in the expectation of the Second Coming. By the late second century it was clear that the end would tarry, and the encratites, who shunned both meat and marriage as though they were evil in themselves, were denounced as heretics, at least by episcopal writers.[3] It did not, however, follow that because Christians had a full span of life before them in the present world they should live like the majority. Sexual intercourse outside marriage was forbidden, as was the marriage of a Christian woman to a pagan whose authority she was bound to defy in the practice of her religion. The ban on the consumption of *eidolothuta*, or offerings to idols, did not imply that any food was unclean, but was designed to prevent the Christian from stumbling into the worship of false gods. It may be that scrupulosity of this kind lent some colour to pagan fantasies of 'Thyestean banquets and

[2] Adult virginity and the sexual innocence of the young are prized in Christian epitaphs: Pietri (1985), 165–76.

[3] Irenaeus, *Against Heresies* 1.28; Brown (1988), 92–3.

Oedipodal copulation', since those who abstain from lawful acts are commonly accused of doing something more nefarious in secret.[4] Nevertheless, the chief task of many synods in the Constantinian era was to decide what worldly business was permitted or prohibited for Christians, thus ensuring that they were visibly set apart from the pagan world.

For the council of Elvira in Spain, which took place in the immediate aftermath of the Great Persecution,[5] idolatry is a more heinous sin than murder (canons 1–3), but it is sometimes equally difficult to atone for having fallen into everyday modes of conduct when a personal vow or ecclesiastical ordinance requires one to abstain. Virgins who fall into dissolute ways and do not repent are excommunicated for ever (13). Marriage to a believer commutes the penalty, but even those who enter the marital state under normal conditions may find themselves condemned to celibacy by widowhood or divorce. A woman who forsakes her unfaithful spouse and marries again can never hope to receive the Eucharist, unless she is prudent enough to wait for the death of the man who wronged her (9). The clergy were permitted to have wives but not to procreate or even to engage in sexual congress (33). Dicing is prohibited (79), as is the lending of money at interest by the clergy (20). Lifelong excommunication is also the sentence for a baptized woman who sells her own body or that of her daughter (12); on the other hand, prostitutes who have mended their ways and married before they 'come to faith' are admitted to the font without delay (44). The Eucharist is to be withheld from a magistrate so long as he holds his office (56); no charioteer may remain in his profession once he is baptized (62); painting is not pronounced to be unlawful, but no pictures are allowed within the church (36).[6]

It appears then that there were no trades, other than that of money-lending, which were forbidden to the clergy but permitted to the laity, as there were trades which were forbidden to the rabbi but permitted to the ordinary Jew. One reason was, no doubt, that Christianity proscribed only occupations that were deemed ungodly or morally perverse; another was that the payment of a salary to the clergy, a schismatic innovation in the late second century, had become common practice in the third, so that they now lived, like the Israelite priesthood before the Temple had fallen, on the offerings of those whom they

[4] Edwards (1992).

[5] Jonkers (1954), 5 (whose text I follow here) dates it to 305; Macmullen (2006), 2 to 310; Lane Fox (1986) 664 to sometime after 312 on the grounds that martyrdom 'is no longer an issue'. The canons as they stand are highly discordant, If we are not to suppose, with Laeuchli (1972) that they record dissensions at the council itself, we may be obliged to posit a history of redaction and augmentation: see Meigne (1975); Muro and Villena (2005); and Sanchez (2008). It is agreed that canons 1–21 at least are ancient.

[6] The witnesses collected by Thümmel (1992) would have applauded this prohibition. On Christian art unknown before Constantine see Jensen (2005), though outside Dura-Europos no decorated churches have been discovered.

ruled and served. To say that the clergy had become a priesthood, however, would be to forget that all priesthood in Israel, like many priesthoods elsewhere, was hereditary, whereas for Christians priesthood precluded a second marriage, if not a first. Even among the laity (who were all priests in the language of the New Testament) such unions are discountenanced, if not punished, while virginity is regarded as a desirable state for any woman, not only (as in Judaism) for one who was set apart as a prophetess or a philosopher. No other ancient nation or society had connived at such widespread indifference to the duty of procreation;[7] it is probable that an even greater number of Christians heightened their eccentricity, in pagan eyes, by abstaining at certain seasons even from foods that they otherwise considered wholesome. Fasting was mandatory for Jews, and certain sects were noted for the severity of their regimen. The Christian episcopate had always regarded those who wished to impose extremes of continence on the whole church as schismatics, if not as heretics; on the other hand, voluntary supererogation (like that which Eusebius ascribes to Origen[8]) was generally admired. Two of the canons associated with the Council of Elvira relate to fasting: one denies that all Christians are bound to practise supererogation on the Sabbath (26), the other (to spare the infirmity of the flesh) decrees that supererogation is lawful in every month except July and August (23). Moderate fasting is presupposed as a general obligation, but there is nothing to show that even the most austere were unremitting in their observance or had deprived themselves for long periods of all food.

In 314 the Council of Arles resolved that actors and charioteers were not to be admitted to communion (canons 4 and 5),[9] that a man whose wife had committed adultery was not to remarry while she lived (10), that a maid who took a pagan husband was to be excommunicated (11), and that clerics who lent money at interest should incur a similar penalty (12). In the East the Council of Ancyra resolved that deacons who disclaimed the gift of continence before their ordination could retain their office at the bishop's discretion when they married (canon 10);[10] adulterers and adulteresses were to be excluded from communion for seven years (20)—a mere sabbatical compared with the twenty-five years of exclusion appointed for those who lay with beasts (16).[11] The canons of Neocaesarea summarily rescinded the orders of presbyters who married (canon 1) and forbade presbyters to attend the feasts of those who had

[7] See Brown (1988), 7–8.

[8] On pagan models (or better parallels) for Eusebius, *Church History* 6.8–39 see Grant (1975); Cox (1983).

[9] Jonkers (1954), 23–8, but a different, and perhaps older version appears as appendix 4 to Optatus, *Against the Donatists.*

[10] Jonkers (1954), 28–35. For collation with the Syriac see Rackham (1891).

[11] Reference is also made in certain councils to clergy who live chastely with women whom they describe as sister; see further Elm (1994), 48–9.

married twice (7).[12] Adulterers were not to be admitted to ecclesiastical office (7); presbyters who confessed to a sin 'in the body' were not allowed to participate in the offering (8); multiple marriage was to be punished with excommunication (3), while a woman who successively married two brothers could be reconciled only at the point of death and on condition of repentance (2). While, therefore, it is evident that chastity was strictly regulated throughout the Christian world, none of these councils fell into the sin of forbidding to marry. They were even further from forbidding to eat, and the fourteenth canon of Ancyra rules that a cleric who will not taste meat in any form is to be removed from office, no doubt on suspicion of being a Manichean.

ORIGINS OF MONASTICISM

Christians in the early fourth century took up more exacting ways of life, the aim of which was to purge both soul and body by the mortification of every appetite but the love of God. Perfect sexual continence no longer sufficed unless it was accompanied by painful austerities in daily regimen, and particularly in diet. Practitioners of such disciplines, forgoing domestic ties and the affairs of the world, sought out the untrodden places, peopling one site after another either singly or in small companies, until at last, as a famous dictum has it, they had made the desert a city. We have no reason to doubt the ancient sources which inform us that monasticism was a new phenomenon; the concept, on the other hand, was familiar enough to mislead a historian seeking notices of primitive Christianity outside the New Testament. In the second book of his *Church History*, Eusebius makes a long excerpt from a work by Philo *On the Contemplative Life*, which some regard as our first account of the Essenes, some as a portrait of a different community, and some as a flight of fancy, perhaps not correctly attributed to Philo. The *Church History* presents it as a veridical description of a Christian school of the apostolic era, each of whose members perused the law and the prophets in a private asylum, taking no measures to humour the needs of the body, while at other times they forgathered to expound the deep sense of the scriptures.[13] Eusebius suggests that Philo gave the names Therapeutae and Therapeutrides to the men and women of this chaste order because 'the name Christian was not then generally known' (2.17.5). This is a gross anachronism but one that tells us something of his own time, as he would not have fallen into it

[12] Jonkers (1954), 35–8.

[13] *Church History* 2.17.10–12. On Eusebius as a witness to the authorship and purpose of the treatise see Taylor (2003), 31–40. On his error as evidence of antiquity of the Christian monastic tradition in his time see Richardson (2004), 153.

had the church of his time been ignorant of, or inimical to, the very concept of monasticism.

And yet the *Church History* must have been completed years before the first experiments of Pachomius. The only such institutions in his own day were the Manichaean communities, cemented by their fivefold vow of poverty, veracity, sexual purity, non-violence, and abstinence from meat.[14] Eusebius, of course, did not take Manicheans for Christians; in the *Church History* they are only heretics, not ascetics. If, however, it seemed to him that their practices were worthy of imitation, it is possible that he misread Philo on purpose, lest the church should appear to lack something that its enemies possessed. If others thought as he did, it can be argued that the presence of the Manicheans in Egypt helped to foster the intensification of ascetic practices within catholic Christianity. Since, as we have noted, such practices in their inchoate form were endemic to Christian life and thought, we ought not to speak of simple emulation, whether conscious or unconscious. We should rather say, in the light of the fact that Manicheans and Christians were acquainted with the same apostolic scriptures and exposed to similar cultural and political circumstances, that Christian practice underwent a natural evolution which might not have seemed so natural but for the precedent that had been set by the Manicheans.

Should we look further east for the origins of Christian monasticism? The passionless equanimity of the Indian sage, who suffered death as the voluntary coda to a life of self-inflicted suffering, was admired by pagans who despised the irrational fortitude of Christian martyrs. Alexander's conquests had extended to the Punjab, and encounters between Greek monarchs and whole communities of renunciants are recorded in both Greek and Indian literature. In detail these are manifestly fabulous, but if the events are fictitious we must account for the diffusion of the legends by some other means of contact. While Buddhist writings are not so easily dated as those of classical antiquity, it is clear that cenobitic or communal asceticism had been established in India long before the age of Constantine, and that comparisons between Pythagoreans and 'Brahmins' had become conventional. Mani was a self-professed apostle, not only of Jesus, but of the Buddha and Zoroaster;[15] it may no accident, therefore, that his sect resembles Buddhism in its organization more than it resembles any religion of the Mediterranean world. Once again we must enter the proviso that any influence will can only have been catalytic. The forms that cenobitic life assumed in ancient India are by no means identical with those that Mani instituted; where analogies have been observed, the dating of the Buddhist texts is too insecure to exclude the possibility of diffusion from west

[14] Lieu (1992), 26. Kephalaion 79 at Gardner and Lieu (2004), 240 advances five reasons for fasting which seem to mirror the fivefold vow.

[15] See further Woschitz (1989).

to east in the wake of the Manichaean exodus from Persia. Moreover, Mani himself was reared among the Elchasaites, a Christian sect who observed a meatless diet and took stringent measures to curb the sexual appetite.[16] To his former coreligionists he will not have been the Gautama of the west but a parody of their own founder—as Plato might have put it, an Elchasai gone mad.

This Manichaean precedent should be taken into account when one considers the theory of Reitzenstein that the church began to treat affliction and self-maceration as goods in themselves because the involuntary blessings of martyrdom had become unobtainable.[17] It is not a strong objection to this theory that the first cells were established in the desert before Diocletian's persecution, because the edicts of 303 took Christianity by surprise after forty years of toleration, during which it would have been easy to imagine that the church and the throne would be at peace for ever. On the other hand, we cannot suspect the Manicheans of embracing a stringent regimen as a substitute for martyrdom, for they had never known relief from persecution in the seventy years that elapsed between the death of Mani and that of Constantine. The Pythagorean lodges also excited the envy of tyrants, but it would seem that for the majority of the inmates this was their first taste of political oppression. Thus there would appear to be no general law which states that ascetic disciplines are always compensatory, developing only after the body has been reprieved from external tribulations. We must grant to Reitzenstein that the Manicheans had few imitators in the third century, and that flight to the desert grew more common during the years preceding Constantine's victory in the east; but if worldly causes must be sought for this, is it not more likely that the first hermits were escaping from persecution, or from the threat of its return, than that they had fallen into spiritual *ennui* within a few tears of its cessation? The chronology of asceticism might be better explained if we surmise that it began as an expedient but grew into a fashion, and once it could no longer be seen as the lesser of two privations the majority chose to temper the ordeal by fasting communally rather than alone.

Causes more specific to Egypt may account for the first migration to the desert. As one of the richest provinces of the empire, Egypt had been an object of fiscal plunder for three centuries, and it was not uncommon for those who were unable to meet these imposts to abandon their estates.[18] Brigandage was often the only means of livelihood open to them; in the meantime the authorities found no other way to redeem the loss of revenue than to increase

[16] See *Cologe Mani Codex* (Bibliography A).

[17] Reitzenstein (1916), 79–81. For criticism, chiefly of his assumption that confessors awaiting martyrdom habitually received visions, see Kirk (1931), 495–502. On virginity as martyrdom in Methodius see Clark (1998).

[18] Lewis (1983), 168–84 and 201–9.

the burden on those who had not yet fled. This combination of legal and illegal depredations drove many more into voluntary exile, the technical term for which was *anachorêsis*, or flight up country. Diocletian's remedy was to attack the symptoms without addressing the cause: his legislation interned the property-holder on his land, while his troops displayed unprecedented vigour in the chastisement of brigands. 'Anchoritic' solitude was a new means of escape for those who could not survive by toil and were unwilling or afraid to live by pillage. This theory is not exposed to the chronological objections that can be brought against Reitzenstein, and it furnishes a reason for the sale of possessions which often preceded the flight, since the property of a man who absconded would otherwise have been forfeit to the state. It need hardly be said that no evidence in its favour can be quoted from the ancient hagiographies, though even in these the spiritual motives of some characters are tempered by worldly appetites. It is likely enough that the motives of the first anchorites differed, as those of other groups differ, and that in many individuals the worldly and the spiritual were so mixed that no biographer could hope to disengage them. If they could not, neither can we: when we read that Antony sold all his goods because he understood this to be the one way to salvation, we may believe or disbelieve, but there is no scientific principle which will establish that the sale is a fact and the reason a mere surmise.

THE *LIFE OF ANTONY*

The fourth-century *Life of Antony* is our principal source of evidence for the dating of his career, and it is not a reliable one. Antony baffles Satan's attempts to drive him from the wilderness at the age of 35. After twenty years as an athlete of the spirit (14), he defies the tyrant Maximinus Daia (46),[19] who as Caesar of the east would have been his temporal overlord from 305 to 313. In chapter 82 he predicts, two years before its occurrence, an eruption of strife which the author, writing after his death, describes as the 'present' affliction of the church. The prophecy thus appears to have been uttered shortly before the end of Antony's life; four chapters later (86), Nestorius is named as the prefect of Egypt, and we know that he held this office from 345 to 352. Jerome, however, gives 356 as the year of Antony's death, and a letter written in 353 by the monk Ammonius indicates that he was still alive in that year. If we combine Jerome's date with the biographer's assertion that Antony died at the age of 105 (89), the year of his birth is 251, and he reached his fifty-sixth year a few months after the accession of Maximinus. This calculation requires

[19] On the tendency of historic persecutors to become stock figures in more fanciful narratives see Barnes (2010a), 137.

us to assign the prophecy to 354, some two years after the demission of Nestorius. If we shift Antony's death to 354, and the prophecy to 352, we shall find him defying Maximinus Daia before the latter had come to power.[20] Worse still, the saint is credited in chapter 86 with another augury of doom, this time in a letter to Balacius, a martial ally of Nestorius, who was bent on rendering Egypt docile to Gregory, the Emperor's nominee to the bishopric of Alexandria. According to his rival Athanasius, it was Gregory himself who received this missive (*History of the Arians* 14); yet Gregory met his wretched end in 345, the first year of Nestorius' prefecture. If that is indeed the date of the letter described in chapter 86, the prophecy in chapter 82 must have been uttered a decade, rather than two years, before the death of Antony. Since Athanasius is also the putative author of the *Life*,[21] this contradiction warns us that the provenance of the text is no more certain than the chronology of the events to which it alludes.

It is the Greek text of the *Life of Antony* that ascribes it to Athanasius, patriarch of Alexandria and formidable champion of the Nicene Creed, which stated that God the Son is consubstantial, or of one essence, with God the Father. In favour of this attribution, it can be said that, notwithstanding his illiteracy, Antony is depicted in the *Life* as an eloquent mouthpiece of the Nicene faith, unmoved by the sophistries of its opponents. Although it has been urged that Athanasius could not have had the personal knowledge of Antony to which the author of this work pretends, that is at best an argument against his veracity, not against his being the author. It has also been maintained that Athanasius, to judge by his dogmatic and expository writings, would not have granted to demons the power of troubling the elect that is permitted to them in this *Life*; to this, however, it seems to be a sufficient reply that every genre has its own laws, and that Antony's war in the desert may be seen as a continuation on earth of the struggle that Christ, according to Athanasius, waged on the cross against wickedness in high places.[22] Finally, it has been argued that the Greek is not the original form of the *Life*, and that the Syriac or Coptic versions exhibit more primitive features.[23] The last judgment is not shared by a majority of scholars,[24] and, even if it is true (as good critics have argued[25]) that the idiom and vocabulary of the Greek are uncharacteristic of Athanasius, the inference that it is not an original work but a translation would be patently invalid.

[20] That is, if Antony dies at the age of 105, the year of his birth will now be 349, and he will reach his 56th year in 304–305.

[21] Brakke (1995), 207 suggests that he is redacting traditions derived from earlier sources.

[22] *On the incarnation* 22–25. See further Louth (1988). Dörrie (1967), 179–82 lists numerous points of correspondence between the *Life of Antony* and the apologetic writings of Athanasius.

[23] Draguet (1980); Barnes (1986).

[24] See Brakke (1994); Rousseau (2000), 100–4.

[25] Perczel (1999); Barnes (2010a), 162–70.

Whoever its author was,[26] the Greek goes under the title *Life and Regimen (bios kai politeia) of the Holy Antony*. Its purpose is clearly to glorify its protagonist, and to hold him up as an ideal to Egyptian monks whose habitual role, from the middle of the fourth century onwards, was to act as a phalanx in defence of orthodoxy as this was defined by the Alexandrian see. Some modern historians have surmised that the eremitic life was an alternative to brigandage for Egyptians who had been ruined by high taxation; as though to forestall this calumny, the life records that Antony was a young man of means who gave up his prodigal ways when he was suddenly touched by Christ's command to the rich young ruler, 'Sell what thou hast and give it to the poor' (*Life* 2; Matthew 19.21). Connoisseurs of classical tropes will remember that a number of Greek philosophers—Antisthenes, Zeno, Polemo, and Plotinus, for example—were also converted abruptly and by a chance word.[27] The austerities that follow, however, bear no resemblance to the disciplines of any Greek school. The humble novice spends some years at the feet of aged hermits who have retired to the desert before him (4); at length he feels called to adopt a more stringent regimen, living on frugal measures of the coarsest food and passing whole nights without sleep (7). He has to weather not only the charge of fanaticism but the assaults of the devil, who whispers to him of the pleasures of home, appeals to his sexual instinct by assuming the form of a beautiful woman, and tries his courage by taking on the shape of one ravening predator after another (5). On one occasion he is so badly bruised that onlookers take him for a corpse (8); on another, a crowd of spectators is drawn to his cell by the din of battle, and they rout his demonic assailants by making the sign of the Cross (13). The devil throws gold and silver before him in vain (11), and reptiles flee at his approach (120). After twenty years of meditation in solitude (14), he emerges to preach a sermon to the host of imitators who have gathered around his refuge. He exhorts them to remember that the goods of this world are as nothing compared with the joys of the next (17), to go on 'dying daily' with the apostle Paul (19; Romans 8.28), and not to expose themselves to Christ's malediction on those who turn back from the plough (20). No demon, however, terrible in aspect can withstand the true servant of Christ (22–30); their pretence of foretelling the future is illusory (31–35),[28] and all their overtures will come to nothing if we practise the patience of Job (29).

[26] Cameron (2000) argues that the Antony of the Greek *Life* is a mirror to the Constantine of Eusebius: both are orthodox in theology, dutiful to the church, frugal in regimen, eloquent in preaching to the converted and the unconverted, vigorous in old age and invulnerable to the assaults of demons.

[27] Diogenes Laertius, *Lives of the Philosophers* 4.3 and 7.2; Edwards (2000), 5. The story of the rich miser who sold all his goods after hearing Proverbs 17.19—see Bauckham et al. (2013), 365—is more likely to be a reprise of the Christian anecdote than a Jewish antecedent.

[28] Cf. *Bohairic Life of Pachomius* 6.

Antony continues to grow in virtue, zeal and discernment (45). When persecution falls upon the Alexandrian church, he ministers openly to the confessors in prison, but the magistrates are too afraid of him to satisfy his desire for martyrdom (46). He retires to the upper Thebaid, where he cultivates his own garden of crops and herbs and receives the homage of the local Saracens (49). His deeds begin to bear a closer resemblance to those of Christ: he brings forth water miraculously for a crowd that is ready to die of thirst (54), goes up a mountain to meditate (51) and then preaches to a multitude, heals a lunatic (57) and a paralysed woman (58), relieves a sick girl at distance (61), and delivers two youths from possession (63, 64). The likeness is never exact, but those who have characterized this work as an 'anti-Pythagorean' narrative are closer to the truth than those for whom Antony is a little more than a Christian simulacrum of the Greek sage.[29] If, for example, the illumination of Antony's countenance at *Life of Antony* 13–14 reminds some critics of a similar episode in Iamblichus (*On the Pythagorean Life* 14–16), why should we not infer that the pagan author is indebted to the stories told of Moses and Elijah in texts which antedate his own sources.[30] This is not to say that the *Life of Antony* owes nothing to pagan models, but that it stands in a competitive rather than a parasitic relation to them. Pythagoras, for example, might perform miracles of clairvoyance, but he never anticipated Antony's vision of departing souls (66), his awareness of another monk's death at a distance of some days' journey (60) or the ecstatic rapture which threw the saint's companions into temporary dismay. Moreover, Antony does not use his authority to found his own sect but testifies on behalf of the church against the Melitians who had set up their own bishop in Alexandria (68), against the Arians who deny the Trinity (69), and against the Greeks who substitute voiceless effigies for the living image of the unseen God (72–79). This appeal from idol to image is very much in the style of Athanasius, who strove with vigour against the same three enemies. The Christlike Antony seldom acts as judge or intervenes in public affairs, although he sets an example to all by prayer and discipline. His death, at the age of 105 (89), is preceded by a meek farewell to his brethren and an injunction to bury his corpse without the extravagances of a pagan funeral (91).[31]

[29] Rubenson (2006), 205; Reitzenstein (1914).

[30] Barnes (1986), 361; Edwards (1993), 169. I do not know why Barnes thinks it probable that the 'pagan' conceit in the Greek is less primitive than its 'Christian' counterpart in the Syriac. Since both redactors were Christians, it is surely more likely that one of them would have superimposed a biblical motif on a profane original than that either would have performed the converse operation.

[31] These strictures are repeated in Athanasius, *Festal Letter* 41, where the practice of exposing the holy man's corpse is represented as a Melitian innovation. If Wortley (2006) has correctly traced it to a belief in the *dunamis* of the holy body (already evident at Mark 5.30), the arguments advanced in its defence may have echoed Porphyry's apology for the veneration of statues, which

THE LETTERS OF ANTONY

In the first chapter of the *Life of Antony* the author sets up his hero as an antitype to the Origen of Eusebius, recording that in his youth he quickly abandoned the study of books.[32] This may not be said to his honour, for the young Antony had much else to repent of; it may not even be true, for in his homily to the monks of Egypt Antony displays a prodigious knowledge of the scriptures, and we have cited a story in which he sends a letter to Duke Balacius. On the other hand, a man who cannot read may still be capable of dictation, which was a universal practice in this period. Whether it was true or not, the popular belief in his illiteracy ensured that the letters of Antony would not be so well remembered as his sayings, collections of which (with those of his real or putative precursors and contemporaries) exist in Greek, Latin, Syriac, Armenian, Ethiopic, Georgian, and Arabic. The Greek alphabetic and systematic collections are regarded as the earliest,[33] though many have followed Bousset in his opinion that the Syriac often preserves the sayings in a more primitive form.[34] Yet if the first monastic community was largely illiterate (as our sources claim), we have no reason to think that even this tradition has been faithful to the Greek or Coptic of the original speakers. No evidence of any compilation before the sixth century survives, and the extant matter is so diverse that Samuel Rubenson, a leading authority on the desert fathers, believes the quest for an aboriginal version to be neither achievable nor worth achieving.[35] If, as James Goehring opines,[36] sixth-century witnesses have piously exaggerated the ignorance of their ancestors, it will not be safe to conclude that any utterance has survived without redaction from the fourth century. The multiplication of variants shows that writing may be as treacherous a medium as speech.

According to Samuel Rubenson, the most primitive version of Antony's letters now extant is the Syriac one, though it lacks the fourth letter, the only one extant in Coptic.[37] The Arabic is avowedly a translation from Coptic;[38] the Greek preserves all seven letters, though it lacks passages which survive in the Arabic and Latin versions.[39] If they are authentic (as their editor, Samuel Rubenson, contends), it is reasonable to assume that the Coptic, fragmentary as it now is, was the original, since ancient sources agree that this was Antony's native tongue. Their content is sometimes such as would be predicted by a reader of the *Life of Antony*. Thus the fourth included a denunciation of the

is mocked by Athanasius at *Against the Nations* 19. These observations add some strength to the case for his being the author of the *Life of Antony*.

[32] *Life of Antony* 1; on its popularity see Larsen (2013), 61. [33] Holmberg (2013), 35.
[34] Bousset (1923). [35] Rubenson (2013).
[36] Goehring (2005). [37] Rubenson (1995), 23 and 31.
[38] Rubenson (1995), 30. [39] Rubenson (1995), 26.

Arians which is not obviously extrinsic to the argument; the sixth exhorts its correspondents not to fear the menaces of demons, to give no credence to their prophecies and to remember that, being fallen beings in origin, they take a pleasure in propagating sin. The eulogy of baptism in the seventh might be thought more apposite in the mouth of a bishop than in that of a monk; it could be argued, however, that for that very reason Antony would have been asked to lend his authority to the sacrament. The first letter is the most difficult to reconcile with the *Life*'s portrayal of Antony as an unschooled sage who throws the plain word of God in the teeth of the Greeks: making liberal use of the philosophical lexicon, it represents the ascetic life as a struggle between the soul and a triple alliance of bodily appetites—natural, sinful, and daemonic—extolling gnosis or knowledge as the medicine for its wounds. The discrepancy suggests that if the letters are forged they were forged in the light of some tradition independent of the *Life*; if Antony himself is the author, much of the *Life* is not history but romance.

PACHOMIUS AND HIS LEGACY

The first life of Pachomius, the most celebrated pioneer of the common or cenobitc life, was written in Sahidic, his own dialect of Coptic.[40] Fragments of ten versions survive, but the only complete representative of this text is an Arabic translation.[41] The longest of the narratives now extant is in Bohairic, another dialect of Coptic, and owes its length to an appendix which describes the government of two Pachomian institutions after the founder's death by his pupils Theodore and Horsiesius.[42] Much of the same matter, with a severe curtailing of the appendix, is contained in the version known as the First Greek Life.[43] Discrepancies between this and the Bohairic life have persuaded the majority of scholars that neither text is a mere derivative of the other; the language of the original on which both depended has still to be determined.[44] The second Greek Life, the most widely known in the middle ages, is now of least interest to scholars of antiquity,[45] as it combines the content of the First Greek life with a collection of anecdotes, known as the *Paralipomena*, which also survives in earlier recensions.

[40] Veilleux (1980), 2. See also Halkin (1979). [41] Veilleux (1980), 425–57.

[42] Veilleux (1980), 23–296, hereinafter cited as B with the chapter number as in Veilleux.

[43] Veilleux (1980), 297–424, hereinafter cited as G, with chapter numbers as in Veilleux. The priority of the Greek is maintained by Chitty (1954) against Lefort (1954).

[44] Veilleux (1980), 5. The labyrinthine controversies may be pursued in Rousseau (1978), 243–7, and in Goehring (1986), 1–23.

[45] Veilleux (1980), 12–15.

Neither the Bohairic nor the Greek can be trusted as a faithful chronicle of events:[46] so much is apparent, for example, from their accounts of the military service for which Pachomius was conscripted in his youth.[47] The Bohairic text asserts that the war was provoked by a Persian invasion of Roman territory in the reign of Constantine (B7), but no such invasion occurred, and it is impossible that Pachomius was forced into the army at any date after 324. The Greek, more circumspectly, speaks of a muster of troops by Constantine against an unnamed tyrant (G4). Again, the mention of Constantine is a flagrant anachronism; since, however, Maximinus Daia had the misfortune to be a tyrant in the eyes of Constantine and his ally Licinius, it has been proposed that Pachomius was enlisted for his campaign against Licinius in 312.[48] Although this theory inverts both the Bohairic and the Greek accounts (Constantine's enemy being now the employer of Pachomius), it is deemed to receive support from the appearance of the name Maximinus in one of the numerous manuscripts of the Second Greek Life—a document of no evidential value, as we have seen. By a similar exercise of credulous ingenuity, it is said that Pachomius must have died in 346 on the grounds that no other year (except perhaps 343 or 349) would be consistent with the testimony of both the Bohairic and the First Greek lives that the day on which he expired, the fourteenth of Pasons or ninth of May, fell forty days after the Passover during which he succumbed to illness (B123; G116). At the same time the statement in the Bohairic life that he was sixty years old is admitted to be incompatible with other 'chronological indications' in these narratives.[49] Even if 'forty days' were a linear rather than a symbolic measure of time, it should already be apparent that these 'chronological indications' are worthless. It must therefore be understood that in the following paragraphs the word 'life' will invariably denote a piece of literature without reference to the actual life—that is, the real acts or experiences—of Pachomius the man.

A Platonist, fresh from reading the *Life of Antony* and more than ever disgusted by the notorious credulity of the Christians, would have found in the life of Pachomius a more sober representation of a more admirable figure.[50] Neither the Bohairic nor the Greek text maintains that Pachomius was self-sufficient in wisdom: he receives instruction from an older sage, much more obscure to any reader of the life, whom he none the less inters with the honours due to a parent (B10–156 and 18). In forming his own community, he imposes a term of silence on his neophytes (B74 and 77, and sets an example of strict vegetarianism, to be followed by all except when he himself

[46] Harmless (2004), 117 believes the narratives to be reliable in outline.

[47] Chitty (1966), 22 somewhat fancifully suggests that the martial experience of Pachomius may have inspired the design of his monasteries.

[48] Veilleux (1980), 267 and 408.

[49] Veilleux (1980), 287.

[50] Pachomius and Pythagoras are compared as masters of animals by Alexander (2006), 21.

perceives the necessity of a concession to bodily weakness (B48). His miracles, such as they are, seldom entail the suspension or reversal of natural laws, but are more commonly feats of clairvoyance which enable him to ascertain the fitness of postulants for the monastic life (B23–25). His reverence for the characters of the alphabet, attested in the Greek life and in his own letters, may be compared to the high estimation of the properties of numbers which distinguished the Pythagoreans at all times, and Iamblichus in particular. He himself, like the Samothracian, was an oracle to his pupils, and only the less proficient were offended by his lapidary judgments. While 'brotherhood' and 'friendship' are not such watchwords in the monastic life as in the Pythagorean communities, two of the most eminent successors of Pachomius, Theodore and Horsiesius, are so much at one in temper and vocation that the death of Theodore cements the union of their souls (B146, 200; G145).

For all that, the similarities prove on inspection to be tenuous or illusory. It was never the avowed object of a Pythagorean to enfeeble his own flesh by his abstinence from meat; yet this was so much an axiom for Theodore, the disciple of Pachomius, that he warned a man under his charge to refrain from eating leeks because they increased the robustness of the body (B79).[51] He was to repent of this admonition, just as others, when rebuked by Pachomius,[52] repented of having denied meat to a man of frail constitution (B48). Such exceptions, characteristic of Paul but not of Pythagoras,[53] reveal a willingness to temper discipline with charity which was both Christian and pragmatic: although it did not receive all who came, the monastery, like the church, was obliged by the teaching of the New Testament to admit inquirers who were not destined to become adepts.[54] The seminars of Plotinus, more hospitable than a Pythagorean lodge,[55] had been less reclusive; neither affords a true analogue to this Christian school in which even the master's precepts possessed authority only because they were laced with passages from canonical texts that could never be subject to scrutiny or rebuttal. Even the rule of silence was designed to make the soul a receptacle for the speech of God (B74), and both the Bohairic and the Greek lives are evidently written on the assumption

[51] For the same belief, giving rise to the opposite counsel, see the *Ten Questions* of a Taoist master at Cleary (1999), 17. Goehring (2001), 242 notes that the community to which Theodore initially belonged was one of three that had existed independently 'prior to their affiliation with Pachomius'.

[52] Porphyry, by contrast, enjoins the meatless diet on the grounds that it is conducive to bodily health: *On Abstinence*, p. 86.4–7 Nauck. Cf. Clark (2005). On the relaxation of abstinence for the sick see Jerome, PL 23, 67A–B (Bibliography A), the oldest extant version of the *Rule of Pachomius*.

[53] See Romans 14; 1 Corinthians 8.4–13.

[54] The *Rule of Pachomius* none the less prescribes that all postulants be examined at the door by the 'father of the monastery': Jerome, PL 23, 73A.

[55] See Porphyry, *Life of Plotinus* 1, where an artist enters the classroom and secretly paints a portrait of Plotinus.

that even a saint can be no true model for believers unless the similitude of Christ himself is visible in the public events of his life.

Accordingly, the ability to recognize and cast out a demon—the power that set Christ apart from both sages and the sorcerers of his time—is also credited to Pachomius, though in his case it is sparingly employed. As in the gospel (Mark 9.31), the father of a demoniac in the petitioner (B44; G44); as in the stories of miraculous feeding,[56] the miracle is effected with a loaf supplied by one of those who are present. From another man, according to the Bohairic life, he cast out demonic host which gave its name as 'Hundred' (B114), thus proving a little less formidable than the legion that had been expelled by his Master (Mark 5.9). In imitation of the latter's humility, he stooped to wash the feet of a disciple (B61). As Christ had promised the faithful that they would tread the snake and the scorpion underfoot (Luke 10.19), Pachomius was able to ignore the sting of the scorpion and remained unmoved when two snakes wound themselves around his ankles as he prayed (B98; G21).[57] On another occasion the illumination of the abbot's face invites comparison with Christ's transfiguration (B114), with the descent of Moses from Sinai which prefigured it, and with the return of Pythagoras from Carmel as this is recounted by Iamblichus.[58] In the closest approximation to a biblical narrative, a woman with an issue of blood is healed when she seizes the garment of Pachomius before he can forestall her (B41; G41). The capacity to heal by inadvertence had been communicated to Peter by Christ, and it would seem that the woman who touched the hem of Christ's robe had acquired a peculiar celebrity in the fourth century, when she came to be identified with the legendary woman who had wiped the face of Christ on the road to Calvary.[59] In the Bohairic life the gospels also furnish precedent for anecdotes concerning the disciples of Pachomius, though there is no direct imitation of the Saviour. Thus Zacchaeus, an emissary from Pachomius to Antony, is said to have been a short man like his namesake at Luke 19.3 (B127[60]); and, whereas in the Gospel of John Nathanael is amazed to learn that Jesus saw him sitting under a fig tree when he was too far away to be visible (John 1.48–50), in the Bohairic life it is Theodore who is praying under the fig tree and Pachomius who is the object of his vision (B85). We must not be too quick to lay the invention of such stories at the door of the biographer, since it is possible that the monks had shaped their lives, or allowed their perception of life to be shaped, by their remembrance of a narrative which all of them were required to have by heart.

By heart, because many of them will have been illiterate; the Greek life records that Pachomius himself could not preach, let alone read, any language

[56] Matthew 14.17 par; John 6.5.
[57] Cf. Acts 28.4–6 and B99, where a scorpion dies after stinging one of the brethren.
[58] *Life of Pythagoras*, 14–16.
[59] See Mark 5.30; Acts 5.15.
[60] This detail is not found in the parallel passage at G.

but the Egyptian vernacular.[61] According to the Bohairic account, the learned Alexandrian Theodore acted as an interpreter for those who knew only Greek,[62] while demonstrating his own humility by his efforts to learn Egyptian (B90). The letters of Pachomius were written in Coptic, and his cryptic allusions to the arcane significance of the Greek characters suggest that they had for him the fascination of the unknown.[63] Coptic is the language of the writings that proceeded from his monasteries (nine in all by the time of his death), and the language into which heterodox Greek compositions were rendered by scribes whose relation to the monastery of Chenoboskion remains undetermined. It has been surmised that the Nag Hammadi Codices (as we call them) were ejected from the monastic library after Athanasius, in his Festal Letter of 367, denounced the use of apocrypha, or spurious additions to the writings of the saints. Only a handful of the codices meet this definition, and the letter affords no proof that Athanasius had commenced an inquisition,[64] or that such an inquisition would have found Chenoboskion to be a hothouse of aberrant teachings. Nevertheless, the admonition shows that not every monk could be trusted to canonize only what Athanasius canonized, and the Bohairic life contains a long quotation, clearly purporting to be biblical, for which no source could have been supplied from an Athanasian copy of the scriptures.

Whether literate or illiterate, the Pachomian monasteries entertained a high reverence for the scriptures. In addition to frugal diet and rigorous discipline of the body, prompt and apt quotation from the sacred book was agreed to be the strongest charm against the assaults of demons.[65] Pachomian foundations were renowned for their orthodoxy, and both the Bohairic and the Greek lives are at pains to demonstrate that fame spoke no more than the truth. The Bohairic life relates that the monastery welcomed Athanasius, that they assisted him in his exile and that they offered every impediment to his pursuers (B28, 89, 96, 124–125, 133, 185, 210; G113, 120, 137–138, 143, 150). We are even told that Antony condoned the Pachomian practice of interrogating visitors, including ascetics of his own circle, in order to ensure that they were not Arians or Melitians (B129)—that is, that they did not differ from Athanasius either in doctrine or in their answer to the question, 'Who is

[61] B89; Veilleux (1980), 281 contrasts *Paralipomena* 27, where Pachomius is miraculously endowed with the gift of tongues. The author of this narrative may have felt that a second Pentecost was owing to this 'unlettered and ignorant' scion of the apostles: Acts 4.13.

[62] Two Theodores are distinguished by implication at B89 and expressly at G94. It is not always easy, however, to ascertain which is intended: see B30 and n. 2 to chapter 89 at Veilleux (1980), 281.

[63] See the next section of this chapter on the writings of Pachomius.

[64] It is commended at B189 and G99.

[65] Brakke (2006), 93, noting also that the texts owed their efficacy to the 'integration of scripture and life'.

the bishop of Alexandria?'[66] The Greek redactor, more learned though not learned enough, misrepresents Bishop Gregory, the imperial substitute for Athanasius, as the leader of an armed rising by the Arians, and recounts (as we might have foreseen) that his attempt to force the Pachomians into his retinue came to nothing. This apologist (who admits that no biography of Pachomius was written by his disciples) betrays his late date when he tells us that Pachomius not only spoke of Origen with aversion but declared that it was only the occurrence of the name of God in the latter's books that prevented him from destroying them (G31). Even if Pachomius could have spoken thus of one whose authority Athanasius treats as unassailable,[67] this argument for the merciful handling of Origen's works was not advanced before his condemnation in 553.

Neither of these lives can tolerate an unresolved feud between Pachomius and Antony, who had passed into the record as another unshakable ally of Athanasius.[68] In the Bohairic life, however, Pachomius contrasts the anchoritic, or solitary path to its disadvantage with the cenobitic, or communal, practice of his own disciples (B105). In both the Bohairic and the Greek lives, the hero refuses an expensive blanket when he is suffering from an illness that threatens to be terminal (B120; G115); we cannot say whether either was written with knowledge of Jerome's life of Paul, in which Antony's last duty to the old hermit is to fetch him a shroud that he might have coveted for himself.[69] We cannot be sure that Antony's testimonials in both lives to the sanctity of Pachomius are fictitious (B133; G120), though we may confidently suspect the Bohairic text of some embellishment when it puts into Antony's mouth the confession that he too would have embraced the cenobitic regimen had it existed when he first retreated to the desert (127). Of these biographies, as of most biographies in antiquity, we can say that they tell us not so much what their protagonists did as what deeds were attributed to them, and what these deeds had come to signify.

Since the two lives give similar accounts of the delegation of offices in a Pachomian monastery, we may presume that both are reproducing an earlier source, although we cannot say how well this source preserves the institutions of Pachomius himself (B26; G28). According to the Greek, which is the more lucid of the two, Pachomius created a number of houses, setting a master over each. The stewards of the first house were to prepare tables and food for the brethren, while those of the second ministered to the sick. Others were to act as porters, receiving visitors 'according to rank' and giving them instruction until they were ready to take on the habit of a monk. Others again were to

[66] Melitians also set up monasteries: Bell (1914), 71–99; Krämer and Shelton (1987).
[67] *On the Nicene Decrees* 67.
[68] On the failure of the latter's attempt to ordain Pachomius see Elm (1994), 362.
[69] See the edition of Kosik (Bibliography A).

superintend the purchase of necessities and the sale of monastic wares, the manufacture of which fell under the scrutiny of another house.[70] Every three weeks the subordinate workers in each house would return to manual labour and a new corps would succeed them. In every house a deputy was appointed to perform the master's duties in his absence, and when a lieutenant stood in for the father of the monastery, he too was entitled to unreserved obedience. The father of the monastery was to deliver three instructions every week, one on a Saturday and two on a Sunday; on fast-days (twice a week) this office fell to housemasters. It is evident that such a developed system presupposes a large community, which was constantly replenished from without, and which, for all its levelling of worldly ranks, could not be wholly indifferent to the social order, the exigencies of commerce or the rhythm of the ecclesiastical year.

WRITINGS OF PACHOMIUS

Rebukes administered to disaffected or rancorous students are reported at length in both the Bohairic and the Greek lives of Pachomius, which make it clear that his friends had all the more reason to go on quoting them as the murmurs had not subsided with his death. The longer of the two surviving treatises that go under the name of Pachomius is said in the title to contain his instructions to a monk who bore a grudge against another.[71] We possess two Coptic and two Arabic versions, which are not identical; none is free of confusion or repetition,[72] and at least one passage appears to have been lifted from a sermon by Athanasius, unless we suspect the patriarch of embezzlement from the writings of his own monks.[73] A precept which assumes that the anchoritic and the cenobitic lives are of equal merit contradicts a speech attributed to Antony in the Bohairic life of Pachomius[74]—a fact which might be cited either against or in favour of its authenticity. The prefatory allusion to Abraham's sacrifice of Isaac is another feature that this homily shares with the Bohairic life,[75] and again it would be hard to determine which, if either, has borrowed from the other. Pachomius is not a man to whom works were ascribed promiscuously, and it is therefore not unreasonable to suppose that this text preserves, if not a specimen of his own dictation, at least an informed recollection of his teaching.

[70] For the rule requiring brothers in the same art to be gathered into the same building see Jerome, PL 23, 67C (Bibliography A). Sleeping alone in a closed cell is forbidden to all but the sick at PL 23, 79A.
[71] Veilleux (1982), 14–49. [72] Veilleux (1982), 2. [73] Lefort (1933).
[74] *Instruction* 22; *Bohairic Life* 127. [75] *Bohairic Life* 1.

The lesson of the opening chapters, reinforced by copious illustrations from the scriptures and daily experience, is that the monk must lay the keystone of the regenerate life through patience. By the cultivation of this virtue, he will learn to bear vexatious thoughts, to be resolute in fasting, to secure his innocence against temptation and to pray without fatigue (8–9). It will even—and this is the burden of the whole piece, to judge by the title and the frequency with which this point is urged—give a monk the strength to rejoice when he sees another receiving greater honours (12; 58). Biblical examples are laid under contribution, not without some straining of the text. Habbakuk and the widow of Zarephath show that works of charity can be performed without great resources (13); jesters should remember that the three children Shadrach, Meshach, and Abednego were immune to the raillery of Nebuchadnezzar (15); Elijah is an emblem of strength, Elisha of obedience to those who are strong in God. Abraham, Lot, Moses, and Samuel are more conventional exemplars of the fortitude that is required when the devil assails us (18); at the same time, the ascetic must beware of his internal enemy's concupiscence, gluttony, and lust (19). Turning to God, with Jacob, is his antidote to all vices, and above all to pride, which hardens the heart unless it is repulsed by eternal vigilance (20). Joshua's perseverance is a pattern for those who mortify their bodies in the desert (22–23). Proficiency in monastic discipline brings its own vices, self-satisfaction and vanity (24). We escape this tool of the devil by remembering that Adam fell from paradise and that Judas was one of the twelve (25). Awaiting the judgment of God (26), and knowing that he does not spare even his saints (27), the adept will bear a harsh word from a brother (29) and bear his afflictions as Paul bore his chains (30).

Those who seek heaven will not cry for Egypt like the Israelites in the wilderness (31–32); they crave the glory of this world (33), though they may 'make careful use of it' (34); they will guard both body and heart from all impurity (35–36), taking pains to reconcile themselves before death to all with whom they are variance (37–38). This is what it means to put on Christ, abjuring the world and passing sentence of death on one's own members in order to receive his body and blood as the food of life (39–42). Reiterated exhortations to perseverance, charity and peaceable conduct are followed by a reprimand to those who treat Paul's admonition to 'take a little wine' as a charter for drunkards (46). Humility is commended once again as the palmary virtue, which will teach the monk to work ceaselessly in fear of wrath and expectation of the eternal crown (47–50). Indolence, avarice, and effeteness are constant foes (51–53) in a world where the young no longer obey the old and the seekers of holiness are as orphans (48–49), but the task of an Israelite is to throw down Pharaoh and lead his people through the sea (54). The devil lies in wait for all backsliders (55), assaulting the monk from the right, not from the left as he 'comes to others' (57). Humility, willing poverty, and forgiveness of others according to Christ's command are inculcated once again (58–59);[76] 'gnostic' is the homilist's epithet for those who remain untouched by the discord that has spread from the churches to the abodes of monks (60). A final chapter of renewed exhortation ends with a prayer to the holy Trinity.

As in the lives of Pachomius, a literal belief in the hidden agency of demons is pervasive in this text, though it is not implied that such temptations render the soul less answerable for its crimes. Citations from the Bible are, for the most part, equally literal, though we have noted the metaphorical allusions to the devil's attacks from the right, and the symbolic figure of Pharaoh in chapter 55 is most probably another of his disguises. Just as demonic subterfuge does not annul our responsibility, so there can be nothing below the surface of a text that overrides its patent meaning. Before we conclude, however, that Pachomius was as hostile to Origen as the Greek life implies, we should consider the second treatise that is attributed to him, a short dissertation on the six days of the 'Passover', which bears no internal marks of forgery or interpolation. These six days, we are told, correspond to the six days of creation, which in turn prefigure six modes of ascetic service: silence, manual labour, copious prayer, and purity of body, mouth, and heart (2). Acts 27.44 reads 'some on beams, some on pieces of the ship, and thus all came safe to land'—a paradigm of evangelical matter-of-factness to any opponent of allegory, but here a template for the division of ministries (3). The Passover is the season in which the faithful mourn with heaven and earth, the rich put off their purple in remembrance of Christ's nudity, and the ascetic takes for his model the king whose final repast was vinegar and gall (4; cf. Matthew 27.44).

It cannot be an accident that five of the six ascetic ministries—all but manual labour[77]—were also defining traits of the Manichaean communities which had lately begun to thrive in Egypt. Pachomius is of course no Manichaean, though he observes the ancient maxim that a wise man learns from his enemies; we may argue on the same principle that his figurative reading of the liturgy does not imply assent to any contestable doctrine held by Origen. This is a true observation from which we learn nothing, since no writing by Pachomius, or alleged to be his, affords evidence of his taking sides in any controversy that might have come before a council of this period. When he affirms in his letters that Christ suffered on our behalf in a palpable body to vanquish death, he does so not in a spirit of correction but to reinforce the norms of belief and doctrine to which his readers already subscribe. What was new to them, and still obscure to us, is his correlation of these received beliefs and doctrines with characters of the Greek alphabet. In the Greek text of the

[76] Matthew 18.22. [77] See Dôrrie (1967), 298–9 on the importance of this feature.

first of the eleven letters which make up the standard collection,[78] we meet such maxims as 'Do the work of the ι, which was called o in the old days'; and 'Sing to the ω lest the ω sing to you.'[79] In the second he asks his correspondent whether ξ and μ are not o, with an admonition not to write δ over ϕ.[80] In the third a pair of consonants, ςϕ, succeeds the injunction to 'remember the groaning of the saints'.[81] In the fourth and fifth, which are extant only in Latin, no such cryptograms appear, but in the Latin text of the sixth (which is all that survives) he explains that, having noticed the sacred characters η and θ in the writing of his correspondent, he answered with ς$\phi\theta\mu$, lest anyone should deny that this is the spelling of his own name.[82] The ninth letter (in its Coptic form) is a litany, in which dicta such as 'the earth has been hidden without price' or 'those who were hidden fled with fear' are introduced by two alphabetic characters and terminate in another.[83] Many of the propositions which make up the Coptic version of letter 11 are sealed by clusters of two or three characters.[84] Like the ninth it has no named addressee; various names appear in the superscriptions to earlier items in the collection, but the arcane matter figures only in letters addressed to leaders of monasteries.[85] It would seem, then, that initiation into this secret language was a perquisite of authority, not the common privilege of the brotherhood.[86]

Signs that in Greek are merely graphic substitutes for sound are hieroglyphs to this Egyptian, each conveying some import either by itself or in combination with another. No parallel is offered by the ululatory strings of vowels in the magical papyri and the Nag Hammadi Codices, which owe their efficacy to recitation. Pachomius has devised a semantic, not a magical cipher, and we might suspect that its function was to protect the sacred truths from espionage or profanation. There is, however, no evidence that Pachomius founded any institution before the victory of Constantine in 324, and why should it have been necessary after that date to throw a veil over teachings which, for the most part, are not mysteries but banalities? In the second century Mark the Mage had correlated alphabetic characters with parts of the body, revealed the mission of Jesus by attaching numerical values to every letter of his name,

[78] The whole collection is extant only in the Latin of Jerome, but Greek texts survive of letters 1–3 and 7 and Coptic texts of letters 8–11.

[79] Veilleux (1982), 51. On p. 78 Veilleux notes that the last sentence, here translated from Greek, is also extant in the Coptic version of Letter 9b.

[80] Veileux (1982), 52–3. Jerome's text, here as elsewhere, replaces the Greek with Latin characters.

[81] Veilleux (1982), 53. This long missive is otherwise free of letter-play.

[82] Veilleux (1982), 67.

[83] Veilleux (1982), 72–4, distinguishing letters 9a and 9b.

[84] Veilleux (1982), 75–6.

[85] It does not occur in Letter 7 (Greek and Latin) or in Letter 8 (Coptic and Latin): Veilleux (1982), 68–72.

[86] Cf. also Methodius *Symposium* 6.136 on the iota.

practised the same expedients on the word *delta* in order to illustrate the properties of the Delta itself, and subdivided the alphabet into consonants, vowels, and semi-vowels to match the arithmetical premisses of his own cosmogony. Another freethinking sect, the Peratae, held that a person's destiny or the outcome of a combat between two persons could be predicted when the letters which composed their names were translated into numbers.[87] Pachomius, by contrast, does not seem to be assigning any talismanic or mathematical properties to the characters, and shows no interest either in the alphabetic ordering of them or in any new concatenation. For the same reason, nothing to the purpose can be gleaned from the anonymous tract *On the Mystery of the Letters*, another product of the fourth century, which professes to elicit, from the shape and order of signs in both the Greek and the Hebrew alphabets, such luminous testimonials to the truth of Christianity that the Greeks and Jews have proved themselves illiterate in failing to discern them. As we shall see in Chapter 8, the author of this tract sometimes reclaims lost characters of the Greek script and sometimes derives his lessons from a fixed aggregate of twenty-two or twenty-four, assigning at different times a different position to the same sign or a different value to its position. Thus his divinations are as variable but seldom so elusive as those of Pachomius; it is certainly not his intention to devise a code for secret correspondence, since he purports to be republishing a manifesto which already lies open to all who are capable of reading. More likely than Pachomius himself to be indebted to the Peratae and Mark the Mage, this treatise holds no solution to his riddles, and illuminates them only insofar as it shows that reverence for the alphabet was no more anomalous in Christian than in Jewish or Platonic circles of the fourth century.

CONCLUSION: THE VALUE OF SAINTLINESS

It is possible to read the lives of Antony and Pachomius without exclaiming, with E. R. Dodds, 'Where did all this madness come from?'[88] Dodds had in mind the athletes of self-chastisement whose sedulous efforts to petrify every vital function seem to us wholly devoid of social utility, unless we echo the half-facetious comment of Dean Inge that if they failed to produce they also consumed very little. Antony too produced little after the act of largesse that preceded his withdrawal to the desert; for much of the narrative he is a recluse who emerges only to travel further into the wilderness and to harangue or

[87] Irenaeus, *Against Heresies* 1.14; Hippolytus, *Refutation* 5.19.

[88] Dodds (1965), 34. For a sceptical view of the thesis that this madness represents the emergence of individuality see Clark (2004), 66–7.

castigate the fellow mortals whose society appears barely more welcome to him than that of demons. Nevertheless the regimen attributed to him is self-denying rather than self-despising: he maintains his radiant vigour throughout an uncommon span of life, and sets an example to his disciples not only by abstinence but by manual husbandry. In the Pachomian fraternities holiness was never a private virtue: communal worship and mutual exhortation were the rule, the care of novices was a recognized duty of senior monks, and no-one was exempt from physical labour. This last proviso would have sufficed in Greek eyes to deprive them of any pretensions to philosophy, which was always the preserve of a leisured class. Among Platonists the contempt for banausic industry was extended to the body: it was Iamblichus, not Antony or Pachomius, who identified the body with the underworld in which the soul suffers the penalty for its sins. We must not forget that Christian asceticism was informed, if not inspired, by a strong belief in the resurrection. Platonists strove to liberate the immortal soul from the perishable body; Christians subjected the body to redemptive discipline in the hope that it would become the deathless tenement of the soul.

The typical philosopher came from a class that was not required to support itself by physical labour. No change of livelihood ensued if philosophers chose, if they often did, to renounce the burdens of civic life and the ties of domesticity; on the other hand, an ostentatious refusal to participate might confer authority of a different kind, as in the case of Apollonius.[89] Porphyry's model philosopher was Plotinus, who, while he did not despise the public virtues, clearly believed that he himself had advanced beyond them; his one political act while teaching in Rome was to persuade the senator Rogatianus to resign his office as lictor on the day when he would have taken up the ceremonial rods (*Life of Plotinus* 7). The city of philosophers that he proposed to found in Campania might have served as a pattern for the Pachomian monastery had he and his colleagues been willing to undertake the project without an imperial subsidy (*Life* 12). Balked of this retreat, he continued to teach in a private house, which was open to all and never more than a temporary place of resort for his students (*Life* 1 and 7). Apart from the Cynics (of whom we hear little in the early fourth century) no philosopher emulated the self-sufficiency of the desert monks, and no intellectual brotherhood contrived, as the Pachomians did, to observe an autarkic regimen while maintaining intercourse with the people of the neighbouring region. Even if the Pythagorean sodalities described by Iamblichus were not fictitious, they existed only in literature in this era. In any case the choice of the sequestered life by pagans never threatened to call the world into judgment, as the monks did by their secession. To make a *polis*, a city, of the desert was to announce

[89] And later for Christian ascetics: Brown (1971).

that one had no abiding city in the empire which had once supposed itself to be eternal.[90] What Cicero said of Romulus, that he alone had converted the ideal city into a real one,[91] could be said with more truth by Christians of Antony and Pachomius. Even if much that is said of them is not true in fact, such legendary accretions were symptomatic of, and also helped to promote, a new mentality which glorified poverty, celibacy, and a mode of life that Aristotle had once declared to be possible only for a beast or a god.[92]

[90] Cf. Hebrews 13.14 and the conclusion in Chapter 1 of this volume.
[91] Cicero, *On the Commonwealth* 1.21.
[92] Aristotle, *Politics* 1253a29–30.

Part II

Religious Plurality

6

Religions of the Vanquished

Under the rule of its emperors Rome had become the crossroads of the world. The satirist Juvenal put the matter differently at the turn of the second century: the Orontes, he hissed, is flowing into the Tiber (*Satires* 1.3). He was not to know that the city of Apamea on that river was to become the seat of two distinguished schools of Platonic thought, first under Numenius, then under Iamblichus of Chalcis. He had no notion of the oriental as a philosopher: it was the Phrygian eunuch, the effeminate Syrian, the superstitious Egyptian, and the venal Greek who tried his patriotism.[1] In fact, however, neither these characters nor their religions were new to Rome in the age of the principate. Aesculapius had been brought from Epidaurus to Rome with acclamation in 293 BC. In 204 BC the Roman matron Claudia Quinta had towed the ship of Cybele over a sandbar in the Tiber.[2] In 186 BC the first unauthorized intrusion of foreign rites had been condemned in the senatorial decree against the Bacchanals.[3] The rigorous inquisition that followed may have suppressed the associated crimes but not the Dionysian cult itself. In the first century BC Latin poets complained, perhaps only half sincerely, of other interlopers: the Great Mother with her turbulent entourage, the castrated Attis, and cow-headed Isis whose holidays furnished girls with an excuse to sleep alone.[4] We have seen that the apologist Arnobius held Rome accountable for all the atrocities that her subjects perpetrated in the name of religion; all could be said to have the protection of imperial law so long as it was only Christianity that was officially proscribed.

How often these extraneous rites augmented or supplanted native practices in the capital it is impossible to say. Franz Cumont, unabashedly drawing a parallel with the quest for new faiths in twentieth-century Europe, set aside the 'oriental' religions as a special class and argued that they satisfied the new desires that were woken when the Romans tired of the formulaic observances in which even their fathers had only half believed.[5] Yet the old books were still

[1] *Satires* 3.78, 6.516, and 15.2ff.
[2] Ovid, *Fasti* 4.305ff.
[3] Livy, *Histories* 39.8–9.
[4] Catullus 63; Ovid, *Amores* 1.8.84.
[5] Cumont (1911).

consulted under Constantine's predecessors and the omens were still taken. So far as it is possible to plot the spread of the eastern cults they tend to follow patterns of migration: that is to say, the majority of their adherents, in the ancient as in the modern world, could trace their origin to the countries in which these cults were indigenous.[6] From the sonorous names that appear on inscriptions we can deduce that some of the richer votaries of the Great Mother or Mithras were Roman citizens, even citizens of distinction;[7] but neither name nor rank is an infallible index of ethnic origin in the imperial period. Problems of interpretation grow more acute in the age of Constantine because the epigraphic evidence becomes sparser even before his rise to power. The present chapter could not have been written at all were it not for the sulphurous eructation of Firmicus Maternus against the 'error of profane religions', published early in the reign of Constantine's successors. Firmicus had been, if not a Christian, at least a toady of Constantine when he wrote his handbook of astrology, the *Mathesis*; the *Error*, though more declamatory, is clearly the work of the same man, who had either been converted to Christianity in the meantime or had acquired new zeal in professing it. It is generally held that his knowledge of astrology, by comparison with that of other practitioners whose works survive, was superficial and limited; for want of other evidence, his invective provides the frame for the present chapter, together with as much corroborative or supplementary information as I have been able to discover. The plan of his work and the change in the Christian temper that it reveals will be discussed in Chapter 14.

PERSIAN MITHRAS?

From the reign of Hadrian to the late third century, stones and monuments bearing the name of Mithras, in a remarkable variety of spellings, are found in every province of the empire. The honorific term most often joined to it is *invictus*, 'unconquered', and numerous inscriptions couple Mithras with the sun, for whom this was also a regular epithet; in fact there are some inscriptions in Vermaseren's compilation of Mithraic remains which name no other deity than the sun. Where there is explicit devotion to Mithras, it is not uncommon for this to be coupled with references to the donor's proficiency in other cults. Thus we read that Alferius Ceionius Julianus Kamerius is at once a father of the rites of the most high unconquered Mithras, a hierophant of Hecate, an *archiboucolos* of Dionysus under his Roman name of Liber, and

[6] Macmullen (1981), 116–27.

[7] See e.g. Duthoy (1969), 103 on the known participants in the *taurobolium* between 319 and 390.

a man who has received the *taurobolium* which qualifies him to perform the rites of the mother of the gods.[8] An inscription from 313, naming Constantine and Licinius as consuls, informs us that Severianus, a father of the rites of the unconquered Mithras, is also a hierophant of Liber and the Hecates, and again a recipient of the *taurobolium*.[9] As late as 377, the Mithraist Rufus Caionius Caeio was yet again a hierophant of Hecate and a 'tauroboliate' minister to the Great Mother.[10] The poor did not hold such positions, and Kamerius is described as a man of senatorial rank, a *vir clarissimus*. From these dedications we learn that the cult of Mithras was patronized by men of high rank who had no sense that they were turning away from the gods of their fathers to a foreign, let alone an oriental, cult.

They had no reason to fear that they might become Persian, since the desultory references to Mithras in Avestan and Vedic literature have proved to be of no help in deciphering the sculpture and iconography of the shrines that his Roman votaries dedicated to him in subterranean caves. A lion-headed statue to 'the god Arimanius' illustrates the freedom of innovation that was permitted to them, for Ahriman, the malign twin and antagonist of the creator, received no cults in the Persian world.[11] No Persian antecedents have been discovered for the ubiquitous scenes of Mithras being born from a rock,[12] his feasting with his worshippers,[13] his carrying of the bull or his subsequent immolation of it with the assistance of a serpent, a dog, a scorpion and his acolytes Cautes and Cautopates.[14] No religion of the east is mirrored in the marble relief which Vermaseren dates to the last years of the third century:[15]

> Mithras in *tunica manicata* and flying cloak is slaying the bull, whose tail ends in one great ear. On the point of the Phrygian cap a star; four more stars are visible to the right of the god's head. The dog and serpent are licking the blood from the wound; the scorpion grasps the testicles. On either side stands a torchbearer: Cautes (l) and Cautopates (r), not cross-legegd. They are dressed in tunics only. Behind the main scene a grotto has been represented: on its border the raven is perched, which grasps with its beak; further a lizard is visible creeping out of its hole. Before the entrance to this grotto Mithras carrying the bull; before the bull's forelegs a serpent. In the upper corner the dressed bust of Sol [the sun] with a crown of seven rays, and of Luna [the moon] with a crescent behind the shoulder. She is looking downwards. On the upper border, above Mithras' head, a crown of leaves on either side of which runs [the inscription of Titus Claudius Hermes to Mithras the Unconquered Sun-God].

8 Vermaseren, 516 at I, 205; also at II, 27.
9 Vermaseren 523 at I, 208 (CIL VI 507).
10 Vermaseren 522 at I, 208.
11 Bianchi (1975).
12 Cf. Justin Martyr, *Dialogue with Trypho* 70.
13 Kane (1975), 150 notes that the report of Justin, *Apology* 66.4 is uncorroborated.
14 Though Schwartz (1975) proposes an Iranian etymology for these names. See further Beck (1994).
15 Vermaseren.

This relief is a picturesque compendium of the questions yet to be answered by the student of Mithraism. We would give as much for a prose account of the myth which underlies the principal scene as for a specimen of Gnostic architecture: in the second century Celsus accused a Gnostic sect of stealing from the Mithraists the notion that the soul will escape the world by ascending through the planetary spheres.[16] Since there are seven planets, and we hear of seven grades of initiation in Mithraism, there is reason to suppose that each of the grades was correlated with a new stage in the ascent. Yet this is conjecture, and though the raven in this relief is no doubt a representation of the lowest grade, we rely on Jerome, a hostile Christian witness, for a full enumeration of the seven.[17] Planets and stars are regularly depicted in Mithraea, yet the order of the planets is inconsistent, and the astronomical patterns irreconcilable with the known configuration of the heavens in this period.[18] The Phrygian cap of Mithras is notorious, but where did he acquire it in the course of his migration from Asia to Europe? Commagene, we might propose, after reading a celebrated article by Roger Beck (Beck, 1988); the same scholar contends that the strange cosmography of the Mithraic caves is an attempt to restore the stars to an ancient alignment which had been marred by the precession of the equinoxes. If that is so, there is all the less reason to think of it as an oriental cult, and all the more reason to be surprised that it was so profoundly misunderstood, not only by the Platonists (who wrongly equated Mithras with the demiurge), but by the astrologer Firmicus Maternus, whose rancorous chapter on Mithraism, written shortly after the death of Constantine, is the longest of the surviving accounts, and perhaps the most opaque.

In his treatise *On the Error of Profane Religions*, Firmicus characterizes each of the mysteries as the worship of an element; yet he never explains what Mithras has to do with fire, the deity (as he tells us) of the Persians and the Magi (Error 5.1). This curious juxtaposition of the name of the people with that of its priesthood, as though they were kindred nations, might be a symptom of ignorance, affectation or textual corruption. If we prefer the last explanation—and no one doubts that the text is riddled with errors—the substitution of Medi for Magi is all the more enticing because the Medes and the Persians form a biblical doublet. On the other hand, the Magi also have their place in scripture, they were regularly supposed to worship fire, and they appear again, with the Persians, in the peroration to what remains of the chapter. As eponymous patrons of *magia*, or magic, they might reasonably be suspected of a secret devotion to Hecate, whom Firmicus, alone of ancient

[16] Origen, *Against Celsus* 6.23–24; cf. Bianchi (1975).

[17] Jerome, Letter 107. The seven grades are: raven, cryphius (?nymph), soldier, lion, Persian, sun-runner, father. See further Chalupa (2008).

[18] See Campbell (1968) on the iconography. Ulansey (1989), 125 interprets Mithraism as a 'cosmological code', while Beck (2006) surmises that the diagrams reconstruct an ideal configuration of the stars.

witnesses, is later to introduce as a second idol of the Mithraists.[19] All this is invidious enough, but less invidious, as Robert Turcan points out, than the association of Mithras with the most powerful and inveterate of Rome's enemies.[20] Why, exclaims Firmicus just before his text breaks off, should this cult of fire be the one vice that Rome borrows from the Persians? The jibe would be piquant for those who were aware that Diocletian—the same Diocletian who had stigmatized the Manichees as a Persian sect—had erected at least one temple to Mithras under the august title of Sol Invictus. This being said, we must grant that Mithras was originally a Persian god, and that until the last quarter of the twentieth century few scholars of any note had denied the Persian origins of his cult in the later Roman world.

No other ancient author, and no discovery yet made by archaeologists, corroborates his assertion that the Persians worshipped fire under both a male and female aspect (*Error* 5.1). In Persian texts a consort named Anahita is sometimes assigned to him,[21] but in this, as in many other respects, the original myth and the subsequent cult are at variance. Our faith in his veracity would be increased if we could infer, when he purports to be quoting a hymn that was 'handed on' to him, that he had been at one time an initiate. The words *tradidit nobis*, however, will bear a looser construction, and even as the author of the *Mathesis* he had denounced nocturnal gatherings of the kind that he would have been obliged to frequent as an adept in these mysteries. The salutation, wherever he found it, is someone's notion of a Greek hexameter, one word of which is evidently corrupt in the surviving manuscript:

Adept of the Cattle-theft συνλεξιε of the Noble Father

'Hunc esse Mithram dicunt', writes the accuser: 'they declare this to be Mithras'. But is 'mystic' or 'father' the referent of the pronoun, and what is the noun that complements μυστά? For the untranslatable συνλέξιε Ziegler proposed to substitute συναλέξιε, 'coadjutor', taking the verse to be addressed to every initiate and Mithras himself to be the noble father;[22] favouring the same emendation, Clemen took the verse to mean that Mithras becomes a partner in the theft of the father's cattle.[23] Nevertheless, the discovery of an inscription to an αγαθός συνδεξίος ('excellency at the right hand') in a

[19] *Error* 5.1, with epigraphic an iconographic warrant, as Turcan shows on p. 206 of his introduction (Bibliography A).
[20] See introduction to Turcan's edition (Bibliography A), 204.
[21] See *Error* 5.3 with the introduction to Turcan's edition (Bibiography A), 212.
[22] Ziegler (1909), 1198 and in his edition of 1907, xxxi–xxxiii, rejecting the identification of the mystic with Mithras and in Cumont (1896–99), II, 532.
[23] Clemen (1901), 351.

Mithraeum at Dura-Europos on the Euphrates has persuaded the majority of scholars to accept *συνδεξίε* as the authentic reading.[24] If it is Mithras himself who takes the right hand of the father,[25] or perhaps sits at his right, one might suspect a plagiarism from Christianity.[26] Yet this would be no more than a verbal borrowing, as the father, on this construction, is to be understood as the hierophant of the mysteries: we may think it strange to speak of Mithras as a mere colleague of his own initiate, but the locutions 'father of Mithras' and 'father of the most high god' are attested in inscriptions at Dura-Europos.[27] The meaning of the noun *βουκλοπίη* is more elusive, since there is no surviving representation of Mithras as a cattle-thief in literature or in art, though in the west both images of his slaying a bull and references to the baptism of his neophytes in the blood of a bull are legion. Porphyry, who mentions Mithras more than once in his *Cave of the Nymphs*, speaks also of a *βουκλόπος θεός*, 'cattle-stealing god';[28] the text, however, is both too cryptic and too uncertain to guide us in the elucidation of any other passage. It may allude, for example, to the most famous exploit of the infant Hermes, or again to the abduction of Geryon's cattle by Heracles. While neither of these Greek figures is identified with Mithras in ancient sources, a case can be made for regarding both as aspects of the sun. The sun himself is a 'cattle-stealing Titan' in the *Orphic Argonautica*,[29] but this too is a cipher to modern scholars, for in mythology the sun is no thief but the owner of a herd unlawfully butchered by the companions of Odysseus. Since Mithras was identified with the sun in late antiquity, we need not doubt that this hexameter is a genuine relic of the ceremonies practised by his Roman devotees.

Firmicus proceeds to his declamatory conclusion (*Error* 5.3). This man, he says is worshipped with secret rituals in the shadowy interior of a cave—a clear acknowledgement that his sins are too heinous to see the light of day and that his sacraments are barbarian fabrications. Mithraism, in this new caricature, is no cult for soldiers, but is all that Christianity was in pagan eyes: a religion of subterfuge, hostile to Rome from its very inception, all the more nefarious because it practised more than it cared to preach. Whereas Platonists like Porphyry superimposed their own philosophy on voiceless pictures, Firmicus repeats words that were overheard by no other witness and describes an image yet to be recovered by archaeologists, but is blind to all the evidence that other students, ancient and modern, have deemed essential to an understanding of Mithraism. If we cannot see how ignorance could be so selective or why dissimulation should be pressed so far, we may hazard a third, more charitable

[24] Cf. Dieterich (1923), 18.
[25] Bidez and Cumont (1938), II, 153 n.2.
[26] Cf. Psalm 110.1, Mark 14.62, Acts 7.55, etc.
[27] Cumont (1975), 196–200.
[28] *Cave of the Nymphs*, 69.16 Nauck; cf. Cumont (1899), 40.
[29] *Orphic Argonautica* 1057. On the text of Porphyry see Edwards (1993b), 123.

conjecture that he had chanced on one of the heterogeneous forms that a religion may assume when it has no scripture, no magisterium and not even, so far as our knowledge goes, an archetypal myth.

But how much remained of any of the practices that Firmicus reviled? Dedications to Mithras are less frequent in the late third century than in the second, and the countenance which the cult enjoyed, or was thought to enjoy, under Diocletian and his fellow-tetrarchs does not seem to have inspired a strong revival of devotion. The African governor Florus, a notorious persecutor of Christianity, set up an altar to Mithras the sun-god at the beginning of the fourth century.[30] In 307 a Pannonian shrine was restored with a dedication to the Augusti and Caesares, to whom the author attaches the epithets Joviani and Herculiani.[31] Whether he reckoned Constantine among the dedicatees we cannot say: the vision of Apollo with which Constantine was credited in the following year cannot have been an epiphany of Mithras, who was not prone to such manifestations or equated by his worshippers with Apollo. Another temple is said to have been erected at the behest of Diocletian and Maximian,[32] and a certain Ursinianus who restored a ruined shrine in Noricum in 311 may also have had an eye to imperial favour.[33] We have noted above an inscription in which Constantine is named only as a consul, but in 315/6 he and Licinius were joint dedicatees of a *centenarium solis*, an edifice honouring the sun, in Mauretania.[34] Less equivocal as an index of Mithraic piety is the dedication in 325 of a German temple to Mithras the unconquered god by the 'raven' Materninius Faustus.[35] In a house dating from the reign of Constantine Jupiter shares a Lararium with Isis, Serapis, Hecate, and others, while a 'door nest to it opens on a lower room, which served as a Mithraeum'.[36] As new foundations become less frequent, so the use of the old foundations dwindles:[37] the excavators of a Mithraeum in Colchester discovered no coins from the reign of any of Constantine's successors,[38] and on another British site, a decadent shrine was rebuilt under Maximian, but the 'total absence of Constantinian issues' shows that the project of restoration was stillborn.[39] We may suspect that patrons were deterred by the known hostility of the Emperor, but in the absence of any positive legislation it is safer to attribute the decline to a general waning of devotion, punctuated by the collapse of masonry but largely independent of political duress.

[30] Vermaseren 1381, at II, 219. [31] Vermaseren 1698 at II, 219.
[32] Vermaseren 722 at I, 259. [33] Vermaseren 1431 at II, 161.
[34] Vermaseren 150 at I, 96. [35] Vermaseren 1315 at II, 125.
[36] Vermaseren 356 at I, 160.
[37] Coins from the reign of Constantine are more abundant at Bingen, but Vermaseren 1341 at II, 103 is not certain that the sire was a Mithraeum.
[38] Vermaseren 829 at I, 289. [39] Vermaseren 844 at I, 293.

ISIS AND OSIRIS

Unlike Persia, Egypt had been a portion of the Greek world for almost three hundred years before it became a province of the empire. During this time Egyptians wrote in Greek, a handful of writers who might have passed as Greeks were called Egyptians, and it was generally admitted that, if antiquity were wisdom, the Egyptians would be the wisest of all nations. Readers of Eusebius will have known that in one of Porphyry's more belligerent treatises members of the Egyptian pantheon bring up the rear in a list of gods whose attributes can be deciphered from their statues.[40] Kneph the demiurge may be represented anthropomorphically, but his dark hue and the wings that veil his head signify the unknowability of the noetic realm.[41] The egg in his mouth, from which the lesser demiurge Ptah emerges, is the cosmos in which the noetic manifests its creative power. The boat which carries the sun surmounts a crocodile as the symbol of the humid atmosphere through which the sun passes. Isis has two aspects, the heavenly and the earthly, and in the second she corresponds to Demeter, representing either the earth or its nutritive energy.[42] Osiris is the Nile or the crop that Egypt owes to its inundation. Horus their child, the vanquisher of Typhon, has the form of a hawk whose brilliant plumage makes him a fitting emblem of the sun.[43] The same Porphyry, according to Eusebius, wrote a letter in a very different vein in which he questioned the rationality of many Egyptian practices; Iamblichus offers a Platonist's apology for them in the character of an Egyptian priest. He is careful enough of his mask to insist that, while a sacred pictogram can be paraphrased in Greek, a magical name will lose its potency if translated from Egyptian into any other tongue. The author of the *Asclepius* makes the same observation, but he too wrote in Greek, and for most Greeks Egypt was above all the land of Isis, whose shrines in the rest of the Mediterranean world had become so numerous only because she had consented to be a goddess of many names.

All the Latin apologists of this period show some familiarity with the myth which recounts the marriage of Isis to her brother Osiris, the murder of Osiris by his brother Seth or Typhon, the dismemberment of his body and his sister's arduous quest to reunite the fragments after they had been dispersed among the cities of Egypt. The story had been recounted at length by Diodorus Siculus and Plutarch, Apuleius had described the festival of Isis in Alexandria and the termination of two civil wars in Egypt had inspired allusions to that country's

[40] The following information is taken from the long excerpt in Eusebius, *Gospel Preparation* III.11.45–13.2, which appears as Fr. 10 in Bidez (1913), appendix 1.

[41] Eusebius, *Preparation* 3.11 = Bidez (1913), appendix 1, 18*.

[42] Bidez (1913), appendix A, 19–20.

[43] Bidez (1913), appendix A, 20.

gods in Latin epic.[44] Porphyry, as we have seen, concurs. Lactantius (unless he is guilty of a simple error) enhances the resemblance by making Osiris not the brother of Isis but her lost child (*Divine Institutes* 1.21). Firmicus, to deprive the leading characters of our sympathy, represents the 'incestuous' union of Isis and Osiris as a breach of her legitimate marriage to Typhon, with whom she appears to have no tie of blood (*Error* 2.3). In the Euhemeristic vein that is characteristic of all the Latin apologists, he purports to have heard that Osiris was a just and benevolent ruler of Egypt and Typhon the jealous rival who dethroned him. This being much the same story that Lactantius, following Euhemerus, tells of Jove and Saturn (*Divine Institutes* 1.11 and 1.14), we need not suppose that it was believed in Egypt. Firmicus has the authority of Porphyry, and perhaps of native traditions, for his allegorical reading, according to which Osiris represents the harvest, Isis the soil, and Typhon the heat of summer (*Error* 2.6). He exhibits no knowledge either of Plutarch's equation of Osiris with the moist element or of a similar interpretation of Isis in the magical papyri; his assertion that the Egyptians venerate water (2.5) is corroborated only by the detail—peculiar to himself and perhaps invented—that the limbs of Osiris were strewn on the river Nile.

The yearly re-enactments of the myth are sketched with studious disdain: 'in their hallowed places they have an idol of the buried Osiris, which they lament with annual mourning, shaving their heads so that by the ugliness of their dishonoured pates they may bewail the wretched misfortune of their king. They smite their breasts, lacerate their arms and open up the scars of old wounds so that by their annual mourning the calamity of a dolorous and wretched death may be reborn' (*Error* 2.3). All other sources agree that it was the custom of the priests to shave their heads as a permanent sing of their vocation, and (according to Apuleius) a preparation for entry into the higher mysteries. Since the obsequies of Osiris were celebrated not only in Alexandria but in Rome at the beginning of every November, we ought perhaps to assume that this description of an annual depilation of the multitude is satirical. For the same reason it cannot be taken as evidence of widespread adherence to the Egyptian cult.

Horus, the offspring of Isis and Osiris, is ignored by Christian authors. Firmicus however, fires a quick volley at Serapis, a Hellenistic amalgam of Osiris with Apis, the god of the Nile to whom Egypt owed its wealth. Risibly deriving the name from the Greek *Σάρρας παΐς*, he argues that the true Serapi was the biblical Joseph (13.2). Porphyry is cited to prove that the blood that is now offered to his human simulacrum is drunk by demons (1.3.3) and that the oracles which proceed from him in this shape, being uttered under coercion, cannot be divine (13.4). For Lactantius Serapis is merely the popular name of

[44] Diodorus, *Histories* 1.14–25; Plutarch in Griffiths (1970); Apuleius in Griffiths (1975); Virgil, *Aeneid* 8.698.

Osiris, but it was also the name employed by Diocletian and Galerius to reinforce their dominion in Egypt. In 303 Serapis and Isis mingled with the Roman gods in the retinue of Galerius on the arch that he erected in Thessalonica as a monument to his eastern victories.[45] Within two years their images appeared on coins which Diocletian struck to commemorate a vote of thanks for his Vicennalia,[46] the twentieth anniversary of his accession. When Maximinus Daia, first the Caesar then the successor of Galerius, contested the eastern empire with Licinius from 310 to 313, his coins predict the decapitation of Serapis by the unconquered sun.[47] Yet Serapis himself takes on a solar aspect both in Alexandrian currency of this period[48] and in a shrine consecrated in 299 by four Egyptian notables.[49] He shares with Isis the honours of a temple built in Rome by Diocletian, who also adorned his palace in Split with eight Egyptian sphinxes[50] and had altars set up to the deities of the land in Philae, one of the most ancient seats of Isis.[51] Here, as R. E. Witt observes, 'a truce was declared between Roman and Egyptian deities'.[52]

It is in the nature of truces to expire, and no true Israelite is at home in the country of Pharaoh. According to Eusebius, Licinius put himself in the role of Saul, and hence beyond hope of accommodation with God or his servant Constantine, when he placed his hopes in a cabal of Egyptian soothsayers, diviners, magicians, and sorcerers (*Life of Constantine* 2.4). The *Historia Augusta*, falsely purporting to have been written by six authors in the reign of Constantine,[53] contains a letter, ascribed to Hadrian but patently fictitious, which alleges that every religious teacher in Egypt—be he Christian, Jew, or Samaritan—is an astrologer, an augur, a magician, and a votary of Serapis (*Florus, etc.* 8).[54] The very patriarch, he exclaims, is forced when he comes to Egypt to pay his devoirs not only to Christ but to his native rival. Even if the *Historia* is as early as Alan Cameron maintains, and even if the patriarch (as Ronald Syme proposed[55]) is Athanasius, this forgery cannot be treated as a document of the Constantinian era. And yet its contents are almost vindicated in the transcript of a trial that certainly took place in this era, in the course of which a group of Donatist bishops was accused of stealing a quantity of wine from the temple of Serapis in Cirta.[56] The wine, it appears, was paid as tax and the temple served, on this as on other occasions, as a treasury. Why they stole it and whether they carried it off in the fiscal vats or in their own vessels we have no means of discovering from this record. Perhaps it was for the

45 Malaise (1972), 213. 46 Alföldi, A. (1937), 30ff. 47 Turcan (1989), 121.
48 Vogt (1924), I, 224. 49 Turcan (1989), 121. 50 Budischowsky (1977), 214.
51 Kakosy (1995). 52 Witt (1971), 239.
53 In fact it is almost certainly the work of one author writing in the last quarter of the fourth century: see Barnes (1978); Rohrbacker (2013).
54 On the literary echoes in this *jeu d'esprit* see Cameron (2010), 759–60.
55 Syme (1971).
56 Optatus, *Against the Donatists*, appendix 1.16 = Edwards (1997), 164.

edification of Christians who spent too much time in the temple of Serapis that the emperor constructed an experiment to show that prayer to this god had no effect on the inundations of the Nile.[57]

PHRYGIAN VICES

Arnobius relates the following version of the myth on the authority of Timotheus, a Hellenistic poet of little charm and caliginous learning (*Against the Nations* 5.5–17). Jupiter, attempting to ravish the mother of the gods, was thwarted and spilt his semen on a rock. From this sprang up the androgynous giant Agdistis, who, unchecked by fear or piety, set about laying waste the works of gods and mortals. Liber, at the behest of the gods, subdued him by drugging a spring with wine, and captured him as he slept in a snare from which he could free himself only by cutting off his genitals. These became the seed of a pomegranate tree; a maiden who ate from this conceived and gave birth to the handsome Attis, who soon became the inseparable companion of Agdistis and the great mother. Midas of Crete, in the hope of drawing Attis into human society, gave him his daughter in marriage, but the feast of betrothal was thrown into confusion by Agdistis. Attis died after severing his genitals as a final gift to Agdistis; the bride took her own life also, and purple violets issued from her blood. When the great mother planted the severed organs of her grandson, a pine grew from them, while the fruit of her own tears was an almond tree. Though Jupiter would not restore Attis to life at the prayer of Agdistis, he provided that the body should not decay, while Agdistis appointed a priesthood to maintain a yearly ritual of mourning. Of all authors before Arnobius himself, Timotheus had been the loudest in his praise of innovation,[58] and, while this bloody cross-hatching of botanical aetiologies with two myths from the *Symposium* can hardly be called original,[59] we may be confident that the tale of Attis had never been told before in such a manner.

Firmicus again adopts a Euhemeristic redaction of the myth, omitting Agdistis and representing Attis himself as a human youth who failed to require the affections of a proud queen. She procured his death, apparently by castration, but then in remorse began to dedicate temples to him, setting up an order of priests to perform an annual rite of emasculation in remembrance of her crime (*Error* 3.1). He also offers an allegorical reading, suited to the theology of the Phrygians for whom earth is the sacred element: Attis is the fruit which is cherished by earth, but must yield to the pitiless scythe and deposit its seed in the ground if it is to be reborn the next year (3.6). This

[57] Socrates, *Church History* 1.10. [58] Hordern (2002), 32–6.
[59] Plato, *Symposium* 190d–192a and 203b–c.

interpretation presupposes a myth in which Attis returns to life, and Firmicus tells us, though elliptically, that the sycophants who erected temples to the 'dead youth' also boasted of his resuscitation.[60] He appears to be unaware that Gnostic and Platonic exegetes of the myth would have been ashamed of such an epilogue,[61] since for them the emasculation of Attis symbolized the withdrawal of intellect from the domain of the senses. As it is one of his aims to unmask the pagan rites as diabolic counterfeits of the true mysteries, we may guess that this variant represents his own assimilation of the tragedy of Attis to that of Christ.

In Martin Vermaseren's compendium of inscriptions to Attis and the great mother, nothing is said of the former's death, let alone of his coming to life, and the name of Agdistis is barely attested. The frequency of dedications falls precipitately throughout the empire in the epigraphic remains of the late third century, and there is no revival under the Tetrarchy or Constantine. Even from Asia Minor, the home of the cult, only three inscriptions of any substance remain, all from the same locality and recording the consecration of a slave-girl to the great mother. Two were commissioned by women—one by Aurelia in 309, the other by Theodote in 311—and the third by Aurelius in 314.[62] In Carthage the pair found a patron in a *vir clarissimus*, a man of senatorial rank, who had already held a host of public offices when he set up an altar to Attis and Cybele in 337.[63] From Rome comes most of our information about the *taurobolium*, the ceremonial draining of a bull's blood into a cup, which we have encountered already on Mithraic monuments where the sponsor was also an adept of the Phrygian mysteries. In 305 a certain Julius Italus records that he 'received' it (*percepit*) when Constantine and Maximian were consuls. [64] Another inscription records that the rite was administered to a woman named Serapias during the consulship of Constantine and the 'younger Licinius'.[65] It has been supposed that the use of the verb *percipere*, which displaces its cognate *accipere* in the fourth century, betokens the adoption of a new rite, in which the initiate, washed and clad in white, lay in a pit beneath a wooden plank and was immersed in the blood of the slaughtered animal. The most vivid accounts of this, however, occur in the vigorous poetry of Prudentius, who, as Neil McLynn observes,[66] may never have witnessed the atrocities that he describes without fear of correction or

[60] *Error* 22.1 with 27.1. If the identification of this youth as Attis is not upheld, the myth of the 'dying and rising god' will not have been so ubiquitous in the ancient Mediterranean world as scholars have supposed: see J. Z. Smith (1987).

[61] Hippolytus, *Refutation* 5.8.40; Sallustius, *Concerning the Gods* 4.

[62] Vermaseren VI, 186, 187, and 188.

[63] Vermaseren, V, 94 (p. 36). See Vermaseren, V, 97 on the same page for an African *taurobolium*.

[64] Vermaseren III, 226 (p. 49) = *CIL* VI.491.

[65] Vermaseren III, 234 (p. 53) = *CIL* VI.507.

[66] McLynn (1996).

reprisal. It would be safer to assume that the change of verb was as arbitrary as linguistic fashions are apt to be, and that any blood spilt in a Roman *taurobolium* of the fourth century was offered to the presiding deities.

ANOTHER VENUS?

Greek and Latin writers were aware of a powerful goddess whose cult originated in the region vaguely known as Syria, though different authors give her different names, or none at all. To some she is Atargatis or Astarte, to Philo the Syrian Aphrodite, to Lucian the anonymous goddess of Syria.[67] Latin readers recognized her by her entourage of effeminate mendicants whose avaricious stratagems disgust the narrator of the *Golden Ass*.[68] To Firmicus the Syrians are Assyrians and their deity a counterpart of Venus or Juno (4.1). He intimates obscurely that this Venus has pretensions to virginity; Juno seems to be a more apt designation if, as he says, the Assyrian goddess is the consort of her own brother. Perhaps he knows something of Baal and Astarte;[69] on the other hand, confusion of eastern goddesses was rife in the Roman world, and it is was certainly his own conceit to decide that this goddess personifies the air because it occupies the place between heaven and earth (4.1), just as her mutilated votaries fall between the two natural sexes (4.2). As Pastorino observes,[70] he had already shown a typically Roman horror of men who renounce their manhood and dress like the other sex in his *Mathesis*; this treatise adds nothing but the admonition that if we fail to give nature her due we are also rebels to the Creator (4.3). There is no reason to think that he had heard the clashing cymbals to which he alludes (4.2), since they are inseparable trappings of the cult in literary caricature.

Firmicus devotes his central chapters to a harangue against Venus, the lewdest of divinities both in her oriental and in her Roman guises. In both her only adepts are the lecher, the pimp and the sybarite; as ancestor of the Caesars and patroness of the Eternal City, she acts as a bridge between the ethnographic chapters and those in which the cultured reader learns that his own traditions condone obscenities which he was wont to regard as all too typical of subject races. But who is the oriental Venus? The evening-star of ancient Mesopotamia was Ishtar, who as her temples multiplied took the form of Atargatis in Syria, of Ashtoreth in Phoenicia, and of Astarte in the

[67] Lightfoot (2003), 10–33 does not believe Cybele and the Syrian goddess to be interchangeable.

[68] Apuleius, *Metamorphoses* 8.27–28.

[69] Wyatt (1995).

[70] Pastorino (1956), 54, citing *Mathesis* 2.94.6.

Hellenized Levant.[71] If we can trust Eusebius, her amoral cult was suppressed by Constantine with exemplary rigour. He exultantly records the desecration of an underground sanctuary, close to the holy sepulchre in Jerusalem, where 'profane altars' had been dedicated to the 'incontinent demon' Aphrodite (*Life of Constantine* 3.26.2–3). At Aphaca in Lebanon, the all-seeing monarch uncovered and destroyed the grove in which effeminate men had deflowered the young, conniving at acts of theft and homicide and inducing women to form their own guilds for the satisfaction of 'unspeakable', 'lawless', and 'incontinent' passions (*Life* 4.55.1–2). Although he asserts that all former practitioners of 'superstition' fled to the Saviour when they witnessed the spoliation of their altars (4.57.1), the historian records the fall of only two more shrines, one dedicated to Asclepius in Cilicia (4.56) and the other the Phoenician Aphrodite at Heliopolis, where her votaries were inveigling both married women and unwed girls into fornication (4.58.1). It cannot be inferred from the *Life of Constantine* that such measures were typical; on the other hand, the infrequency with which they are recorded may prove only that Eusebius was better acquainted with his master's policy in the neighbourhood of Palestine than in other parts of the empire. No reader of the *Life* can fail to discern a profound antipathy to the worship of Aphrodite; but whether this should be ascribed to its author or his hero we cannot pretend to know.

THE GOD OF WINE

In his account of the origins of the Bacchic or Dionysian mysteries, Firmicus adds human flesh and bones to the skeletal narrative which Clement of Alexandria appears to have derived from an Orphic poem. No earlier pagan version of the story is extant, and we cannot say whether Euhemerus was his source or merely his model when he tells us that Liber (the Roman name for Dionysus) was the illegitimate son of Jupiter, king of Crete. He adds that, fearing the wiles of his consort Juno (6.1), the king appointed guards to watch the child, until at last his absence gave her the opportunity to suborn them (6.2). Using toys and a mirror to lure the young prince from the throne which had been entrusted to him by his father, they murdered him in a secret place and concealed their crime by devouring every part of him but the heart. This was the portion of their accomplice Minerva, the daughter of Jupiter, who presented it to him on his return as evidence and solace for the crime (6.3). Having destroyed the murderers with a thunderbolt, the grieving father set up the usual obsequies (6.4), at which the mutilated priests of Liber were required

[71] See Graf (1995), 122; Wyatt (1995), 208 on Astarte and Lucian's Syrian goddess.

not only to dance and clash their cymbals but to tear apart a live bull with their naked hands and gorge themselves on its bleeding flesh (6.5). Firmicus is the only ancient witness who imputes this atrocity to his male contemporaries:[72] in myth the *omophagia* is performed by maenads, the maddened female votaries of the god, while Greek inscriptions suggest that the civic rite of this name was a tamer affair, carried out under strict regulation.

Like his fellow-monotheists Arnobius and Lactantius, Firmicus grows satirical in counting the avatars of pagan deities.[73] There was, he tells us, a second Dionysus in Thebes, an incontinent seducer of women, who, after having been justly unmanned and banished by Lycurgus, found a new career in pandering to the lusts of others When Lycurgus commenced a second pursuit, Dionysus fled with the gang of eunuchs who were now his sole companions (6.7). In the midst of their debaucheries, however, Lycurgus surprised them and drove them over a precipice into the sea. The commemorative rituals mimic the states in which he found them—some brandishing snakes, some tearing animals limb from limb, some merely supine with intoxication (6.8). The Christian polemicist contrasts the turpitude of the latter-day Roman with the probity of the republican consul Postumus, who in 186 BC had induced the senate to issue a decree suppressing the bacchanals (6.9); this is a less than tactful hint that the emperors must assume the role of the enervated senate, but he does not say where, outside the pages of Livy and his own imagination, they will find anything worthy of their vigilance.

Firmicus has now aligned each of the elements with an oriental cult, and therefore insists on a Euhemeristic reading of the myth of Dionysus. Proponents of physical allegory who see in this emasculated rogue a personification of the sun are charlatans (7.7). Turning to Eleusis, he insists that the rape of Persephone was another act of aggravated violence which does not lend itself to a palliative reading. Persephone (or Proserpina) was not (as some say) the moon, but a Sicilian maid, and her suitor a neighbouring peasant who because of his affluence was known as Pluto (from the Greek *ploutos*, meaning 'wealth': 7.1). Failing to seduce her, he snatched her away, whereupon her mother Ceres raised an army of local sympathizers (7.2–3). Pluto could escape only by driving his team into a lake, whose waters closed over him and his reluctant paramour. The grieving mother, following idle rumours that her daughter had been seen alive (7.4), arrived at last at a place that was henceforth to be known as Eleusis, from the Greek word that denotes a 'coming' (7.5). Here, though disappointed in her quest, she taught the inhabitants the hitherto unknown art of cultivation (7.6). Then she took her own life, but because it is the way of the

[72] Pastorino (1956), 84 notes that Aelian (*Varia Historia* 12.34) speaks only of a calf, while in Euripides (*Bacchae* 735–745) this banquet is at most an occasional feature of the cult.

[73] Cf. *Error* 16.1 on the five Minervae.

Greeks to honour their benefactors as divinities, the Eleusinian mysteries were created in remembrance of her sorrows.

Although he has juxtaposed the two myths, Firmicus does not explain himself by pointing out that Dionysus was honoured together with Demeter and Persephone at Eleusis. Evidence is wanting for the continued celebration of the Eleusinian mysteries in the Constantinian era. They do not figure in the treatise of Iamblichus *On the Mysteries*, though he defends the use of intoxicating vapours to induce ecstasy in the prophetess at Delphi and the priests of other shrines. In his *Protrepticus* or *Exhortation to Philosophy* he makes only a passing allusion to the necessity of initiation into the lesser mysteries before one essays the greater. Here, as elsewhere, the Pythagorean brotherhood replaces the mystic guild. Porphyry at least gives substance to the apologist's sallies against the allegorical reading of the Dionysian mysteries. What better emblem of the soul's peregrinations could there be, he asks, than the furniture of the caves in which these rites are celebrated?

> Let the stone bowls and amphorae be symbols of aquatic nymphs; for these, being ceramic (that is, from baked earth) are symbols of Dionysus. This has an affinity with the gift of wine from the god, because the fruit of the vine is warned by heavenly fire. Moreover, stone bowls and amphorae are particularly appropriate to the nymphs who preside over the water that flows from rocks. But what could be a more appropriate symbol than these for the souls that descend to generation and the fashioning of bodies? (Porphyry, *Cave of the Nymphs*, 65.19–66.4 Nauck)

In another passage Porphyry, assuming throughout that Homer's cave of the nymphs is a representation of the cosmos like the caves dedicated to Mithras, explains the presence of bees in the cave by noting that these insects were sacred to Demeter, that Demeter's daughter Kore was identified with the moon, that the moon (by virtue of her horns, we presume) is also a bull, that bees (according to legend) are born from the carcass of a bull, and that the 'cattle-stealing god' is the one who leads souls into the realm of generation (69.2–16). It is Firmicus himself, as we saw above, who affords the best evidence that this deity is Mithras; since he shows knowledge of Porphyry's treatise on oracles, it is possible that he was also acquainted with his writings on the interpretation of myth. The essay *On the Cave of the Nymphs* is only a remnant of a much larger corpus, but even here we encounter an allegorical reading of the Bacchic mysteries and a physical allegory equating another Eleusinian divinity with the moon. Porphyry also couples these Greek deities with Mithras, on the principle (as he said in his treatise *On the Return of the Soul*) that every people has found its own way of restoring the soul to communion with the gods. He had not, however, found a universal way, and may have held, in conscious opposition to Christianity, that there was no such way to be discovered. While Firmicus is equally eclectic, his aims run counter to those of his Greek informant. For him it is the mysteries themselves that stand in need of an interpreter, and there is one text—not a Greek fable but the word of God—that brings to light their origins. Judgment is thereby passed both on the deceivers and on the deceived; Porphyry falls under both descriptions when he attempts to redeem the blemishes of Homer by expedients which belie the obvious meaning of the text.

BAAL AND THE AFRICAN SATURN

In chapter 12 of his diatribe against false religion, Firmicus has one contemptuous sentence for Saturn, who 'fearing for his kingdom, devoured his sons' and then took refuge in Italy to escape the son who survived. Thus he concurs with other Latin authors in identifying the Cronos of Greek mythology with the Saturn who had passed into Roman legend as the patriarch of a prosperous though frugal age when Italians still lived only by the plough. Nothing is said of the African custom of offering human victims to a deity named Saturnus, which had been cited by both pagan and Christian writers in previous centuries to illustrate the pernicious consequences of superstition. It is possible that his silence betrays his ignorance of African affairs, notwithstanding his dedication of the *Mathesis* to a proconsul of Africa; or perhaps it simply corroborates the archaeological evidence for the atrophy of the African cult of Saturn in the fourth century. There is equally cogent evidence that the worship of Saturn flourished in Numidia, a province to the west of Carthage, up to the time of Constantine, though it cannot be proved that human sacrifice was practised after the Emperor Hadrian's suppression of this rite in the second century. The practice was brought to Africa by the Phoenician founders of Carthage, and Marcel Leglay,[74] whose collection of epigraphic and literary testimonia has not been superseded, concluded that the cults of two Semitic deities, El the high god and Baal the lord of popular devotion, had coalesced in Africa with indigenous traditions. Excavations at the shrines of other gods in Africa have revealed similar conflations in iconography and ritual; the pre-eminence of Saturn in Numidia exemplifies the tendency to henotheism, the elevation of one god to the first place in the pantheon, which was characteristic of North Africa in ancient times. As for his name, Leglay was more inclined to derive it from the Etruscan Satre, notwithstanding the numerous monuments which portray the god holding a sickle, the typical attribute of the Roman Saturn. In favour of his opinion, it can be said that the patrons of the African cult were seldom Romans of distinguished rank or polished education. On the other hand, we have seen that the Roman Saturn

[74] Leglay (1966).

was the Greek Kronos, whom mythographers had long identified with the Phoenician El.

Such questions will be of little consequence to the present study if the African Saturn is merely one more god who received his death-blow from the militant Christianity of the fourth century. Quite a different thesis was maintained, however, by W. H. C. Frend in his seminal book *The Donatist Church*, which, for all that has justly been said against it, is even today the most impressive attempt to prove empirically what no one denies to be probable a priori—that conflicts of religions in the ancient world were frequently exacerbated, then as now, by undeclared hostilities between different ethnic groups or social classes. Frend held that the secession of a group of Numidian bishops from the Catholic Church in 311, following the succession of Caecilian to the bishopric of Carthage was an example of such a conflict. The public accusation against Caecilian—examined in 313 by a Roman synod and found to be baseless—was that one of the bishops who consecrated him, Felix of Abthungi, had been guilty of *traditio* during the Great Persecution, that is, of complying with the demand to hand over copies of the scriptures to be burned. Frend attached more weight to another story, preserved in a text known both as and as the *Acts of the Abitinian Martyrs*,[75] according to which Caecilian, as a deacon to Bishop Mensurius in the early years of the persecution, had kept peace with the Romans by intercepting supplies of food to Christian prisoners, thus ensuring that they would starve. Catholic opponents of the Donatists maintained that they had been suborned by a woman named Lucilla, who had cherished a grievance against Caecilian ever since he forbade her to hour the relics of a false martyr. All three of these narratives imply that the schismatic bishops placed a high value on defiant suffering, and that the Catholic Church in their eyes was a school of compromise and sycophancy.

Taking account of their Numidian origin, Frend argued that in condemning the friends of Rome, whose church had its centre in the capital, they were giving voice to the resentment of a colonized people. Numidia, he argued, had not only been the cradle of Donatism but was proved by archaeology to be the region in which it enjoyed the most concentrated support throughout the fourth century. He could quote the opinion of André Berthier, the leading authority on Tunisia in the Roman era,[76] that the majority of excavated churches in the southern province had embraced the schism. Electing to believe the catholic sources which alleged that the Circumcellions—lawless and masterless gangs of brigands who revered neither power nor property in Africa—were acting at the behest of the schismatics, he surmised that Donatism was as much a peasant revolt as a provincial insurrection. God for these sons of the soil was the latest alias of Saturn, the Phoenician Baal or Moloch,

[75] Frend (1952), 110–11, 116, 150, 308.
[76] Berthier (1942), on which see now Michel (2005), 105–6.

whose savage cult had been brought to Africa by the founders of Carthage and taken up with zeal by the native Berbers. The research of Jules Toutain was thought to have proved that Saturn was above all a rural deity,[77] and the equation of the rural with the vernacular seemed to be warranted by epigraphic traces of the use of Punic and Berber in the hinterland of Carthage. Donatism, ethnic marginality, and the cult of Saturn were therefore coextensive, and the Donatists drew into their orbit every movement of secular defiance: is it not all too probable, then, that Christian zealots of Berber and Punic extraction had found in dying for Christ a substitute for the oblations that their fathers had offered to a more jealous god?

Nevertheless, it is generally held that the theory will not withstand a more reflective examination of the data. Few scholars now accept Frend's early dating of the *Passion of Saturninus*, or his assumption that an earlier text is always more veridical.[78] A Punic or Berber inscription cannot tell us whether this was the only language of its readers or was used alongside Latin. Bilingualism is sometimes a mark of low economic status, sometimes of high intellectual culture; inscriptions, insofar as they afford evidence of literacy, cannot be adduced as evidence of the former.[79] James Rives has pointed out that dedications to African gods by local dignitaries were often accompanied by professions of loyalty to the empire;[80] while it may be true that African images of Saturn are free of Romanizing features,[81] artistic independence is no clear proof of contumacy or defective education. It is not a historical law that every puritan is a militant: if the Donatists were the only fanatics in Africa, who but they could have been responsible for the defacement of Saturn's images which Andrew Wilson attributes to the 'anti-pagan fervour' of the fourth century?[82] Even Frend's important premiss that Saturn was predominantly the god of the Berbers and not of their Roman masters is open to challenge.[83] It was always in the interest of the catholic party to represent their opponents as barbarians in provenance, in conduct, and in culture; nevertheless, Donatus was the putative bishop of Carthage, not of Cirta the metropolis of Numidia, and he obtained enough of a following in that city to raise a doubt in the mind of the emperor and secure the endorsement of an eastern synod.[84] Of his mental cultivation we know nothing; the letters of his cronies which are preserved by Optatus are barely specimens of Latin prose.[85]

[77] Toutain (1920). [78] Dearn (2004).
[79] For bibliography see Rebillard (2013), 66–7. [80] Rives (1995b), 142–50.
[81] Wilson (2005). [82] Wilson (2005).
[83] Goddard (2010), 122–30, though I do not dwell on this point as I suspect that archaeology will never resolve such questions.
[84] Edwards (1997), 29, citing Augustine, *Against Cresconius* 3.38.
[85] Optatus, *Against the Donatists*, appendix 1.

THE MOST HIGH GOD

Around 338 the church received a neophyte in his middle years, whose god of choice hitherto had been Zeus Hypsistos, Zeus the Most High.[86] Neither this Gregory nor the bishopric of Nazianzus which he subsequently held would be of interest to us but for his son and namesake, who became one of the most celebrated doctors of the church. On the other hand, inscriptions throughout the empire attest the popularity of the cults of Zeus Hypsistos and Theos Hypsistos, though neither has left a clear trace in literature. In the Septuagint the epithet translates the Hebrew El Shaddai, which functions as a personal designation for the God of Abraham. Philo applies it to God as the omnipotent Creator, and the angel's promise to Mary at Luke 1.35, 'the power of the Most High will overshadow you' introduced this Jewish circumlocution into Christian parlance. When we find no noun coupled with it but *theos*, we may reasonably surmise that the epigraphists were anonymous Jews or Gentiles of the 'godfearing' persuasion, who had adopted certain outward forms of Judaism without the illicit rite of circumcision. This is all the more probable when some further salutation such as *eulogêtos* ('blessed') or *pantokratôr* ('almighty') has been added, or where the inscription is found in the vicinity of a synagogue or some other Jewish site. It is not so likely when the venue is Delos, Apollo's island, or when the dedicatee is a female deity (as in one inscription from Lydia) or when (as in Dacia) the prudent worshippers address a whole company of the 'highest gods'. In many localities the name Zeus predominates, and, while it is true that Zeus shares a number of attributes with the 'Most High' of the Septuagint, it remains possible that the difference in nomenclature is explained by the existence of two distinct religious guilds.

In two important articles on the Hypsistarians, Stephen Mitchell points out that the epithet *hupsistos* is attached in many inscriptions to the names of particular deities and not to the bare noun *theos*.[87] He does not endorse the inference of Glen Bowersock that there were many hypsistarian cults which had nothing but the epithet in common;[88] he is equally unwilling to follow Ustinova in identifying every bearer of the epithet with a sky-god of Egyptian provenance.[89] He surmises that two Hypsistarians, naming their own gods differently, might none the less agree, as a modern Christian and a Muslim might agree, that they were worshipping the same god because each worshipped only one.[90] He

[86] Elm (2012), 50.

[87] Mitchell (1999) and (2010), 170–4, though Zeus predominates. At (2010), 174–9 Mitchell observes that offerings to the highest god were often made by 'humble' persons without the ostentation that we observe in other cults.

[88] Mitchell (2010), 185; Bowersock (2002), 361.

[89] Mitchell (2010), 185; Ustinova (1999).

[90] Mitchell (2010), 188.

also suggests that the typical Hypsistarian might have belonged to the race of godfearers who, according to some historians, lived on the margins of the synagogue, observing certain Jewish rites and eschewing other cults but without undergoing circumcision.[91] It is possible that the typical Hypsistarian was also a Jew, a Samaritan, a polytheist, or even (though the historians might deplore it) a tipsy Christian in the multitude that gathered to adore the god of Abraham at one of his oldest haunts. Eusebius cannot bring himself to recount the profanations which the emperor suppressed by immediate fiat as soon as he learned that the Saviour had shown himself to Abraham at Mamre in the company of two angels; nor does the bombastic letter of Constantine to Macarius of Jerusalem, which Eusebius transcribes in full, add any detail to his repeated assertions that the rituals performed at Mamre are 'worthy of execration'. It is Sozomen, another Palestinian, who informs us that the impurity of the festival lay in the indiscriminate mingling of the chosen with the unchosen:

> Here some prayed to the god of all; some called upon angels, poured out wine, burnt incense, or offered an ox, or he-goat, a sheep or a cock. Each one made some beautiful product of his labour, and after carefully husbanding it through the entire year, he offered it according to promise as provision for that feast, both for himself and for his dependents. And either from honour to the place or from fear of divine wrath, they all abstained from coming near their wives, although during the feast these were more than ordinarily studious of their beauty and adornment. Nor, if they chanced to appear and take part in the public processions, did they act at all licentiously. Nor did they behave imprudently in any other respect, although the tents were contiguous to each other and they all lay promiscuously together. (Sozomen, *Church History* 4.2.4, NPNF translation)

Thus little can be said to the discredit of this festival. Yet Sozomen records with approbation that when Constantine learned of this promiscuous gathering from his mother-in-law Eutropia,[92] he wrote at once to reproach Macarius and the bishops of Palestine for their indolence. Having paraphrased the transcript in Eusebius (which the latter too describes as a 'rebuke to us'[93])

[91] Mitchell (1999), 15–21; (2010), 189–96. *Theosebes* may not have been a term with a fixed definition: see Reynolds and Tannenbaum (1987), 53–67.

[92] Constantine appeals to the Most High God when denouncing Apollo (Eusebius, *Life of Constantine* 2.48, 2.51.1) and when informing Aelafius of his desire for the universal triumph of Christianity (Optatus, *Against the Donatists*, appendix 30).

[93] 'Learning that the one and self-same saviour who had recently manifested himself to the living had also made divine appearances to God-loving men in Palestine by the oak which is called Mamre, he ordered that there too a splendid house should be erected to the God who had become visible. Therefore a royal fiat went forth to the secular rulers through the letters dispatched to each, commanding that his injunction should be carried out to the last word, while to us who are writing this history he sent instructions with a more detailed argument, a fair copy of which I have decided to include in the present work in order to give an accurate notion of this God-loving man's solicitude. Here, then, word for word, is what he wrote, rebuking us on

he adds that, once the impious custom had been suppressed with the help of Phoenician bishops, no strange altar or oblation was allowed to profane the site.

Constantine's measures in Palestine invite two observations. The first is that the bishop whom he appointed as his executor was Macarius, as though Jerusalem rather than Caesarea were the metropolitan see, at least in matters touching the purity of religion. The second is that, if he pursued a policy of forbearance, it did not extend either to cults that were plainly daemonic (as in Jerusalem) or to those which as at Mamre, were admitting difficult neighbours on easy terms to the household of the Most High God.

THE QUESTION OF DIVINE UNITY

Those engaged in the practice of religion are seldom scholars: they do what we know without knowing what they do. If we, as scholars, none the less feel bound to ask whether the cult of God Most High was monotheistic, an answer cannot be given until we define the term 'monotheism'. Dedications to a named divinity as the 'one god' or simply the 'one' are preserved in inscriptions from almost every Mediterranean province of the Roman Empire throughout its history.[94] The majority of scholars are agreed, however, in holding these to be instances not of monotheism but of henotheism, the exaltation of one deity against or above the rest. Peter van Nuffelen, following Henneck Versnel,[95] enumerates three forms of henotheism: 'the exaltation of one god above the others, the *reductio ad unum* of many divinities, and the assumption by a single god of the role of many others'. It can be argued that the second and third are mutually convertible: such monism, as it might be called, may take the form of a philosophical speculation that all the gods are in fact one god or an inscription saluting some particular god as the one who is all.[96] In either case, however, it might be argued that a reduction of many to one is neither monotheism nor true henotheism, which always implies the choice of one from many. We might offer 'theistic monism' as a less

account of the acts which (as he had learned) were being performed there: *Constantine Victor, Supreme Augustus, to Macarius and the other bishops of Palestine,* etc.' (*Life of Constantine* 51–52).

[94] Belayche (2010) maintains that such formulae are not 'theologically exclusive' (p. 158), but imply that the deity was 'alone of its type' (p. 166). At the same time it was adopted by Christian neophytes and by Samaritans who wished to distinguish themselves from rival worshippers of the same deity: see Trombley (2001), 260 and Markschies (2010), 107.

[95] Van Nuffelen (2010), 18; Versnel (1990), 35–6.

[96] Versnel (2011), 300 judges a salutation to Isis, *tibi una quae es omnia* ('to thee who alone art all') to be 'as close as Hellenistic henotheism ever gets to monotheism'.

misleading expression; it might be urged, however, that our reluctance to speak of 'monotheism' is baseless, for the statement that all the gods are one must logically entail that there is no more than one god.

Yet abstract logic is one thing and practice another. Cult in the Roman world, as John North observes, is always polytheistic in its outward character:[97] even one who opined that Apollo, Jupiter, and Bacchus were all epiphanies of the sun would readily worship Apollo, Jupiter, and Bacchus under their traditional names. Even the Neoplatonists who maintained that the One is god did not draw the inference that *theos* has no plural. They applied this term to a multitude of beings, and (with the exception of Plotinus[98]) they were willing to join in popular devotions to these same beings, the gods of the poets and the priests: they themselves wrote no hymns to the One. Thus they differed irreconcilably in their linguistic behaviour from the Christians: the latter might sarcastically echo the usage of the pagans when they announced that all the gods of the nations were idols, but when they were expressing their own convictions they denied that more than one being could bear the name God. When Trinitarian Christians of the fourth century were accused of being tritheists without knowing it (the Father, the Son, and the Spirit being three objects of worship who were not identical), they went to ingenious lengths to prove that three can also be one.

Granting all this, we may say, and granting that Christians in the Roman world were henotheists (or as some might prefer to say, monolatrous theists), is it not still true that their monotheism, as I have hinted, is not so much a distinct position as a peculiarity of language? If Christians held that the gods of the nations are really fallen angels—believing all the while in the reality of these creatures and their superhuman powers—they are confessing the existence of the gods by another name. Furthermore, while Christians may be forbidden to venerate the unfallen angels, it cannot be denied that certain texts in the scriptures of Israel describe them as 'gods' (Exodus 15.1; Psalm 82.1 and 6).[99] As for the Trinity, even the subtlest attempts to reconcile the threefold worship with the unity of the Godhead in this period are likely to strike most readers as fallacious. A number of modern scholars have therefore argued that the difference between the Christians and the Platonists in the fourth century is chimerical, the costly result of building a dogma upon a semantic nicety. Nevertheless, as historians we cannot doubt that it was a difference which was visible to both sides, that it inspired polemic and quickened the zeal of martyrs. We may add that beliefs are known by their

[97] North (2010), 37, with the caveat that the term 'polytheism' should not be thought to define a 'religious position'.

[98] Porphyry, *Life of Plotinus* 10.45.

[99] See Assmann (2003), 13 on the polarity between the true God and false gods in the Old Testament.

effects, and that the consequences of Christian monotheism were unmistakable once the church had acquired political hegemony in the empire. They were also, as far as we know, unprecedented: it has been argued that the vigorous propagation of a cult of the sun by Aurelian in the third century explains the manner of Constantine's conversion and the profusion of solar imagery in Christian texts and monuments of his era,[100] but we have no clear proof that Aurelian's proselytizing was accompanied by a commandment to forsake all other gods.

CONCLUDING REMARKS

However common it was for the cult of God Most High to serve as a preparatory school for Christian monotheism, the same cannot be said in the age of Constantine of the other cults which are often reckoned among the alternatives to Christianity in the 'market-place of religions'.[101] If the paucity of information is evidence of anything,[102] it suggests that Cybele and Mithras were losing adherents even before the conversion of Constantine enhanced the allure of Christianity. On the other hand, we cannot compile statistics for the growth of Christianity in the third century, or even adduce good reasons for supposing this growth to have been continuous; we certainly have no reason to suppose that they were so numerous by the beginning of the fourth century as to render it impossible for the other religions to flourish. In Egypt, where Christianity showed unusual vigour, a study of papyri indicates that it accounted for less than a fifth of the population;[103] the common estimate that it accounted for 10 per cent of the empire as a whole does not seem unduly parsimonious.[104] It would be difficult, in any case, to say what was entailed by a conversion from Mithraism to Christianity, since it was rare for a cult to exercise that universal vigilance over the lives and thoughts of its adepts that was typical of a philosophy. For this reason Christianity defined itself as a

[100] Wallraff (2002); this argument can withstand the observations of Berrens (2004) on the frequency of solar imagery in Platonic texts. See, however, Barnes (2011), 18–23 against the use of this evidence to impugn Constantine's profession of Christianity.

[101] Cf. North (1992).

[102] Macmullen (1981), 127 maintains that decline in the number of inscriptions betokens only a scarcity of stonecutters.

[103] Bagnall (1982).

[104] See Stark (1997) and Hopkins (1998). For comments on the sociological algorithms employed here see Edwards (2006b) and Barnes (2007), 201—though Stark, p. 12, anticipates the latter's triumphant objection that the curve of growth, if prolonged, would result in a figure which exceeds the population of the whole empire. My objection is not that he fails to provide for the levelling of the curve, but that he assumes without evidence that this levelling occurred only in the fourth century, and not, say, two centuries earlier.

philosophia, not as a *thrêskeia* or *cultus*, and (as we have seen) its apologists in the fourth century took Plato and Aristotle for their interlocutors, not the priests of Isis and Cybele. It was not unusual for the same man or woman to participate, or even to officiate, in more than one pagan cult, and it was therefore only the Christian—we may add, the devout and knowledgeable Christian—who would feel obliged to choose between Christ and Mithras. Even then this would not so much resemble a choice between two coats in the market-place as a choice between a coat and a pair of gloves.

Thus it can be said of Christianity, as Jacob Needleman said of the 'new religions' of the west in the latter half of the twentieth century,[105] that the needs which they addressed in this new environment were not those to which they had ministered, and continued to minister, in their eastern homelands. Nevertheless, we cannot say of the fourth century, as we can surely say of the twentieth, that the general conditions of life had changed so much as to render it all but impossible to retain faith in hereditary norms and usages. No doubt the novelty of the Christian gospel was enticing to some and repellent to others; before we assume, however, that it was always an antidote to a sense of emptiness, dispossession, or estrangement, we should remember, as a historian of modern witchcraft remarked some years ago, that even unusual choices are not always born of need.[106]

[105] Needleman (2009), 229–43.

[106] Hutton (1999), 403: 'a taste for vintage wine or a love of painting landscape is not automatically regarded as a compensation for other, scarce or unobtainable rewards'.

7

Religions of Transformation

It was common in the first half of the twentieth century to maintain that late antiquity saw the birth, or at least the proliferation, of personal religion. No one hitherto, it was said, had recounted his own conversion with the fervour of Apuleius in his novel the *Metamorphoses* or *Golden Ass*; no one had kept such a sedulous record of the epiphanies and good offices of a tutelary god as Aelius Aristides in his *Sacred Tales*.[1] The same phenomena could be adduced by Christian scholars to prove that the Mediterranean world was athirst for a new religion,[2] or by sceptics to support a diagnosis of widespread anxiety, of which Christianity was the terminal symptom.[3] The *parti pris* in each of these theories is obvious: we flatter ourselves today that we are more dispassionate and less ingenuous in our handling of ancient literary sources. Apuleius, after all, is writing fiction, and Aelius Aristides is a sophist, a professional creator of personae whose venal prayers, if he really addressed them to Asclepius, barely deserve to be called religious. The collapse of the city-state, which was once supposed to have set the uprooted spirit free to choose its own gods, is now thought to have been greatly exaggerated; on the other hand, even when the city-state was the only political unit to which a Greek could belong, philosophers such as Heraclitus, Socrates, and Plato could espouse their own forms of piety, while the Orphic leaves are addressed to a small community of initiates. Nor should it always be assumed that personal religion is private religion: as Plutarch reminds the Epicurean Colotes, it was possible for the common folk, and even for the learned, to engage with heartfelt jubilation in a collective rite.

Nevertheless, the evidence suggests that there were seasons of growth and attrition not only for certain religions of the Roman Empire but for certain types of religion. Those which were commonly held to be of oriental provenance (Christianity included) flourished under Marcus Aurelius and the Severans; by Constantine's time the majority of these (Christianity excepted) were

[1] See Nock (1933). [2] Festugière (1954).

[3] Dodds (1965). For an evaluation of the concept of 'anxiety', which appeared to have been put to death by Brown (1978) but is now showing signs of reanimation, see Athanassiadi (2006).

on the wane. The movements which, by contrast, originated or achieved prominence for the first time in this period have left few traces in lapidary texts or in iconography: they are known today primarily, some entirely, from the esoteric writings of their own adepts. Some of these texts have been preserved by Christian scribes, while others survived in the teeth of episcopal censure. In the twentieth century, all have been adduced as antecedents to Christianity, sometimes as distinct enunciations of a diffuse and amorphous religion of *gnosis*, or knowledge. Such theories, however, tend to accentuate only the affinities between Manichaean, Hermetic, alchemical, and gnostic literature, giving little weight to differences which might suggest a diversity of origin, and sometimes constructing a common genealogy for them to which no ancient documents bears witness. What these literatures certainly have in common is that they inculcate, as the goal of religious discipline, a transformation of the self, conceived as a disclosure and liberation of the divinity within. For this reason they stand at once in a symbiotic and an antagonistic relation to Christianity, to whose triumph some or all of them owe their tenuous survival.

MANICHEANS

Mani, the founder of the sect named after him, began to preach in 241 and briefly enjoyed the patronage of Sapor I of Persia. For this reason, and because he named Zoroaster among his teachers, Manichaeism was depicted by its first opponents and by later scholars as a Persian religion; it was as a foreign cult, not a Christian sect that it was repressed by Diocletian in 302. Yet Mani also styled himself a pupil of Jesus and Paul (not to mention the Buddha) and a Greek papyrus published in 1970 contains a text purporting to be his own account of his life, in which he claims to have been reared among the Elchasaites, a Christian sect that professed to maintain the purity of the body by daily immersion and a diet that excluded not only meat but wheaten bread and vegetables.[4] Years of reflection, punctuated by visions, taught the young Mani that no diet could be sinless and that lustration defiles the waters more than it purifies the flesh. The new regimen that he and his disciples adopted required the elect to eat only vegetables, but to escape the guilt of killing them by entrusting the preparation of their food to an order of acolytes, or 'hearers'. These practices were justified by a myth of his own devising, according to which the primordial state was one in which light and darkness formed two separate and coextensive kingdoms, one ruled peaceably by the father of light

[4] See Cologne Mani Codex (Bibliography A) with Gardner and Lieu (2004), 46–9.

while the other was under the sway of five vicious archons.[5] The darkness began to yearn for the light, thus threatening to obliterate the frontier between the kingdoms. The father clad his own son, Primal Man, in light, and sent him forth to battle, but this champion was vanquished and a portion of his armour consumed by the archons.[6] Five new powers were dispatched for his rescue, and he was woken from his comatose state by the living spirit, who planted the stars and other heavenly bodies in the firmament and excited the lust of the archons, thus inducing them to ejaculate the light that they had swallowed. But two new demons arose, ingested the light and peopled the darkness below the firmament with their own creatures.[7] Adam's body and those of his descendants belong to this lower, animal realm, which is doomed to perish; yet here and there within these walking sepulchres there are sentient remnants of the fallen light. These are the elect, whose duty it is, by pursuing a vegetarian diet and thus increasing the concentration of spirit in their own bodies, to release the greatest possible quantity of light from matter when they quit the present world.

We need not doubt that, if we possessed their esoteric commentaries on the myth, we should find that allegory was as serviceable an instrument to the Manichees as it was in Augustine's vindications of the Old Testament against their strictures. It is evident, for example, that their Primal man is the archetype of those to whom Paul says, 'Awake, thou that sleepest and God will give thee light' (Ephesians 5.14). But Augustine, a 'hearer' for nine years, nowhere hints that the light and darkness might have been understood by the Manichees as states of the soul. A Greek polemic, which seems to have been composed at the beginning of the fourth century, is equally lacking in hermeneutic charity.[8] The author, Alexander of Lycopolis,[9] was once believed to have been the Christian bishop of that city; the most recent commentary in English characterizes him as an 'Alexandrian Platonist',[10] yet we cannot

[5] See Gardner and Lieu (2004), 168–72, translating Augustine's Latin text entitled *The Epistle called Fundamental*. In the footnotes to this section, I shall also give some illustrative quotations from the Coptic text entitled The *Kephalaia of the Teacher*, translated by Gardner (1995). Since these originated in the third century, a full discussion of them lies outside the scope of this book.

[6] At *Kephalaion* 89 in the Medinet Mani version, cited by Gardner and Lieu (2004), 208, we learn that 'the enemy of lights constructed [the cosmos] after the likeness of a man', so that ribs became the firmament, his lungs the race of birds, his liver the quadrupeds, etc. On the discovery at Medinet Madi see Böhlig (1994).

[7] At *Kephalaion* 69, cited in Gardner and Lieu (2004), 205–8, the sun and moon do not share in the obloquy which is thrown upon the other five planets and the twelve signs of the zodiac. The latter are drawn in pairs or triads from each of the five realms of darkness, and each of the five malign planets is ruled by the offspring of a different element.

[8] Against the misuse of hermeneutic charity see Beduhn (2002), 261–6.

[9] According to Gardner and lieu (2004), 38, it is probable that the Coptic Manichaean texts discovered at Medinet Madi in 1933 originated in Lycopolis (Assiut).

[10] Van der Horst and Mansfeld (1974), 27–36 demonstrate that he holds tenets which are commonly found in Platonists before Plotinus, e.g. that no intelligible is contained by another

deny him a knowledgeable sympathy with the Christian religion. His exordium is that Christianity, though a simple religion, has been corrupted by the vainglorious strife of a succession of teachers, each outdoing his predecessors in the absurdity of his confections (pp. 3–4 Brinkmann).[11] The essence of Christianity is defined as the belief that *to poiêtikon*, the productive cause, is the noblest,[12] the eldest and the cause of all; with this, we are told, all philosophers will concur. This might have been the sentiment of a Platonist, but only of one who was ignorant of Numenius, Plotinus, and Iamblichus, for all of whom the demiurgic intellect was inferior to the first principle. Platonism colours the representation of the Manichaean cosmology, where soul is substituted for primal man and we learn what no other source reveals, that the dissipation of light was likened to the rending of Dionysus by the Titans in Orphic myth (p. 8 Brinkmann).

The argument, never scriptural, rests largely on premises that would have been endorsed by any Platonist. The first of these is that matter is not a substance or a body but the malleable substrate from which bodies are formed by the imposition of properties.[13] If the primordial matter of the Manichees is already a body, it must already have been informed by soul;[14] if it is not a body, it cannot be an agent and thus cannot encroach upon the good.[15] If God, as the Manichees say, is a creator, yet the matter of the present world is not his initial substrate, it will be necessary to postulate a different species of matter as the substrate for those creatures who inhabit the realm of light (p. 10). Furthermore, if God and matter are by nature immiscible, a third entity will be required to bring them together, though even this would be possible only if certain logical conditions are satisfied (p. 13). Thus, if both God and matter are incorporeal, neither can contain the other; if one is corporeal and one

intelligible, and that soul and attribute occupy the same ontological plane. Again they observe (pp. 37–8) that he imputes to his opponents a conflation of body and matter which is typical of the Stoics, and suggest (pp. 39–42) that his conception of the World-Soul is anticipated in Plutarch.

[11] Van der Horst and Mansfeld note, without arguing that Alexander is indebted to Porphyry, that he and the latter frequently coincide in their teaching on the nature of matter (pp. 19–27). This would not preclude Alexander's being a Christian, even if one were to accept the dubious conjecture that he is borrowing from Porphyry's assault on this religion. We have only to think of Tertullian's co-option of Stoic arguments in his treatise *On the Soul*, or of Origen's exhortation to 'spoil the Egyptians' at *Philokalia* 13.

[12] Van der Horst and Mansfeld (1974) 49 cite Acts 17.24.

[13] At p. 5 Brinkmann Alexander alleges that the Manichees identify matter with chaotic motion, thus contradicting both Plato, who describes it as a receptacle of properties (*Timaeus* 49a6–51a7), and Aristotle, for whom privation and matter are synonymous (*Physics* 190b17–191a22).

[14] See p. 10 Brinkmann with Van der Horst and Mansfeld (1974), 61 n. 227; also pp. 25–6 Brinkmann.

[15] See p. 9 Brinkmann, with Van der Horst and Manfeld (1974), 60 n. 221 for the allusion to the Stoic distinction between passive matter and the productive agent.

incorporeal, the former cannot trespass upon the latter (p. 14). If both are corporeal, each will tend to its own place if they are differently constituted, while if both are of the same element they will seek the same place eternally, not in consequence of a temporal aberration (pp. 13–14). If matter is evil, its striving for the light is at odds with its nature, and therefore this salutary upward motion must have been imparted to it by God (p. 15). If matter and God are not to be equipollent, we must assume that matter is weaker than God; but if it is evil by nature, it can be weakened only by becoming less evil, which can mean only that it participates in the good (p. 18). Once the plasticity of matter is granted, it cannot be maintained that any being who is compounded of soul and matter is incapable of aspiring to the good (p. 23). The author adds that in endowing the moon with its capacity for illumination the Manichees show themselves ignorant of astronomy (p. 30). Scientific reasoning, however, is not to be looked for in fanatics who fail to grasp that when the poets speak of giants or the Jews of fallen angels, they are offering a mythological adumbration of the noetic realm.

Christ, the Manichees tell us,[16] is an intellect (p. 7); they fail to perceive that, since the intellect enters the body only at the age of seven,[17] the incarnate saviour cannot have been Christ for the first seven years of his life (p. 35). Of Christ, the author exclaims, they know so little, that they pronounce his name as Chrestos, the Greek for 'good' (p. 34). Second-century apologists who had seized upon this inadvertent compliment were also acquainted with the myth,[18] retold in the book of Enoch, which represents the giants of Genesis 6.4 as the fruit of sexual intercourse between angels and mortal women. At p. 37 Alexander flippantly couples Greek tales of the giants with this Jewish fable, to which no allusion is made in any other Platonic writing. In short we cannot maintain, without a battery of ancillary hypotheses, that our author was a pagan. More probably he was a Christian who had been to school with the Platonists, and was resolved to defeat the Manichees by a priori reasoning without appeal to any contested word of revelation. We should call him an economic polemicist rather than a Platonizing Christian, though his comments on the abuse of myth suggest that he brought a subtler hermeneutic to the sacred text than many of his co-religionists.

[16] Gardner and Lieu (2004), 181 n. 6 observe that this equation of Christ with intellect is attested in the Sabuhragan, a Middle Persian text composed by Mani himself. As an example, of further mystification, Alexander might have cited *Kephalaion* 8, as quoted by Gardner and Lieu (2004), 218–19, where Christ employs ten chariots in his descent. For other texts see Franzmann (2003).

[17] This is an unusual position for a Christian; contrast. Origen, *First Principles* 1.7.1; notwithstanding the evidence assembled by Van der Horst and Mansfeld (1974), 30, it is not clearly attested in the Platonic tradition either. On the significance of the seventh year see *Kephalaion* 32 at Gardner and Lieu (2004), 204–5.

[18] Justin Martyr, *First Apology* 4.

How numerous were the Manichees in the Roman Empire of the early fourth century? We can say with assurance only that they were especially conspicuous in North Africa. In a rescript to the proconsul of Africa, written from Alexandria in 302 (or, as some think, a few years earlier), Diocletian condemns the Manichees as a sect of Persian origin who, in embracing the 'savage laws and nefarious customs' of that hostile nation, have overturned the traditions which the Romans received from their ancestors, fomenting civil unrest in an otherwise docile population.[19] The magistrate was commanded to burn not only the books but the leaders of the sect, and also to put to death any of their adherents who would not recant, while claiming their estates for the public exchequer. Half a generation later, the Alexandrian presbyter Arius took advantage of the notoriety of Mani when he implied in an insolent letter to his bishop Alexander that unless the latter endorsed his own view that the Son, or Second Person of the Trinity, is 'from nothing',[20] he would fall into the Manichaean error of imagining the Godhead as an extended domain of light, of which the Son was a consubstantial portion, a *homoousion meros*.[21] He names three other heretics—Valentinus, Sabellius, and Hieracas—who were also thought to be of Libyan or Egyptian provenance, but the tacit charge of sympathy with Mani was all the more bruising because a predecessor of Alexander[22] had censured the Manichees in an encyclical letter, of which a fragment survives in a papyrus of this era.[23] The author warns his flock that the Manichees worship the creature rather than the creator, and quotes a prayer to bread—'They say, *another brought this to me; I am guiltless*'[24]—as an instance of the fatuity into which this error has led them. The jibe became notorious: it was reproduced in Cyril of Jerusalem's attack on the sect, and in the *Acts of Archelaus*, now extant only in Latin, which profess to record the public mortification of the heresiarch in debate with a catholic bishop.

Manichaeism has been called a world-religion,[25] and it took forms in central Asia that belied the Christian origins of its founder. We have seen that to Diocletian it was a Persian distemper, and we have no evidence that he regarded Christianity, which he treated with comparative forbearance, as the genus of which Manichaeism was the species. Nevertheless, every writer in antiquity

[19] *Collatio Legum Mosaicarum at Romanarum* 15.3; Corcoran (2000).

[20] Theodoret, *Church History* 1.5.5.

[21] Athanasius, *On the Synods* 16.

[22] Gardner and Lieu (2004), 114 date P. Rylands Greek 469.12–42 to the late third century, following Roberts (1938), 42–3.

[23] See Beduhn (2002) for a comparison between Rylands Papyrus 469, *Acts of Archelaus* 10 and Cyril of Jerusalem, sixth catechetical lecture.

[24] That is, the meal was prepared by their *auditores* or hearers to spare them the guilt of killing.

[25] Mirecki (2006), 569.

who describes the system presents it as an aberrant form of Christianity,[26] and Coptic texts from Medinet Madi, like the Greek autobiography of Mani himself, are instinct with biblical images and allusions, densely mustered and deftly adapted. Mani was indebted, by his own account, to the Buddha and Zoroaster, but he professed to be not merely a disciple or admirer of Christ but the paraclete promised in the Gospel of John. The same verses were applied to Mohammed, not by himself but by his later apologists. In the Zoroastrian empire of the Sassanids, Manichaeism was extinguished; in the west it survived Diocletian and prospered for centuries under Christian rulers, most of whom took vigorous measures for its suppression. It is not absurd to surmise that it prospered because it had the status of a heresy and not a new religion, so that those who wished to escape the hegemony of the Catholic Church could adopt it without divorcing themselves entirely from the faith in which they were reared. That seems to have been the position of Augustine, who also confiscated and copied books of which their putative owners professed to know nothing. It is possible, then, that having been suppressed as an upstart religion in one empire, Manichaeism survived in another because it was persecuted as a sect.

HERMES TRISMEGISTUS

'Hermetica' is the name given to a corpus of seventeen Greek texts, together with a Latin rendering of the lost Asclepius, which purport to reproduce the discourses of a divine revealer, the 'thrice-great Hermes', sometimes in dialogue with his pupils Asclepius and Tat.[27] Asclepius is the Greek god of medicine, Tat a diminutive form of Thoth,[28] the Egyptian god of wisdom, and Hermes Trismegistus the Greek equivalent of Thoth in his divine character. Excerpts from other writings ascribed to Hermes are preserved by Stobaeus, a Byzantine anthologist, and Hermes is also credited with a voluminous body of magical and astrological writings, few of which propound the distinct philosophy that we know as Hermetism. Even under his Greek name he was evidently a figure of some antiquity in Egypt; Plutarch refers to secret books of Hermes (*Isis and Osiris* 61) and Apuleius was suspected of magic on account of his devotion to the god, whom he carried about with him in the

[26] Ammianus Marcellinus, *Histories* 15.13.2 speaks of the Manichaeans as a 'superstitious sect' whom Constantine interrogated with the help of an interpreter. Since this is the only evidence of his dealings with them, we cannot tell whether Constantine regarded them as heretics or pagans.

[27] See Fowden (1993), 1–11 on the relation between these and other Hermetic writings.

[28] Fowden (1993), 29–31 notes that he comes to be perceived as a son of Thoth, just as a second Hermes was invented to act as translator to the writings of that Hermes who is Thoth.

form of a wooden effigy.[29] Of Hermes the philosopher, however, we hear nothing before the third century. Even then the system that Iamblichus ascribes to him in his treatise *On the Mysteries* is not easily reconciled either with the Hermetica or with native Egyptian sources. Professing to know of many books, perhaps 2000 in number (8.1), which had been translated from Egyptian to Greek by authors 'not unskilled in philosophy' (8.4), he asserts that for Hermes the first God is superior to the intelligible, and even to the self-sufficient Good, his second god, who is the source of all essence and entity (8.2). According to a second scheme, the first god is the indivisible One which contains the noetic and the noeric (that is, the intelligible and the intellectual), and is to be worshipped in silence alone (8.3). Subordinate to this solitary monad is the demiurgic intellect, whom the Egyptians call Amon, Ptha, and Osiris, he is the parent of the Ogdoad, a comity of four masculine and four feminine powers who govern the lower cosmos. Hermes also teaches that we possess two souls, the lower of which is subject to the fate that governs the transient natural order, while the higher, by exercising its capacities with the assistance of the gods, may become a free citizen of the intellectual realm.

Apart from the Ogdoad, there is little here that is Egyptian, and the first principles are more Iamblichean than Hermetic. We may wonder why Hermes appears under his Greek name, when Ptah and the other deities of Egypt are always spoken of by their native appellations. A similar question could be put to the Hermetica, where Hermes is the chief speaker in the majority of dialogues but, like his interlocutor Tat, his occasional proxies—Isis, Osiris, Horus, and even (if Peter Kingsley is right[30]) Poimandres—are always called by Egyptian names, or names that admit of an Egyptian etymology. The same principle whereby Thoth, the Egyptian god of wisdom, became the Theuth of Plato and the Taautos of Porphyry seems to dictate that Tat in the Hermetica will never be more than a secondary instrument of revelation. Thoth in fact was never what his putative counterpart was to Greek philosophers and mythographers—the messenger of higher gods and thus the herald in the present world of posthumous or supernal mysteries;[31] even had any god performed this office for the dwellers on the Nile, no Greek would profit by the disclosure unless it were given in his own tongue. Hermes, whose name is derived from the root which is also the root of the noun *hermêneia* ('interpretation') is not so much Thoth translated as translation itself personified, the *interpretatio Graeca* masquerading as the original of which Egypt herself possesses only the ectype. Both in Iamblichus and in the Hermetica we read of terms employed by Egyptian sorcerers and priests which lose their potency when translated into Greek;[32] the very fact, however, that these admonitions

[29] See *Apology* 31, 42, and 61–5 with Fowden (1993), 199.
[30] Kingsley (1993).
[31] On the many parallels that can be drawn see Fowden (1993), 22–3.
[32] See *Corpus Hermeticum* XVI.2; Fowden (1993), 30 and 37–8; Copenhaver (1992), 201–3.

are phrased in Greek precludes the inference that this language is uniformly inferior to Egyptian as a vehicle of theology. To say that Rilke cannot be translated into English is not to say that German is superior to English or even that the Germans are better poets. At the same time, it would be false to conclude that the supposed interpretation is merely a fanciful substitute for the original. Comparison of both the *Hermetica* and *On the Mysteries* with the fruits of two hundred years of hieroglyph-reading and papyrology has revealed that these works were not created *ex nihilo* by the Greek imagination, though the indigenous matter has often been tendentiously adapted. If Christians could maintain that words which God had uttered once for all in Hebrew became intelligible only when read in Greek under the guidance of four Greek-speaking evangelists, it was not absurd for the Platonists to imagine that a true theology could arise in Egypt, yet remain dark to its own adherents until Athens, Apamea, or Alexandria had furnished tools for its elucidation.

It was not the custom of Platonists to asseverate, with the Christians, that one cult was ordained by God while all the rest was idolatry. Porphyry spoke for all when he denied that there was a universal way to liberation: in its vulgar or pandemic form, every cult is superstitious, but the mirror of philosophy shows us the mystery within the mirage, the divine behind the demonic. We may suspect him of making Platonism itself a middle way, but the charge would not be wholly just, as Platonism took diverse forms, and Porphyry was not in all respects a disciple of Cronius and Pallas, whom he accepted as his mentors in the decipherment of Mithraic iconography.[33] Nor was there a single canon of rites that all Platonists were required to vindicate: each chose his objects of rational devotion from the shrines where Christians scoffed and the multitude worshipped without understanding. Thus Mithras is not to be found in the extant writings of Iamblichus, while Isis and Hermes are absent from those of Porphyry. For Christians one cult was as delusive as another, and in the third century Hermes, if he was mentioned at all, was ranked among the false teachers of philosophy. Tertullian represents him as the teacher of Plato, adding, on the authority of the second-century Platonist Albinus, that, according to Hermes, once the migrating soul has assumed a body it can never escape from finitude (*On the Soul* 33.1). Cyprian cites him, with Ostanes the Persians, as a witness to the incomprehensibility of God;[34] Arnobius knows him only as a teacher who is invoked by the *novi viri*—evidence, if we will, that they were followers of Iamblichus rather than Porphyry.[35] Egyptian Christians of this epoch had neither good nor ill to say of their fellow-countryman, and it was left to another North African,

[33] Turcan (1975), 62–79.
[34] *That Idols are Nothing* 6, though the attribution to Cyprian is contested.
[35] See Chapter 2, this volume.

Lactantius, to complete his expatriation by co-opting him as a witness to the antiquity of the gospel.

Hermes takes his place alongside the Sibyl in Lactantius as a seer whose claim to be heard rests not on his status in a canon of approved writers but on his antedating the canon altogether (*Divine Institutes* 2.8). Whereas the Sibyl, however, was a venerable name to the Romans, Hermes Trismegistus will barely have been a name to many, Lactantius identifies him with the fifth Mercury of Cicero,[36] who in Egypt is called Thoth. This Hermes, we hear, confirms the Euhemeristic account of Saturn's birth (*Epitome* 14.2–4), but those who garnish the altars of such deified men should learn from him that the true God is both fatherless and motherless.[37] It is this God, according to Hermes, who has formed us in his image as composites of a perishable body and a soul that cannot die.[38] Yet Hermes also posits two gods, the Creator and the visible world that he brings forth in his own likeness (*Epitome* 37.4–9). The Christian apologist has performed a sleight of hand here, since the Greek that he quotes is not an allusion to the incarnation and a Christian cannot affirm the divinity of the cosmos. He adopts Hermetic language again, this time not so tendentiously, to explain that the title Word, when given to that which is invisible in Christ, does not connote audible speech and pertains to him only by analogy, as the inexpressible agent of the Ineffable.[39] The primacy of the Father and the deity of the Son are jointly upheld in the formula 'demiurge of the one and first god', where 'one' and 'first' are a pagan's epithets for the Second Person of the Trinity (*Institutes* 7.18.4). The antiquity of Hermes (who was later to be identified with Enoch[40]) enables him to testify that the beings whom the world reveres as daemons are fallen angels (*Institutes* 2.14). Just as he sees the beginning of things more clearly than the pagans, so he foresees the impermanence of all sublunar glory. We owe to this Latin apologist our few Greek remnants of an important treatise, the *Asclepius*,[41] which predicts that faith will wane and a day will come when the gods desert their Egyptian shrines.[42]

The Sibylline oracles to which Lactantius appealed were Jewish or Christian forgeries.[43] Can the same be said of the Hermetica? Scholars have returned a partial affirmative with regard to two texts, the first and the twelfth in the corpus, which contain the name *Poimandres*. In the first, where it is

[36] Cicero, *Nature of the Gods* 3.22.56; Lactantius, *Divine Institutes* 1.6.1.
[37] *Divine Institutes* 1.7.2 and 4.13.2; *Epitome* 4.4.
[38] *Divine Institutes* 7.4.3 and 7.13.
[39] *Divine Institutes* 4.7.2 and 4.9.3.
[40] Van Blundel (2009), 183–4.
[41] *Divine Institutes* 4.6.4 and 7.18.4.
[42] It is now agreed that no part of this tract should be construed as an allusion to the destruction of Egyptian temple under Theodosius: see Copenhaver (1992), 239, citing Dunand (1977). On the other hand, the traditional ascription of the Latin text to Apuleius has few defenders other than Hunink (1996), whose argument is countered by Scotti (2000).
[43] Lightfoot (2007), 18–23 and 51–94.

understood to signify 'mind of the sovereignty',[44] Poimandres is the chief speaker and the cosmogony that he unfolds is reminiscent at many points of the Mosaic account and of rabbinic annotations to this narrative. In the thirteenth treatise, *Poimandres* is styled the 'mind of the sovereignty' once more (13.15), although a subsequent pun suggests the etymology *poimên andrôn*, 'shepherd of men' (13.19). In this text the hymns to God as *ktistês* or creator would sit more naturally on a Jewish tongue than on that of a Greek, to whom 'Demiurge' would have been a more familiar term for the framer of the cosmos.[45] Richard Reitzenstein saw evidence of a Christian borrowing from the first Hermeticum in the *Shepherd* of Hermas: in both texts a mouthpiece of revelation is asked for his name, and in both, if we accept the Greek etymology for Poimandres, the reply is 'I am the shepherd'. This is questionable reasoning, if only because we cannot be certain that the *Poimandres* is the earlier writing. In the light of an allusion at *Poimandres* 16 to a 'mystery that was hidden until the present time' (cf. Romans 16.25; 1 Cor 2.7), it seems at least as reasonable to argue that the Hermetic author was drawing on Christian tropes as that these tropes were initially his but reappeared at intervals in unrelated Christian texts.

Christian he is certainly not: if he is one thing only, he is (as we now say) a Middle Platonist. The *Poimandres*, as the first treatise is titled after its narrator, recounts the creation of the noetic or intellectual universe by the unfathomable wisdom of the Father (8). Next it tells how the waters below were illumined when the filial Godhead shone forth under the aspect of the Anthropos, or androgynous primal man (12). The reflection of this heavenly man is taken captive when he becomes enamoured of the material realm (13), and the rest of the work, together with the majority of the treatises that follow it in the corpus, is devoted to the liberation of the slumbering soul. This begins with the rediscovery of its supernal origin and is not complete until it has escaped the material cosmos to rejoin its creator in the noetic realm. This transcendence of the noetic, the natural immortality of the soul and the presence within it of latent *anamnesis*, or recollection, are cardinal tenets of Platonism. On the other hand, it is at Genesis 1.28 that human beings are made in the image of God, at Ezekiel 1.26 that God assumes the refulgent form of a man, and at Genesis 1.3 that the illumination of the deep by light marks the beginning of creation.[46] The fall of the Anthropos, or heavenly man, is a Gnostic conceit; the *Poimandres*, however, describes it as a mystery that was hidden before the ages (16), thus evincing a knowledge of Paul.[47] It also plots an itinerary for the soul through the seven planetary spheres (23), a notion for

[44] For other interpretations of *authentia* at *Hermetica* 1.2 see Copenhaver (1992) 96–7 and Kingsley (1993).

[45] Zuntz (955).

[46] See further Pearson (1981).

[47] The putative author of Ephesians 3.9.

which the Platonist Eubulus had sought analogues in Persian rather than Egyptian teaching.[48] Throughout the Hermetica affirmations that the true God is bodiless, invisible and superior to all that thought and speech can express are couched in the vocabulary of Plato and other Greek philosophers. The centrepiece of the fourth treatise, a *kratêr* (or cup) for the rejuvenation of souls, suggests a different Greek etymology for the name Poimandres and may number among its models the mixing-bowl in which the Platonic demiurge combines the elements. The cosmogony of the third treatise, on the other hand, seems to borrow more from Genesis than from any Greek or Egyptian ancestor. The Corpus Hermeticum is a palimpsest of many cultures, not a Greek paraphrase of the Egyptian *Book of the Dead*.

More representative of Hermetic literature is the *Discourse on the Eight and Ninth*, discovered at Nag Hammadi, in which meditation on his previous reading enables an unnamed pupil of Hermes to rise—in mind alone, without any change in bodily location—to the spheres beyond the planetary hebdomad.[49] The ascent is crowned by a hymn to the invisible, eternal and immutable lord of all, which is also in part a prayer for self-knowledge, and the neophyte is advised to make a record of it on tablets of turquoise stone. This coda is less typical of Greek than of Jewish or Egyptian literature, but a similar journey, culminating again in an anthem of praise, is commemorated in the thirteenth treatise of the Hermetic Corpus. Neither the Coptic *Discourse on the Eighth and Ninth* nor the shorter *Prayer of Thanskgiving* in the same codex contain any elements that are discernibly Christian, yet their presence among the Nag Hammadi Codices testifies to a Christian interest in their contents.[50]

For all that, there is evidence that for Christians of a stricter persuasion Hermes was not an ally but one head of an ancient hydra. A short tract, wrongly ascribed to the martyr Anthimus and more probably by Marcellus of Ancyra or one of his satellites,[51] maintains that Valentinus was the first to speak of three hypostases and that the Arians who make Christ a second god or second cause are the dupes of Hermes and of Marcion's dissident pupil Apelles. This is the only writing of the fourth century that fathers Arianism on Valentinus (a figure abominated by the historical Arius), and the only one that clearly treats the use of the appellative 'second god' as a diagnostic of heresy rather than as a concession to polytheism. It appears, though he does not state his objection, that the author could not reconcile the word 'second' with the axiom that God is one, which is stated to be a canon of orthodoxy at the beginning of the treatise. Furthermore, his assimilation of the 'Arian' view to that of Hermes signifies that for him what is second to God can only be his

[48] Porphyry, *Cave of the Nymphs* 60.1–14 = [Numenius], Fr. 60 Des Places.
[49] On its affinities with other Hermetic texts see Scarpi (2011), 65–71.
[50] These are numbered 6.6 and 6.7 in the *Nag Hammadi Codices*.
[51] Richard (1949). For the text see Mercati (1901) and Scott (1936), 155–61.

creature, and thus (as Arius said) 'out of nothing'. This is not true (in the sense that opposes 'creation' to 'begetting') for Origen or Eusebius, the two authors before Nicaea who speak of Christ as a second god.[52] It is true, no doubt, that all these authors *assume* the inferiority of the Son; what they *affirm*, however, when they make use of the locution 'second god' in their apologetic writings, is that Christians, though not polytheists, acknowledge two divine subjects. 'Second god' implies, that is, an iteration rather than a gradation of divinity: the adjective 'second' does not suffice of itself to determine whether the Persons are equal or unequal. Whether or not this treatise is a fair specimen of polemic, it is one more piece of evidence that Hermetic literature in the age of Constantine was almost the sole preserve of Christians, serving at times as a larder of apologetic arguments, at others as food or seasoning for speculative theology, and at others again as a test for poisoned meats.

GNOSTICS

'Gnostic' is the name given in antiquity to a number of groups, all putatively Christian, which have in common the absence of a named founder and a claim to the knowledge (*gnôsis*) of an arcane sense which has not been grasped by the common reader of scriptures or practitioner of mysteries. Common to all is the teaching that we are not so much creatures of spirit and flesh (in the language of the New Testament) as spirits imprisoned in matter; *gnôsis* is held up by all as the means, and the *sine qua non*, of liberation. Some, though not all, regard this world as the product of a tragic, though perhaps inevitable, fissure in the realm of spirit; at the same time, they assert the continuity of matter and spirit as substances, antipodal though they are as domains of knowledge or moral action. Early Christian writers hold that the more seductive heresies of Basilides, Valentinus, and Marcion were drawn from a Gnostic well, although the term 'Gnostic' was seldom or never applied to any of these teachers before the fourth century.[53] Most scholars today accept this genealogy, though many would resist the extension of the term 'Gnostic' to cover all cosmogonies that deny the original goodness of creation.[54] This is a modern usage, though some have unjustly laid it at the door of Irenaeus and his fellow-heresiologists.[55] Nothing, could have further from the intent of these first witnesses than to represent Gnosticism as a united movement, offering an alternative to Catholic theology which was rooted in older traditions, and even

[52] See Edwards (2006a).
[53] See e.g. Irenaeus, *Against Heresies* 1.30. On the construction of genealogies for heresy see Mansfeld (1992).
[54] Brakke (2011). [55] King (2005).

perhaps in traditions older than the New Testament. On the contrary, they take pleasure in noting that each new system deviates from the last, and that they are held together by nothing but their determination to compromise the purity of the gospel. It is the evidence of these Church Fathers, together with that of the Neoplatonist Porphyry, that has been adduced in the last three decades to prove that 'Gnosticism' is a chimaera, and to justify the restriction of the term 'Gnostic' to that circle which was known under this description to Irenaeus. The adjective 'Sethian' is also used on the authority of Theodoret,[56] a historian of the fifth century; it is generally believed that we possess original documents of this sect, at least three of which—the *Zostrianus*, the *Allogenes*, and the *Apocryphon of John*—are expressly said by Porphyry or Irenaeus to be of Gnostic provenance.[57]

These texts have come to light only in the last 125 years. A version of the *Apocryphon of John* was shown in 1896 to agree in content with Irenaeus' synopsis of an unnamed writing current among the 'Barbelognostics';[58] two further variants, differing greatly from this and from one another, were discovered in 1946 at the Egyptian site of Nag Hammadi, together with mutilated copies of the *Zostrianus*, the *Allogenes* and numerous other writings, hitherto unknown and largely heterodox in character.[59] The word 'heterodox' is not an anachronism, since the Nag Hammadi manuscripts are agreed to date from the second half of the fourth century. It is evident, however, that the majority of the texts have already undergone a long history of redaction, and that transcripts of all or most of them must therefore have been current in the age of Constantine. It is not so easy to ascertain who read them or for what purpose. Because they made use of papyrus from the neighbouring monastery of Chenoboskion, it has been surmised that the scribes themselves were members of this Pachomian house, which therefore cannot have been such a citadel of orthodoxy as such foundations are commonly supposed to have been.[60] But even if were certain that the copying was performed inside the monastery—and of course, since they were discovered outside it, this is far from certain—we could not say whether the texts were acquired as edifying additions to the library or only for the purpose of refutation. Again we cannot say whether they were discarded in reluctant deference to an episcopal edict or to make way for other books which were of more interest to a new generation of monks. The fact that all our versions survive in Coptic may be an accident of time and geography: even if it were proved that they had ceased to be read in Greek, it would not follow that the perusal of them was always a conscious

[56] Theodoret, *Compendium* 1.14.

[57] Porphyry, *Life of Plotinus* 16; Irenaeus, *Against Heresies* 1.29. See further Rasimus (2010).

[58] Schmidt (1896); Irenaeus, *Against Heresies* 1.29.1.

[59] On the discovery see Doresse (1960); Robinson (1981).

[60] See further Goehring (2001). For the unsubstantiated theory that the codices were ejected from the monastery to anticipate a purge by Athanasius, see Meyer (2007), 6–7.

assertion of ethnic difference, let alone of ecclesiastical disaffection. And above all, we must remember that the survival of Gnostic literature is no proof of the continuing existence of a sect, even supposing that 'sect'—in contrast, say to 'movement' or 'tradition'—would be the most judicious term to describe the milieu of these texts in their original form, a century or more before the accession of Constantine.

The first and most ornate of the codices, commonly styled the Jung Codex,[61] contains five untitled treatises, of which one alludes to (or is perhaps a version of) the Valentinian *Gospel of Truth*, while the others appear to presuppose the Valentinian doctrines that the present world is the product of divorce between will and wisdom in the Godhead, that the antidote to error for the captives in this world is gnosis or knowledge, and that those who escape carry with them not the gross body but an envelope of spiritual flesh. If scholars are right to assign the *Gospel of Philip*, a text in the second codex, to the same category, we learn from it that the Valentinian adept was required to pass through five rites of emancipation—baptism, chrism, the Eucharist, redemption, and the inexpressible union with Christ in the Bible chamber.[62] Another group of texts, in which the world is said to originate from a descent or inclination of divine wisdom towards the subjacent realm of matter, are now by general agreement described as Sethian, although that term is poorly attested in antiquity. Three of them, the *Apocryphon of John*, the *Allogenes*, and the *Zostrianus*—were also known to Greek witnesses, who have no other name than 'Gnostic' for those who read them. In some modern reconstructions, a liturgy of five seals is the common element in the heterogeneous literature of the Sethians; others divide this corpus between Sethians and Ophites, though the latter name too was in ancient times and surely pejorative.[63] A number of cognate works bear the name of Thomas the Twin: of these the *Gospel of Thomas* is by far the best known, and is now more often characterized as 'encratite' than 'gnostic'.[64] A fragment of Plato's *Republic* and a portion of the *Asclepius*, a Hermetic work which also survives in Latin, are often cited as evidence that the library does not represent the interests of any one sect; against this some would argue that the Plato has been purposely mistranslated in order to give it a Gnostic bent.[65]

There is little to suggest that catholic writers—or even would-be Catholic writers—of the Constantinian era were aware of such opponents. The Council of Nicaea makes no reference to Gnostics; in Egypt Athanasius and Alexander are equally silent; to Eusebius the Gnostics (in the wider acceptation of that term) are figures of history but not contemporaries. Arius, in maintaining his

[61] On its history see Robinson (1977).
[62] *Nag Hammadic Codices* Ii.3. On the Valentinian school see Thomassen (2006).
[63] Turner (2001); Rasimus (2009).
[64] See the essays collected in Uro (1990). [65] Jackson (1985).

own position against Alexander, insinuates that only a Valentinian would describe the Second Person of the Trinity as the offspring of the First; but Origen had incurred, and Tertullian had anticipated, the same objection,[66] and no acquaintance with any living Valentinian is implied by this attempt to re-light spent powder. A rhetorician of this epoch, Marius Victorinus, was later to avail himself of passages from Sethian texts in a refutation of Arianism, composed in the wake of the Council of Sirmium in 357.[67] Victorinus, however, was in the autumn of his years at the time of his baptism; since we can hardly suppose that his new fathers in Christ would have pointed him to the *Allogenes* as a magazine of arguments against heresy, it is more likely that he encountered it while still a pagan, and thus without the canons of discernment that would have been applied by a bishop or a monk.

Even in their present form the *Allogenes* and *Zostrianus* may not have seemed contemptible to this scryer of hieroglyphs and incantations; if their authors were pupils of Ammonius Saccas, as I have conjectured, they had as much right as Porphyry to be treated as expositors of an authentic though eclectic Platonism.[68] While Porphyry sides with his master in this particular altercation, there are elements in his own teaching for which we can now find only Gnostic antecedents. In his letter to Marcella, written towards the end of his life, he enjoins the practice of four cardinal virtues, faith, love, truth, and hope. This tetrad, which appears to be unanticipated in Platonic literature, is attested none the less in the *Gospel of Philip,* a Valentinian text which many scholars date to the second century.[69] Whichever is the earlier, it may be less profitable to speak of one text as depending on the other than to suppose that they represent divergent branches of a stream that was still undivided a generation before Plotinus. Some of his own contemporaries accused him of plagiarism from Numenius of Apamea, and, although the best critics judged otherwise, the influence of this seminal thinker on Porphyry, Amelius, and Theodorus of Asine was uncontested. Numenius, however, was by his own account a disciple of the Brahmans and an admirer of the Jews, though what he knows of the Septuagint could easily have been gathered outside the synagogue from Christian or Gnostic sources. He is certainly more at one with the Christian Gnostics of his own day than with any of his successors in the Neoplatonic tradition when he frames a myth which depicts the sensible universe, not as a purposeful creation, but as the product of a rupture in the demiurgic intellect. What we might call hybridity in the Platonism of the fourth century, therefore, is an inheritance from the second, though the partial

[66] Tertullian, *Against Praxeas* 8.2. On Origen see Chapter 8, this volume.

[67] Tadieu (1996); Moreschini and Tommasi (2007), 29–31; but cf. Abramowski (2007).

[68] Edwards (1989). On Porphyry's allegation that they had forsaken the ancient philosophy see Igal (1981).

[69] *Nag Hammadi Codices* II.28.74–75; *Letter to Marcella* 24.

bifurcation that was effected by Plotinus ensures that nothing manifestly contradictory to Plato will be permitted to invade the thought of Iamblichus and his successors. It could be said of him, as of any Platonist, that he understood his own system as an alembic in which he had at last reassembled the limbs of a philosophy that had come down to posterity in fragments; this alchemical metaphor is peculiarly apposite in a period when, as we shall see, the science of alchemy comes of age as a universal medicine for the soul.

ZOSIMUS: GNOSTIC, CHRISTIAN, ALCHEMIST

Is alchemy a religion? It is not, but through the centuries it has been pursued with religious assiduity by adepts of every faith. Too often despised in modern time as a venal or naive precursor of chemistry, it did not aim, in the hands of its nobler exponents, at the manufacture of gold from baser metals, or even at the prolongation of life in the present world. Reitzenstein, Jung, and others have taught us to see it as a sacrament without a church, in which the mingling of elements symbolized the action of spiritual forces on the ignorance or callosity of the inner man who clings to his prison of flesh.[70] We cannot say whether this is true of the earliest extant treatise in Greek, implausibly ascribed to the philosopher Democritus of Abdera, since it is little more than a catalogue of titrations which are not easily reproduced in the modern laboratory. It is certainly true, however, of the dialogue between Cleopatra and the mage Ostanes, in which the queen undertakes to explain how the higher descends to the lower, how the lower is raised to the higher, and how the blessed waters lave the fettered corpses in Hades. In the age of Constantine this tradition is represented by Zosimus of Panopolis, an Egyptian by topography, but enough of a Greek to express himself in the style of a philosopher.

The few who have heard of Zosimus today are perhaps most likely to have encountered him through Jung, for whom he was a Daedalus of the inner life, transmuting the plastic imagery of dreams into the salts and solvents of a utopian science, and cradling in his own dreams the homunculus who returns in Goethe's *Faust* as a cryptic emblem of rebirth for the modern soul. Jung may have learned of Zosimus from Richard Reitzenstein, in whose eyes the homunculus was none other than Primal man, the Aryan counterpart of Adam, whose avatars appeared in Vedic, Avestan, and gnostic literature long before the birth of Christ. Jung and Reitzenstein are not incompatible, but the second is more amenable to historical criticism. I shall argue here in favour of Scott's designation 'Christian Gnostic',[71] which acknowledges, in contrast to Reitzenstein,

[70] Reitzenstein (1904); Jung (1967).

[71] Scott (1936), 114 speaks of a blend of Christian Gnosticism with pagan Platonism.

that Christianity was already an established point of reference for Zosimus, as it also appears to have been for the Hermetic and gnostic authorities whom he invokes. His metaphysical principles are set out with unwonted clarity in his *Treatise on the Omega*, addressed to the lady Theossebeia, who, as the biblical origin of her name suggests, may be not a real person but a personification of Christian godliness.

He assures Theosebeia that he is no purveyor of novelties, but the trustee of an ancient wisdom which is opened to discerning eyes in the work of Nicotheus, 'the hidden one'.[72] This name occurs only once elsewhere in Greek, and then it is nothing more than a name in Porphyry's list of five apocalyptic writings which were cited by the Gnostics of his day. Traces of the other four (*Zoroaster*, *Zostrianus*, *Messos*, and *Allogenes*) were discovered in 1946 at Nag Hammadi in Egypt; a cursory allusion to Nicotheus in another Coptic text of Gnostic origin, the Bruce Codex, had been known since the nineteenth century, but nothing has come to light that would enable us to say how much Zosimus owed to his lost apocalypse. He need not have consulted Gnostic texts to learn that each of us is two beings, an outer man and an inner man—the outer man purblind, gross, and subject to natural vicissitude, while the true abode of the inner man is not the visible cosmos, but the sphere of the incorporeal and eternal. To those who are not philosophers only the palpable is visible, fate is sovereign, and the same fate tosses them from one delusion to another. Skilled interpreters of the poet Hesiod will perceive that the inner man is represented by Prometheus, the outer man by his less discerning brother Epimetheus (*Omega* 6); but in fact there is only one true name for the father of humankind, though it admits of numerous interpretations:

> The Chaldaeans, the Parthians, the Medes and the Hebrews name him Adam, the interpretation of which is virgin earth[73] and bloody earth and rutilant earth and carnal earth.

Zosimus concludes that, while among 'us' (that is, the Egyptians) the first man is named Thoth, the Hebrews profess to have received the name Adam from the angels (*Omega* 9). Reitzenstein and others have detected an echo of a motley text from the second century, whose custodians, styled Naassenes or snake-worshippers by Hippolytus, preferred to be known as Gnostics. The Naassenes in fact assert that the first man has been given various names by ancient nations, but they agree with the alchemist in assigning a different Adam to each tier of reality (*Refutation* 7.4–5, 8.5–6). Thoth, he writes, is the name of the outer man, while the proper name of the inner man remains secret (*Omega* 10). The deliverance of this inner man from fate is accomplished by

[72] *Treatise on the Omega* 1. See Jackson (1978), 40–1 and (1990), with Baynes (1933), 83–4 and Porphyry, *Life of Plotinus* 16.

[73] Cf. Justin Martyr, *Dialogue with Trypho* 22.1; Tertullian, *On the Flesh of Christ* 17.

Jesus Christ, who, by a familiar play on words, transforms man, who is called φώς in the Greek of Homer into the incarnation of φῶς, or light (*Omega* 10). From the invisible heaven Christ and his retinue of light teach the elect below to slay the carnal Adam (13); the rulers of the material realm, however, falsely imagine that they can subject man to fate by imprisoning him in a body of four elements (11). This error finds a parallel in the *Apocryphon of John*, a second-century writing widely held to be of the same provenance as those employed by the Gnostics of Plotinus. Common to the these Gnostics, the *Zostrianus* and the *Apocryphon* is a claim to the possession of an otherwise unknown book by Zoroaster; for Zosimus Zoroaster is the antitype to Hermes, one espousing and one rejecting the use of magic in the deliverance of the soul (7.2). This was a dispute in which Neoplatonists had argued on both sides. Zosimus, for his part, is a Christian who contends that the soul's redemption is possible only because the incorporeal Son of God has taken upon himself our coil of flesh:

> [The adept] must not strive with necessity, but, leaving nature and judgment to her disposal, progress by seeking himself alone, and once he has come to know God, must hold fast to the unnameable triad,[74] letting fate do as she will to the clay that is hers, that is the body. And when you are so minded, he says, and live in this way, you will see the Son of God becoming all things for the sake of the holy soul, so that he may draw her from the place of fate to the incorporeal. See him becoming all things—God, angel,[75] suffering man. (*Omega* 7)

Was it heterodox to hold that more than one species of rational creature has been set free by Christ? This tenet was later attributed by hostile critics to Origen, and there is evidence in his writings that he held it. It is not among the culpable propositions that were ascribed to him at the beginning of the fourth century—which is as much as to say that, if he held it, it was not yet heresy. It is the intention of Zosimus to be orthodox: so much is clear from his vilification of Mani as an 'emissary of the Persians, who has made all human beings subject to fate'.[76]

In another work, recording visions under the title *Memoirs*, the renewal of the inner man is effected by y a series of immersions in the crucible which the one undergoing the sacrifice has prepared for himself in his character as priest. The first immolation is that of a man of copper:

> Having heard his voice as he stood by the bowl-shaped altar, I asked to learn from him who he was. And he answered me in failing accents, saying, 'I am Ion, the priest of the sanctum, and I suffer intolerable violence. For one came in haste at

[74] Jackson (1978), 44–5 takes the members of the triad to be Mind, Logos, and either the cosmos or humankind.

[75] Cf. Isaiah 9.6.

[76] On the name Manichaios as the solution to a riddle in chapter 14 see Jackson (1978), 54.

eventide and seized me, lacerating me with a knife, tearing apart the harmonious fabric and flaying the whole of my head with the sword that he wielded. He kneaded my bones with the flesh, and with the fire in is hand he burned me until by changing my bodily form I learned to become spirit.' And as he said this to me and I pressed him to speak, his eyes became blood and belched forth all his flesh. And I saw him utterly transformed into a maimed homunculus as he fell upon himself, rending himself with his own teeth. (*Authentic Memoirs* 10)

Jung compares the fourth treatise of the Hermetic corpus, in which mind is set forth in the midst of souls as a 'mighty chalice' in which we are exhorted to immerse ourselves (the Greek verb is *baptizein*) if we wish to know the Creator.[77] We are given to understand that the baptized have chosen the bodiless in preference to the bodily, and that ascent to the Creator requires us to pass through increasingly subtle orders of corporeality until we are united at last with his incorporeal oneness. There is, however, no allegory of dismemberment, and this, of all the Hermetica, is the one that might be most plausibly construed as a Christian sermon under camouflage, a symbolic conflation of baptism and the Eucharist, which for the primitive church were both instruments of participation in the death of Christ. The cup of Zosimus also might be understood as a eucharistic chalice in which the believer undergoes burial with Christ in order to share his resurrection;[78] such an interpretation, however, need not presuppose the perusal of any hermetic text. Reitzenstein's hypothesis that the red man is to be identified with the heavenly Anthropos of the *Poimandres*, and more remotely with Gayomart, the Adam of the *Zend-avesta,* also assumes too much while leaving much unexplained. Nor can a sound comparison be drawn with other myths in which the dead are resuscitated by immersion, for the variants in which the body undergoes dismemberment are the ones in which it does not return to life.[79]

The memoirs of Zosimus go on to describe encounters with other metals, each perhaps representing an altered state of the soul. The syncretistic character of his philosophy is most evident in the recipe for the union of the 'spirit of fire' with the 'stone of alabaster' that occupies the thirteenth and final chapter of his narrative. This, he declares, is the incommunicable mystery that the prophets could not disclose in speech, but only by tacit gestures; this

[77] Jung (1967), 73 n. 21. His appellation 'vessel of Poimandres' is not warranted by the text of *Corpus Hermeticum* 4, though *poimandria* signifies a cauldron in Greek. Scott (1936), 111 reproduces a short text from Zosimus in which the allusion to Hermeticum 4 is juxtaposed with the name Poimandres as though to imply an etymology from *poimandria*.

[78] Eliade (1977), 120 hints at an analogy between transmutation and the change of elements in the Eucharist. On pp. 176–7 he likens the dismemberment of Zosimus to that of Dionysus, interpreting both as symbolic rituals of initiation. Yet neither here nor in his chapter on human sacrifice (54–9) does he find another instance of self-dilaceration by the alchemist.

[79] See Matthews (1991), 68–9; Dodorus Siculus, *Histories* 4.54.2.

is the *pharmakon*, the therapeutic mystery, of the Mithraists. He goes on to extol the virtues of the pearl, a Christian symbol of the kingdom, which inspired at least two Gnostic allegories. In one the pearl is the object of redemption, though the one who seeks it becomes in turn a figure to be redeemed;[80] in the other, preserved in the Nag Hammadi Codices, the seller of pearls Lithargoel is revealed to be Christ himself.[81] The designation 'Christian Gnostic' is certainly true, so long as it connotes not adherence to any of the sects that were so described by ancient witnesses, but a religious sensibility akin to that of the Naassenes, who professed to concentrate all the mysteries into a single creed.

The voluminous works of Zosimus include treatises *On the Sacred and Divine Art of the Making of Silver, On the Substances that Support the Four Metallic Bodies according to Democritus, On Treating a Unique Tincture, On the Sulphurs, On the Preparation of Ochre, On the Measure of Yellowing, On the Final Reckoning*, and *On the Philosopher's Stone*, as well as *The True Book of Sophe the Egyptian on the Divine Lord of the Hebrews*. For the most part they consist of recipes for combustion and mixture, attenuation and dilution, sublimation and refinement, the detailed scrutiny of which would exceed my competence and the patience of most readers. Yet cheek by jowl with long accounts of the whitening of one metal or the liquefaction of others we come upon an elusive reference to the extraction of 'divine water', or an aphorism of a more obviously religious character, such as 'spirit is better than soul' or 'you must unite the male and female'. This last is also a precept of the apocryphal Gospel of Thomas and of a document, otherwise orthodox, which quotes it as an authoritative saying.[82] The authorities cited by Zosimus himself are never Christian: where he is not invoking Democritus, Hermes, or Agathodaemon (the 'good daemon' often identified with Hermes), he will turn to Moses or to Maria the Jewess, who reappears in Byzantine and Arabic works on alchemy as a prophetess of the Hellenistic era.[83] It would be as perverse to doubt as it would be credulous to believe all his citations. He has evidently no animus against Jews, which need not make him any worse a Greek or a Christian; and evidently he was as much a philosopher in his own eyes as Iamblichus or Numenius, capable like them of divining truth in all localities, though often enough it was only by letting down his own philosophy into the well that he could be sure of drawing up what he wished to find.

[80] See *Acts of Thomas* 108 at Elliott (2005), 487–91.

[81] See *Acts of Peter and the Twelve Apostles* (*Nag Hammadi Codices* VI.10) with Meyer (2007), 356–60.

[82] Gospel of Thomas 105; 2 Clement.

[83] See Patai (1994), 60–80.

CONCLUSION: CREED AND PRACTICE

Evidence for the theory, let alone for the practice, of alchemy outside the works of Zosimus is meagre. The baptism of which he dreams could be described as a rite of initiation, but to surmise that it had a liturgical equivalent outside his dream, and hence that there was a liturgical community—an alchemical church, as it were—is to reason in ever-widening circles. That one of his correspondents bears the name Theossebeia suggests that women patronised groups of adepts as they patronised philosophers or hosted Christian gatherings in this period. We may guess that such groups were apt to be small; it may be for that reason, and not because they cultivated secrecy, that they figure so little in the surviving records. The *Suda*, a Byzantine lexicon of uneven quality,[84] is to be read with caution when it asserts, in its entries under 'Diocletian' and 'chemistry' that after suppressing a popular commotion in Egypt Diocletian had the works of the alchemists put to the flames lest they should go on manufacturing the gold which had subsidised the insurrection. This otherwise unattested decree is most probably an embellishment of Diocletian's rescript against the Manichees, on the principle that an Emperor who persecutes one religion will persecute all and that religious solipsism is always accompanied by political unrest.

We cannot be any more certain that the authors of the Hermetica ever formed a visible guild. A tradition of writing may be carried on without a community of adepts, as some commentators on Orphism have maintained and every student of Sibylline literature will acknowledge.[85] Our evidence suggests that the intention of the first Gnostics was to restore the primitive vigour of the church, not to set up discrete communities outside it.[86] Mani, by contrast, was the founder of a new religion, and Diocletian's edict does full justice to its independent status. Elsewhere, however, we meet it only as an 'enclitic' phenomenon—that is to say that, like Gnosticism and Hermetism, it is never found standing free of Christianity.[87] Of course the church was not a willing prop to either the Gnostics or the Manichees, and when it acquired the power to persecute them it did so with zeal and mixed results; nevertheless, the material collected in this chapter shows that a history of Christendom in this era will be defective if it records only the suppression of diversity and the stilling of every voice that refused to join the episcopal choir.

[84] See now the Adler edition (Bibliography A).

[85] Linforth (1941).

[86] Julian, Letter 40 indicates that distinct communities of Arians and Valentinians existed in the fourth century.

[87] Lieu (2007) observes that in Egypt they styled themselves Christians.

8

Jews and Judaism

The term *Ioudaios* (*Judaeus*) in ancient sources, like 'Jew' today, denotes at once a religion and a race. In the Old Testament Judah is first the name of one of Jacob's sons, then of the tribe that claimed descent from him, then of the southern kingdom of Israel in which that tribe was numerically dominant. The Greeks who encountered only the remnant of Israel after the fall of the northern kingdom to Assyria and the return of the southern tribes from their exile in Babylon, applied the name *Ioudaios* without discrimination to anyone who claimed descent from Jacob or observed the Mosaic law. Notwithstanding occasional conversions—including that of an entire people, the Idumaeans[1]—the majority of those who embraced the *politeia*, or way of life, which came to be known as Judaism also regarded themselves as members of an *ethnos*, or race, which had faithfully cherished the customs of its fathers. As practitioners of an ancestral religion, they were able to obtain privileges and exemptions from the Roman government; at the same time they were intermittently harassed, though not always with impunity, by the mob, by local magistrates and even by the emperor. There is little evidence that they sought neophytes from the pagan world under Roman dominion,[2] but in some localities at least the synagogue was open to a class of uncircumcised *theosebeis*, or 'god-fearers'.[3] The temple at Jerusalem was still the notional centre of the cult, although the priests had ceased to minister at its altars after the conflagration of AD 70. In the wake of Bar Cochba's abortive revolt, Hadrian founded the Roman colony of Aelia Capitolina on the ruins of Jerusalem and forbade the Jews to inhabit the neighbouring territory. Even before this date the true centres of Jewish culture in the Roman Empire were Alexandria and Rome; nevertheless, the code of law for all Jews in the age of Constantine was the Mishnah, compiled in Palestine by men who had not yet given up all hope of the reunion of the people with the land.

To the authors of the New Testament, the plural noun *Ioudaioi* always signifies the people of the old covenant, who remain hostile to the Saviour and

[1] Cohen (1999), 135–9. [2] *Contra* Simon (1986).
[3] Reynolds and Tannenbaum (1987), 53–67.

his church.[4] It may also be employed with specific reference to the inhabitants of Judaea (the Roman province which succeeded the kingdom of Judah), but never without the religious connotation.[5] No believer is called a Jew in Christian literature unless, like Paul and Peter, he was born into that community;[6] when Paul himself avers that the true *Ioudaios* must be so in spirit, not only in outward practice,[7] he does not imply that a Gentile could become a Jew in spirit without conforming to the practice. The people of the new covenant initially styled themselves not Jews or Christians, but Israel or the twelve tribes,[8] thus appropriating the name which, as they knew well enough, was also the self-designation of those whom the rest of the world called Jews. It was therefore to be expected that when a Christian legislator came to the throne he would make it apparent that the Jews were to him not only a peculiar people but a stiff-necked and benighted one, who wrongly accorded themselves a place of honour in the divine economy. These expectations were not fulfilled by any violent persecution or forced conversion; instead, as we shall see in the present chapter, the emperor and his satellites promoted strategies of usurpation which ensured that the Jews would feel themselves to be strangers in their own land.

THE JEWS OF PALESTINE

In Palestine the first half of the fourth century was a period of want and tribulation. The scarcity of coin, to which a rabbi had alluded in the third century,[9] was not ameliorated, here or elsewhere, by Diocletian's policies; as the exactions of the imperial fisc became more oppressive, frequent droughts curtailed the dwindling revenues of the farmer, and by 350 almost every independent holding had been surrendered to a great landowner, who may in turn have struggled to obtain some profit from his dispersed possessions.[10] The Jewish population of this territory was a remnant of the nation that had been purposely scattered by Hadrian when he founded the Roman colony of Aelia Capitolina on the ruins of Jerusalem in AD 135. We do not know the size

[4] See esp. 1 Thessalonians 2.14–15; 2 Corinthians 11.24 (in sharp contrast to 'Israelites' at 11.22).

[5] Lowe (1976) believes this to be true throughout the Gospel of John.

[6] Galatians 2.14–15; Acts 22.3. At Galatians 2.13 the observance of Jewish dietary laws is hypocrisy in a Christian.

[7] Romans 2.28, sometimes cited as a gloss to Revelation 2.9 and 3.9. This, however, may also refer to Christian passing as Jews to escape persecution.

[8] James 1.1; Romans 11.26.

[9] Stemberger (2000), 13, quoting Rabbi Levi at *Canticle Rabbah* 2.5.

[10] Sperber (1978), 136, cited by Stemberger (2000), 16.

of this remnant in the fourth century: the tale of the Empress Helena's discovery of the True Cross, which reckons the number at a thousand, is only a tale.[11] The right of the Jews to occupy their own land was guaranteed by the imperial recognition of a patriarch in Jerusalem. In the late fourth century he held the title *vir clarissimus*, which indicates senatorial rank,[12] and could exercise influence, if not authority, over the governance of Jewish communities outside Palestine.[13] Constantine, on the other hand, accords no political title to him in his legislation; it is arguing in a circle to maintain that we do not have the original wording of his laws,[14] just as it is arguing in a circle to surmise that the patriarch owed his exaltation to Diocletian because no Christian would have granted such a privilege to the Jews.[15] We shall see that Constantine was not uniformly harsh in his dealings with the synagogue; if there is any truth in the story that patriarch Hillel was forbidden to calculate the date of the Passover by traditional means and therefore introduced a fixed calendar, we cannot be sure that Constantine was the ruler who forced his hand.[16] To Constantine the norms of Jewish observance would have been of no interest once the Nicene Council had established a rule for the computation of Easter that prevented any alignment of the two feasts.

Epigraphic and archaeological studies have revealed that there was no 'zone' which the Jews were not obliged to share with Gentiles.[17] Conversely, there was no distinguished city of the region—not even Philistine Gaza, now a showpiece of Greek learning and pagan worship—which did not have its quorum of Jews.[18] Rabbinic schools were flourishing in Tiberias, Sepphoris, and all centres where the Greeks formed a majority.[19] Despite its name, the Talmud Yerushalmi is a product not of Jerusalem but of Galilee, where the rabbis had come to think themselves superior to their rivals of the south.[20] There is evidence that they were now regarded, or at least regarded themselves, as a privileged group within the synagogue;[21] at the same time they built their own houses of instruction, and two illustrious figures of this epoch, Abun and Yirmeyah, came all the way from Babylon to teach in the academy of Tiberias, which was also the seat of the patriarch.[22] When Abun had new gates fashioned for this splendid edifice, the Palestinian Mana rebuked his profligacy by quoting Hosea 8.14: 'Israel has forgotten her maker and built

[11] Edwards (2003), 68 and 82.

[12] Stemberger (2000), 235, citing *Codex Theodosianus* XVI.8.8.

[13] Stemberger (2000), 242–3, citing Libanius, Letter 1251, though, as n. 25 reveals, some doubt attaches to the identification of the political intriguer in this letter as the patriarch.

[14] So Stemberger (2000), 235.

[15] Stemberger (2000), 236 rebuts the arguments of Dothan (1983), 68.

[16] Stemberger (2000), 250–1, responding to Dothan (1983), 68 and Avi-Yonah (1976), 166.

[17] Millar (2010), 45.

[18] Millar (2010), 33.

[19] Stemberger (2000), 271. The school at Lydda was now defunct: ibid., 274–5.

[20] Stern (2010), 147.

[21] Stemberger (2000), 278–9.

[22] Strack and Stemberger (1991), 102–4.

palaces'.[23] But Mana, it seems, was a man of the past who, rather than submit to the usurpations of the patriarch, was later to quit Tiberias for Sepphoris.[24] One notable zealot for purty, Rabi Abbahu, was the first to pronounce it unlawful to drink the wine of the Samaritans.[25] According to one account he had seen a pagan taking part in one of their festivals; according to another, he denounced them for accepting wine from the Romans in a time of scarcity. In a third scenario, the Samaritans make libations at the behest of Diocletian when they might have claimed the indulgence which he had granted to the Jews.[26] As Stemberger observes, the one stable element in these narratives is the ascription of the ruling to Abun; since, however, false tales as well as true grow in the telling, this is not so much a proof of the historicity of the ruling as a testimony to his reputation.

Certainly his vigilance did not prevent the growth of the Samaritan population. Their own chronicles record that they acquired sufficient confidence in their numbers to rebel under the captaincy of a certain Baba Rabba.[27] The cause of revolt, as always, was an edict that would have forced the Samaritans to break their law, and the recruits were paid with funds that would otherwise have been swallowed by the Roman fisc. The Emperor Alexander was defeated, and the Romans turned for assistance to the Arabs and Jews, but the Emperor Gordian failed to make good his promise of restoring the temple in Jerusalem. After a further series of victories, Baba was lured to Constantinople by the Emperor Philip, and his captivity put an end to the insurrection. All three autocrats (Alexander Severus, Gordian III, and Philip the Arab) are of the third century, but Philip resides in Constantine's new capital, while Gordian's courtship of the Jews foreshadows the policy of Julian. Some scholars have therefore argued that the story is true except for all its details, and that Baba first raised his standard in the first half of the fourth century; but surely it is futile to base historical conjectures on such reveries as to ask which Caesar really invaded Britain in the reign of Cymbeline.[28]

SOME LITERARY EXPERIMENTS

A history of Jewish literature in the age of Constantine cannot be written. We can date most Christian texts to the nearest decade with some diffidence, but we are fortunate if we date a Jewish text to the nearest century. We can be

[23] Stemberger (2000), 272, citing JSheq V.6.49b.
[24] Stemberger (2000), 273, though there is much speculation here.
[25] Stemberger (2000), citing JAZ V.4.
[26] The reference is to the fourth edict of 304, unless Diocletian has been confused with Decius.
[27] Stemberger (2000), 222–6. [28] See further Stenhouse (1995).

reasonably certain that the Mishnah, the great compilation of rabbinic sayings, had already been augmented by some version of its sequel, the Tosefta.[29] The *Targumim*, or Aramaic paraphrases of certain scriptures, are of an earlier period, but may have undergone revision in the fourth century.[30] The *midrashim*, or legal commentaries, have been assigned both to the fifth century and to the third.[31] Visionary narratives of ascent through a series of *hekhalot*, or celestial palaces, were almost certainly current by the beginning of the fourth century, though we cannot be sure that any extant specimen, such as the book now known as 2 *Enoch*, was in use.[32] Even the inscriptions which can be confidently dated to the fourth century are sparse and fragmentary. The *piyyut*, or hymns, are perhaps the only literary form to have been invented in our epoch.[33] Our difficulties are all the greater because we have so little evidence that anyone who was not a Jew was acquainted with Jewish literature of this period or with its authors. Even the learned writings of Eusebius do not contain the allusions to intercourse with living Jews that we encounter from time to time in those of his master Origen and his disciple Jerome.

One text, whatever its date, deserves our attention because it is surely the earliest specimen, and perhaps the inspiration, of the alphabetic mysticism which makes its first appearance in the Platonic and Christian literature of the Constantinian era.[34] The *Sefer Yetzirah*, assigned by its devotees to the time of Abraham, is one of the numerous works of which scholars say only that it was probably composed between the second and the sixth centuries.[35] It opens with a stanza proclaiming that the titles of God have been engraved in the thirty-two paths of wisdom—these being (according to Aryen Kaplan) the thirty-two episodes of the creation as related in the first chapter of Genesis.[36] Next we are told that God created the universe with three books—text, number, and speech—all four of these words being represented by the same three consonants in Hebrew.[37] In the second stanza, the twenty-two 'foundation letters' of the Hebrew alphabet are divided into three mothers, seven

[29] Reichman (2010), 18 opines that the Tosefta 'originated' in the early third century, but was 'vigorously reworked over a considerable period of time'.

[30] Hayward (2010), 238 tentatively assigns Targum Neofiti, Targum Psalms, and Targum Job to the fourth century.

[31] Stemberger (2010), 131.

[32] Schäfer (2010), 265–7 and 275.

[33] Van Bekkum (2010), 217.

[34] For its antecedents see the Josephus, *Against Apion* 1.8.38–40 and 4 *Ezra* 14 (2Esdras 16), 45–6, trans. Box (1917), 113, in both of which the number of books in the canon is equal to the number of letters in the alphabet. Note also the reverence accorded to the letters *aleph*, *daleth* and *lamed* at *Damascus Document*, Statute XV.1 at Vermes (2011), 138. At John 3.14 and Justin, *First Apology* 60.1 the letters *tau* (the Cross) and *teth* (the serpent) would appear to have been conflated.

[35] See Kaplan (1990), xviii–xxv; Scholem (1987), 24–5. For a general survey of numerological mysticism in Jewish thought of the Roman era see Holdrege (1996), 168–72.

[36] *Sefer Yetzirah* 1.1, pp. 5–14 Kaplan.

[37] SY 1.1, pp. 19–22 Kaplan.

doubles, and twelve elementals.[38] The Mothers are *aleph, mem*, and *shin*[39]—the first, the midmost, and the last but one; we later learn that *mem* hums, *shin* hisses, and *alef* is the breath of air that decides between them.[40] The doubles—that is, the letters which can express two sounds, are *beth, gimel, dalet, kaph, peh, resh*, and *tau*.[41] Before naming the members of each class, however, the tenth stanza declares that all twenty-two characters were engraved and carved as breath from breath, and that one breath proceeds from them.[42] As the characters were engraved with water from breath, so the throne of glory was engraved with fire from water.[43] Three of the twelve elementals—*yod, heh*, and *vau*—are successively arranged in each of their six permutations to seal the extremities of the divine name.[44] When the letters are divided again into five phonetic orders, each of these three elementals is found to inhabit a different order.[45] Each of the Mothers is king over one of the elements, *alef* over the breath of creation, *mem* over water, *shin* over fire.[46] Each of the doubles corresponds to a planet and is king over one of God's blessings;[47] each of the elementals has its own month and its own astrological sign.[48]

The Christian counterpart of the *Sefer Yetzirah* is a formidable treatise, *On the Mystery of the Letters*, which has recently been dated to the fourth century by its editor, Cornula Bandt.[49] According to this author the earliest alphabet was the one that he calls Syrian, vouchsafed to the world by Enoch before the Flood.[50] After the fall of the Tower of Babel, however, each of the nations introduced its own corruptions, Hebrew alone preserving the original deposit.[51] The Greek script has lost has been augmented by two characters, *psi* and *xi*, while the Hebrew *vau* is now represented not by the lost *digamma* or (*episêmon*), but by *omicron*.[52] For all that, it is the Greek letters whose outlines furnish visible emblems of the first four days of creation and of the works that God wrought on each. The author reckons one work on the first day, two on the second, three on the third, four on the fourth; when the ten letters depicting them are added to the initial four, fourteen of the twenty-two have been deciphered.[53] These last eight represent the works of Christ, who was circumcised on the eighth day in obedience of the Law, but gathered the saints into an everlasting Sabbath or octave, of which the Law was merely an adumbration,

38 SY 1.2, pp. 22–32 Kaplan.
39 SY 3.2, pp. 140–2 Kaplan.
40 *SY* 2.1, pp. 95–100 Kaplan.
41 *SY* 4.1, pp. 159–62 Kaplan.
42 *SY* 1.10, pp. 71–3 Kaplan.
43 *SY* 1.12, pp. 77–80 Kaplan.
44 *SY* 1.13, pp. 80–7 Kaplan.
45 *SY* 2.3, pp. 102–8 Kaplan.
46 *SY* 3.7–9, pp. 152–5 Kaplan.
47 *SY* 4.7–4.14, pp. 174–84 Kaplan.
48 *SY* 5.7–10, pp. 214–28 Kaplan.
49 Edition by Cordula Bandt, *Der Traktat 'Vom Mysterium der Buchstaben'* (Berlin: De Gruyter, Texte und Unterusuchungen 162, 2007).
50 *Buchstaben*, pp. 148.10–14 Bandt and 182.16–18.
51 *Buchstaben*, pp. 148.15 and 184.5–12 with pp. 56, 59, 64, 76, and 78 of Bandt's introduction.
52 *Buchstaben*, pp. 164.18–166.18 Bandt; p. 160.7 Bandt.
53 *Buchstaben*, pp. 122–30 Bandt.

like the eight souls in the ark.[54] It is also true that the first three letters represent a trinity of elements in the world above, the next three a trinity in the world below. The *delta* has the triangular form of the first plane figure, and is consequently a fit symbol of the earth which affords a foundation for all other creatures.[55] Each of the twenty-two letters also stands for an episode in the life of Christ, while the seven vowels, occurring as they do at irregular intervals, can be likened to the seven great interventions of God in history, which were separated by unequal epochs.[56]

This we may call the iconic interpretation of the Greek characters; another, non-pictorial signification can be accorded to each, however, if we study the names of their Hebrew archetypes. These, it should be said, are not the meanings that would be found, then or now, in any primer of Hebrew. Some fantastic glossary of his own enables the author to match the first four letters with four things antecedent to the creation of light,[57] which is signified by the fifth letter (*hê*), while *vau*, the sixth, denotes simply a sign (*sêmeion*). It therefore stands for Christ himself, who appeared in flesh at the end of the sixth millennium;[58] the absence of a letter corresponding to it at this point in the Greek alphabet is providential, for this lost cipher is one of three discarded elements which collectively stand for the Trinity.[59] The term 'elements' is given to the characters because they have been arranged for our edification; the Greeks have fallen into idolatry because they imagined, on the contrary, that the characters are so called by analogy with the *stoicheia* or elements of creation. The twenty-two books of the Septuagint are the speech of God the Word,[60] who is not to be numbered among his works, although for our sakes he has elected to take on flesh. The translation of God's speech into legible ciphers is an anticipatory act of condescension, which makes every letter a hieroglyph of two created things as a testimony to the coupling of the human and the divine in the incarnation.[61] It is Christ himself who embodies the wisdom of letters, proclaiming 'I am alpha and omega, the first and the last' (Revelation 1.8).[62]

The letters preceding *vau*, the symbol of light, represent the blindness of the Greeks; the next ten answer to the Ten Commandments, and the final eight are once again reserved for the people of God.[63] The Jews who claim this title for themselves forget that the alphabet was given to the nations long before the Creator made a special covenant with Israel. The Greek language has been sanctified by the translation of the scriptures; we are edified by its very

[54] *Buchstaben*, pp. 138–48 Bandt.
[55] *Buchstaben*, pp. 118.15–19, 122.19–20, 124.25–26 Bandt.
[56] *Buchstaben*, 178.4–180.12.
[57] *Buchstaben*, pp. 126.16–27, 180.29 Bandt.
[58] *Buchstaben*, p. 176.9–14 Bandt.
[59] *Buchstaben*, p. 174.5–8 Bandt.
[60] *Buchstaben*, p. 184.1–2 Bandt.
[61] *Buchstaben*, pp. 196.5–200.20 Bandt.
[62] *Buchstaben*, pp. 106.23, 108.17, 110.22, 156.8, 158.12, 180.14, 182.11, 194.4–5, 200.13–14, 202.7 Bandt.
[63] *Buchstaben*, p. 193.1–7 Bandt.

imperfections, which permit us to correlate Greek and Hebrew letters according either to their sounds or to the positions that they occupy in the respective alphabets. Thus whereas omicron is the phonetic equivalent of *vau*, omega corresponds by position to *tau*, the symbol of consummation to the symbol of the Cross.[64] Every use of the Greek abecedary is thus an unwitting vindication of Christ; the very persecutors—Nero, Hadrian, Maximin, Diocletian[65]—are condemned in every syllable of their own edicts against the church. The reference to Hadrian, more commonly held up as an example of a good emperor who refrained from persecution, suggests that the author regards his dispersion of the Jews as an act against God. While his contempt for the Jews as false custodians of the scriptures is everywhere manifest, and while we can hardly imagine any prototype for this text which was free of reference to Christ, it is not impossible that he found his model in Jewish literature, which had long borne testimony in all its branches to a belief in the mystical properties of letters.

Josephus and a forger writing under the name of Ezra agreed that the number of books in the Hebrew canon was equal to that of the letters in the alphabet, though one was speaking of the Hebrew alphabet, the other of the Greek.[66] The Hebrew alphabet provides a frame for the longest Psalm,[67] and in a vision of Ezekiel, much cherished by the church, the letter tau is stamped on the foreheads of those who bewail the abominations of Israel (Ezekiel 9.4). This name means 'cross', while the name of the letter which represents the aspirated form of *tau* is *teth*, denoting a serpent. The Messiah of Israel shows that he is aware of this equivalence in the Fourth Gospel, when he tells Nicodemus, a ruler of the Jews, that the brazen serpent which Moses lifted up in the wilderness was a portent of his own Cross.[68] The Book of Revelation, in which the same Messiah proclaims himself *alpha* and *omega*, is shot through with the imagery of Jewish apocalyptic, and may therefore have originated in circles close to Qumran, where similar reverence was accorded to *aleph, lamed*, and *daleth*, the A, L, and D of the Hebrew alphabet.[69]

CHRISTIANS VERSUS JEWS

Whether or not we can speak of a persecution of Jews in this era, A. H. M. Jones was evidently right to detect a 'theological animus' which had not been

[64] *Buchstaben*, pp. 186.32–3, 200.7 Bandt. [65] *Buchstaben*, p. 116.5 Bandt.

[66] Josephus, *Against Apion* 1.8.38–40; 4 Ezra 14 (2 Esdras 16), 45–6, trans. G. H. Box, *The Apocalypse of Ezra* (London: Haymarket, 1917), 113.

[67] Psalm 119; see also 9, 10, 25, 34, 37, 111, 145, and Proverbs 31.10–31.

[68] See John 3.14 with Numbers 21.9 and Justin Martyr, *First Apology* 60.1.

[69] *Damascus Document*, Statute XV.1. See G. Vermes, *The Dead Sea Scrolls in English* (Harmondsworth: Penguin, 2011), 138.

apparent in pagan measures against them, or even in the stock charges of misanthropy and antinomianism.[70] A chorus of witnesses tells us that 'the Jews' continued to furnish causes of enmity by doing ill to the church wherever they could. In the Acts of the Apostles they harry Paul with canine tenacity; in early martyrologies that exacerbate pagan hatred and whisper that Christians who prefer to live will be welcomed in the synagogue.[71] Whole books of vituperation and forced exegesis had left them unmoved, and according to some reports they had been not only accomplices but instigators of pagan violence against the church under Diocletian. Thus we read that the magistrate who ordered the execution of Basil, bishop of the Chersonese, was acting on information received from Jews;[72] they were duly confounded in the reign of Constantine when Basil's successor walked through fire unharmed, and thus presented Jews and pagans alike with an irresistible motive for conversion. Another atrocity, also expiated in the reign of Constantine, was the killing of a Jew named Lucius by his own father after his defection to Christianity.[73] We may not be 'on the border-line of history and myth',[74] but well beyond it when we hear that the burning of a soldier named Carterius proved too slow for a Jewish onlooker, who relieved his impatience by driving a spear through his heart. Two accounts of the death of Paul, another of Diocletian's martyrs, state that he owed his crown to the Jews who formed a majority in his native Diocaesarea.[75] In this case, however, we can observe the growth of the legend, for Eusebius, our earliest informant, does not say that Paul was denounced by Jews, but only that as he expired he uttered a prayer for both Jews and pagans. Having seen how little value can be attached to these records of Jewish animosity to Christians in the Roman world, we need no scales to estimate the likely truth of anecdotes which represent them as gadflies to the church in Persia under Shapur II.[76] We need only remember that even in the third century the pagan who caused Valerian to renew the persecution was described by the impossible locution 'synagogue-leader of the magi',[77] as though to imply that the Sassanids, who conquered and captured Valerian shortly after the publication of his edict against the Christians, were not merely the protectors but the confederates of the Jews.

Eusebius, who preserves this phrase in reproducing a letter by Dionysius of Alexandria, does not hold the Jews accountable for any persecution in his *Ecclesiastical History*. He does not spare the *Christoktonoi*, the Christ-killers who failed to recognize their own Messiah, and his excerpts from Josephus' account of the Roman sack of Jerusalem are longer and more lurid than they

[70] Jones (1964), 92–3. [71] *Martyrdom of Pionius* 13. [72] Parkes (1961), 133.

[73] Parkes (1961), 133–4, noting that narrative falsely imagines Judaism to have been subject to legal penalties in 312.

[74] Parkes (1961), 139. [75] Parkes (1961), 135. [76] Parkes (1961), 140–3.

[77] Eusebius, *Church History* 7.10.4, quoting Dionysius of Alexandria on Macrianus.

would need to be if his sole aim were to prove that Christ had been a genuine prophet.[78] In the first two books of his *Church History*, however, he repeatedly extols the antiquity of the Jewish nation and the service that it has rendered to the rest of the human race by its observance and dissemination of the Mosaic Law. While he insists that the true religion of Abraham was republished to the world only through the ministry of the incarnate Word, he does not deny that the Jews have always been, and remain, the same people as the Hebrews who were set apart from the earliest times by the purity of their faith.[79] Josephus, for example, is a reliable historian of the Hebrews because he is one of them (3.9.5); the Maccabean martyrs are also Hebrews (3.10.6), and the Jews of the church in Jerusalem are 'true Hebrews', in contradistinction not only to unconverted Jews but to Gentile Christians (4.5.2). While the names 'Hebrew', 'Israelite', and 'Jew' are not interchangeable, there is no strict or consistent differentiation of usage. The error of the Jews is to imagine that the Law has furnished them with a perfect knowledge of the mysteries; only those who are Hebrews in faith perceive that the angel whom Abraham saw at Mamre (1.2.7) was the same being who revealed himself to Daniel as the glorified Son of man (1.2.24–26).

In the seventh book of the *Preparation for the Gospel*, on the other hand, the Hebrews are an older race than the Jews, deriving their name from Eber, an antediluvian forefather of Abraham, whereas the Jews can trace their ancestry no further than Judah, one of the sons of Joseph (7.6). Another etymology suggests that the word means 'passengers' or sojourners, and the spiritual progenitor of the Hebrews was Enos, the son of Seth, who, as the first to call on the name of God was the primordial man in a truer sense than his fallen grandfather Adam (7.8). Enoch is the second and Noah the third of the Hebrews commemorated in the scriptural narrative. None of the three was circumcised, since none was a prey to any irregular passion; immediate communion with God from birth to death dispensed them from the observance of any written law. The first of their successors after the Flood was Abraham, whose circumcision did not subject him to any law, but was either a sign of his faith in the promise of multitudinous offspring or a mark by which the fidelity of his offspring might be tested (7.8). Isaac, Jacob, and Joseph all reveal themselves by their acts to be genuine Hebrews; Jacob is the father of twelve tribes, although all twelve fall under the appellation 'Jew' when this is applied to those descendants of the Hebrews who submitted to the legislation of Moses. Moses himself, no less than Paul, deserves to be called a 'Hebrew of the Hebrews' (7.7), but the rest of the people had forfeited this name after their growth in numbers brought them into proximity with their venal and impious neighbours. The covenant which God made with them at Sinai was neither a token of their sanctity nor a means of sanctification, but a yoke for stiff necks,

[78] *Church History* 3.6, citing Josephus, *Jewish War* 5.10.
[79] *Church History* 1.2.22; cf. Johnson (2006), 94–125.

a chastisement and a testimony to the hardness of heart with which Jesus had so often taxed his countrymen. The Jew is now as much a lost child of Adam as those who make no claim to descent from Abraham.

The law is conducive to holiness so long as its provisional character is not forgotten. The perennial mistake of the Jews, according to Eusebius, is to force an impoverished sense on texts that were written in the fullness of inspiration. Oracle after oracle which had borne no fruit in the time of the prophet himself is found in the *Commentary on Isaiah* to have been fulfilled at last by the Incarnation and the sowing of the church. Others, not yet fulfilled, are more perspicuous to the church than to the synagogue because their consummation is prefigured in some writing of the New Testament.

CONSTANTINE AND THE JEWS

Constantine is frequently regarded as an oppressor of the Jews, although his legislation is temperate by comparison with that of his mediaeval and modern *epigoni*.[80] One of his laws permits the appointment of Jews to the governing council of a city, with the rider that, in order not to break with ancient custom, two or three may remain unburdened by any civic obligation.[81] Appointments of this kind, though honorific, were seldom coveted, as those who held them were also required to subsidize public works and entertainments, and to ensure (at their own expense, if necessary) that the city paid its taxes. A second law provides that no such duties shall be imposed on Jews who devote themselves entirely to the synagogue or administer the law;[82] it adds a clause sparing all Jews who are not of the decurial class, and stipulates that members of this class may not be compelled to go abroad on public business. Thus, while the first Christian emperor may have deprived Jews of the universal exemption that they enjoyed under pagan rule, he never denied them the limited immunity that he extended to other religious groups in accordance with pagan custom. This parity was a consequence of measures that a Jew could only applaud, since they allowed him to occupy a position of dignity without garnishing the altars of strange gods.

That not all Jews were born Jews in this period is evident from a law of 336 which provides that if a Jew 'has not shrunk from circumcising' a purchased slave, whether a Christian or one of another religion, the slave is to be set free.[83] Eusebius purports to know of another decree, or another version of this

[80] Linder (1987), 138–44. [81] *Theodosian Code* 16.8.3.

[82] *Theodosian Code* 16.8.2.

[83] *Sirmondian Constitutions* 4, dated 21 Oct 335, but issued at Carthage in March 336. It is possible that the law does not apply to slaves who were born in captivity. Stemberger (2000),

one, which deprives the Jews of the right to own Christian slaves on the grounds that those who have been ransomed by the Saviour ought not to be subject to his murderers.[84] Whether or not these were his own words, Constantine could be vehement in his legislation against Jews who opposed themselves to the triumph of Christianity. In endorsing the *Sentences of Paulus* in 315, he ratified a law which banished citizens who allowed themselves or their slaves to be circumcised, sentenced to death the doctor who performed the operation, and imposed deportation or execution on Jews who had bought and circumcised a slave of another race.[85] In one of his own enactments he does not go so far, but stipulates that Jews are to die by burning if they harass members of their own 'savage sect' who have turned to the worship of the true God, and that anyone from the people (*ex populo*) who joins their 'nefarious sect' shall be punished according to his desert.[86] Whether *ex populo* means 'from the Christian laity' or 'from the Roman people',[87] the phrasing of the decree is more illiberal than its content, but the content is fierce enough to suggest that Constantine was perplexed by the reluctance of the Jews to take advantage of his inducements to conversion, and vexed to find that his measures had not put an end to Christian apostasy.

We must hold him entirely responsible for the acrimonious diction of the letter which enforced the Nicene resolution on the date of Easter.[88] For over a century Rome and Alexandria had enjoined on the whole of Christendom the practice of commemorating the resurrection on the Sunday after the full moon following the vernal equinox. The alternative, or Quartodeciman, custom was to make Easter coincide with the fourteenth day of the Jewish month Nisan,[89] which, as the day of preparation for the Passover, was also that of the Passion.[90] Objection was made to this, not only on theological grounds—the Passover was the sacrifice of saints, whereas the death of Christ was inflicted

38–9 compares a law of Constantius, *Theodosian Code* 16.9.2 and notes that *Theodosian Code* 16.8.22 ascribes a similar law to Constantine, of which no original text survives.

[84] *Life of Constantine* 4.27.1. Eusebius reports this law solely with reference to the benefit that Christians derive from it, as did Edwards (2006b), 143. Neither of us is guilty, as Barnes (2007), 198 alleges, of asserting that the law applied only to Christians, though the extension of it to other *sectae* may be intended to encompass heretics and schismatics rather than pagans.

[85] See Stemberger (2000), 35–7, citing Theodosian Code 16.8.1 and (for the approval of the *Sentences* in 228) *Theodosian Code* 1.4.2.

[86] *Theodosian Code* 16.8.1, traditionally dated to 315, though Stemberger (2000), 36 prefers 329, while Avi-Yonah (1976), 174 attributes it to Constantius in 339. The law quoted above from *Constitutions of Sirmium* 4 also provides that a Jew who molests a convert to Christianity is to suffer in proportion to the severity of his crime.

[87] See Barnes (2007), 199.

[88] Eusebius, *Life of Constantine* 3.17–19.

[89] *Life of Constantine* 3.18.4. Socrates, *Church History* 7.18 distinguishes this Asiatic practice from the observance of the 'day of resurrection', which the Novatianists adopted in defiance of the Nicene resolution.

[90] See further Cameron and Hall (1999), 259–60.

on him by sinners—but on the grounds that the Paschal calendar was determined by codes intelligible only to the Jews. It had not hitherto occurred to any bishop to remind his co-religionists that these Jews were the same sinners who had shed the Saviour's blood; in Constantine's letter, however, this is the sovereign argument,[91] reinforced by the observation that, because the Jews adhered to a lunar calendar they sometimes 'wandered so far from the truth' as to keep the same festival twice in a year—that is, between one vernal equinox and the next.[92] Eusebius echoes these tendentious strictures when he writes in his *Life of Constantine* that one purpose of the Council of Nicaea was to put an end to the use of the Jewish reckoning. No reference to the holiday is found among the canons of Nicaea as these are now preserved, though a canon of uncertain date and provenance, attributed to the synod of Antioch in 341, purports to ratify the Nicene excommunication of those who celebrate Easter 'with the Jews'.

JERUSALEM, THE HOLY CITY

Ambition and curiosity had always furnished the moneyed classes of the ancient world with incentives to travel.[93] The statue of Zeus drew multitudes to Olympia, the air of Athens nourished many a lesser mind than Plato's, and who would not wish to verify with his own eyes that, compared to Rome, other cities were like shrubs beneath a cypress?[94] But pilgrimage, the visiting of holy sites to honour their holiness and enhance one's own, was a Christian practice,[95] only partially foreshadowed in the annual journeys of Israelites to Jerusalem for the Passover or in purposeful expeditions like the one described in the *Letter of Aristeas*. Again, not only Jews but Greeks and Romans travelled far to salute a tomb, but Christ had done many other things before his death that were worthy of a memorial. Around 333 the Bordeaux Pilgrim, wrongly naming giving the name Bethsaida to the pool of Bethesda, places it first in a list of sacred trophies.[96] While he makes no mention of the angel who was said

[91] On the Jews as 'Lord-killers' see *Life of Constantine* 3.19.1.

[92] Cf. Socrates, *Church History* 7.18, where it is alleged that the Samaritan Passover never falls before the vernal equinox.

[93] Walker (1990), 41–50 denies that Eusebius would have attached this epithet to Jerusalem or any site in Palestine, except insofar as they were hallowed by association with past events. Contrasting *Demonstration* 6.18.50 with *Tricennial Oration* 9.15, he argues that the Bishop of Caesarea took increasing pains to prevent the singling out of the rival see as a site of pre-eminent holiness in Palestine.

[94] Dio Chrysostom, *Oration* 12; Virgil, *Eclogues* 1.25.

[95] For general studies see Hunt (1982); Dietz (2010).

[96] Stewart (1887), 20. Douglas (1996) denies that this traveller was in fact a pilgrim; for Elsner (2000a) he exemplifies the rapidity with which literary conventions were adapted to a new

to have stirred the waters of this pool in some Latin versions of John 5.2, he was shown a secret place nearby in which Solomon was supposed to have tortured demons.[97] The tower from which Satan tempted Christ to throw himself down was also pointed out to him, as were the mountain of the Transfiguration, the pool of Siloam, the garden of Gethsemane on the Mount of Olives, the site of the betrayal of Christ by Judas, the house of Caiaphas the high priest, the palace of Pontius Pilate, the pillar at which Christ suffered flagellation on the way to the Cross, the hill where he was crucified and the tomb from which he rose.[98] His guides had not forgotten the palm-tree from which the crowd tore branches to welcome the new king into Jerusalem; even the stone which was destined to 'become the head of the corner' in one of his parables had acquired the solidity of a real artefact.[99]

Innovating on a confused text in the Gospel of Matthew, the Christians of Jerusalem were now displaying the vestiges of the nails which had been used in the crucifixion of the prophet Zacharias.[100] If the supposed executioners were Romans, it ought to follow that Zacharias had been identified with the father of John the Baptist rather than with either of the prophets called Zechariah in the Old Testament. It is unlikely, however, that such questions were carefully weighed by an informant who imagined, or was content to hear, that the ruined temple in which these events were commemorated had been built by Solomon.[101] He was also shown the tomb of the prophet Isaiah, another monument which a Jew might have been less disposed to look for than a reader of the New Testament. One relic which was certainly of more consequence to that people than to Christians was a stone at which they bewailed their expulsion from the land of Israel, not far from two statues of Hadrian which had no doubt been erected when he founded the Roman colony of Aelia Capitolina on the remains of the ancient city.[102] Although he mentions the site of David's palace, together with both the house and the tomb of Isaiah's contemporary king Hezekiah of Judah,[103] the only other sovereign to whom the pilgrim alludes is Constantine, and only because he had founded a church 'of wondrous beauty' in the vicinity of Christ's tomb.[104] He is happy to observe, with an inapposite quotation from Isaiah, that the city which boasted seven synagogues now contains but one.

Jerusalem was clearly the centre of a widespread traffic, for the pilgrim had already seen the well at Sychar where Christ asked a Samaritan woman for water,[105] as well as the baths which the god-fearing centurion Cornelius had

purpose—in this case the topographic embodiment of the scriptures—by the beneficiaries of the Constantinian revolution. Its counterpart in the writings of Eusebius is the *Onomasticon*.

[97] Stewart (1887), 21. [98] Stewart (1887), 23–4.

[99] Stewart (1887), 21; cf. Matthew 21.42 and Psalm 118.22.

[100] Stewart (1887), 21; cf. Matthew 23.35. [101] Stewart (1887), 21.

[102] Stewart (1887), 20. [103] Stewart (1887), 22–3.

[104] Stewart (1887), 24; cf. 27. [105] Stewart (1887), 18.

endowed in Caesarea.[106] After leaving Jerusalem, he was able to contemplate the tomb of Lazarus near Bethany and went on to find confirmation of the book of Joshua in Jericho. He recalls that in the course of this journey he saw the very cup that Elisha had used in the performance of a miracle.[107] As is well known, he makes no allusion to any exhibition of the True Cross, although legend attributes the rediscovery of this relic to the Emperor's mother Helena in the last years of his reign.[108] The believer might propose that Helena's excavations took place in the years following the pilgrim's observations, or that the Cross was exhibited only at Easter, as the later *Travels of Egeria* imply.[109] No one will doubt today that our extant narratives of the 'advent' or 'invention' of the Cross are replete with legend: we may deny without hesitation that Macarius, the Bishop of Jerusalem, was a convert from Judaism, or that the Cross was found in the company of those on which the two thieves had been crucified, and could be identified only when it proved capable of resuscitating a corpse.[110] We are also free to doubt that the Cross which Egeria beheld at that portentous ceremony had ever stood on Golgotha. For all that, once the tale is stripped of its fanciful concomitants, it may be true that something was brought to light under the direction of the empress and was subsequently paraded, with the usual mixture of subterfuge and credulity, as the instrument of Christ's passion.

Harold Drake[111] suggests that a letter by Constantine, enjoining the construction of new church near the holy sepulchre, may contain an oblique commendation of this discovery:

> Such is the grace of our Saviour that words seem to lack the capacity to give fitting expression to the present marvel. For the memorial (*gnôrisma*)[112] of his most holy Passion, long since hidden under the earth for so many cycles of years, has now, through the destruction of the common enemy, shone forth to his liberated servants in a manner that passes all astonishment. (Eusebius, *Life of Constantine* 3.30.1)

Does the noun *gnôrisma* denote the Cross or the sepulchre itself? The former interpretation would be more true to the common use of the term, but the

[106] Stewart (1887), 17. [107] Stewart (1887), 25.

[108] Her journey to the east is attested at *Life of Constantine* 3.42ff., and reconstructed in detail by Odahl (2003), 285–9.

[109] Wilkinson (1971), 137.

[110] See Borgehammar (1991); Drijvers (1992); Edwards (2003). Helena is, however, credited by Eusebius, *Life* 3.43 with the foundation of new churches at the sites of the nativity and the ascension.

[111] Drake (1985a), also citing Cyril of Jerusalem's account of the discovery at *Catechetical Orations* 4.10 10.19, and 13.4. Cf. Dietz (2010), 114–16.

[112] The argument of Rubin (1982), 83 that this term signifies the Cross rather than the tomb is rejected by Cameron and Hall (1999), 282–3, as also in the commentary of Bleckman (Bibliography A), 350.

excavation of the tomb is more securely attested.[113] Eusebius says nothing of this trophy when he recounts the excavation of the cave which contained the *martyrion* of the saviour and the erection of the Church of the Holy Sepulchre on the same site at the Emperor's command (*Church History* 3.27–28).[114] The floor, he tells us, was of polished marble, the external walls of perfectly fitted stones; the roof was crowned with lead against the elements, but the spectator within looked up at a sea of the purest gold, which caused the whole building to glitter.[115] The church was flanked on each side by two porticos, and three gates were placed on the eastern side to admit the congregation. Opposite these gates a hemisphere—possibly the altar—rose to the summit of the church, and was encircled by twelve columns, each surmounted by a silver bowl from the emperor's treasury. The building was adorned throughout with ornaments of unutterable beauty.[116] While he adds that churches were established at Bethlehem and elsewhere in Palestine, the historian gives us to understand that this one was established as a testimony to the emperor's peculiar reverence for the holy city.[117]

CONCLUSION

Jacob Neusner has argued that in the interval between the composition of the Mishnah and that of the Palestinian Talmud, the Jews of Palestine lost sight of the sapiential theory—the philosophy, to use his term and Philo's—that informs every verse of the Mishnah, and had begun instead to cultivate Judaism as a religion.[118] He means by a philosophy a system of thought which determines the order, value, and higher significance of every phenomenon; in the Mishnah he detects just such a conception of the world as a unified hierarchy of masters and subjects with the Creator at its apex. The fiscal, commercial, and punitive ordinances of the early sages, he finds, are governed by general principles of fair traffic and distribution which had not

[113] Biddle (1999).On the archaeology of the church, see also Walker (1990), 235–81.

[114] *Life of Constantine* 3.28. As Wilken (1992) observes, the cave is not found in any passion narrative; Eusebius perhaps wished the place of Christ's interment to mirror that of his birth. Walker (1990), 46–7 contends that the cave if 'holy' to Eusebius not because it possesses any sanctity of its own but because it inspires faith in the saints.

[115] Stemberger (2000) points out that the dome was added a decade after the dedication in 335.

[116] See *Life of Constantine* 3.33–40. As Cameron and hall (1999), 276–7 point out, this account does not support the theory of Taylor (1993), 141 that Constantine orchestrated the discovery of the cave because he had already resolved the set up a shrine to the Cross.

[117] On the remains see Galor and Bloedhorn (201), 134–6. For a commentary and a plan of the church see Cameron and hall (1999), 274–91.

[118] Neusner (1999).

been laid down in such a compendious form since Aristotle. In the Talmud the presuppositions of the Mishnah are retained but without reflection on the divine economy to which they bear witness; precepts are given solely with a view to their application, and the one who obeys them faithfully will be conscious not so much of cosmic harmony or the unfolding of God's plan as of his own righteousness, his immunity to natural and political vicissitude—in short, of his self-sufficiency as a Jew. In keeping with this shift from the world to one embattled portion of it, the object of the midrash *Genesis Rabbah* is to demonstrate that Israel is the first love of the Creator, that his dealings with her have always corresponded to her merits, and that every event in history subtends the future glorification of the chosen people. *Leviticus Rabbah* has a similar purpose—to assure the Jews in exile that the covenant is not dissolved, the land not lost, the Temple and the ministry of its priesthood not extinct, though temporarily in suspense.

If this is a fair appraisal of the lot of the Jews in the later Roman Empire, how far can we hold Constantine responsible for this deracination of a whole people? His purification of the cult at Mamre has been described in a previous chapter; he also made it his task to establish the worship of the true God in Palestine where it had not yet been offered. According to Epiphanius of Salamis, he commissioned a convert, Joseph of Tiberias, to plant new churches even in localities were he found no Christian settlement; Epiphanius may for once be worthy of credit, not only because he himself was Palestinian by birth but because he is reproducing Joseph's own account of his travels from site to site in the teeth of the intrigues and enchantments of the Jews.[119] Joseph's claim to have been a disciple of Hillel II is of course unverifiable, as is the tradition that he founded the House of Peter at Capernaum[120] and the Church of the Multiplication at Tabhga by the Sea of Galilee.[121] What we can say with confidence is that Epiphanius illustrates the common view among Christians of his time that the Holy Land belonged only to them. The tone of Constantine's legislation is always contumelious, and, as a modern scholar observes, he describes the Jewish institutions of Palestine in terms that would befit a rival church.[122] It was all the easier therefore to subject them to laws resembling those which were being enacted for the restraint of heretics—all the easier too for the opponents of such a heretic as Arius to revile him as a Jew.[123] Eusebius, by contrast, chooses his words with the specious temperance of a historian when he undertakes to prove from their own scriptures that the Jews had never been the true people of God. No doubt the likenesses of the apostles

[119] See Epiphanius, *Panarion* 30.4 and 11–12.

[120] Stemberger (2000), 76 finds the speculations of Testa (1972) more imaginative than compelling.

[121] Murphy-O'Connor (2008), 220 and 278 notes that the plan is identical to that of the House of Peter.

[122] Linder (2006), 155.

[123] Cohen (1999), 191–4.

Paul and Peter, which he counted among the treasures of his native Caesarea, were in his mind happy prefigurements of the numerous conversions which took place in that city after the accession of Constantine.[124] Although it has been surmised that a 'passage at arms' between him and Macarius of Jerusalem gave rise to one of the Nicene Decrees in 325,[125] Jerusalem's determination to make itself the cynosure of the Christian world is supported by his own writings. Whatever the bishop gained was lost to the synagogue and even if Jews were subject to no coercion or expulsion, it was inevitable that their numbers in Palestine would be depleted, and that Babylon would henceforth have no rival as a nursery of holiness and a school for the application of the Law.[126]

[124] *Church History* 7.18.1. Such trophies are not incompatible with the argument of Eusebius; supposed letter to Constantia, which denounces only the veneration of the image of Christ. On its questionable status see Barnes (2010b).

[125] Stanley (1970), 182–3.

[126] See further Solomon (2009), xxv–xxxvi.

Part III

Christian Polyphony

9

The Religious Integrity of Constantine

The religion of the New Testament (if it is a religion) is not one into which its adherents were born, but one into which they were reborn by *metanoia* or conversion.[1] The sudden, catastrophic change in conduct and mentality that this word implies was not asked of participants in other ancient cults; analogues can be found in the biographies of philosophers, but even they were not subject to the same tests of sincerity that the church applied to its neophytes. The philosopher showed his purpose by assiduous attendance on one master, until he became in turn a master to others, under some label such as Peripatetic, Platonist, or Stoic which originated in the Athens of the classical or Hellenistic period. Yet, while allegiance to one named institution was the norm, it was equally normal to blend the tenets of the founder with those of his rivals, so that the lessons which one man received from a Platonist might be indistinguishable from those that another received from a Peripatetic. A Christian, on the other hand, was required to forsake all other gods, to shun not only the heathen but the heretic, and to live by precepts strange to the world which were far more severely enforced than those that regulated the conscience of the typical philosopher. It has often been observed that Constantine's faith was never an obstacle to his ambition, and that in his political acts he treated pagans with a moderation bordering on indulgence. Hence it has been surmised that he was dishonest in his profession of Christianity, or that he failed to grasp what his new religion demanded of him. Historians wrestle with discordant accounts of his conversion,[2] which agree in ascribing one decisive experience to him, but cannot agree with regard to its date, its location or its content. In modern times they have contested not only the date but the reality of the conversion, maintaining that while the emperor was a Christian when he spoke to the church he addressed the pagan world in a different character; others, though they argue that he was privately and publically a Christian, opine that he was not orthodox, or rather that in

[1] On conversion as a problematic category see Morison (1992).

[2] Elliott (1992a) does not produce enough evidence to persuade me that Constantine was already a Christian in 306.

the murky altercations between Eusebians, Marcellans, Homoousians, and Arians he did not know his right from his left.

VARIATIONS ON A LEGEND

The first Christian to ascribe a portentous vision to Constantine is his contemporary Lactantius, who does not name his informant, and does not say that the experience was followed by an immediate conversion:

> In his sleep Constantine was enjoined to inscribe the celestial sign on the shields and thus to seek the issue of battle. He did as he was commanded, and inscribed Christ on the shields by marking a line through the letter X and giving it a circular inflexion at the top. (Lacantius, *Deaths of the Persecutors* 44)

Since the basic figure was an X, the result would be an approximation to χ, the first letter in the Greek spelling of the name Christ. Having obeyed the command he advanced to battle the following day, and drove the forces of Maxentius into the Tiber with so much loss of life that his panegyrists were hard put to excuse it.[3] Almost a quarter of a century later, Eusebius purports to heard the sworn statement of the emperor that, at some unspecified place and time in the west, he had been surprised, about noon, by the spectacle of a cross of light above the sun. The following night, the 'the Christ of God appeared to him, holding the same sign' (*Life* 1.29). In giving this name to the apparition, Eusebius is speaking from subsequent knowledge, and what he goes on to describe is, properly speaking, not the sign itself but the representation of it which was immediately commissioned by the emperor (*Life* 1.30). This, as he can testify from acquaintance, was a gilded spear, crossed by a transverse bar and wreathed with gold, within which were inscribed the first two letters of the name of Christ, the *P* (English R) passing through the centre of the *X* (English CH). From the top of this cross hung a banner bearing the legend 'In this sign you shall conquer' (*Life* 1.31). Some time before this revelation, Constantine had resolved to commit his fortunes to the supreme God, without yet knowing whom he worshipped (*Life* 1.27); now he discovered among his advisers some who were able to tell him that the name of this god was Christ (*Life* 1.32).[4]

Real events, when they move us, are unconsciously augmented in each retelling, and this later account is surely, as E. R Dodds surmised, a 'secondary elaboration' of the original narrative.[5] It is hard to understand why Constantine should have failed to point out the celestial anomaly to anyone else at the

[3] *Latin Panegyrists* 6(7).5.3 and 10.4.
[4] This account is accepted with little modification by many historians, e.g. Odahl (2003), 92.
[5] Dodds (1965), 47 n.1.

time of its occurrence; one might ask how a banner large enough to be legible to one observer could have eluded other eyes. Eusebius must have been forgetful or inattentive if he failed to grasp that the promise of victory was vouchsafed on the eve of a battle; although he records that the cross was inscribed on the shield of the emperor's troops, this episode is separated by many chapters from his account of the vision. In both redactions we are left to wonder why either God or the emperor's own subconscious should have elected to communicate with him by the medium of the Greek alphabet; the symbol XP, commonly called the *labarum*, does not appear as a military ensign before 317, although some scholars have maintained its pagan origin.[6] No doubt it can be urged that these inconcinnities prove the good faith of Eusebius, who would have written more competently had he been free to devise his own narrative; but, once so much is granted, it seems more reasonable to surmise that he has combined two recollections, or has simply misunderstood the imperfect Greek of Constantine, than to insist that his account must be more veridical because it was confirmed by the emperor's oath.

That Constantine was prone to visions,[7] or fertile in the invention of them, can be deduced from an early panegyric, delivered at some time from 308 to 310, which reminds him that his destiny has been sealed by an encounter with Apollo bearing a crown:[8]

> For I believe, Constantine, that you saw your Apollo, with victory at his die, offering your crowns of laurel, each of which carries the presage of thirty years. (*Latin Panegyrics* 6. 21.3)

Apollo and the crown are the only details in this anecdote, and neither appears in later accounts of Constantine's conversion. Yet Peter Weiss has argued,[9] to wide acclaim, that this pagan courtier is describing in his own way a real epiphany which was then repeatedly staged under different lights by our Christian impresarii. The core of truth, he maintains, is the crown, or rather a solar halo of which the crown is the mythological remainder. A solar halo, according to Weiss, is apt to appear from a clear sky as a 'double crown formed by bright, cross-shaped concentrations of light around the sun'. Being the

[6] Grégoire (1927–28) derives the word from *laureum*, 'laurel'; Bruun (1966), 61 suggests that the prototype was the Egyptian *ankh*, while Drake (1976), 73–4 derives it from a solar emblem used in Constantine's Danubian homeland. For his appearance on coins see Frakes (2006), 104–5.

[7] See further Macmullen (1968). Cameron (1997), 259 observes that this return to his father's god (Eusebius, *Life of Constantine* 1.27) resembles Moses' encounter with a burning bush from which he was addressed by the 'God of his fathers' (Exodus 3.6).

[8] For commentary see Lieu and Montserrat (1996), 73–6. Constantine in fact reigned for a little over thirty years in the west; but Nixon and Rodgers (1994), 248–9, interpret the omen as a promise of life beyond the usual span.

[9] Weiss (2003). Cf. Barnes (2011), 74–80.

product of 'sunlight refracted through ice-crystals in the higher levels of the atmosphere', it is often accompanied by iridescence, and Weiss observes that, in his neglected account of the vision, the erudite though playful Philostorgius refers to both a circle and a rainbow. Noting (or asserting) that in Latin a 'halo-image' is called a corona, and summarily deciding that Apollo is 'his late-antique equivalent Sol', he concludes that the corona of the Latin panegyrist, understood here as the laurel crown of victory, is the sign that was fabulously represented by Eusebius as a banner proclaiming 'in this sign you will conquer'. As Weiss says, it does not follow from the orator's petition that the epiphany took place within the temple of Apollo. He surmises, not improbably, that it occurred in the course of a march. The 'authenticity' of this later account is 'in no way impugned' by the fact that it represents a 'subsequent, Christian interpretation'. Nor need we doubt, adds Weiss, that this apparition was the catalyst for the dream, which may thus be regarded as the final aftershock of the commotion that the emperor had experienced in another place and long before he had any quarrel with the pagan gods. Eusebius, writing later, has been favoured by his sovereign with a more primitive version, and no one will find it difficult to discern the 'cross-shaped rays' in his account, though we must be ready to explain away the embellishments which could not have formed part of any natural vision.

Weiss's theory has been cordially received in certain quarters; yet few modern scholars outside the narrow circle of Constantinian studies share his faith that truth can be attained by the permutation of selected elements from discordant narratives. If we are to follow this method, should we not do as Robert Graves enjoins,[10] and take account of every narrative, late or early, including those in which Constantine's conversion is an episode in a late campaign, the response to a miraculous cure from leprosy or a calculated overture to the one god who will pardon him for the murder of his own son?[11] The answer will be, of course, that the first accounts are the most likely to be veridical, and that the kernel of fact will emerge when we strip away the husk of fiction. Thus we ignore the tendentious introduction of the figure of Christ in the story which Eusebius professes to have received on oath from the emperor; we discard the clear assertion of Lactantius that the vision occurred at night. It cannot be maintained, however, that any detail is less essential than another to the story as it is told by either of these ancient witnesses, and in such a case, as Chesterton said long ago,[12] to give up the detail is to give up the story. The futility of attempting to deduce history from legend has been

[10] Graves (1955), vol. 1, 22–3.

[11] Lieu and Montserrat (1996), 102; Edwards (2003), 62–3; Julian, *Caesars* 336b–c.

[12] Chesterton (1960), 162–3: 'If somebody said that he had met a man in yellow trousers who proceeded to jump down his own throat, we should not exactly take our Bible oath or be burnt at the stake for the statement that he wore yellow trousers.'

proved repeatedly in biblical study, which is equally capable of reducing every event in the life of Christ to myth and of unearthing a natural cause for every fabulous occurrence in the Book of Exodus. No reader of Lactantius or Eusebius would imagine that either author is describing a solar halo,[13] and anyone who contends that tales of this kind do not win an audience unless they are true in substance should remember the angels of Mons.[14]

CONSTANTINE IN HIS OWN WORDS

All history warns us not to deduce the religious beliefs of a monarch from his political morality. When he publishes his convictions we must take him at his word, unless we possess some less tendentious record that allows us to contradict him. Constantine has not left us a journal or any intimate correspondence; the inevitably public character of his surviving utterances is in fact the best guarantee of their sincerity, for he could not have hoped in speeches, edicts or official rescripts to be one man to the church and another to his pagan subjects.[15] No doubt we must set aside the letter to Aelafius, an otherwise unknown prefect of Africa,[16] which concludes with the hope that the catholic religion may prevail throughout the empire. On the other hand, few scholars contest the authenticity of a letter of October 312,[17] which accompanies a subsidy to the ministers of the 'holy catholic religion' in Africa, and ends with a prayer that Caecilian, bishop of Carthage, may be preserved for many years by the 'divinity of the great God' (Eusebius *Church History* 10.6.4). Eusebius appends the emperor's simultaneous mandate to Anulinus, the pagan proconsul of Africa,[18] to relieve 'the clergy over whom Caecilian presides' form all public liturgies, alluding to the dangers which arise from the contempt of that religion 'in which the highest reverence for the most holy power in heaven' is maintained, and contrasting these with the benefits that accrue when the servants of the true god 'devote themselves without hindrance to the observance of their own law' (*Church History* 10.7.1–2). When the same

[13] We should perhaps be willing to be reminded of the light 'above the brightness of the sun' that Paul purports to have witnessed at Acts 26.13, and of the 'splendour outshining the sun' that is extolled in the opening sentence of the *Oration to the Saints*.

[14] The story by Machen (2011), in which a rearguard of angels covers the British retreat, is a pure invention, which owes its fame to the frequency with which it was subsequently corroborated by supposed eyewitnesses.

[15] See the collection of references by Girardet (2013), of which I have made grateful use in the following paragraphs.

[16] Perhaps Elaphius: Corcoran (2000), 331.

[17] On the manifest Christianity of Constantine in this letter see Maraval (2013), 22–4.

[18] Odahl (2003), 116 is impressed by the rapidity with which Constantine had mastered the Christian faith.

Anulinus informed him of the charges that had been brought against Caecilian by the malcontents who were soon to be known as the party of Donatus, Constantine wrote to Miltiades, Bishop of Rome, assuring him of his reverence for the 'lawful' catholic church and appointing him the president of a mixed tribunal of bishop from Gaul and Italy (10.5.20).

This synod pronounced in favour of Caecilian, or rather of his consecrator Flexi of Abthugni, who had been accused of handing over copies of the scriptures during the Diocletianic persecution. Since however, it failed to appease the Donatists, Constantine convened a general council at Arles, declaring, in his letter of invitation to Chrestus of Syracuse, that the dissidents had prove themselves unmindful of their own salvation and of the reverence due to the 'most holy religion', which he once again expressly equates with 'the catholic sect' (Eusebius, *Church History* 10.5.21–22). Eusebius justifiably treats the letters to both Miltiades and Chrestus as extensions of the document, now commonly known as the 'edict of Milan', in which Constantine and Licinius had proclaimed the liberty of all religions in the empire. The authors were aware that Christianity was the one religion suffering duress in the provinces ruled by their dissident colleague Maximinus, and, in preparation for the war against him they declared the abrogation of his measures to be a necessary condition for retaining the goodwill of the god who had hitherto been their patron (10.5.16). Once again it is only the Catholic Church that is to enjoy the benefits of emancipation; that Constantine stops here of declaring himself a Christian is less remarkable than that he should have persuaded his pagan ally to go so far.

All the texts cited so far are the effusions of a newly converted Christian. For a reasoned account of Constantine's decision to be a man of one god, we must turn to his *Oration to the Assembly of the Saints* which is appended as a fifth book to Eusebius' *Life* of him. If genuine (as most now hold it to be), this declamation sheds more light on the beliefs and motivations of the author than the writings of any of his imperial predecessors apart from Marcus Aurelius. The title—misremembered by Eusebius, who thus acquits himself of the suspicion of having forged it—might have suited an allocution to the senate. Since it is clear none the less that the implied audience is a Christian one, it subverts the conventions of apologetic, the stated brief of which had hitherto been to avert persecution, not to avenge it, so that the emperor was more likely to be the addressee than the speaker. The stated occasion is the 'day of the passion', but the natural inference that this is Good Friday has been denied on the grounds that no such holiday was observed by Christians in this period. As to the year of delivery, estimates range from 313 to 328; in the space at our disposal, it will be possible only to summarise the text and to set out my reasons for holding it to be an early composition, which bears witness to the clarity and vigour of his convictions at a time when he was not yet sole master of the Roman world.

THE *ORATION TO THE SAINTS*

Eusebius records that it was the emperor's custom to draft in Latin the speeches which were then translated by other hands for delivery to a Greek audience (*Life* 4.32). He adds that one of these, under the title 'Of the Assembly of the Saints', will be appended to his *Life of Constantine*. The ponderous oration which appears in manuscripts as the fifth book of the Life is in fact entitled 'To the Assembly of the Saints'. If this will not suffice to prove that Eusebius is neither the translator nor the true author of the speech, we may add the speaker's own confession that he was not brought up in the knowledge of the true God, which contradicts the historian's claim that Constantine returned to the monotheism of his father;[19] we may also note that when he inveighs against the persecutors he does not name Galerius as the true instigator of the measures which disfigured the later years of Diocletian. We must therefore assume that the speech has come to us as Eusebius found it, and it is obviously improbable that, writing so soon after the death of Constantine, he could be mistaken as to its authorship. The only scholar to doubt its provenance in recent years is Richard Hanson, who rightly perceives that the speaker alludes to Apollo's shrine at Daphne, but assumes without good reason that he must therefore have witnessed Julian's consultation of the oracle at Daphne, which resulted in a calamitous attempt to remove the bones of the martyr Babylas from the neighbouring soil in which they had been interred in 351.[20] The shrine was already celebrated before that date, and no doubt the translation of the saint's remains to that place had been a calculated affront to the god whose oracles were believed (and were said by Constantine himself[21]) to have exacerbated Diocletian's enmity to the church.

If Constantine is the author, what can be said of the date, the venue and the occasion of delivery? The opening sentence proclaims that it is the 'day of the Passion', which ought to mean the day now called Good Friday.[22] It is possible that this was not yet a date in the ecclesiastical calendar;[23] by the reckoning that Constantine approved, however, the celebration of Easter fell invariably on a Sunday, and no one who knew the gospels would fail to deduce that the previous Friday was the anniversary of the crucifixion. If it was not yet an ecclesiastical holiday, a layman would have all the more opportunity to test the patience of a Christian gathering with a speech that, in its present form, could

[19] *Oration* 11. For criticism of the theory that Constantine's father Constantius was a solar monotheist see Smith (1997).

[20] Hanson (1973) on *Oration* 18. Daphne was in any case a stock theme for declamation: see Aphthonius, *Progymnasmata*, p. 15 Rabe.

[21] Eusebius, *Life of Constantine* 2.48–52.

[22] So Barnes (1976b), maintaining an earlier date than Barnes (2001b).

[23] Hall (1998), 92.

not have been delivered in less than two hours.[24] That the audience was a Christian one is obvious enough, although the conventional description of the senate as a *sanctus coetus* ('sacred assembly') may be parodically echoed in the title.[25] On the other hand, we cannot be sure that this audience heard the speech in its present form. It was by no means rule in antiquity that the spoken oration should be identical with the published text, and there is one passage in the Oration—an acrostic poem attributed to the sibyl—which could hardly have been deciphered by an audience at first hearing whether the native language of that audience was Greek or Latin.[26] The doubt implied here cannot be resolved, for even if our text is Greek translation from a Latin draft, we cannot be sure that the purpose of translation was to enable Constantine to speak in Greek.[27] Moreover, when we speculate on its purpose we must remember that the bare text of a speech reveals at most the intention of delivery, and is no guarantee of performance. Even if Constantine was no Isocrates, rounding his periods for the inner ear, we can cite the case of Cicero, who could not deliver his second speech against Verres because he had already won his case.

Of the intended or imagined audience we may guess that it had some reverence for the sibyl, though it may not have comprehended, or been asked to hear, the full text of the oracle. Since a few of the verses had already been quoted by Lactantius in Greek, and a full Latin text, imperfectly preserving the acrostic, was known to Augustine,[28] Constantine's appeal to this authority would have served him as well in the west as in the east. On the other hand, the audience is expected to take an interest in a detailed commentary on the Fourth Eclogue of Virgil, a text which may have been rendered into Greek before the fourth century but was never canonical for those who knew it in this guise.[29] It has been maintained that where the Greek translates the Latin poorly in the *Oration* the author's commentary is apt to follow the Greek; I hope, however, to have shown elsewhere that the commentary always presupposes the Latin original, though not always in a form that coincides

[24] See Gerlach (1998) and Edwards (2007), 57. If Barnes (2013) is right to maintain that Constantine was the first to celebrate Christmas on December 25, may he not be credited also with the institution of Good Friday?

[25] Woods (2002), 498. This observation favours Rome as the place of delivery, although Woods does not draw the inference.

[26] *Oration* 18. The partial citation of the same Greek verses by Lactantius, *Institutes* 7.19.9 seems to me a sufficient reply to the argument of Potter (2013), 337 that the presence of this oracle implies that the speech itself was composed in Greek.

[27] Lane Fox (1986), argues for delivery in Greek, and any scholar who maintains a date of delivery after 324 must surely concur.

[28] On parallels between the oration and Lactantius see Bolhuis (1956); De Decker (1978).

[29] *Oration* 19–21. See further Baldwin (1976); for the argument that the commentary presupposes the Latin text see Kurfess (1936); Ison (1985a).

with the printed texts in use today.[30] It need hardly be said that if Constantine delivered the *Oration* to an audience of Latin speakers, he did so before the permanent translation of his residence to the east.

An early date is also suggested by the superscription: Since Constantine assumed the title Victor (*Nikêtês*) after his deposition of Licinius in 324, it was once agreed that its absence in the exordium to the speech ought to betoken an earlier date of composition.[31] This inference is supposed to have been refuted in recent years by the citation of a letter from Constantine to King Sapor of Persia, certainly written after 324, in which this title is omitted (Eusebius, *Life* 4.2). One might object that it would have been presumptuous (not to say truculent) to make use of it in correspondence with a foreign power over whom he had not yet obtained a victory. In any case, when certainty eludes us we must deal in probabilities, and, since we find this appellation in almost every document which is known to have been composed by the emperor after 324, its absence in any other text must heighten the probability that this text was written in an earlier period of his life.

If the speech was delivered, or intended for delivery, to a Latin-speaking audience before 317, what is the likeliest venue? Trier, the most regular seat of Constantine before his year, has been reasonably proposed,[32] and it is perhaps the strongest argument in its favour that this important city is nowhere mentioned under its own name in the *Oration*. The fact that Rome is named is urged by Robin Lane Fox as a proof that it cannot be the 'dearest city' anonymously commended for its loyalty.[33] This reasoning would exclude not only Rome but the eastern city of Nicomedia, which had not been proposed when Lane Fox made his case for Antioch. But the principle that one cannot use a name alongside a sobriquet is not universally followed in the rhetorical prose of late antiquity, and for Timothy Barnes the naming of Nicomedia is an element in what is 'almost a formal proof' that this was the destination of the speech.[34]

Perhaps the strongest evidence in favour of Rome is Constantine's apostrophe at the beginning of chapter 2 to the 'pilot' and 'nurse' of the Christian world.[35] Whether, with Heikel, we take the pilot and nurse to be one subject, or maintain with Barnes that the nurse is the church while the pilot is its bishop,

[30] Edwards (1999). We may add that only a Roman would salute Virgil as 'Maro', and that Lactantius had already adduced the fourth Eclogue as a Messianic prophecy (*Institutes* 7.24).

[31] Ehrhardt (1980).

[32] See now Girardet's edition of the *Oration* (Bibliography A). Giradet argues that the Oration was most probably delivered in the wake of Licinius' victory over Maximinus Daia, and that, whether the date is 314 or 315, Constantine is more likely to have been in Trier than in Rome or Milan.

[33] See chapters 22 and 25 with Lane Fox (1985), 778. Rome is mentioned in 22, Nicomedia in 25.

[34] Barnes (2001b), 29, proposing 325 where Bleckmann (1997), proposed 328.

[35] This venue was suggested by Drake (1985b), though neither here nor at (2000), does he fix the (initial or intended) date of delivery at 315, as Edwards (1999) and (2007a) proposes to do.

there was surely no congregation that was more likely to have been deemed worthy of this compliment.[36] Constantine's professions of love for Rome as a city were broadcast to the Latin world by his early panegyrists,[37] his benefactions during the pontificate of Silvester I were numerous, and Silvester's primacy among western bishops was acknowledged in his absence, though not without irony, by the Council of Arles in 314.[38] Trier, by contrast, held no place of honour in Christendom, and even Nicomedia, for all its political eminence, could not pretend to any ecclesiastical distinction. At no time could a ruler of any tact have bestowed such accolades on Eusebius, the bishop of that city, who was formally deposed in 325 for the opinions which were already being impugned as heresies some five years earlier. Under Constantine we cannot speak of a papal monarchy, or even of a universal primacy, but we can say that no eastern church—not even Alexandria, let alone Antioch, Thessalonica, or Byzantium[39]—held such a lofty and secure position of esteem.

As for a date, it is true that Constantine cannot have been in Rome at Easter in 313, 314, or 316, and that many scholars hold a date of 315 to be equally impossible.[40] Here we need only reiterate that even an emperor cannot accomplish all that he intends. Nor need we accept that similarities between the style of the speech and that of texts which date from the latter half of Constantine's career afford good evidence for a date of composition after 320. The literary remains of the younger Constantine are meagre and, being extant (as they were drafted) largely in Latin, seldom admit of minute comparison with later works that owe their survival to Greek translators and historians. What we possess of his writing from these early years reveals that a predilection for leonine bombast, trite hyperbole and arduous circumlocution was native to him, and did not overtake him suddenly after his seizure of the eastern capital in 324.

THE *ORATION* AND ITS THEOLOGY

The orator commences by declaring that it is now the date of the Passion. After this his discourse falls into three parts. The first (chapters 2–10) puts the case for monotheism: the pagan gods, with their diverse births and characters,

[36] Barnes (2004a), 353.

[37] *Latin Panegyrics* 4(10).11.2; 5(8).2–3; cf. Eusebius, *Life of Constantine* 1.39 on the salutation of Constantine in Rome.

[38] *Latin Panegyrics* 4(10) and 12(9).16; Optatus, *Against the Donatists*, appendix 4.

[39] For arguments in favour of these venues see Piganiol (1932) and Mazzarino ((1974), esp. 109.

[40] Barnes (1982), 72 quotes a letter sent in Constantine's name from Trier on April 28 315 (Optatus, appendix 8). Since, however, this is a rare case in which his order was not signed by his own hand, it could be adduced as evidence that he was not in Trier at that date.

cannot maintain the concord of the universe, and their immoralities prove that they are either living demons or dead mortals. The notion that the world exists by chance is indefensible, as a mighty and benevolent creator would be needed to appease the eternal conflict of the elements. Plato had an inkling of the truth, but no philosopher has understood how the sum of things is governed by the Father through the offices of the Son. Next (in chapters 11–19) he extols the voluntary abasement of the Son in his incarnation. A god in human form, replete with virtue and inalienable wisdom, Christ has opened up the path to heaven by his teaching. Having manifested his philanthropy by his willingness to suffer, he imitates his Father's magnanimity by waiving his revenge for a certain interval, during which he enlightens every nations with the brilliance of his resurrected glory. His life and vindication were foretold by the Hebrew prophets, but the most persuasive arguments for pagans are a Sibylline acrostic which predicts the Day of Judgment and the Fourth Eclogue of Virgil, which celebrates the birth of an unnamed infant as the prelude to a returning age of gold. Finally (chapters 20–26), the speaker declares his personal adherence to the Saviour. He apostrophizes Decius, Valerian, and Aurelian, the three persecuting emperors of the third century, and cites himself as a witness to the calamitous effects of the Great Persecution initiated by his predecessor Diocletian in 303. He claims that those successors of Diocletian who have perished most ingloriously were those who had compounded their defiance of the imperial constitution with the oppression of the church. He ends with the praise of Christ, whose wise and merciful dominion he will never cease to acknowledge and proclaim.

The theology of this sermon, for the most part, is formulaic enough to have satisfied any bishop of his epoch. That God is one, that Christ the Word is in some sense his Son, that his feats on earth attest his Messianic status and were prophesied in the Old Testament—all these are commonplaces in apologetic literature and in dialogue between churchmen of different parties. There are, however, points at which scholars detect an inclination to the heresy of Arius who denied the coeternity of the Father and the Son and held that the latter was begotten or created 'out of nothing'. Their arguments are sometimes unsustainable: the ascription to Christ of two births, one from the Father and one from Mary, may be redolent of the myth of Dionysus,[41] but has also been a perennial canon of ecclesiastical orthodoxy. A passage that affords more plausible grounds for the suspicion of Arianism occurs in chapter 10, where Constantine endorses the conventional view that Plato had come within sight of the Christian doctrine of the Trinity:

> And Plato himself, who excelled all others in gentleness and first accustomed human intellects to rise from the sensible to the intelligible and the things that are

[41] Graves (1956), vol. 1, 56.

> always thus, the one who taught us to look up to things above, did well when he postulated the god above being, then made a second god subordinate to this one, dividing the two essences numerically, while both shared one perfection and the essence of the second god received its concrete existence from the first. For the maker and governor of the universe is clearly sublime, while the other after him, in submission to his commandments, refers to him the cause of the constitution of all things. According to the exact account then, there would be one God who exercises care over all things and takes thought for them, having set all things in order by his Word. And the Word is himself God and the child of God,[42] for how could anyone escape the greatest error, for how could anyone escape the greatest error if he gave any other name than the appellation 'child'? For the father of all[43] would rightly also be called the father of his own Word. So far then Plato was insightful; but in what follows he is found to err from the truth, introducing a host of gods and assigning a form to each, which became a pretext for greater error among the most unreasoning people, who did not look towards the providence of the Most High, but worshipped images of [the gods] which had been transformed into human types and those of other creatures. The result is that a nature and discipline which were excellent and worthy of highest praise, mixed with such shortcomings, are in an impure and defective state.

Though Constantine speaks of Plato, 'second god' is the terminology of Numenius, a second-century Platonist to whom Porphyry, Plotinus, and Theodorus of Asine were all believed to owe more than they acknowledged.[44] Since he does not apply the same locution to Christ himself, it is remarkable that this passage should have been held up as evidence of the emperor's adherence to the heresy of Arius, which may not even have been formulated at the time when the speech was first prepared for delivery. As we have seen in Chapter 6, Marcellus of Ancyra might have concurred; Eusebius, on the other hand, employs it when he is writing for those who are not well-schooled in the faith, and it comes handily to Lactantius as a pagan approximation to the true doctrine.[45] We cannot cite the phrase 'second god' as an index of Arian sympathies in this period, any more than we could argue from the emperor's use of the formula 'child of god' (*Oration* 9) that he was already familiar with the Nicene Creed.

What is clear enough is that in his own mind he was a Christian, and therefore nothing but a Christian. Throughout the *Oration*, Constantine speaks of pagan myths and practices with unqualified contempt. Even if they were real—if their tombs and monuments were not pointed out by their own votaries—the pagan gods would set us examples only of strife, impurity and petulance; each is at best a smallholder in the universe, and as a group they could not hope to maintain the harmonious balance of the elements. Idols are

[42] Cf. Acts 5.32. 'Servant of God' is also a possible translation. See further Ison (1985b).
[43] Cf. Plato, *Timaeus* 28c.
[44] See Chapter 3, this volume.
[45] See Kraft (1955), 213 on the possible influence of Hermetism.

human figments, while the fables of poets are charters for depravity. Nothing more edifying can be expected of the rites which are engendered by these myths, and yet it is not, at the time of speaking, the emperor's purpose to suppress them:

> Away with you, impious ones (for this command is laid on you on account of your incorrigible sin) to the slaughter of victims and sacrifices, your revelry and feasting and carousing, as you profess to offer worship while you devise unbridled pleasures and debaucheries, and pretend to make sacrifice while you are in thrall to your own pleasures. For you do not know any good, nor the first commandment of the great God, who gave laws to the human race and committed the government of their lives to his child so that those who lived rightly and with discretion should, according to his child's judgment, obtain a second life that was good and happy.

What can be made of this scornful injunction, in view of a contemporary historian's testimony that after Constantine had won control of the east he forbade not only provincial governors but the populace to erect statues, to practise divination or to offer sacrifice?[46] All this is related by Eusebius before he comes to the Council of Nicaea, which took place within seven months of Constantine's victory over Licinius in November 324. It is clear that if his statement is true, and his ordering of materials is strictly chronological, the *Oration to the Saints* could not have been delivered as late as 325. If, as is more probable, he has interrupted the narrative of events in order to make a convenient digest of the laws that Constantine issued as sole emperor, we must assume that this prohibition of sacrifice was a later ordinance, not even foreseen in the immediate aftermath of his success. It is commonly acknowledged that, whatever he may have decreed, he did not put an end to the custom of sacrifice, and that no text of the law to which Eusebius alludes is found in the Theodosian Code. While this silence does not refute Eusebius, it leaves us seeking a witness to corroborate his report.[47]

CONSTANTINE'S LEGISLATION

It is natural to suppose that the acts of Constantine as statesman and legislator will throw some light upon his personal religion. We cannot assume, however, that he must have been a tepid or equivocating Christian if he aimed at anything less than a complete annihilation of paganism. A king who means to rule—and a king must rule—should be wise enough to know that he cannot force or suborn the conscience of an entire population. Even a Christian

[46] Eusebius, *Life of Constantine* 2.45.

[47] See Chapter 10 in this volume.

monarch who did not fear his subjects might adopt a policy of tolerance, not in spite of his Christianity but because of it, on the principle that coercion is inferior to persuasion as a means of winning souls. Failure to sack a temple, to smash an idol or to baptize by reluctant immersion might be evidence of weakness or impiety in a mediaeval potentate; in the Roman world it betokened a desire to reconcile the faith of the ruler with the ancestral cults through which the various peoples under his sway had been wont to express their acquiescence. Even the retention of symbols traditionally associated with the pagan gods would not be proof of divided allegiance, since a Christian could simply put his own construction upon them, leaving pagans to misunderstand them at their own peril. Christian apologists had urged since the second century that, although they acclaimed Christ as the sun of righteousness and turned to the east in the morning when they prayed, they were not worshipping the sun;[48] solar imagery on Constantine's coinage thus affords no proof that he was a solar monotheist at heart, any more than the legend '*fidei defensor*' on British coins affords any proof that the monarch is at heart a Roman Catholic. The arch in Rome, which attributed Constantine's victory first to Jupiter Optimus Maximus and then to an unidentified *numen*, testifies to the prudence of the senate, not to any subterfuge or temporization on his part.

A thoroughgoing suppression of pagan rites and places of worship would of course be an undeniable mark of Christian zeal, if not of a Christian spirit. Libanius, writing two generations after his death, has been quoted to demonstrate both that he passed an evil law against sacrifice and that he made 'absolutely no alteration' in the forms of worship.[49] Neither statement is likely to be more true than it needed to be to fulfil his rhetorical purpose on each occasion, but the second is more consistent both with Constantine's retention of the title Pontifex Maximus and with the letter of thanks for his favour that he received in 326 from a priest of the Eleusinian mysteries.[50] The papyrus which preserves this cannot prove that he was equally accommodating ten years later; had tolerance died with age, however, we might expect to hear of numerous measures against the pagans in Eusebius, the one ancient witness who ascribes to Constantine a general decree against sacrifice. Yet even he records the destruction of no more than a handful of shrines, with an exultation no doubt born of his pleasure in having something to say against those who accused the emperor of excessive lenity. These assaults (as we saw in Chapter 6) included the removal of idols from the site of the Holy Sepulchre in Jerusalem, the expulsion of every trace of paganism from the new city of Constantinople, the abolition of eunuch-priests in Egypt, the purification of

[48] Malachi 4.2; Tertullian, *Apology* 16.10.
[49] Bardill (2012), 285–6; see Chapter 10, in this volume.
[50] Bardill (2012), 304.

the rites performed in honour of Abraham at Mamre, the razing of two temples of Aphrodite in Phoenicia which had been nurseries of lewd practice, and the destruction of a Cilician shrine in which the healings allegedly performed by Asclepius rivalled those of Christ. In all these cases Constantine's zeal was intensified by the manifest profanity of the site or by some clear impediment to his own plan for the glorification of God. Let us now turn to the evidence of his legislation.

1. In 320 Constantine repealed the law which allowed the state to confiscate the property of a man who died without legitimate issue.[51] Eusebius hints that the measure was designed for the protection of ascetics, but, so far as is known, there were no exponents of eremitic or monastic piety in those provinces which were under the sway of Constantine in this year. In any case, ascetics would already have divested themselves of all possessions, whether by donating them to the community that they had entered, by giving them to the poor in accordance with Christ's injunction and Antony's example, or by testamentary disposition to their more worldly relatives. Although such acts were subject to annulment before the law permitting this was repealed by Constantine, the Christian was in no worse case than any pagan philosopher who had elected not to marry. It could be argued that the clergy, in the west as in the east, stood in more peril than their pagan counterparts because an unmarried man ordained to the Christian ministry was not encouraged to take a wife. But in this period most conciliar rulings on that question were made in the east, where Constantine was not yet emperor; moreover, even if it could be proved that clerical celibacy was a norm in the west, we should not forget one other powerful class that would have welcomed relief from the penalties of childlessness—the very class whose conduct the law had been designed to regulate when it was introduced by Augustus.[52] Senatorial families had great wealth to dispose of and perennial difficulty in producing legitimate heirs; there was no other order so capable of repaying the exchequer for its indulgence, and none that would feel such a need of it, if half of what we hear of the fiscal rapacity of Maxentius is true.
2. A law of 321 permits divorce by mutual consent, but restricts the grounds on which either party has a unilateral right to dissolve the marriage. A woman may cite only murder, sorcery and sacrilege, while a wife found guilty of sorcery, adultery or working as a procuress has no appeal against her offended husband.[53] Since Roman law had hitherto permitted either party to dissolve the union merely by sending a letter to

[51] *Theodosian Code* 8.16.1; cf. Grubb (1993), 122–6.
[52] See further Clark (1993), 150–6.
[53] *Theodosian Code* 3.16.1; see further Grubb (1993), 129.

the other, we may assume that any new impediments would have been approved by the Christians of the empire, to whom Christ had forbidden divorce except on one condition—*porneia*—the meaning of which is still debated.[54] It may be that the law was designed to bring about as close an approximation to Christian teaching on the indissolubility of marriage as the subjects of Constantine could be asked to bear. Rather than ask why it was not more stringent, we should reflect that even Christian societies have been obliged to find ways of breaking an intolerable yoke, and that Constantine himself (the son of a concubine) contracted more than one marriage. At the same time, it is likely enough that Christians were not the only group to deplore the inconveniences that arose from serial marriage, with its inevitable counterplot of contested dowries, unresolved intrigues, and supplanted heirs.

3. A law enacted when Constantine and Licinius shared the consulship extended to Christian minsters the exemption from municipal obligations that had long been enjoyed by members of other priesthoods.[55] As similar provisions had been made long before on behalf of pagan temples, and were not to be rescinded during the reign of Constantine or his immediate successors, this measure secured equality for the Christians, but with no recognition or promise of hegemony.[56]
4. Two decrees of 321 declare the *Dies Solis* ('day of the sun') to be 'venerable' and 'illustrious because of its veneration'. Litigation is pronounced to be inconsistent with its dignity, and a complete cessation of work in the towns is also enjoined, though agricultural labour is exempted on both occasions. There is reason to suspect, as Girardet notes, that these pronouncements merely ratified previous acts of legislation.[57] The practice of freeing slaves by *manumissio in ecclesia*, reserved for the Sunday in 321, is attested, without restriction to any particular day of the week, as early as 316.[58] Earlier still is an inscription in which Constantine grants the citizens of a Pannonian spa extraordinary permission to hold a market on a Sunday for the duration of the next year.[59] This is the exception that 'proves the rule', in the only logical sense that can be

[54] Matthew 19.9, more liberal than Mark 10.11 or Luke 16.18.

[55] *Theodosian Code* 16.2.2, reinforced with reference to the minor clergy at 16.2.7 (AD 330). In both decrees the peculiar sanctity of the clerical office is affirmed. At 16.8.4 (331 AD) similar immunities are guaranteed to 'fathers of synagogues'. Cf. 16.8.2. At Eusebius, *Church History* 10.7.2 the privileges are restricted to catholic clergy. On the rigour with which these curial duties were commonly enforced by Constantine see Pietri (1983), 74–5.

[56] See Barnes (1981a), 50 on the debate as to whether bequests to the church were also immune from taxation under Constantine.

[57] Girardet (2008), 344–57.

[58] Girardet (2008), 352–5, citing *Codex Justinianum* 1.13.1.

[59] Girardet (2008), 355–7, citing *Corpus Inscriptionum Latinarum* III, 4121.

can be attached to that stale adage. In 321 a Sunday Sabbath will therefore have been no novelty under Constantine's jurisdiction; how much of a novelty was it when first promulgated? If a papyrus of 313 has been read correctly by scholars, Thursday had already been appointed as a day of rest in Egypt, perhaps by Diocletian, whose patron Jupiter was also the god after whom this day was named.[60] There are cryptic intimations in authors of the second century that the observance of the Jewish holiday was not uncommon among the Gentiles.[61] The earlier the date that we assign to it, the less reason we have to assume that Constantine's choice of Sunday had a Christian motive. The fact that he does not use the term *kuriakê* (i.e. the Lord's Day) as Eusebius does in reporting him,[62] may be a proof of nothing but that *Dies Solis* was the name by which the day was universally known; it may also bespeak a desire to avoid offence, to express a belief in the unity of religions or simply to promote the cult of the sun. Constantine, as is well known, makes abundant use of solar imagery on coins,[63] in statuary and even in religious proclamations, though a discussion of the competing inferences that these facts have prompted will be postponed to a later section of this chapter.

5. Provision is made in a law of uncertain date[64] for the referral of a case, at the request of a single litigant, from a civil court to the 'hearing' (*audientia*) of a bishop, who will judge according to the *lex Christiana*, the Christian law.[65] The meaning of the last phase is obscure, and in later reports of such appeals the judge—or arbiter, as he is often styled—proceeds according to the 'Roman' (that is, the civil) law. But these are not the circumstances envisaged by Constantine, for he does not make the bishop an arbiter—a referee acceptable to two parties who have yet to reach agreement—but an autocrat whose decision will supersede one that has been rendered, or was about to be rendered, in a previous court. To confer such authority on a single prelate in a case where neither litigant was a Christian would be to give the church a greater and more universal power than is accorded to it in any other act of Constantinian legislation.[66] It is therefore reasonable to

[60] Girardet (2008), 343, citing *Oxyrhynchus Papyri* 3741. Cf. Barnes (1997), 656 n. 47.

[61] Tertullian, *Against the Nations* 13.4.

[62] *Life of Constantine* 4.18.1. Tertullian, *Apology* 16.11, is content to write *dies solis*.

[63] See especially Bruun (1966), 243–8.

[64] Perhaps 318. The authencity of an addendum in the so-called Sirmondian canons is doubted by Drake (2000), 325. See further Vessey (1993).

[65] *Theodosian Code* 1.27.1. Corcoran (1993), 111–13 doubts that Licinius can have been a party to it. There are, however, many untested assumptions in his argument that the chief beneficiary would have been an Arian bishop, Eusebius of Nicomedia, and that this fact would have been urged against Licinius by his Catholic detractors.

[66] Drake (2000), 323 understands this law to mean that the case can be taken to the bishop by the will of either party. Humfress (2011) argues that the consent of both parties was required and that the judgment of the bishop was referred to the court in which the proceedings began.

assume that the law was intended only for trials in which at least one of the parties was already a professing Christian.

6. A law of 316 ordains that the crimes of those who had been condemned to the games or the mines should be branded not on the face but on the limbs, so that the punishment would not mar the 'likeness of celestial beauty'.[67] The circumlocution may have been intended to give a more universal colour to the sentiment; or perhaps he was not yet ready to offend his pagan subjects by adopting the biblical usage 'image of God' in a public document.[68] Whether he avowed a Christian motive when he abolished crucifixion as a mode of judicial punishment we cannot say, as neither the date nor the text of his decree has been preserved.[69] In the rescript of 325 which put an end to execution by gladiatorial combat, he begins by deploring all bloody entertainments, yet does not extend the scope of his ruling, here or elsewhere, beyond the judicial practice of *damnatio in ludum* 'condemnation to the games'.[70]
7. A law of uncertain date prescribes fearsome penalties for the abductor of a virgin, for those who abet him and for the virgin herself if she be found guilty of consent.[71] Slaves who assist the criminal are to be burned alive; if the nurse is an accomplice, her mouth and throat are to be sealed with molten lead. This conversion of a private tort into a heinous crime protected the domestic merchandise of all families, not only those who were Christian; but only a Christian legislator would have echoed the casuistry of Deuteronomy 22.23–27, where rules are laid down for determining the culpability of the molested virgin. Constantine in fact exceeds the rigour of Moses by passing a law which relates to all virgins, not merely to those already betrothed. He also adds a new clause which states that parents are to be punished if they connive at the abduction.[72] While there may have been instances in which one parent plotted against the other, or impecunious parents found it expedient to have their daughter stolen without a dowry, it is possible that Constantine had in mind the latter-day Thecla who had pledged herself to virginity for life. Such a woman was almost certain to be a Christian, and an outlaw in her own family even if they were Christians also; it may therefore have appeared that her resolve could be protected only by sanctions of unprecedented severity.

[67] *Theodosian Code* 9.40.2. [68] Genesis 1.26, 28; 9.6.

[69] Sozomen, *Church History* 1.18.13; cf. Aurelius Victor, *Caesars* 41.4.

[70] *Theodosian Code* 15.12.1. On the continuance of the games see Macmullen (1990), 167 and Wiedemann (1995), 156–7.

[71] *Theodosian Code* 9.24.1.

[72] Abduction was a traditional means to marriage, though perhaps a decadent custom, at least among Romans, in this period: Arjava (1996), 37–41.

NOTES ON TOLERATION

When the new city of Constantinople was created from the 'Severan embellishments' to the old Byzantium in 330,[73] no temples were dedicated to pagan deities and no gladiatorial shows reminded Christians of their tribulations under pagan rulers. In the forum, however, a porphyry column supported a colossal image of Constantine, the extravagance of which became a mark for pagan satire. If Christians could not charge him with a breach of the Ten Commandments (which forbid not the making of images but the worship of them), there must been some who thought its crown of seven rays more worthy of an idol. Later observers took it for a representation of Helios the sun-god, while apologists for the Christian emperor guessed that he had transformed an existing statue of Apollo.[74] Since, however, Constantine is often depicted in a similar fashion on the coins of his reign,[75] we need not doubt that this monument was designed for him and under his direction. We should not be too quick to infer that his Christianity was a fraud, that he was at heart a solar monotheist or that he was simply too ignorant to grasp the exclusive claims of his religion:[76] his own words, far less open to interpretation than any visual icon, prove the contrary. Up to his time there was barely such a thing as Christian art, and he had no choice but to avail himself of icons and motifs that were already familiar to his pagan subjects. The choice that he made on this occasion would not have seemed an unnatural or an impious one to those who regarded him as the earthly surrogate of Christ, the sun of righteousness; Christ's own votaries, after all, had not refrained from facing the dawn in prayer when they saw that this practice had led some pagans to mistake him for a solar deity.

Inscriptions are also monuments—in purpose at least the most public, the most enduring and the most perspicuous media of political discourse. In a rescript preserved in marble at Orcistus in Galatia, Constantine restores the city to its ancient status and releases the inhabitants from the duty of subsidizing the cults of the city to which Orcistus had been annexed. Although their petition was only for civic honours and exemptions, he grants it all the more readily because the majority of them are 'of the true faith'.[77] Against this unsolicited profession of Christianity we may set the decree recorded in an inscription at Hispellum, where the citizens had requested, without disguising

[73] Potter (2013), 259. On the novelty of the choice, and the reasons for it, see Grig and Kelly (2012), 6–9.

[74] Fowden (1994).

[75] Barnes (2011), 18–23 is rightly critical of attempts to deduce the paganism of Constantine from such traditional emblems.

[76] Cf. Bardill (2012), 36.

[77] For text, translation and commentary see Chastagnol (1981), who argues that this inscription marks the first stage in the separation of pagan religion from the state.

their paganism, that their priest should no longer be bound to undertake an arduous journey to Volsinii, and that instead they should be permitted to build a temple of their own.[78] Constantine replies without censure, endorsing the dedication of a temple to his own family, the *gens Flavia*, and that every year a priest appointed by Umbria should stage both plays and gladiatorial shows within the new precincts. As he makes the further provision that the rites at Volsinii should not be suspended, it might seem that this inscription, set up perhaps as late as 335, is a document not only of toleration but of connivance with religions that any Christian would have judged to be superstitious. It should be observed, however, that he does not undertake to subsidize the temple (which was already under construction) and stipulates that it must not be defiled by irrational beliefs. Worded, as he himself implies, in accordance with ancient custom, this clause was no doubt intended to exclude rites of the kind that he had already suppressed in the eastern provinces. He could justly claim that these rites would have been offensive to the senate that suppressed the Bacchanals in 186 BC; if therefore his imperial predecessors had been more indulgent to lewd and exotic abuses, this was all the more reason for him to demonstrate by his legal policy that a Christian—and only a Christian, as the Latin apologists argued—could be trusted to uphold the virtues to which Rome owed her greatness.

Among the principal causes of Rome's prosperity, says Polybius, was her custom of uniting religious with political office.[79] Constantine agreed, and by retaining the ancient title Pontifex Maximus he gave notice of his intention to regulate all religious practice in his empire. Eusebius records that he also styled himself the '*episkopos* of those outside'.[80] The conventional translation of *episkopos* as 'bishop' has led a modern scholar to wonder why he should claim this status rather than that of a priest.[81] In his own tongue the word for 'priest' would be either *presbyter*, an elder, or *sacerdos*, a performer of sacrifices: it is hard to imagine what either of these terms would have conveyed had he applied it to himself. It will not be possible even to pose this unanswerable question if we restore to *episkopos* its original sense of 'overseer' or 'superintendent', which it still bore in the scriptures and in the political nomenclature of Greek communities. Whether *episkopos* represents the Latin *episcopus* in the original dictum or has been substituted for a different term, it implies here not that Constantine pretends to any ecclesiastical office,

[78] For text, translation, and commentary see Gascou (1967), who dates the inscription to 337 and argues that the Constantine's purpose was to empty the ceremonies of religious content, since he was powerless to suppress them. Cf. Cameron (2010), 141. Bardill (2012), 286, endorsing the date of 337, holds Constans to be the true author.

[79] Polybius, *Histories* 6.56.

[80] Angelov (2014) maintains that this royal episcopate was limited to those outside the church but within the empire.

[81] Rapp (1998), 594–5.

but that the office that he performs for 'those outside' is the political complement to the pastoral ministry which is exercised by bishops within the church. The new title invites comparison with another which, although it had long been current among the Latin-speaking clergy, had not yet been employed without satire. Tertullian had raged against a bishop of bishops, a *pontifex maximus*—surely the Bishop of Rome—who had made terms for the readmission of apostates, murderers and adulterers to communion (*On Modesty*). Cyprian had declared, in his preamble to the seventh council of Carthage, that 'for us there is no bishop among the bishops, for all of us await the judgment of God'. If Optatus can be trusted, Constantine's first response when the Donatists sought his arbitration was an echo of this saying. We need not doubt that, as an intelligent man who read his own tongue with great fluency, he was fully aware of what he had left unsaid; when, therefore, he styled himself the '*episkopos* of those outside', he will have known that he was eschewing the title 'bishop of bishops' for a second time.

10

The End of Sacrifice

Paraphrasing rather than quoting the laws that his hero promulgated as emperor of the west, Eusebius attributes to him a general prohibition of sacrifices (*Life of Constantine* 2.45). Scholars have seldom noted that his evidence is partly corroborated by Optatus of Milevis in his tractate against the Donatists (2.15), though this Latin author also fails to reproduce the exact words of the statute to which he alludes. The absence of any such interdict in the Theodosian Code has led many scholars to suspect that our Christian witnesses have exaggerated the scope of legislation which, to judge by the third and fourth books of the *Life*, was applied selectively to cults that offended the emperor by their prurience or their parodies of Christian symbolism. Even if Timothy Barnes is right to argue that some vestiges of this measure have survived in other documents,[1] it cannot be maintained that sacrifice ceased in the reign of Constantine: had that been so, the Theodosian Code would not contain the law against sacrifice which was issued by his sons. In this they purport to be upholding the policy of their father, but do not make reference to a particular statute. Of course, no Roman autocrat could enforce his legislation through the tentacular institutions of the modern state, and the Theodosian Code is only the flotsam of a much larger body of juridical matter. We cannot, then, infer that a law was not passed because we have no record of its enactment and no proof of its execution; we can infer that the cessation of sacrifice, which is undoubtedly a phenomenon of the fourth century, was not the result of any one edict framed by Constantine.

In part it was the result of mass conversion to Christianity, the impact of which on the pagan religious economy, already attested in the second century, could only be increased when imperial policy began to favour those who renounced the old gods. Some historians argue that animal sacrifice was already in decline before this period, though we do not see any evidence of

[1] Barnes (2011), 6 cites an ambiguous allusion in Libanius, *Oration* 1.27; at *Oration* 30.6–7, however, Libanius plainly says explicitly that it was not Constantine but his son who put an end to sacrifice. On Palladas see Barnes (2011), 127–31 and the final chapter of this book. See also Barnes (2004b).

this atrophy in the stereotypical arguments of the Christian apologists. It is possible that the Christian ban on sacrifice became efficacious only when the effect could have been achieved by other means; since it failed to extinguish the beliefs that accompanied sacrifice, the pagan remnant was forced to adopt a new form of cult that involved no public offerings. While it was new it was not unheralded, for the first extended critiques of pagan sacrifice that survive are those of Porphyry, and the *Letter to Anebo* which is commonly attributed to him drew forth a defence of sacrifice from Iamblichus which was also a corrective to popular notions. On the other hand, Christianity, for all its railing against the inhumanity and superstition of pagan rites, could not entirely dispense with sacrifice or with the premiss that some shedding of blood was necessary to seal our peace with God.

THE RATIONALE OF SACRIFICE

When God says through the mouth of a prophet 'I desired mercy and not sacrifice' (Hosea 6.6), this has generally been understood to mean that he desires mercy more than sacrifice. When Jesus turns this saying against the Pharisees (Matthew 12.7), he is passing judgment on the unmerciful application of the law, not on the practices of the Temple, participation in which is assumed at Matthew 5.23–24 to be obligatory once the offices of love have been fulfilled. At Romans 12.1 Paul exhorts believers to present their bodies as a living sacrifice, and when he proclaims at 2 Corinthians 2.15 that he and his fellow-workers are a 'sweet savour of Christ to God', he is alluding to the act which 'Christ our Passover' is said to have performed on behalf of the saints at 1 Corinthians 5.7. The author of 1 Timothy 4.6 expects to be 'poured out' in the last of the mortifications that he has suffered for the gospel. Nowhere does the apostle say, however, that a believer ought to shun the Temple, any more than a Platonist, whose philosophy was a 'preparation for death',[2] took this to mean that he should bring no further oblations to the gods. The Epistle to the Hebrews, however, argues that the regular iteration of these rites was sufficient proof that they had never been efficacious and that now they had been rendered obsolete (10.11), together with the priests who had been appointed to celebrate them, by the all-sufficient death of Christ on an altar 'outside the city' (13.10–12). It is not clear whether either he or Barnabas was writing long enough after AD 70 to be sure that the Temple has been destroyed beyond hope of restoration; Barnabas brings his case not merely against the continuance of animal sacrifice, but against the Mosaic law and the bloody practice of

[2] Plato, *Phaedo* 64a.

circumcision, maintaining that from the outset God's intention was that the ceremonial ordinances should be observed in spirit only, not by the mutilation of the flesh.[3] Nevertheless, the more common opinion in the early Christian centuries was that carnal circumcision and animal sacrifice were legitimate but provisional institutions, to be at once consummated and superseded by Christ's death on Calvary.

Of pagan sacrifice Paul had said that, since it was offered to demons, a believer could take no part in it (1 Corinthians 10.20–21); at the same time, an idol being 'nothing in the world' (1 Corinthians 8.4), no harm could come of eating the meats that were sold in the shambles, apart from the offence that this might give to the weaker brethren (1 Corinthians 10.25–29). Even the consumption of these remnants was prohibited after sacrifice to the pagan gods became a test of loyalty to the empire;[4] fear of enthralment to demons precluded not only the killing of animals but libations, bloodless offerings, and the scattering of incense.[5] Apologists denounced the obscene and savage concomitants of the pagan ceremonies, hinting that it was impossible to defend the slaughter of brutes without condoning the murder of humans. According to Tertullian, this atrocity had in fact been practised in Africa up to his father's time,[6] while Minucius Felix speaks as though it were not yet obsolete (*Octavius* 9.5). Hadrian was supposed to have suppressed it,[7] while in Rome it had been abolished in 97 BC by senatorial edict;[8] Tatian asserts none the less that the cults of anthropophagous deities were still flourishing in his day at no great distance from the city (*Oration* 29). Arnobius found in Ovid that King Numa had substituted bloodless offerings for the human victims that the gods demanded;[9] no being who craves such nourishment, he retorts, can be truly divine, and if it is claimed that the worshipper must sacrifice to atone for his transgressions, it is not repentance to expiate a sin by a greater sin. Pagans retaliated by accusing Christians of Thyestean banquets and Oedipodal conjugations, on the principle (already laid down by Tacitus with respect to the Jews) that those who despise whatever is lawful for others will consider nothing unlawful among themselves.[10] To

[3] See esp. *Barnabas* 9.4 with Carleton Paget (1994), 51–63.

[4] See Revelation 2.14 and Finn (2009), 73–5.

[5] On the intimate connection in Greek society between the eating of meat and animal sacrifice, see Burkert (1983) and Detienne (1979). Paul, however, can reject sacrifice without proscribing meat, and thus stands in an obverse relation to the early Pythagoreans, who, as Rives (2011) points out, rejected meat without offering a critique of sacrifice.

[6] *Apology* 9.2, on which the comments of Barnes (1971), 21–9 are still exemplary.

[7] Lactantius, *Divine Institutes* 1.21; Porphyry, *Abstinence* 2.56; but cf. Hughes (2013), 129.

[8] Pliny, *Natural History* 30.13, cited (with most of the references in this paragraph) by Nasrallah (2011), 151.

[9] Arnobius, *Against the Nations* 5.1; Ovid, *Fasti* 3.289–326.

[10] See Edwards (1993); Rives (1995b) observes that atrocious rituals were most commonly imputed to barbarous and primitive nations.

Justin, Athenagoras, and Tatian it became apparent that every pagan cult was the contrivance of some demon, a fallen angel, who thus procured not only a surfeit of incense but unlimited dominion in the souls of his credulous adepts.[11] Those who refuse to sacrifice become willing hecatombs to these unseen tyrants; as Origen boasts, however, it is the demon who flees the courage of his victim, and God himself who receives the fragrant offering.[12] God is a man-eater, says the *Gospel of Philip*;[13] in the last times the sacrifice of beasts gives way to the spiritual sacrifice of men.

No vindication of sacrifice appears to have been attempted by a pagan before the third century AD. The reason is, no doubt, that it had never been impugned as an institution. There were groups who abstained, and philosophers who framed arguments for abstaining, from the sacrifice of meats, but Christianity was the first religious movement that denounced not merely certain kinds of offering but the altars on which they were offered. The Pythagoreans acknowledged the duty of sacrifice, though in most circumstances they offered only wine and grain. Traditions recorded by Porphyry in his *Life of Pythagoras* represent the sage as a trainer of carnivorous athletes and an occasional practitioner of animal sacrifices.[14] The hero of the treatise by Iamblichus *On the Pythagorean Life* abstains from all meat and imposes a similar ban on those of his followers who can bear it, though sparing use of meat and even sacrifice are allowed to the less proficient. In the same work he persuades the priest Abaris that the future is more legible in mathematical symbols than the entrails of an ox. What these symbols were Iamblichus does not tell us, but in his work *On the Mysteries* he concedes that the majority, who lack the philosopher's intimacy with the gods, commit no wrong if they appease the daemons with more tangible offerings. Moreover, insofar as it serves as a lesson in detachment to the worshipper, the renunciation of material goods may be a preparation for the higher modes of sacrifice. Porphyry, by contrast, has often been supposed to hold two philosophies, one of which lays down specific precepts for the feeding of our oppressors in their heavenly, sublunar, and subterranean fiefs, while the other strictly forbids us to comply with their exactions. As a closer scrutiny of his writings *On Philosophy from Oracles* and *On Abstinence* will indicate, any discord in his thought has been purposely magnified by the witnesses who preserve what remains of the first of these two books.

[11] Justin, *First Apology* 45; Athenagoras, *Embassy* 26; Tatian, *Oration* 19 and 29.

[12] Origen, *Against Celsus* 8.38–44. His strictures on the complicity of philosophers (8.63–64) are echoed by Porphyry, *On Abstinence*, p. 170.9–14 Nauck.

[13] *Nag Hammadi Codices* II.62.34–63.1. See 55.1–5 on the abrogation of animal sacrifice.

[14] Porphyry, *Life of Pythagoras* 15 (athletes) and 36 (an ox, but anomalously).

PORPHYRY *ON ABSTINENCE*

In its sacerdotal ordinances the Mosaic Law consistently distinguishes bloody from bloodless sacrifices; both kinds were equally subject to the interdict on all offerings that were not made in the temple at Jerusalem and under the direction of its priests. The fall of this institution, which greatly reduced the frequency of both kinds of offering if it did not put an end to them altogether, came to be understood by Christians as the judgment of God on the carnal interpretation of the law and an intimation that the temple cult had been only a transient foretaste of the one sacrifice, Christ's Passover on Calvary, which put away sin for ever (Hebrews 9.29; 10.12). To the author of the epistle to the Hebrews, it is self-evidently absurd that sin should be expiated by the blood of bulls (10.4); on the other hand, while Christ is metaphorically described as the first-fruits of the resurrection (1 Corinthians 15.20), the New Testament never denounces the literal offering of the fruits of the soil to God. Later in this chapter we shall ask whether the Eucharist was perceived in this epoch as a bloodless sacrifice superseding those of the Temple. In pagan literature it is often difficult to ascertain whether 'sacrifice' means the slaughter of beasts or the offering of fruits; we have far too little evidence to corroborate Nilsson's thesis that animal sacrifice waned in favour of bloodless oblations after the classical period,[15] or Louis Robert's detection of a monotheistic tendency in the Roman world which subordinated sacrifice to prayer.[16] For Christians all forms of pagan sacrifice were equally sacrilegious, since the crime lay not in the killing but in the presentation of the gift to demons: those were expelled from the church in the aftermath of the Decian persecution had often been convicted only of scattering incense, or at the worst of offering bread and wine.[17] Animal sacrifice, the habitual target of both pagan and Christian satirists, also tends to be treated as a norm in modern scholarship, even where it is differentiated from the bloodless practice. Nevertheless, the distinction is of capital importance to one pagan author of the late third century, who condemns the traditional rites of immolation with a fervour that would scarcely be explicable if they had been as moribund as Nilsson and Robert suppose.

The four books *On Abstinence*, which survive intact apart from the ending of the fourth book, are addressed to Castricius Firmus, a disciple of Plotinus who had supported his dying master from his own household in Campania while Porphyry remained in Sicily.[18] It was, however, Castricius who had proved the less faithful pupil, abandoning the vegetarian diet that Plotinus

[15] Nilsson (1945).
[16] Robert (1971), 610, cited by Petropoulou (2008), 86.
[17] On the decree and its consequences see Rives (1999).
[18] *Life of Plotinus* 2; *On Abstinence*, p. 85.2 Nauck.

had inculcated. Porphyry's admonitions, which are not intended only for Castricius, imply that the consumption of meat is always a concession to vice and error; nevertheless, he protests that he is not agitating for the repeal of laws that have hitherto governed states and peoples. His arguments are counsels of perfection, and for the most part philosophical, not theological in tenor: one need not be a theologian to maintain that beasts are as rational as men (187.6ff.), that the principle of benevolence should be extended to all species, or that even if some animals must be killed for the protection of our own lives and resources, it does not follow that we should eat them (133.4ff.). The reasoning is not always altruistic, since a philosopher has a duty to cultivate his highest faculties, and Porphyry subscribes to the homoeopathic assumption of some medical writers that the eating of brutes gives rise to a brutish temper in the soul.

It is in Book 2 that he demonstrates the futility of animal sacrifices. There are, he maintains, three motives for sacrificing: to honour the gods, to thank them and to obtain from them what is necessary to life. But a god cannot be honoured unjustly, cannot be thanked for injustice, cannot be moved by an unjust petition. The sacrifice of animals is theft because, when we kill a living creature, we part it from its soul against its will (142.21–143.3). We do not commit any such robbery on the plant—this perhaps in answer to the Manichees—because plants will drop their fruits in time even if we refrain from plucking them (143.3–15). The most archaic rites are those which honour the gods by the kindling of fire, the element that is closest to them in nature (135.20–21); that plants were the first consumable things to be offered is evident from the universal practice of the nations (156.1–10). Historical research and the diversity of customs, on the other hand, reveal that animal sacrifice arose in one place after another from adventitious causes as virtue withered or want prevailed. In one place humans turned upon their own kind for lack of food; on another an ox was rashly killed in anger (158.15–160.24); in both a laudable instinct led the murderers to devise new rituals of propitiation, but they then fell into the error of supposing that it was the murder itself that rendered the gods propitious. Barbarians spill human blood on their altars to this day (156.10–22); the Greeks abhor such victims, but the selfishness of their motives is apparent from the fact that they sacrifice only animals that they can use for meat.

Yet we are not the sole authors of our crimes, though we bear the guilt of them. Below the incorporeal and immutable source of being, and below the world-soul, which is not defiled by anything in the world that it governs, human affairs are administered by two races of daemons, one uniformly benevolent while the other has a capacity only for evil.[19] To the good daemons,

[19] See Johnson (2013a), 96–8 on the rigidity of Porphyry's distinction between the daemons and the gods.

we owe the tools of art and agriculture and the tempering of the climate to our needs (167.8–20 Nauck). Earthquakes and tempests, famine and plague are the visitations of evil daemons, who wish to terrify us into worshipping them because their aerial bodies hunger insatiably for the smoke and incense that arises from our altars (169.10–15).[20] They perfect their stratagem by spreading the false belief that it is the highest gods who desire these vicious offerings, though the truth, as our shrines and oracles inform us, is that the gods accept only bloodless gifts and only when they are tendered with a pure heart. The sorcerers whom the daemons employ as lackeys promise us purity but have none to bestow; on the contrary, they persuade us to go on sacrificing animals because they know that the soul remains earthbound after a violent death and that its presence attracts the daemons in greater numbers (175.6–176.2). It is these evil daemons who teach us the art of haruspication from the entrails of the dead beast (172.2–3): the philosopher who is indifferent to the honour and wealth of this world will have nothing to do with these stimulants to cupidity. With the assistance of the good daemons, who warn us in dreams of the machinations of their evil counterparts (171.4–12), he will learn to spare his body everything that foments passion or occludes judgment, dining only on vegetables and offering to the gods only what he eats, in order that his soul may join them at last in their serenity, alone with the alone.

PORPHYRY'S *PHILOSOPHY FROM ORACLES*

Plutarch had no notion of such calculated maleficence in high places.[21] Numenius, Porphyry's second-century mentor, has spoken of a ceaseless war between demons of dusk and dawn,[22] but he was as much a Gnostic as anyone could be without being a Christian in antiquity. Porphyry, who denounced the Christians and disarmed the Gnostics, takes a view of demons that would have seemed, if anything, too jaundiced to a Christian, for in crediting them with power to shake the earth and change the climate he implies that God does not restrain his vassals. It may be for this reason that it is not *On Abstinence* but a more encyclopaedic treatise *On the Philosophy to be Derived from Oracles*, that was commandeered in the interests of the gospel by Eusebius. The original is lost, but in a study of religious conflict in the age of Constantine, a synopsis of this tendentious redaction, taking due account of the redactor's

[20] Marx-Wolf (2010) asserts that these acts are also ascribed to demons in patristic sources, but I have not been able to trace them. She opines, with Simmons (2009) that Porphyry hoped to unite all seekers in a universal way to liberation; although Johnson (2013a), 105–10 also gives some countenance to this view, I am inclined to think that, in saying that he could not find such a way, Porphyry is mocking the Christian claim that there is one way and no other.

[21] On his demonology see Brenk (1977).

[22] Numenius, Fr. 37 Des Places.

subterfuge where it is evident, will be more instructive than any utopian effort to restore the treatise to its pristine form.[23]

The first extract in Eusebius, which appears to come from the proem to the opening book, declares that none of the oracles collected in the treatise has suffered change or augmentation, but for occasional corrections to the syntax, metrical supplements and pruning of otiose matter (Fr. 303.15–22 Smith). Wherever, then, the reader of this collection meets a philosophic doctrine, it is not because the editor has insinuated his own thoughts into the text but because the gods have a natural propensity to speak the truth. (Eusebius has evidently performed his own rites of exculpation here, for in the passages that he transcribes there is not an atom of philosophy.) The veracity of the oracles will be gauged best by those whose one concern in life has been the liberation of the soul. To those of mediocre understanding the gods are so formidable that even Pan, a mere acolyte of Dionysus, has been known to leave nine men dead by a sudden epiphany. The sarcasm of Eusebius stifles Porphyry's defence of the ritual acts which enable worshippers to approach their gods without fear of annihilation, but the oracles that he retains prescribe the dedication of water to Hera (Fr. 309.11), the beating of timbrels in honour of Rhea (309.6), the mourning of Osiris (309.14) and the orgiastic cult of Dionysus (307.20ff.).

The principal expositor of divine mysteries is Apollo, and from him we learn that gods are of four orders—chthonic or earthly, marine, subterranean, and celestial—each demanding the sacrifice of a different kind of victim. To the gods of earth one offers four-footed animals, which, in keeping with their habitat, must be black (Fr. 315.29–34). A trench must be dug for offerings to subterranean powers; to those who live above the soil we raise altars (315.35–37). Winged fowl suffice the other gods, and these again must be black for those who dwell in the dusky ocean (315.20). White birds are the portion of the supernal gods, the whole carcase being presented to those of the air, while those of the aether and upper heaven require no more than the extremities (315.21–25). Precepts for the fashioning of images follow. Those of Pan should be goat-legged, cloven footed and two-horned; Hecate's should be white-robed, while her waxen effigies should bear a lamp, a whip and a sword and be encircled by the figure of a snake. Her colours should be white and red and gold, which, like the three trophies, reinforce her triple character; this in turn corresponds (as we learn elsewhere) to the three divisions of the soul and to the demiurgic and unitive power which Hecate exerts in all three provinces of matter.

It will be observed that the gods who figure most largely in this account are not those whose oracles were most frequently consulted in antiquity; there

[23] Johnson (2013a), 132 defends the consistency of Porphyry on the grounds that he never advocates the blood-sacrifices which he describes in this work.

were indeed few local shrines of Hecate, who was most often invoked in witchcraft, though she was both a more public and a more potent deity in Hesiod. In Porphyry's time, however, the famous oracles were extinct, and among the utterances that he has collected are some that exhort the Greeks to learn from revelations to other peoples . Apollo couples the Hebrews with the Chaldaeans as wise races who paid due reverence to the 'king who is born of himself'. Porphyry is relying on some other source than the Bible when he adds that the Hebrews had also embraced the Chaldaean notion of seven heavens, each identical with one of the planetary spheres (Fr. 324.15–18). For Eusebius, however, it is enough that one of Porphyry's gods should testify to the wisdom of these barbarians, and all the better that he should be Apollo, who, according to Eusebius' *Life of Constantine*, had planted the iron in the soul of Diocletian by complaining that his freedom to prophesy had been curtailed by the 'righteous on earth'.

Porphyry's second book defines the instruments and the bounds of divine activity. A long oracle divides angels into three classes: those who are always in the presence of the Almighty, those who depart to carry out his errands or convey his decrees and those who intone perpetual hymns of praise. In addition to these ministers, there are evil demons, subjects of the Egyptian god Sarapis, who must be exorcised in preparation for the approach of gods. It is to them that the ignorant offer bloody and unwholesome sacrifices, and their reward is to be puffed up with crass vapours which give rise to wordless gibbering and bombast (Fr. 326.26–34). Whether these squatters are driven out by force or suborned by rituals of appeasement, the recipient of the prayers will be Pluto, tyrant of the nether world—whom the oracles know, however, to be identical with God (326.8–12). Apollo tells one suppliant that he cannot reveal himself until the daemons have received their tribute of wine, milk, fruits and entrails; on another occasion, when asked to foretell the sex of an unborn child, he replies that she will be a girl by the edict of the stars. This edict would appear to be identical with the will of Zeus, yet Zeus is not the donor of any oracle in Porphyry's collection. The lesser gods, if constrained to speak in an unpropitious season, can avoid deception only by giving notice that the response will be untrue.

The excerpts that Eusebius appears to have culled from the third book of the *Philosophy from Oracles* mark little advance on the other two, except that Apollo warns us still more candidly of the impending deceit, while Hecate finds a number of ways—all futile—of protesting against the coercive importunity of their suitors. Verses ascribed to Pythagoras make Hecate submit to the conjurations of a 'mortal man', while other lines prescribe expressly that incantations should be accompanied by a 'mortal flute'. Eusebius adds acid to his own scorn by citing Porphyry's exclamation that no teaching could be plainer, or more consonant with the character of the gods and the physical world (Fr. 349.11–16). An oracle attributed to Hecate declares that the ignorant followers of Christ are wrong to revere him as a god, although he exercised the most august of the faculties that pertain to the divine element in the soul. Such blasphemy is not easily forgiven, and Eusebius encourages his readers to think of Porphyry as a vacillating hypocrite who truckles in the *Philosophy from Oracles* to the beings whose machinations he condemned in his work *On Abstinence*.[24] The caricature is subtle enough to transform an enemy into a grudging ally, as Porphyry cannot redeem himself without speaking like a Christian. What Apollo was to Porphyry the latter is to Eusebius—a witness, albeit a disingenuous one and under compulsion—to the truths that he is predisposed by nature and self-interest to conceal.

PORPHYRY AND ANEBO

Scholars are now less confident than they once were in assigning the superstitious works of Porphyry to his youth and the more rational ones to the years that followed his sojourn with Plotinus.[25] For one thing, the author of the *Life of Plotinus*, at the age of sixty-seven, was still more credulous than his master had ever been. For another, the *Philosophy from Oracles* cannot be so early a work, as it speaks of a life spent in the study of such phenomena. Finally, the *Letter to Anebo*, which is commonly assumed to be the fruit of this Indian summer of rationality, frames questions to the Egyptian priests which would not have needed to ask if he had written books in which they were already answered. This document survives now in two polemical redactions: a long extract or epitome in Eusebius' *Preparation for the Gospel*,[26] and a piecemeal refutation in the treatise *On the Mysteries* attributed to Iamblichus. These versions agree in the spirit but not in the letter; since it is likely that both appeared in the age of Constantine, the following summary will draw on both without endeavouring to decide which is the more faithful.

How is it, Porphyry wonders, that the priests invoke the gods as their superiors, yet command them as inferiors?[27] Why is spotless purity demanded of the postulant when the gods themselves not only assist us in lechery, but command it? How can gods as powerful as the sun and moon be awed into speaking the truth by threats which they know to be fictitious? Are they children, to believe that a man can open the pit of Hades or disperse the limbs of Osiris once again?[28] The Egyptians may profess to have seen their

[24] Cf. Addey (2014), 93.

[25] See Bidez (1913).

[26] *Preparation* 5.10; see also 5.7 and 14.10. A reconstruction is attempted by Sodano (Bibliography A).

[27] See Eusebius, *Preparation* 5.10 for much of the matter in this paragraph.

[28] Cf. Iamblichus, *On the Mysteries* 6.5.

deities ensconced in mud or seated on a lotus,[29] or even changing form to match the constellations of the zodiac; but in that case they have failed to unmask the products of their own fantasy, having no conception (according to their apologist Chaeremon[30]) of any deity who is not a physical element. If all this is said in riddles, can they not divulge the meaning of the riddle? Why are all their mysteries wrapped up in barbarous terms which (we are told) will not bear translation into Greek?[31] We cannot suppose that Egyptian is the language of the gods, or indeed that they use any language heard among mortals. Clearly these are the sophistries of jugglers and impostors—all the more futile because, if the higher gods are impassible, then none of our menaces, prayers, and immolations can subdue them, while the lower gods will be too weak to do us service. Useless as it is in securing happiness, this mummery is not even equal to its stated purpose: no god and no good daemon will be cajoled or intimidated by such arts.

Sacrifice raises a paradox that is calculated to seem intractable: why should the gods, who batten on the smoke from our altars, require us to abstain from eating meat before we approach them?[32] And why, if they are defiled by such repasts, are the practitioners of 'theagogy' required to make use of animal carcasses?[33] What utility is there to the gods in such oblations, or to the worshipper who offers them? Eusebius, who goes on to juxtapose passages from *The Philosophy from Oracles*, declares exultantly that in the *Letter to Anebo* it is the 'noble gods' who crave our sacrifices. Why then did Porphyry not foresee the response given by Iamblichus—that our offerings are made not to gods but to daemons[34]—which is only an iteration of his own teaching in other works? One possible solution, though it seems never to have been hazarded, is that Porphyry was not after all the author of the letter, which is nowhere attributed to him in the text of *On the Mysteries*.[35] Another, less audacious, would be to reckon it among his juvenilia, surmising as a corollary that the rebuttal by Iamblichus was a late showpiece, written to prove that it could be written, just as Origen wrote *Against Celsus* to ensure that his dead adversary would not go unrefuted. The third, and to many (no doubt) the most seductive, would be to read the letter, not as an ingenuous statement of the author's difficulties, but as a 'maieutic' exercise, a piece of midwifery on the part of a tutor who hoped to bring forth just such a rejoinder as the one that we

[29] Cf. Iamblichus, *On the Mysteries* 7.1–3.
[30] Cf. Iamblichus, *On the Mysteries* 8.4.
[31] Discussed at more length in *On the Mysteries* 7.
[32] Iamblichus, *On the Mysteries* 5.1; cf. Augustine, *City of God* 10.11.
[33] Iamblichus, *On the Mysteries* 6.1–2.
[34] See e.g. *On the Mysteries* 5.10 and 14. On the hierarchy of superhuman agents see Book 1.
[35] A similar opinion has been entertained with regard to a lampoon *On Sacrifices* ascribed to Lucian.

possess under the title *On the Mysteries*—a rejoinder that Porphyry's earliest detractors found it politic to ignore.[36]

GODS AND DAEMONS: IAMBLICHUS, *ON THE MYSTERIES*, BOOK 1

It is generally agreed that the author of this tract *On the Mysteries* is Iamblichus. He nowhere, however, identifies himself, any more than he names Porphyry as the author of the *Letter to Anebo*. His pseudonym Abammon has been understood to mean both 'heart of Amun'[37] and 'father of Amun':[38] in either case it includes the name of a deity who at an early date had been worshipped in Egyptian Thebes as father of the gods and then, when Thebes became the capital of the New Kingdom, had been conflated with Ra to assume the chief place of honour in the Egyptian pantheon. The choice of such a figure as his mouthpiece suggests that Iamblichus was aware that the function of a priest in Egypt was not so much to sacrifice as to provide a rationale for religious practices. The name, on the other hand, is explained by Saffrey as a calque on the Greek word *theopatôr*,[39] 'father of gods', applied by the Neoplatonists to one who had reached the loftiest plane of virtue, thereby freeing his intellect from its mortal dross.

Porphyry's cardinal error, says Abammon, is his assumption that all superhuman beings form a single class, differentiated only by locality and bodily condition. The higher gods, the daemons, the archangels, the angels and the heroes differ in essence as in rank. The essence of the highest gods precludes individuation, for deity is pure intellect, identical with its thoughts and grasping all thought in the undivided unity of truth (1.6–7). The more remote a class of beings is from the unity of the ruling principle, the greater will be the difference among its members; nevertheless, it owes this difference not to matter but to the qualities imparted by higher entities from which it receives its form (1.10). Heroes, daemons, and gods alike are properly incorporeal, and hence imperceptible to our physical senses. Bodies, when they employ them, remain extrinsic (1.17), and therefore heroes, daemons, and gods alike are immune to the passions that afflict their votaries (1.10). It is in fact our own rebellious spirits that we propitiate when we offer prayers to wrathful gods, and the evils that we hope to avert by sacrifice are born of our own false reasoning and desire (1.11).

[36] Cf. Addey (2014), 130–6.
[37] So, though tentatively, Dunand (1963), 137.
[38] Saffrey (1971), 235.
[39] Saffrey (1971), 237–8. Cf. Porphyry, *Sententiae* 32.

Whereas daemons represent the creative and generative powers of deity, heroes represent those which communicate life and shape the conduct of the soul (2.1). Archangels and angels rank between the gods and daemons; archons of are two kinds, the cosmic or sublunary and the material or hylic. The first resembles the gods in its stability while the second is diverse in aspect, turbulent in action. Gods are simple and uniform in aspect; archangels and angels may fall short of their simplicity, but do not adopt such heterogeneous guises as the daemons (2.3). Gods are immutable, even in semblance; archangels fall short of them in 'sameness', but even angels, though inferior, cannot yet be said to change. Daemons, however, 'appear at different times in different forms' (2.3). It is from the gods, but often through these intermediaries, that prophecy comes as a voice to the receptive soul that tarries on the frontier between sleep and waking. The less rational souls of women, or of males unmanned by ecstasy, are favoured because they offer less resistance to divine communication (1.11). To propose that it is only through cosmic sympathy that the irrational and inanimate can become portents is to suggest that we acquire knowledge from something lower than the intellect (3.15–17). It is true that the harmonious and immutable revolutions of the stars furnish the data of astrology, because this motion has been impressed upon them by the eternal gods (3.30); it is also true, on the other hand, that augurs base their predictions on anomalies which, if they contradict the instincts of the bird, must be deemed preternatural (3.16).

WORKING UPON THE GODS (BOOKS 4–6)

It is true that there are daemons who effect their illicit purposes through just but unlearned ministers (4.7), and that such practitioners frequently make sue of a natural sympathy between the elements (4.6). This, however, is only a further proof that the wisdom by which gods judge good and evil is not immanent to the world or to our own unassisted faculties. For all that, we cannot deduce that matter, which the gods shun, can never be of service to their devotees. Priests are required, as Porphyry notes, to keep themselves unpolluted by the smoke of animal sacrifices (5.1), and it is patently absurd to suppose that the gods are allured by the 'odours of living things'. It is equally true that, since the gods possess no matter, nothing material can nourish or pollute them (5.4), but this is not to deny that the altar has at least a pedagogic role in the economy of worship. Sacrifice is, as many say, a channel of cosmic sympathy, though Iamblichus means by this not a mechanical chain of causes but the friendship that obtains between creator and creature, the ruler and the ruled (5.8–9). As there are many such relations, so there are many forms of sacrifice, each (when duly performed) releasing the influence of the god to whom it is offered (5.10). This is not the highest or the least fallible mode of intercourse with the gods, as we learned above, but it serves for those—the great majority—who have not progressed so far as to live entirely in the intellect. The prayers of the true theurgist—of the mind set free from the carousel of worldly desire and sensuous delusion—are extolled and illustrated in the last chapters of Book 5.

If it is asked why priests are required to keep aloof from human corpses, but not from the carcasses of beasts (6.1), the answer is that the animal form has never housed a divine soul and is thus not rendered unclean by its departure. It is in any case not through the animal's flesh but through its emancipated soul that we approach the divine, for while this soul retains some likeness to ours, it acquires some kinship with the daemons by the mere fact of having shed its carnal envelope (6.3). A corpse creates no defilement in a daemon, because these superhuman beings are not susceptible of corruption (6.2). But now it seems that Iamblichus has bared his flank to the next thrust: How can beings so impassible be intimidated by the threats of mortals? The great ones, he replies, suffer no coercion (6.5): it is not such potentates as the sun and moon but lower agents—senseless, limited, irrational—who permit themselves to be overawed, or perhaps the terrestrial daemons, not because they are compelled but because they are not so indifferent as the higher powers to the threat of sacrilege (6.6). Furthermore, it is possible that the magician gains an ascendancy over lesser gods by becoming one with their overlords, whose symbols he employs (6.6).

Iamblichus thus has in common with Porphyry the belief that there is more than one order of superhuman being, and those who appear to humans in the most palpable and variable form belong to the lowest of these orders. He denies, however, that they can act independently of the loftier intelligences; indeed, they would not wish to do so, for they owe their power, their form, their essential unity to the devolved activity of the gods, and, while they are not immune to perturbation and vanity, they are not so prone to either as their human worshippers. Thus we hear nothing of their insatiable greed or of their tyrannical exaction of sacrifice from entire communities; sacrifice is treated almost as though it were a private transaction between the priest and his deity, and the former is more likely than the latter to practice coercion. Even in this case he is making use of a potency higher than the daemonic, though in putting it at the service of his own cupidity he proves himself a magician rather than a philosopher. The true benefit of sacrifice to the worshipper is the immolation of his own base desires. We may be sure, then, that as the celebrant advances in virtue and discernment, he will abandon animal sacrifice, as Iamblichus intimates in his life of Pythagoras. For Porphyry animal sacrifice is an ineluctable evil; for Iamblichus it is a good so long as the adept is capable of nothing better. He can hold this view because he does not concur with Porphyry in attributing rational souls to brutes, and can therefore deny that the act of killing them entails defilement. On the other hand, he offers only the rudiments of an apology for civic sacrifice and its concomitants, and to a Christian eye his admission that the gods require no sacrifice would be a sufficient argument for the abolition of all such practices. Why, if we have access to the highest god, should we slaughter even a dumb beast for the purpose of cajoling, coercing, or propitiating a lesser entity? And how could any such offering bring about the regeneration of the inner man, which Christ, as the one high priest and spotless victim, has now made possible by setting up his own Cross as an altar for the passions and infirmities of the flesh?

ARNOBIUS AGAINST SACRIFICE

A recent study contends that one of the cardinal premises of sacrifice in the ancient world was 'misrecognition'—that it to say, the reciprocity between deity and donor was established by a symbolic exchange with no pretence that the things exchanged were in fact of equal value.[40] If there was such a principle, it was misunderstood or purposely ignored in every Christian polemic. Arnobius, introducing his seventh book *Against the Nations*, declares that, having exposed the vanity of idols, he will now speak briefly and plainly 'of sacrifices, of the slaughter and immolation of victims, of libations, of incense and of all that makes up this category' (6.27). A pagan interlocutor protests, 'Do you hold that there ought to be no sacrifice whatsoever?'; it is not I, says Arnobius, but Varro who answers 'None' (7.1). It seems that the great antiquarian had argued, no doubt in jest, that beings of wood and stone have neither sense nor appetite, and thus can neither desire our service nor resent our injuries (7.2); Arnobius maintains that the conclusion at least is true, because the name 'god' can denote only one species of beings, which is unconfined by a body and superior to all passions (7.3–4). No deity succumbs to the weakness of pleasure, let alone the pleasure of killing which is unworthy even of mortals (7.5). Nor can we think them susceptible to anger unless we impute to them our own possibility and ephemerality (7.6). To avenge themselves on those who failed to serve them would be petulance, not justice; when did they show themselves in person to promulgate their arbitrary laws? (7.7–8). If they were justly angered by our sins, they would not allow us to purchase forgiveness (7.9), nor would they visit the penalty on an unoffending beast, which differs from us only in being incapable of rational speech—or rather, incapable of speech that we can decipher (7.10). At this point two inconsequential chapters are given over to the argument that if those who

[40] Ullucci (2012), 120–2.

attribute everything to fate are correct, the gods themselves cannot mar or improve our fortunes (7.11–12). If it is true after all that by moving them we can move the world, we must assume that the rich will always be in more favour than the poor, though even the gods will be unable to make a choice between two rich nations which are about to meet in war (7.13).

If it be urged that altars are erected not to suborn the gods but to honour them (7.14), we may ask how it can be an honour for them to receive praise from their inferiors (7.15) and to be surfeited on bloody sacrifices (7.16). We cannot be sure that the food that we lay before them with such pure hands is more edible to them than the diet of our domestic animals would be to us if they started to offer us similar devotions (7.17–18). No law of reason tells us why one deity should spurn the meat that another consumes with relish (7.19), and how it can be obligatory to divide our oblations according to sex when all philosophers know that the gods, being bodiless, are neither male nor female (7.20)? If it were true that each god has a partiality for beasts of a particular colour, reason would enjoin us to offer them only the hide, not the bones (7.21). Only if they were prone to human jealousy would one of them begrudge his favourite nutrients to others (7.22); if there are virgins among them, their chastity can be honoured in better ways than by the slaughter of virgin beasts (7.23). It is said that we must sacrifice to avert the wrath of malign gods and procure the favour of those who are more propitious; it seems, however, that they are malign or propitious not by nature but according to our capacity to bribe them (7.24). And what bribes are these—these entrails, these extremities, these inedible herbs—that would be repudiated with disgust if they were set before the worshipper himself (7.25–26)? Arnobius comes at last to incense, scoffing that the fathers of the Romans pleased their gods for centuries without this new condiment (7.27). Today, however, custom prescribes that we gather only the resin of certain trees, although the gods would need nostrils keener than ours to distinguish the forbidden aromas from those that are mandatory (7.28–29). As for the wine that is poured on incense, that is not an aliment for the gods but for those who suffer from ill health (7.30); the argument that wine is a token of honour is laughed to scorn again (7.31); if we set aside ceremonial wine with a written formula, to ensure that some remains for common use, could not the gods say that they have been cheated of all the liquor that we omit to consecrate (7.32)? Even if one were to grant that incense and wine are fit gifts for deities, how can their dignity be enhanced by garlands, by washing their statues and laying them in bed, and by the obscenities perpetrated in their names (7.33–34)? Proceeding to a comparison of the true religion with that of the Roman populace, Arnobius contends that it is because they insult their gods with corruptible offerings that the pagans believe these gods to be like themselves (7.35). Even if there are gods who come into being and live (as the pagans suppose) by treachery and caprice, there must be a higher divinity to whom the origin of these gods is known (7.36). Even if we waive the question whether there are many gods or one, it is all too evident that pagan theology is the fruit of opinion, and that only Christians worship an object worthy of their devotion (7.37–38).

Porphyry had argued only for the abolition of animal sacrifice; to a Christian any offering to a false deity was sinful, whatever the character of the victim. Arnobius, however, knowing that true conviction is achieved when the opponent becomes a witness against himself, does not reason only on Christian premises: taking his stand on ground that is common to Porphyry and Iamblichus, he proves to his philosophical interlocutor that all sacrifice, whether bloody or bloodless, is equally vulnerable to the objection that a being who requires any human sustenance must be something less than a god.

THE CHRISTIAN ALTAR

We must take care not to imply more than we mean when we say that the triumph of Christianity marked the 'end of sacrifice'.[41] It is true that the epistle to the Hebrews, in proclaiming Christ as the great high-priest and intercessor, also proclaims the supersession of the Levitical priesthood, whose offerings in the temple were merely overtures to the last and perfect oblation on the Cross; it is true that generations of apologists repeated the Psalmist's dictum that no sacrifice is required by God but that of a contrite and humble spirit. But at the same time, the words that we render 'new testament' signify the new covenant in the blood of Christ, which was prefigured in his pouring of the wine at a meal which was to furnish the pattern for annual and weekly commemoration of his death in the Lord 's Supper or Eucharist. Three of our five canonical narratives style this meal a Passover and when Paul wrote 'Christ our Passover has been sacrificed for us' (1 Corinthians 5.7), he and his correspondents knew that the Passover was a regular feast, not a once-for-all ceremony like circumcision. Most early Christian writers agree that the bread and wine administered at the Eucharist were received by the believer as the body and blood of Christ himself. While this does not mean that the Eucharist itself was regarded as an immolation,[42] it had become customary, even before the Constantinian era, to attach the language of sacrifice to the rite.[43] The questions that have divided theologians, therefore, cannot be set aside by the historian: If

[41] Stroumsa (2009). Cf. Aufferth (2012), 10–11.

[42] Hanson (1985), 83–112 notes: the eucharistization of bread at Justin, *First Apology* 60 (cf. Irenaeus, against heresies 5.2.2); the presentation of gifts at 1 Clement 444.4; the offering of the first-fruits of creation at Irenaeus, *Against Heresies* 4.29.5; the oblation of prayer at Tertullian, *On Prayer* 28.1; the inward sacrifice at *Didache* 11.

[43] On sacrificial and sacerdotal language in Cyprian see Bévenot (1979); Hanson (1985), 104–5.

Christians could celebrate the Eucharist while denying the efficacy of any offering but that of Christ, could the new repast be in any sense a continuation of sacrifice?

It might seem that we can save the ancient church from contradiction by distinguishing between bloody and unbloody sacrifices. Philosophers deplored the shedding of blood, not the act of oblation; the Epistle to the Hebrews has no quarrel with the offering of first-fruits, but only with the useless expenditure of the blood of bulls. Thus, we might argue, the matter is simple enough: the animals were to be spared, but bloodless sacrifice went on. There is indeed no doubt that the bread and wine were brought to the altar in the fourth century as an offering from the people to God; the question remains, however, What does this offering signify if the physical elements are supposed to become, in some sense and at some point in the ceremony, the body and blood of Christ? If we subscribe to the understanding of sacrifice as an 'eating of the God', the conclusion that the eating of the bread and wine is a spiritual or symbolic immolation of the Saviour is almost inescapable. The corollaries of this inference are disquieting, for the wine represents (or rather, is) the blood of God (Acts 20.28), and outside the church no blood, not even token blood, could be drunk with piety, even at a token sacrifice. In ancient discourse, however, so far as this is recoverable, sacrifice is never the ingestion *of* the deity but the consecration of something *to* the deity, and it can be maintained that at the time when the bread and wine are offered, they are still nothing but bread and wine. On this account, the body and blood of Christ are tendered, not by the people to God, but by God (that is, jointly by the Father and Son) to the people. There remains a further offering to be made in response to the gift, but this is the highest of all spiritual oblations, the contrite and humble heart which will enable the believer (in Paul's words) to present his body as a 'living sacrifice' (Romans 12.2).

In his *Demonstration of the Gospel* Eusebius declares, conventionally enough, that the slaughter of animals has now given way to spiritual and unbloody sacrifices.[44] Lest 'unbloody' be taken to signify 'cereal rather than carnal', he goes on to quote the dictum of the Psalmist that no sacrifice is acceptable to God but a contrite and humble spirit. The body and blood of Christ are present not as a new oblation but as a memorial of the one first offered on Calvary; in return the worshippers offers a body cleansed of impurity and an intellect free of malice. As Daniel Waterland pointed out long ago,[45] if this able writer had regarded the physical elements of the Eucharist as a sacrificial offering, he would not have said in his *Commentary on Isaiah* that the saints will go on celebrating the Eucharist in heaven when bread and wine have passed away.

[44] See especially *Demonstration* 1.10 with the commentary of Waterland (1896), 376–7.

[45] Waterland (1896), 376–7, citing *Commentary on Isaiah*, p. 400.29–33 Ziegler.

But why, if the dispensation to the Jews was already a shadow of things eternal, was it suffered to pass away on earth? Eusebius wrote his treatise *On the Pasch* to show that the old has not been extinguished in the new, but partly retained and partly transfigured. Seven days of unleavened bread and one meal on the flesh of a sacrificed lamb were prescribed in the annual celebration of the Jewish Passover (Exodus 12.1–15). For Eusebius these foods remain historically and symbolically distinct yet indissociable, as the first day of unleavened bread is the day ordained for the slaughter of the lamb.[46] Christ, by observing the Passover on this day, showed himself a true son of his people;[47] the Jews who postponed the meal until the second day in order to arrest him betrayed the law that they were professing to uphold.[48] Eusebius is guilty of either sophistry or miscalculation here, for in Jewish reckoning the line between days is drawn at dusk, not at midnight, so that the evening of the first day precedes the sacrifice which is performed in the hours after sunrise, and the consumption of the lamb takes place the next evening, which in this computation is the evening of the next day. Furthermore he has silently, if not negligently, conflated the chronology of John's Gospel, in which there is no bread or wine and Christ dies on the day of preparation for the Passover meal, (John 19.14), with that of the other three, in which Christ celebrates the Passover on the eve of his crucifixion, that is (by Jewish reckoning) earlier on the same day, which is the day of preparation *for the Sabbath* (Mark 15.42). These accounts imply that Christ and other Jews were observing the feast according to the same calendar (Mark 12.1); by contrast, the only meal to which John refers is the one that the Jews were to eat on the evening that followed the crucifixion.[49] The two chronologies are irreconcilable, unless we assume that Christ and the priests were using different calendars and that this fact escaped all four of our canonical witnesses. Since Eusebius cannot attribute either error or ignorance to the evangelists, he preserves the truth of the gospel by convicting the Jews of treason to the law. Thus the historicity of the gospel is vindicated by the letter of the law, and it is not the Jew but the Christian who proves to be a consummate literalist.

At the same time, the Passover of the Jews must be shown to have been a provisional rather than a permanent institution if Christians are not be found remiss in their failure to sacrifice a lamb and superstitious in their transformation of a yearly rite into a weekly celebration.[50] The proof of its impermanence is simple enough: the Temple is in ruins and the Jews, alone of nations,

[46] On the marvellous properties of the number 7 see Eusebius, *On the Pasch* 5 at *PG* 24 700b–c.

[47] On the Eucharist as a Passover meal see Jeremias (1955). On Christian appropriation of the festival see Dix (1945), 337–41.

[48] *On the Pasch* 12 at PG 24 705b–c.

[49] At *On the Pasch* 9–10 (PG 703c–d) Eusebius makes much of their superstitious refusal to enter the governor's palace for fear of defilement before they consumed the Passover.

[50] *On the Pasch* 7 at PG 701b.

are forbidden to follow the customs of their fathers. The statutes of Moses can be honoured only by those who recognize their prefigurative character—by those, that is, who receive the flesh of the martyred lamb within, in the form of teaching, and whose bodies receive, as an earnest of faith, a mark representing the blood that the Jews were required to daub on the lintels of their doors. As the blood of the original victim averted the angel of death, so the mark on a Christian's forehead repels the demons who conspire against his faith. In this theological alchemy there is no strict correlation of the outer man with the literal sense and the inner man with the spiritual or allegorical sense. The mark applied to the body is palpable enough,[51] but it is a symbol of a symbol, a figurative memorial of the real blood which, when shed in an obsolete ritual, had meaning only as an adumbration of the work of Christ, whose sacrifice was the cause of its obsolescence. The historical fact of the crucifixion exposes the historical relativity of the Mosaic code; it is the incarnation, and the physical suffering of the Word, that deliver us from merely somatic notions of obedience, with a promise of life to body and soul alike.

The eating of unleavened bread is not in itself a metaphor but a literal reproduction of Jewish practice and of the act on which it is founded. Nevertheless it is figurative in import, as it represents the nourishment of the soul by the Word within.[52] We are not told whether the bread also goes proxy for the lamb; if it does, the astute historian has once again united two repugnant traditions, in one of which the bread stands for the 'body which is broken for you',[53] while in the other the body of Christ is likened to the paschal lamb of which 'not a bone was broken'.[54] The wine too is symbolic—but of what? Of the blood that Jesus shed for his elect, we may say; but if the literal drinking of blood would be the seal of a magical covenant or a political conspiracy, what is betokened by the metaphorical drinking of it?[55] Eusebius shirks the question, and our hermeneutic difficulties are compounded by the absence of any allusion to the sacrificial character of the Eucharist; there is no description of the order of service, and no indication that anyone had the duty of presiding, let alone that he was regarded as a priest.

That the celebrant was required to be a cleric is made clear in the life of Pachomius.[56] Fearing strife and envy, we are told, he would not admit clerics

[51] *On the Pasch* at PG 24 706d. Eusebius appears to be unaware of Origen's caveat that it is not the Cross but the Passover—not the sacrifice of sinners but that of the saints—that stands in a typological relation to the Eucharist. That is to say, the Eucharist is Christ sacrificed but not his sacrifice. See Buchinger (2005), 722–31.

[52] *On the Pasch* at PG 24 706 a–c: 'We ought to eat the Pasch with Christ, purging our souls of every leaven of sin.'

[53] Luke 22.19; 1 Corinthians 11.24.

[54] Exodus 12.46, quoted at John 19.36.

[55] Dölger (1934).

[56] Greek life 27; Bohairic life 25. According to Veilleux (1980), 271 the Eucharist at this time was celebrated twice every week, on the Saturday evening then on the Sunday morning.

to the monastery; instead he built a church in the local village, which was growing ever more populous, and received the Eucharist there every Saturday evening with his flock. When the number of inmates reached a hundred, a second church was built within the grounds, where a visiting cleric performed the service on Sunday mornings. Presiding at the Eucharist, then, was a clerical prerogative; in this era the exposition of it seems to have been a task for bishops. Constantine, though he preached to an 'assembly of the saints' on the 'day of the passion', made no reference to a forthcoming Eucharist.[57] Lactantius, taking up an old distinction between the gifts that are made to the gods in perpetuity and the sacrifices performed on fixed occasions, goes on to explain that Christians offer no gift but integrity of soul and no sacrifice but thanks and praise (*Divine Institutes* 6.24–25). A sermon ascribed to Pachomius contrasts the Jewish tabernacle,[58] a place of ritual offerings, with the new tabernacle built by Christ for the Gentiles, which is not a place at all but the perfection of obedience to the Law. For these witnesses Christianity has put an end not only to slaughter but to all material sacrifice.

CONCLUDING OBSERVATIONS

The Eucharist is patently not a perpetuation of sacrifice as this was known in the Mediterranean world. A formally bloodless rite cannot expiate the guilt engendered by the necessity of killing; understood symbolically, on the other hand, as the ingestion of the flesh and blood of one who was both man and God, it does not reinforce but rather annuls the traditional bifurcation between the human and the divine.[59] These notions of expiation and bifurcation were equally foreign to its prototype, the Jewish Passover; the Eucharist resembled the Passover also in that, far from cementing the bonds of civil society, it set apart the children of God in a world still peopled largely by the godless.[60] Nevertheless the two rites differed greatly, not only because the Eucharist was celebrated at other times than Easter, not only because it had never required any lamb to be brought to the Temple, but above all because it was not a domestic meal at which the father recited the story of deliverance to his household.[61] The sphere of the Christian priest—for by the fourth century he was a *hiereus* and not only a *presbuteros* or 'elder'[62]—was neither the household nor the Temple, but the basilica in which the catholic faith was

[57] *Oration to the Saints* 1. [58] Veilleux (1982), 47–8.

[59] See my comments above on the contrasting approaches of Burkert and Detienne.

[60] See again Buchinger (2005), 722–31. [61] Cf. Exodus 12.26–51.

[62] Note that it is only in the biblical tradition that the priest is par excellence one who sacrifices. On the protean usage of the term(s) connoting priestly functions in the Roman world see Beard (1990).

preached to the assembled people of one locality. Often (and in contrast to his Jewish and pagan counterparts) he was a man without a family, as the marriage of those already ordained was repeatedly forbidden by ecclesiastical synods.[63] He thus became, in Christ's words, a eunuch for the kingdom of heaven, whose loyalty to the unseen world was not compromised by the necessity of making provision in this one for his heirs.[64]

The Eucharist administered by this celibate caste, however, took over at least one function of sacrifice—the consecration of a public space in which all classes and sexes met to affirm their dependence on, and loyalty to, a common social order.[65] The authors whose positions have been compared in the present chapter were all philosophers, and their question was therefore, how can sacrifice to the gods be an act of rational piety? They have nothing to say of sacrifice as a collective rite, of the bonds that would be weakened by its cessation, or of the economic loss that would result from the suppression of the traffic in beasts for the altar.[66] Christians might have urged that one performs a social duty by excising a cancer from the body politic; pagans who were not Platonists would have asked how any disorder can be cured by the removal of the heart.

[63] See Chapter 5, this volume.

[64] See Matthew 19.12; cf. 1 Corinthians 7.33 on the advantages of virginity.

[65] Cf. Durkheim (1961); on the significance of the abrogation of public sacrifice after Constantine see Zachhuber (2013), 12–13.

[66] Contrast the final observations of Pliny in Letter 96.

11

The Bible of the Constantinian Church

Eusebius, the biographer of Constantine, records with pleasure a momentous commission which he received in his office as Bishop of Caesarea. Remarking on the sudden proliferation of Christian numbers in this city,[1] the watchful sovereign adds that provision must be made for the education of the new converts:

> It seemed fitting to give this direction to Your Understanding, that you order fifty codices[2] of the divine scriptures to be transcribed with ornate leather bindings by skilled calligraphers who know their art well, so that they may be easy to read and serviceable for use. The preparation and use of these are necessary, as you know, to the teaching ministry of the church. Instructions have also been sent to the chief administrator of the diocese,[3] that he may furnish all the materials required for this project. (Eusebius, *Life of Constantine* 4.36)

The production of fifty Bibles will have been not only a difficult but a contentious enterprise. To the labour of the scriptorium must be added that of determining the content of the codices at a time when no fixed canon of the Old Testament or the New was universally received. Eusebius, as the first author to have studied the development of the canon and the most copious expositor of the scriptures in this era, will claim our attention frequently in the first half of this chapter. He, of course, was a bishop whose congregation remains invisible; in the next chapter, however, we shall see how the fourfold narrative (or rather the threefold narrative) of the gospels was retold by a Christian layman for a world in which the classics taught in pagan schools were the soil and seed of intellectual culture.

[1] Clear evidence, against Stark (1997), that Constantine's accession must be taken into account in any attempt to plot the growth of Christian numbers.

[2] Literally 'bodies'. Mango (1985), 34–6 suggests that one copy was destined for each church in Caesarea. Cameron and Hall (1999) are no doubt right to challenge the inference, but, rather than accuse Eusebius of 'exaggeration' in the reproduction of an imperial mandate, we may assume that Caesarea was acting as the scriptorium of Palestine.

[3] The administrative diocese of Oriens at this time comprised sixteen provinces. See further Barnes (1982), 141–2.

THE OLD TESTAMENT: CANON AND INTERPRETATION

In Protestant societies, the Old Testament consists of thirty-nine books translated directly from the Hebrew, apart from some lingering idioms from the period when the Latin Vulgate was the Bible of western Christendom. This was largely the work of an angular and irascible scholar of the fourth century, Jerome of Stridon, who, to the great disquiet of his Latin contemporaries, forsook the Greek which had hitherto been the basis of all translations in order to restore the *hebraica veritas*, the Hebrew truth, of the original.[4] It is not clear whether this locution implies that the Hebrew is more true than the Greek or rather that it elucidates the true sense of the Greek, which, being a calque upon the Hebrew, is often more obscure than the text that underlies it. It was not his stated intention to excise from the canon those texts that existed only in Greek, and certainly this was not the result of his labours. To this day, fourteen books which have no Hebrew archetype are interlaced with the other thirty-nine in Orthodox and Roman Catholic versions of the scriptures; Protestant translators do not neglect them, though they are always set apart from the Hebrew canon as 'apocryphal' and 'deuterocanonical' books, and omitted altogether from the popular editions. Even when the Septuagint, or Alexandrian rendering, was accepted as the work of the Holy Spirit,[5] it appears that the authority of a book was sometimes thought to be impaired if it was not attested in Hebrew. Origen, for example, found it necessary to argue, in answer to Julius Africanus, that even the puns in the Septuagintal Book of Daniel do not prove that any portion of it was initially composed in Greek.[6] His own enumeration of the texts whose Hebrew origin he had verified include the two books of Maccabees, of which there are now no versions in that language.[7] On the other hand, authenticity is not the test of authority, for, while Solomon himself wrote only three books, the putative Wisdom of Solomon is equally canonical.[8] Biblical scholarship after Origen was immeasurably indebted to his Hexapla, a collation of the Septuagint with the later and more accurate translations of Aquila, Symmachus and Theodotion, side by side with the Hebrew substrate and a transliteration of this into Greek characters.[9] From his own practice, however, it is clear that he acknowledged the validity of Septuagintal readings which were not coterminous with his Hebrew text, though he did not subscribe to the claim of Justin Martyr that the Septuagint preserves matter which

4 See Kamesar (1993), 41–72.
5 See e.g. Justin, *First Apology* 1.31; Epiphanius, *On Weights and Measures* 3–11.
6 Eusebius, *Church History* 6.31.3; Origen, *Philokalia* 16; Routh (1846), 224–8; Buzási (2009).
7 Eusebius, *Church History* 6.25.2.
8 Origen, *Commentary on the Song*, proem, p. 75 Baehrens.
9 See Dorival (2013).

had been purposely suppressed by later redactors of the Hebrew when they saw that it furnished unanswerable prooftexts to the church.

Origen's exegesis was as seminal as his scholarship, though it set an example rather than a norm for subsequent commentary. He did not (as his detractors in the fourth century alleged) deny that what is related as history in the Old Testament is veridical; he believes more literally in the garden of Eden and in the Flood than his modern critics who accuse him of failing to grasp that Christianity is a 'historical religion'.[10] It would be just to say that he has no grasp of historical criticism, if we mean by this that he saw the plenary inspiration of God in every verse and would not have conceded that its meaning could be circumscribed by the finite vision of its human author.[11] If he appears at times to make light of history, it is only because he holds that the same authority which guarantees the inerrancy of the literal sense (in every case where the literal sense is binding) has also impregnated the text with at least one higher sense. It is not enough that God should have performed a great work on behalf of our fathers; the text must also work upon the highest faculties of the reader's soul—to use his own term, upon the 'spiritual senses'[12]—to open mysteries which were hidden from those who read the text before the incarnation, and thus prepare a way for ascent to immediate communion with the author of the text, who is also its universal subject.[13] It is to demonstrate the incompleteness of the literal reading that the Spirit has sown an occasional stumbling-block, in the form of a passage which is superficially too absurd or atrocious to be reconciled with the teachings that the church has received from Christ.[14] Every rational student, Jew or Christian, will perceive that the anthropomorphic terms applied to God in the scriptures are metaphorical; on the other hand, only those who see in Solomon a prefigurement of Christ will be able to pass beyond the literal reading of the Song of Songs, a text that Jewish teachers are obliged to withhold form the laity, since they can neither endorse the literal nor expound the mystic sense.

No determination of the Old Testament canon appears to have been undertaken, either by a synod or by a single author, in the age of Constantine. No oecumenical ruling, indeed, was ever secured. Athanasius, in a festal Letter of 367, commends the Hebrew canon but insinuates Baruch while relegating Esther to the deuterocanonical appendix.[15] Africa continued to uphold the Septuagintal canon without discrimination between the Greek and Hebrew

[10] On the evidence that Origen rejected the literal sense of Genesis 3.21, where God sews coats of skin for Adam and Eve, see Heidl (2003), 139–50.

[11] See especially *Philokalia* 5.

[12] Origen, *First Principles* 1.1.9. For an inventory of passages with astute discussion see Rahner (1979).

[13] Torjesen (1986); King (2005).

[14] Origen, *First Principles* 4.2.9.

[15] Brakke (1995), 321–32. For a tabulation of all fourth-century canons see McDonald (1995), 268–70.

writings, and without granting that the authority of a text was to be measured by its antiquity. Eusebius, in his *Ecclesiastical History*, reproduces lists of the Hebrew books from Melito of Sardis and from Origen,[16] but neither agrees in all respects with the Jewish canon of his time or of ours, and neither contends that only the texts that he has enumerated ought to be deemed authoritative. Nor is there evidence of a sustained comparison of the merits of different versions before Epiphanius of Salamis wrote his treatise *On Weights and Measures*, a full generation after the death of Constantine. Among Latin writers of the early fourth century, Lactantius quotes the Old Testament most often and with most latitude: 'blessed is he who was before he was born' is a biblical saying for him, though not found anywhere in the Septuagint.[17]

THE CANON OF THE NEW TESTAMENT

Eusebius, in the third book of his *Ecclesiastical History*, divides the texts that have been received at any time as scripture into three classes. The first contains the *gnêsia*, the writings of undoubted authenticity, among which he reckons the not only the 'holy quaternion' of the gospels but the Acts of the Apostles, although this latter work is cited much less frequently in earlier Christian literature (3.25.1). To these he adds the epistles of Paul, fourteen in number by his own count, though with the caveat that Hebrews had been shown by Origen not to be the work of the Apostle and had not been accepted by the Roman church (3.25.2; cf. 3.3.5 and 6.25). The category of *gnêsia* includes for him only one of the three epistles ascribed to John and only one of the two that bears the name of Peter. He also admits the Apocalypse of John, though acknowledging that some reject it. The second class is that of the *antilegomena*, or disputed writings, which are 'recognized by many' but not by all—that is, not by all whom this historian would embrace as his co-religionists (3.25.3). These books include the second and third epistles of John, the second of Peter and those of James and Jude; Eusebius does not say whether or not he would rank himself among the many, though he intimates that the authorship of a work is not, for him at least, the test of admissibility to the canon. The third class is made up of writings which passed current as scripture at some time but are now rejected by the Catholic Church (3.25.4). Among these rejected books the *Shepherd* of Hermas had been defended with some

[16] Eusebius, *Church History* 6.24.14, 6.25.2.

[17] Lactantius, *Divine Institutes* 4.18; Irenaeus, *Demonstration* 43 with Armitage Robinson's introduction (Bibliography A), 22–3.

vehemence by Origen only a few years after Tertullian pronounced it worthless. The *Teaching of the Apostles* will be a variant of the *Didache*, a homiletic and liturgical text of some antiquity; Rufinus, a younger admirer of Origen, tells us that another version of this, under the title *Doctrine of Peter, or the Two Ways*, was acknowledged by the Latin church, along with the *Shepherd* of Hermas as an 'ecclesiastical' writing which, although not strictly canonical, was conducive to edification.[18] Also rejected, according to Eusebius, are the *Apocalypse of Peter*, the *Acts of Paul*, and the Epistle of Barnabas. Some, he observes, would add the Apocalypse of John, and also the *Gospel to the Hebrews*, which was in use among the Ebionites, or Palestinian Christians, who professed to represent the original following of Jesus (3.25.5). For Eusebius himself, however, these works are not rejected but 'in dispute'.[19]

In the course of his *History* Eusebius remarks that other writings such as the letters of Ignatius or the first epistle of Clement, have been treated as scripture by reputable authors. Since it had not been a universal custom to draw up lists of canonical books, it would appear that an author is deemed to have accorded canonical status to a writing when he quotes it in the same manner as he quotes Paul or the four gospels. On this premiss the *Gospel*, the *Acts*, the *Preaching* and the *Apocalypse of Peter* are declared to be inauthentic because no ecclesiastical writer has drawn upon them. This is a tendentious reading of the historical evidence, and we might ask how the criterion is to be squared with the practice of numerous orthodox writers, before and after Eusebius, who endorse the fourfold canon of the gospels but quote sayings from other sources as genuine utterances of Christ. Jerome believed for a time that he possessed the Hebrew archetype of the Gospel of Matthew (and hence that he had discovered the *ipsissima verba* of Jesus) but never proposed that his 'Nazarene Gospel' ought to supplant the Greek text in the canon.[20] There is evidence that shepherds of the church in previous centuries had proscribed the public reading of texts that they none the less accepted as canonical,[21] and conversely that they countenanced the private perusal of texts that no one had proposed to add to the lectionary. Eusebius, however, takes no account of such fine questions, and the most that can be gathered from his researches is that we ought to be wary of positing a linear and cumulative 'development of the canon'. It cannot be assumed, in other words, that the process was always one of addition—first Paul, then the gospels, then the Catholic epistles and the

[18] Rufinus, *Commentary on the Apostles' Creed* 38 at Heurtley (1911), 160.

[19] Those who follow Hahnemann (1992) and McDonald (1995), 209–20 in favouring a fourth-century date for the Muratorian fragment allege that at *Church History* 5.8.11 Eusebius implies that the Wisdom of Solomon was regarded by some as a writing of the New Testament. No such inference follows unless we are willing to say the same of Justin Martyr, whom he goes on to name as another author cited by Irenaeus.

[20] Ehrman and Pleše, 207.

[21] *Muratorian Fragment* 72–73 at Hahneman (1992), 7.

Apocalypse—if only because all evidence indicates that the Apocalypse commanded far more authority in the second century than the Gospel of Mark. By the fourth century Mark's place was secure, although no commentary had been written on his Gospel; the Apocalypse, on the other hand, had lost credit in some quarters, notwithstanding the elucidatory labours of Victorinus of Petau. A generation after Eusebius, Cyril of Jerusalem omits it from his catalogue of New Testament books;[22] in the 39th Festal Letter of Athanasius, on the other hand, it is as much a part of the canon as the other twenty-six books which are now to be found in all printed copies. We may continue to wonder why a letter from Jesus Christ himself to Abgar of Edessa, believed to be authentic by Eusebius (*Church History* 1.13.1), never found its way into Greek or Latin codices, and whether the epistle to the Laodiceans which Marcion ascribes to Paul was identical with the one that appeared in Latin Bibles of the Middle Ages, to be excised once and for all by the Council of Trent.[23]

Least of all is it possible to determine whether Constantine had any intention of fixing the biblical canon, or any sense that it was open to contestation, when he gave Eusebius the task of supervising the production of fifty copies of the scriptures. We need not suppose that only Caesarea received such a mandate; in fact it is beyond doubt that one of our oldest codices was created elsewhere. Discovered by Tischendorff in 1844, and dated by palaeographers to the first half of the fourth century, the Codex Sinaiticus comprises the whole of our New Testament (with a few omissions), together with half of what was once a complete text of the Septuagint; the list of contents is completed, however, by the Epistle of Barnabas and the *Shepherd* of Hermas (though the latter is mutilated).[24] The *Shepherd,* as we have noted, was regarded as an ecclesiastical book by certain Catholics, and, since the epistle of Barnabas incorporates a sermon on the two ways it is possible that this, for some readers, was the second book in that category.[25] Optatus of Milevis, quotes it as scripture after 370 (*Against the Donatists* 1.21); to Eusebius, on the other hand, both Hermas and Barnabas were rejected books, of no more authority than the *Acts of Paul* or the *Apocalypse of Peter* and less eligible for admission to such a codex than the *Gospel to the Hebrews.* There is therefore no foundation for the theory that Sinaiticus was one of the texts produced at the behest of Constantine;[26] its mere existence demonstrates that Caesarea could not set the norm for every other scriptorium, and that it was no more possible then than now for an astute Christian to say 'I will have the scripture but not the church'.

[22] *Catechetical Homily* 4.36, at Heurtley (1911), 79.
[23] Jerome, *On Famous Men* 5.
[24] See Metzger (1987), 207.
[25] See further Aldridge (1999).
[26] So also McDonald (1995), 182–9.

EUSEBIUS ON THE OLD TESTAMENT

Eusebius perceived that without the Old Testament the church had no reply when Jews or pagans demanded its credentials of antiquity. He was also aware that if the church cited Moses as its prophet, Jews would countermand the summons on the grounds that those who disowned the Law had lost their share in the covenant that God made with the Israelites at Sinai: as any student of Origen's work *Against Celsus* knew, it was not only Jews who could frame this charge with eloquence. His remedy is to urge that the Jews were not the true people of God but apostates from a faith that was older than the Law. The name 'Hebrew', he says in the first book of the *Ecclesiastical History*, should be given to all who lived lives pleasing to God not only after but before the Flood, and pre-eminently to Abraham, the father by blood of the Jews, but the father in spirit of all who inherit the faith which made him righteous in the sight of God. The Hebrews, in the common acceptation of this term, can boast a noble and ancient literature, but in the scheme of providence—or, as we might say, in Paul's sense at Philippians 3.5—the Hebrew is not the Jew but the Christian. If (with Justin Martyr) we give the name 'Christian' to all, from Adam to Abraham, who 'enjoyed the testimony of righteousness', we imply that one may be a member of the elect without being circumcised or subject to arbitrary rules of abstinence. Thus the church is furnished with a genealogy that the Greeks cannot emulate, for even Moses has the advantage of Homer by some centuries, while Eusebius calculated in his *Chronicle* that Abraham had flourished 835 years before the fall of Troy. The argument too, though novel, has an irreproachable pedigree. It is reminiscent of Origen, for whom the gospel is the liberation of that natural righteousness which had been fettered among the Jews by circumcision; and it also looks back to Barnabas, who maintained that the church had inherited the Law inscribed on the tables which Moses broke when the Jews had proved themselves unworthy of it by their adoration of the golden calf.

The *Chronicle* of Eusebius must be reconstructed from its Latin, Armenian and Byzantine derivatives.[27] While much must therefore remain uncertain, we can say with confidence that his project would have led him to favour the Septuagint against the Hebrew even if this choice had not already been inculcated by the New Testament and the traditions of the church. The ages of the patriarchs before the Flood, as given in the Hebrew, imply that they begat children long before reaching the prime of life, and thus provided the sanction that the Jews desired for their custom of early procreation. In the Greek text an edifying divergence from the Hebrew is apparent wherever the age of fatherhood might be deemed premature. Eusebius does not

[27] On its sources see Mosshammer (1979). For a discussion of its genesis see Burgess (1997).

surmise, as Augustine did, that the authors of the Septuagint had corrected the Hebrew text in the belief that the 'years' of the patriarchs were lunar revolutions, each constituting less than a twelfth of a solar year. He is, however, minded to apply this corrective to the Egyptian and Chaldaean chronologies, which contradict the biblical account by reckoning their dynastic histories not in thousands of years but in myriads, or even in hundreds of thousands. By substituting lunar for annual cycles, the 29,400 years of Manetho can be reduced to 2206, and thus the history of Egypt can be brought within the biblical span, though only if the Septuagint is once again assumed to be more accurate than the Hebrew. The nations have erred in one respect, the redactors of the Hebrew in another: Christian scholarship vindicates the infallibility of the scriptural record without conceding a monopoly of knowledge to the Jews.

The *Commentary on Isaiah* is the longest surviving work in which Eusebius attempts to prove that Christians, not Jews, are the true interpreters of prophecy. Since it makes frequent reference to the commentary of Origen (now largely lost), it might be expected to take him as a model. It is not long before we hear, in tones that can only remind us of Origen, that when God summons earth and heaven to be his witnesses at Isaiah 1.2, earth represents the literal or 'somatic' reading and heaven a higher one (p. 4.38–40 Ziegler). It is one of Origen's characteristic sleights to impose a figurative sense upon some passage in his text by mere divination, and then to hold it up as a charter, furnished by the text itself, for the 'tropic' or 'allegorical' reading of other passages. Both adjectives are used elsewhere in the *Commentary on Isaiah*, perhaps more liberally than is typical of Origen's extant writings.[28] Again, though Origen certainly set the precedent, the *Commentary* surpasses his extant writings in the frequency with which it juxtaposes different versions of the same passage, without according unique authority to any of them. While the Septuagint is often fuller, the Hebrew too can speak for the church, as for example at Isaiah 9.6., where the occurrence of the divine name El in the Hebrew makes it clear that the prophesied child is no mere prince (66.16–24 Ziegler). This is an instance of typological rather than allegorical exegesis: the term 'God' is to be taken literally, not tropologically, but the man to whom it pertains could not have been pointed out to Isaiah's contemporaries.

At the same time, this commentary is not the mere echo of Origen's, and has not imbibed his determination to find the elusive figure of Christ in every vision, parable and affliction of the prophets. The longest relic of Origen's exegesis of Isaiah is his discussion of the epiphany in chapter 6, where he asks not only how the prophet saw but who was seen, concluding in response to the second inquiry that the seraphs who stood on either side of God were the Holy Spirit and the pre-existent Christ. Eusebius is less concerned to fathom the

[28] For allegory see pp. 20.8 and 90.13 Ziegler; for allegory of tropes p. 3 and for an allegorical trope p. 90.14.

experience of Isaiah, and is content to let angels be angels, though he grants that they are endowed with 'certain powers which are divine and productive of certain things beyond expectation (38.26–27). These powers are signified by the wings of the seraphim which they conceal their own faces, not that of the Lord (38.31–39.1). It is not an axiom for him, as for Origen, that every passage in scripture must carry a spiritual sense.[29] His opinion is rather that the allegorical sense must be invoked when the literal proves to be inadequate, and conversely that where the literal is sufficient it should not be amplified:

> Here and before we have observed the principle that in the prophetic discourse some elements are delivered literally, without any need of a figurative allegory, whereas others force the use of the allegorical figure (*tropos*) even on those who would wish it otherwise. For example, the rational method (*logos*) obliged us to give a figurative interpretation to the 'rod of the root of Jesse' and the 'flower', yet it was not proper also to allegorize Jesse; again, it was necessary to treat what was said of beasts as metaphorical figures for certain kinds of men, but not also to understand figuratively the nations over whom [the Messiah] was said to rule. In the same way it is necessary in the present passage [Isaiah 19. 1–6] to concede that Egypt is the visible territory of the Egyptians, but to understand its sea and its river allegorically. (p. 90.112–20 Ziegler)

Such alternation of literal and figurative exegesis is not to be found in Origen. It does not follow that the whole commentary has come down to us as Eusebius composed it, and there are passages which force us to doubt the integrity of the transmission. An allusion to the temporary idolatry of the Jews, the ascription of a tutelary role in the lower cosmos to the sun and moon, the equation of death 'the last enemy' with the devil, the suggestion that the serpent was the first of created beings and the appeal on two occasions to the historical erudition of a 'Hebrew' are all untypical of Eusebius, but easily supplied with analogues from Origen, though not with any that are verbally identical.[30] The parallels are collected in an appendix to this chapter, but it lies outside the purpose of this study to decide whether they are transcripts which Eusebius failed to eliminate when adapting the work of Origen or interpolations by another hand.

In the longest of Eusebius' extant commentaries, the Psalms are read, both separately and in sequence, through the prism of Christian theology. Psalmody, according to his preface, is the praise of God on an instrument, while the noun ωδη, which occurs with increasing frequency towards the end of the Psalter, denotes the exercise of the voice alone.[31] Allegorically, the psalm corresponds to the virtuous exercise of the body and the ode to that of the

[29] See also Hollerich (1999), 90–4, 97–9, and 155–8.
[30] Dependence on, though not quotation of, Origen is noted by Hollerich (1999), 148–9.
[31] *Patrologia Graeca* 23.72d.

contemplative faculty;[32] either can exist alone, but the perfect coinherence of knowledge and virtue is the ideal that is represented by the marriage of instrumental and vocal melody. This human ideal is the subject of the first psalm, where the man who has not walked in the way of the wicked is not a token individual but, as the definite article indicates, that One who stands for all, the Son of Man.[33] It also applies protreptically to other human beings insofar as they participate in him. In the 150th Psalm, as they are numbered in the Septuagint, the hortatory tone gives way to the alleluia that the saint will utter when he receives the plenitude of grace.[34] We owe this pedagogic arrangement to Ezra, who after returning from exile reassembled the psalms which had been dispersed with the other treasures of Israel and divided them into five books, commencing with those ascribed to David.[35] The psalmists had set a precedent by working the mystery of salvation into the structure of their own compositions—for example in that of Psalm 22, where, though the author is David, we cannot doubt that the proper subject is the Saviour. Even had he not pronounced the opening verse on the Cross, there is no other man who could have said of himself that 'his salvation is remote from the sins ascribed to him'.[36] (The Hebrew does not mean this, but Eusebius elects to follow the wording of the Septuagint because this is the text to which others appeal when they question the Messianic character of the psalm.) When he exclaims 'I am a worm and no man',[37] we may take this as an allusion to the miraculous birth by which Christ entered into our vile condition. We have all the more reason to do so when he goes on to intimate that he was not born as we are but 'cast upon thee from my mother's womb'. In the succeeding verses we can read a graphic record of the indignities that he suffered on our account. In verse 23 he tells us for whom he suffered by apostrophizing first those that fear the Lord, then the sons of Jacob. The sons of Jacob are evidently Jews by race, but those who are named before them are the Gentiles who have supplanted them by imitating the faith of Abraham.

EUSEBIUS ON THE NEW TESTAMENT

One task of Christian scholarship was to illustrate the concordance of the gospels, so that no one could say that it lacked the testimony of two or three witnesses which was required to establish truth. Another—addressed by Origen in his commentaries and his response to Celsus—was to harmonize texts where they seemed to differ, or else to make a theological virtue of their

[32] *PG* 23.65c–d. [33] *PG* 23.75c–d. [34] *PG* 24.74d–75a.
[35] *PG* 23.74c–d. [36] Psalm 22. At *PG* 24.204b.
[37] Psalm 22. At *PG* 24.206c.

discrepancies. Eusebius addressed the first task in his celebrated canons, which left their progeny in mediaeval synopses of the four gospels. He knew of a certain Ammonius, who had set passages from the other three gospels against the corresponding texts in Matthew; this method, however, seemed to him injudicious as it preserved the structure of Matthew alone while making rubble of all the other narratives. His own expedient was to draw up ten tables or canons, one to contain the passages that appeared in all four gospels, the second for those that were common to Matthew, Mark, and Luke, the third for Matthew, Luke, and John, the fourth for Matthew, Mark, and John; the next five were for material common to only two gospels, the fifth being dedicated to Matthew and Luke, the sixth to Matthew and Mark, the seventh to Matthew and John, the eighth to Luke and Mark, the ninth to Luke and John. The tenth was the receptacle for passages that appeared in only one gospel. He next divided each gospel into sections, assigning to every section both a sequential number and (in red) the number of the canon to which it belonged.[38]

Eusebius may thus have been among the first to discover that (with the exception of a few phrases) there was no material common to Mark and John that was not also common to Luke and Matthew. When he collates the testimonies and precepts of the evangelists in the fourth book of his *Theophanies* (now extant only in Syriac) he draws on Mathew, Luke, and John with an evident partiality for Matthew. In the first book he argues that there must be one supreme cause of the universe; in the second he inveighs against the worship of the elements, the deification of mortals and the worship of passions and virtues as though they existed independently of the worshipper; in the third he demonstrates that the Christ of the gospels is the Son and Word of God, a second cause, who in his ministry on earth has accomplished more, by his healing of sickness and his subjugation of demons, than the imaginary heroes and divinities of the nations. In the fourth he proceeds to a circumstantial proof of Christ's authority, his beneficence and the indefeasibility of his promises. He commences with the healing of the centurion's servant, following Matthew so far as can be determined from the Syriac. There follows a mosaic of quotations on the calling of the disciples to be fishers of men, to which the coda is Christ's command to baptize all nations at the end of Matthew, reinforced by his words to the disciples on the road to Emmaus, which only Luke preserves. Matthew is now sole witness for the consecration of Peter as the rock of the church, the parables announcing the rejection of the Jews and their supersession by the Gentiles and the speech predicting the run of the Temple. Luke is summoned again, as the one who prophesied more clearly the destruction of Jerusalem itself, and, as in the *Ecclesiastical History*, corroborative passages are added from Josephus' history of the Jewish War.

[38] Grafton and Williams (2006), 194–200.

We hear from John at least on the necessity of worshipping God in spirit rather than any house of stone, on the mission of Christ to sheep who are not of Israel after the flesh, on the gathering of the harvest through his passion and on the glorification of Peter by a similar mode of death. From Matthew Eusebius now collects a warning of general persecution, particular admonitions against false prophecy and imposture, injunctions to holiness, auguries of schism and the parables which foretell that some will fall after hearing the gospel for a season, and that other false believers will be winnowed from the elect on the final day. Finally, although neither this information nor the parables of the Sower and the Wheat and Tares are peculiar to Matthew, the signs that will precede the last day are enumerated according to his text.

To prove the necessity of the New Testament as a sacred book, it was not enough to show that the gospels spoke with a single voice: it was also necessary to show that they spoke against the Jews without being unfaithful to the God from whom the Jews had received their scriptures. The rejection of the old Israel is a pervasive theme of the *Commentary on Luke*, which, in its extant form at least, is not a continuous work of exegesis but a series of annotations to discrete lemmata, or sections, of the text. We are told with little ado that the house of Jacob over which Christ will reign (Luke 1.33) is made up, not of his kinsmen after the flesh but of those who come to him in faith.[39] The quotation which follows—'the power of the Holy Spirit will overshadow you' (Luke 1.35) is perhaps an oblique apology for this spiritual reading; it also prepares us for the juxtaposition of the first of Luke's beatitudes—'blessed are the poor' (6.20)—with Isaiah's proclamation that God has anointed him to preach good news to the poor, the broken-hearted, the blind, and the captive (Isaiah 42.1; cf. Luke 4.18).[40] Similar passages furnish a key to the parable of the feast, in which (as Luke records it) an unnamed man decides to hold a banquet and sends out messengers with invitations, only to be met by false excuses, borrowed from the code of war in Deuteronomy (Luke 14.15–24; Deuteronomy 20.5–7). This, it appears, suffices to prove that the recusants are Jews.[41] New messengers are dispatched to the streets and lanes with invitations to the poor, the maimed the lame and the blind—to the people, that is, for whom Christ worked the miracles which awoke faith among the Gentiles. This is the repast of which the Psalmist says 'You have furnished a table for me and my cup runs over' (Psalm 23.5).[42] The salutation which inspired the parable, 'blessed is he that shall eat bread in the kingdom of God' (Luke 14.15), acquires a deeper sense when we compare Christ's saying 'I am the bread of

[39] *PG* 24.538b. [40] *PG* 24.538d–579a.

[41] *PG* 24 588a. Eusebius goes on to distinguish three classes of those who are summoned to the feast at vv. 21–23: those who have strayed in the broad ways, those who hide malignantly in alleys and those who inhabit the nether world represented by the hedges.

[42] *PG* 24.573c.

Life' at John 6.48. The existence of a variant in Matthew,[43] on the other hand, raises difficulties of another kind than are raised by the plurality of Greek renderings from the Hebrews of the Torah. It is only in Matthew that the story is introduced as a parable of the kingdom, that the occasion is a wedding, that the celebrant is a king and that he raises an army to punish those who slight him. Nevertheless, the analogy is close enough persuade us that Luke's parable has 'something to do with the kingdom'; a tropological reading will allow us to equate the wide street with the path of the flagrant sinner and the narrow lane with that of the man who tries to cloak his sins.

THE OTHER EUSEBIUS

It was a younger namesake of the historian, Eusebius of Emesa, who first declared that allegory is always out of season. Of his Greek only fragments remain, but he is generally agreed to be author of a number of biblical commentaries and homilies which are extant today in Latin and Armenian. None of these can be dated, but, since he was present as Bishop of Emesa to witness the deposition of Eustathius of Antioch in 328,[44] Eusebius was almost certainly preaching in some capacity before Constantine's annexation of the east in 324. If we may judge him from his surviving works, his characteristic question to the text was 'why was it written?' and his characteristic question to the congregation was 'What does it ask of us now?'[45] In his *Commentary on Luke*, preserved in Latin, he maintains that the former question cannot be answered if we take the short way of the allegorist for whom a fig is no longer a fig and an ass no longer than ass.[46] This could be read as a stricture on Origen, for whom an ass or a fig in any passage of the scriptures represent all that is represented by an ass or a fig in any other passage; it may also be read as an unabashed rejoinder to Porphyry's jibe that those for whom statues are merely statues might as well suppose that books are nothing more than woven papyrus. But should we deduce that Eusebius made it a rule not to look beyond the immediate context and historical occasion of the text that he was expounding? No ancient critic followed such a rule; few modern exegetes find it possible to do so unless they have ceased to attach any normative or didactic value to the text.

[43] Matthew 22.1–10, which, according to PG 24 576b–d is not the same parable.

[44] Winn (2011), 32, citing Socrates, *Church History* 2.9.4 and Sozomen, *Church History* 3.6.2. On Eustathius see Chadwick (1948) and Burgess (2000). Woods (2003) identifies Eusebius of Emesa with the orator whom Ammianus Marcellinus calls Eusebius Pittacus.

[45] Winn (2011), 68–73.

[46] Winn (2011), 79, quoting *On the Fig Tree* 8.

Thus, if we put the commentator's question, 'Why it is written that Abraham was commanded to kill his son Isaac?', the Jew has no reply;[47] the Christian knows, of course, that this unconsummated rite prefigures the willing and efficacious death of Christ, the true seed of Abraham. As in many other of his comments on the Old Testament, he quotes the Hebrew and Syriac versions,[48] noting with approval here that, in contrast to the Greek, they assert that the lamb which was to be substituted for Isaac was suspended by its horns, so that it more obviously prefigured the crucifixion.[49] Thus he not only accepts but embraces the typological reading when he can find a text to sanction it; he also holds the figurative reading to be mandatory wherever the literal sense would imply that God can repent or does not have certain knowledge of the future. In his view theology teaches us not only when the literal sense cannot be sustained but what other sense we ought to seek in place of it. On the other hand, he declines to imitate Origen in drawing out a spiritual sense from every text for the edification of the reader. The literal sense, where it can be preserved, is always sufficient; if it seems to halt, it is better to make it whole than to discard it. Eusebius looks beyond the literal sense to the event itself, embellishing the narrative, as Philo had done, in order to fill a lacuna or to bring to light the hidden motivations of the actors. In his cursing of the fig-tree Christ exhibited the power that he had chosen not to exert against the Jews; the angel who attacked Moses is the last in a series of emissaries who freed the patriarchs from the fear of men by instilling a wholesome fear of God.[50] It is not without reason therefore that scholars assign Eusebius (with a slight anachronism) to the Antiochene school of exegetes,[51] who held, in contrast to Origen, that their task was not to sublimate the language of the text but to recreate the circumstances of composition, the matter of revelation being not so much the word as the event and the scheme of providence that it exemplifies.

CONCLUDING NOTE ON ALLEGORY

In histories of ancient criticism the Alexandrian school, which sought the meaning of the text as a whole through assiduous scrutiny of its parts, is set against the Pergamene school, which leapt from passage to passage, not so much explaining the text as explaining away its anomalies.[52] The biblical

[47] Winn (2011), 74, quoting *On the Resurrection* 1.25.
[48] For the debate regarding his sources see Ter Haar Romeny (1997), 47–88.
[49] Testimonia collected with commentary by Ter Haar Romeny (1997), 323–31.
[50] Winn (2011), 82–3, quoting *On Moses* 9–12.
[51] Ter Haar Romeny (1997), 89–100. [52] Canfora (1990), 48.

exegetes of the early fourth century were undeniably of the Alexandrian persuasion; for students of theology, however, this term connotes a taste for allegorical or figurative reading, which is contrasted to its disadvantage with the more literal methods that we associate with the school of Antioch.[53] By the 'literal' sense we understand the one that emerges when a competent reader gives each word in the text the meaning that it would commonly bear in such a context. 'Meaning', however, is an ambiguous term, comprehending as it does both the sense of the word, which is given to us by the dictionary, and its reference, which is established anew each time the word is applied to some real object. The sense of a word and its reference are not logically concurrent: sometimes it is possible to identify the referent without grasping the sense of what is being said about it, and sometimes we understand the sense of an utterance without knowing to what it refers. In the majority of biblical texts the literal sense, as we have defined it, will indeed be clear to a reader with sufficient linguistic competence. The reference too is obvious, for the most part, in the historical writings of the Old Testament, but frequently elusive in those of the prophets. When modern critics encounter such obscurities, for example in Isaiah 53, they commonly look for a cryptic reference to some notable contemporary of the author. The task, therefore, is to fit a name to the utterance, and if certain expressions, literally construed, prove not to be consonant with the known character and history of the chosen figure, allowance will be made for the poetic trope and the visionary conceit. We are far too slow to admit that when we read the text in this way we are reading it as allegory, inasmuch as we are giving 'another' sense to certain terms than the literal one. It is for that very reason that Eusebius of Caesarea disowns such readings and insists that we take the referent of the prophecy in Isaiah 53 to be Christ, the one person of whom it is literally true.

Thus it is we who harmonize the sense of the biblical text with its supposed reference, Eusebius who deduces the reference from the literal sense. We may feel that the fallacy in his method is exposed when he oscillates between a specious and a hidden referent in his interpretation of the same passage; similar conclusions were reached, however, by the masters of the later Antiochene school when they applied the same pedantic literalism to biblical prophecy. They differed from Eusebius in their reluctance to find a Messianic tenor in the majority of Psalms: like him, they assumed that a monologue in the first person should be construed as the utterance of a single speaker, but it seemed to them more natural to identify this speaker with the author, relating the content of the Psalm to the circumstances of his time. This is only to say, however, that they were more sparing in the use of an expedient which they agreed to be legitimate in due season. On the other hand, they are opposed to

[53] On the perfidious character of the term 'allegory' see Young (1997), 161–80.

him in principle and not only in application when it comes to the augmentative use of allegorical reading, not to elucidate a difficulty, but to give an oblique sense to words that are plain enough in their literal sense. This is the practice that we are wont to call Alexandrian in honour of Origen, who believed that the text had never been fully interpreted until it was given a sense that brought the student closer to God. The introduction of the new sense entailed a shift of reference from the original subject to one of more universal import—commonly the soul, the church or Christ—for which no reason could be derived from the text or its inconcinnities. On the modern view this is lawful in sermons but not in exegesis: to us, as to the Antiochenes, the handling of prophetic texts in the *Demonstration* seems to fall well short of the rigour promised by the title of this work. Eusebius of Emesa is less speculative, more hostile to the superimposition of an arbitrary reading. For all that, like his namesake of Caesarea, he permits himself a free choice between textual variants, and (as we have seen) the symbolic value of a particular reading is for him a legitimate principle of choice.

APPENDIX

Parallel Passages in Eusebius and Origen

The Repentance of the Synagogue

Eusebius. Having said these things about those who of old were blind, he turns the discourse against those who of old were close to God, but *had turned away to the former things,* speaking cryptically of those of the circumcision, of whom he says, *but they have turned away to the former things.* Next, as though showing them the conversion of the nations, and from what error they had converted in *coming into light* from darkness, he adds these reproachful words to them in their idolatry: *Be ashamed with shame, you who put your trust in graven objects, who say to molten figures, 'You are our gods'* [Isaiah 42.17]. For true it was that after the conversion to godliness of the nations that of old had practised idolatry, the race of the Jews was ashamed (*On Isaiah* p. 275.5–13).

Origen. What is it that the synagogue received from the church? I think that what is to be understood by this is what Moses wrote: *I shall lead you into emulation of those who are not a nation, I shall stir up your anger against a foolish nation* [Deuteronomy 32.21 Septuagint]. And thus the synagogue received this profit from the church, that it should no longer worship idols. For seeing that those who were from the nations had undergone such a conversion to God that they no longer acknowledged their idols, revering none but the one God, the synagogue was ashamed to go on worshipping idols (*Homilies in Exodus* 2.4, p. 50 Heither).

The First Creation

Eusebius. Once these things have been accomplished, the last enemy that shall be destroyed is death [I Corinthians 15.26] . . . Now who was this but the one who from the beginning seduced the first man in the paradise of God and cast him down from his station by God? This one was the crooked snake and serpent, fittingly so called because he and crawled on the ground and lay in wait for the feet of humans in the hope that he might bite one and infuse his deadly poison into him so as to cast him down from the straight path that leads to God (*On Isaiah*, p. 172.5 and 11–16).

Eusebius. To these words he adds *This is the beginning of the Lord's creation, made in order to be the sport of his angels* [Job 40.19]; and again he says, *this is the king of all that are in the waters* [Job 41.26]. And what is said in this passage resolves a doubtful question, teaching that life was granted to him in order that he might be the sport of the holy ones of God (*On Isaiah*, p. 173.12–18).

Origen. The better interpretation, as regards the second saying [Job 40.19], is that, while those beings who have come to exist in the body are many, the first to have been embodied is the one called the serpent, also styled elsewhere the great sea-monster whom the Lord has put under his hand. And it is necessary to ascertain whether, when the holy ones were living a life in blessedness that was absolutely immaterial and incorporeal, the one called the serpent, falling from the pure life, became the first of all who deserved to be bound to matter and body. This then would be what God proclaimed through whirlwind and cloud when he said *This is the beginning of the Lord's creation, made to be the sport of his angels*. On the other hand, it is also possible that the serpent was not the beginning of the Lord's creation once and for all, but rather that he was the beginning [only] of that numerous class of beings who have been made the sport of the angels in the body, whereas it is possible for others to exist in the body in quite another manner (*Commentary on John* 1.96–98, p. 21 Preuschen).[54]

The Heavenly Servitors

Eusebius. Next *the sun* itself too will be ashamed, when it sees those who of old were illuminated by its light undergoing judicial conviction and retribution; and likewise *the moon will be confounded*, as one who has no part in the correction of those who were impious on earth.... [H]aving served the will of God for a long age, they will *be confounded and shamed* in the day when they witness the punishments of the impious who were living under their rays (*On Isaiah*, p. 160.27–33).

Origen. The sun and the moon are said to be *subject to vanity* [Romans 8.20], placed in bodies and appointed them to the office of giving light to the human race. And he says that *this creature is not willingly subject to vanity*. The reason is that they did not willingly undertake to perform this ministration tor vanity, but since it was the will of him who made them subject, [they undertook it] *on account of him who made them subject*, since he promised those who were made subordinate to vanity against their wills that, once their ministration of this mighty work was complete, they were to be *liberated from this servitude to corruption and vanity* when the time came for the glory of the redemption of the sons of God [Romans 8.21–22] (*First Principles* 1.7.5, pp. 92–3 Koetschau).

The Master

Eusebius. Now the Hebrew used to say that Somnas was high priest, a man of impious and profligate character, who went so far as to betray the people and defect of his own accord to Sennacherib the king of the Assyrians (*On Isaiah*, p. 147.25–27).

Eusebius. Again, with regard to this passage [Isaiah 40.1] the Hebrew used to say that that God had not consented to the will of Hezekiah, because, having had made his request on his own behalf while saying not a word on behalf of the people, he had been worthy of blame in the eyes of God. For this reason the prophet goes on to say, '*Comfort, comfort my people*', *says God* (*On Isaiah*, p. 247.6–12).

Origen. For what the Hebrew teacher handed down was as follows: since the origin and end of all cannot be comprehended by any excepting only our Lord Jesus Christ and the Holy Spirit, therefore (he said) Isaiah spoke under the form of a vision of two seraphs only, who *cover with two of their wings the face* of God, *with two his feet, while on two they fly, calling and saying to one another, 'Holy, holy, holy, Lord God of hosts; the whole earth is full of thy glory'* (*First Principles* 4.3.14, p. 345 Koetschau).

[54] Origen goes on to say, as in the following passage, that the sun and moon are not enslaved for their sins.

Origen. Now as one prepares to commence the exposition of the psalms, let us take as our principle a beautiful dictum handed down to us by the Hebrew as a general rule for the whole divine scripture. For this man used to say the whole God-inspired scripture, on account of its obscurity, was like a single house containing many locked quarters. By each of these quarters lies a key which is not the one that belongs to it. And thus the keys are scattered among the quarters, not corresponding severally to the ones next to which they are laid (*Philokalia* 2.3).

12

Celebrating Christ

The authors of the New Testament, to judge by their own words, called themselves not Christians but *pneumatikoi* or *hagioi*, the 'spiritual' or the 'holy'. It was the pagans of Antioch who named them after their founder (Acts 11.27), and what every pagan knew of them henceforth was that they worshipped a crucified sophist who at the time of his death was hardly known outside his native Galilee[1]. Celsus, who may have given his work the title *True Logos* in mockery of the prologue to the Fourth Gospel, protests that if Jesus had been the Word made flesh he would not have been so timorous in the face of death or so elusive in his resurrection. The gods whom Porphyry quotes in his *Philosophy from Oracles* declare that Christ was a righteous man, but that only the ignorant take him for a deity.[2] Many of the first Christian apologists, on the other hand, confine themselves to promoting monotheism, and say nothing of the incarnation, let alone the Cross. The exegetes and castigators of heresy who followed them in the third century could not imitate their reticence, but no discursive vindication of the gospel narrative, to explain how God could be man and why he was bound to die, appears to have been attempted even by Origen or Tertullian.[3] It was not until the reign of Constantine that the crucifix took root at the centre of Christian piety, becoming a fixture in hitherto undecorated churches.[4] Whether or not the emperor inspired this trend, he encouraged it by inscribing the cross on the shields of his troops and striking coins in which the solar imagery was replaced by the chi-rho symbol.[5]

[1] Lucian, *Peregrinus* 13. [2] Augustine, *City of God* 19.23.

[3] On the derisive *Acts of Pilate* which were circulated by Maximinus Daia, *c*.312, see Eusebius, *Church History* 9.5.1 and 9.7.1 with Ehrman and Pleše (2011), 320.

[4] Grigg (1977). Kee (1982) repeatedly argues that the efficacy of the Cross as a means of atonement is neglected by Constantine and his apologists; true enough, if mediaeval piety is the standard of comparison, but was the atonement one of the 'central doctrines of the Christian faith' (p. 112) in the age of Constantine?

[5] Eusebius, *Life of Constantine* 1.30–31. Note also at *Life* 2.7–8 the display of the Cross in battle, the 'pitching of its tabernacle' beside the army at 2.12 and its status as a trophy at 2.16.

We do not know exactly when his future biographer, Eusebius, completed his *Demonstration of the Gospel* as a mighty sequel to his *Preparation*. The heir to over a century of biblical exegesis and synodical discipline, he undertook in the same work to convince the Jews that Christ was the Messiah, to rescue him from pagan doubts and calumnies and to expose the falsehood of heretical teachings with regard to his divinity, his manhood and his relation to the Father. Because of his apologetic purpose, he passes over the nicer questions that he was later to address in his rejoinder to Marcellus. No doubt the book was therefore all the more warmly received by those who held, with Constantine himself, that God had raised him up to put an end to discord within the fold as well as to outward molestation. On the other hand, whatever the author's merits as an apologist, he does not pretend to have found a style that is worthy of Christ or the triumphs of his earthly representative. A richer sacrifice of praise, more suited to the advent of the second Augustus, was offered by Juvencus, a Latin imitator of Virgil, who imposes harmony on a protean narrative by selectively intersplicing passages from all four gospels, making no allusion to the intestinal discords of the church.

THE *DEMONSTRATION OF THE GOSPEL*

Eusebius explains the purpose of the *Demonstration* in the proem addressed to Theodotus, Bishop of Laodicea. Having confuted the pagans from their *own* books in the *Preparation*, he will now enlist the Hebrew prophets as witnesses to the truth and divine authority of the Christian religion. It will be shown that they foretold the incarnation of the Word of God as a child, his miraculous birth from the womb of a virgin, his glory and his tribulation, his death, his resurrection and exaltation and the mission of the Spirit (1.1.2). The inexorable working out of God's design will be illustrated not only from the history of Israel but from the turning of other nations to the gospel (1.1.8); the failure of the Jews to construe their own scriptures, and the punishment that they incurred (1.1.7), will be rehearsed not in a spirit of animosity, but with the aim of showing that this apparent frustration of prophecy was its vindication (1.1.11). Once it is understood that the prophets were speaking to the world, it will be obvious that the pagan representation of the Christians as apostates (1.1.15) is as baseless as the Jewish charge that Christians have dishonoured God by abandoning the ceremonial law (1.1.16). The Church upholds the essence of the Law against the misguided attachment of the Jews to its accidents, and in doing so forestalls the accusation that it has taught Greeks to forsake their own culture in favour of a barbarous and irrational superstition (1.2.1–2).

The historian now proceeds to show, from the words of Moses himself, that before there were Israelites or Jews there were men like Enoch and Noah who were righteous in the sight of God and teachers like Jacob who dared to inveigh against the pandemic flattery of idols (1.2.3). Among these patriarchs Abraham was chosen to be the father of many nations, though it is evident that there are whole peoples on earth who cannot their lineage back to him (1.2.13). The inference that his fatherhood is spiritual rather than biological is confirmed by a perusal of the Mosaic Law. On the one hand it repeatedly prescribes the performance of rites in a certain place which would be conveniently accessible only to those in its immediate vicinity (1.3.3–26); on the other hand, it is prophesied that from one tribe of the twelve a prince would arise who would govern not only the other tribes of Israel but all the peoples of the earth, however distant they might be from the appointed shrine (1.3.45; Genesis 49.10). Moses, in establishing the old covenant, proclaimed[6] that after him there would be a second prophet and lawgiver (1.3.42, 1.4.5–7); when he records the anointing of Abraham by Melchisedek, a priest before there were Sabbaths or circumcisions (Genesis 14.19), he shows that this benediction was not contingent on the observance of the Law (1.4.6, 1.6.1). The Psalms and the prophets alike declare that God desires no hecatombs but the upright heart within and selfless obedience in all our acts.[7] At the same time, God's preference of Abel to Cain at Genesis 4.3 reveals that animal sacrifice has a privileged role in the divine economy (1.10.4): its expiatory character is proved by the dictum of Moses that 'the blood is the life' (1.10.8; Leviticus 17.11), while Jeremiah's lament that he is led as a lamb to the slaughter prefigures the offering of a nobler victim (1.10.17; Jeremiah 11.19). This victim is Christ, the lineal scion of Abraham, the exemplar of perfect righteousness and, according to John the Baptist, the 'lamb of God' (1.10.17; John 1.29).

The second book addresses the Jewish objection that the prophecies were intended only for Israel (2.1.1). Eusebius replies to this with an arsenal of passages, from Genesis to the last books of the canon, all predicting that the promises sown through Abraham will be reaped by all the nations.[8] Texts can be adduced in equal number to show that when the Saviour comes among his own people they will conspire against him, and that in consequence the majority of those who are children of Abraham by blood alone will not enter into God's rest. The prophets say with one voice that only a remnant of the first Israel will receive the blessing;[9] the complement of the new Israel will be made up, as Paul foretold, of those who were formerly children of

[6] Deuteronomy 18.18; Jeremiah 31.31; Isaiah 2.3.

[7] E.g. Psalm 40.6 at 1.10.27; Psalms 50.14 and 141.2 at 1.10.33; Isaiah 25.1 and 6 at 1.10.30–31.

[8] E.g. Genesis 18.17 at *Preparation* 2.15; Deuteronomy 32.43 at 2.1.12; Isaiah 9.1 at 2.1.23.

[9] Isaiah 37.31 at 2.3.137; Micah 2.11 at 2.3.145.

wrath but have now believed in Christ as Abraham believed.[10] The second book is thus of a piece with the first, naming no interlocutors but the stiff-necked 'children of the circumcision'. One might suppose that Eusebius deemed his argument with the pagan world complete, were it not that in the introduction to his third book he sets himself the task of refuting pagan aspersions on the life and character of Christ. This abrupt shift of audience has been imputed lack of art or vacillation in purpose;[11] perhaps it reveals nothing more than that Eusebius set out to discharge in a single work the tasks that Justin Martyr had undertaken in separate writings, the *First Apology* and the *Dialogue with Trypho*. Eusebius may have been shrewd enough to foresee that the majority of his readers would be Christians, who would not complain that his treatise lacked coherence if it furnished them with a catholic defence against two distinct bodies of assailants. The pagan Celsus, after all, had delivered the opening chapters of his polemic through the mouth of an imaginary Jew.

The scriptures continue to supply the matter for the third book and the seven that follow. Citing prophecy after prophecy as though no one would question their inspiration, Eusebius contends that if these oracles were not fulfilled in Christ they had never been fulfilled at all. It was foretold that the servant of the Lord would be born in Bethlehem[12] and of a virgin,[13] that he would rise from the dead,[14] and that he would rule all nations (cf. 3.3.5): among all the kings and prophets anointed under the old covenant, there is not one of whom a fraction of this is true. Moses may have worked miracles, but they were mere foreshadowings of greater wonders, a testament to his veracity but also to the necessity of a successor.[15] Again it was foretold that the sceptre would not depart from Judah until the desired of the nations appeared (Genesis 49.10); and Christ was born in the times of Augustus and Herod, when Israel had surrendered her visible throne to foreign kings (3.2.33–38). A digression reminds the Greeks that it was Porphyry, the great calumniator of the church, who denounced the slaughter of animals (3.3.10); Apollonius of Tyana, who was often accused of sorcery by those who put any trust in his hagiographers, is also adduced as a critic of animal sacrifice (3.3.11). Anyone who contends that Christ was a sorcerer, on the other hand, must explain how he could effect his cures without any charm or instrument (3.4.21–31), and why his apostles required their converts in Ephesus to collect and burn all the

[10] There are echoes of Romans 11.5 at 2.3.133 (cf. 2.3.122); Matthew 20.16 at 2.3.143.

[11] Laurin (1954), 370–3.

[12] *Preparation* 46, citing Micah 5.2; cf. Matthew 2.6.

[13] *Preparation* 3.2.51, citing Isaiah 7.14; cf. Matthew 1.23.

[14] *Preparation* 3.2.60, interpreting Isaiah 53.10–12. The entire prophecy is applied, as convention prescribed, to the expiatory work of Christ. Cf. 3.2.70–71, interpreting Psalm 16.10.

[15] *Preparation* 3.2.8; 3.2.13–14, setting Exodus 16.4 against Matthew 16.8; 3.2.20.22, setting Numbers 12.10 against Matthew 8.2; Exodus 31.18 and 8.9 against Luke 11.20.

writings of the magicians (3.6.16; Acts 19.19). If it be urged that the miracles are fictitious, it must be asked why his disciples, having suffered persecution in every quarter, were ready to go on hazarding their lives for a conscious lie (3.4.43–45).

The doctrine of the fourth book is avowedly more arcane (4.1.1), and a dissertation on first principles is required before Eusebius can proceed to the biblical evidence. The existence of God, as the first, sublime, eternal and unbegotten cause of the universe, is admitted by all (4.1.5–8); knowledge of the Son, on the other hand, is common only to the Christians and the Hebrews, though the latter fall short of the truth in their refusal to confess his divinity (4.2). Since analogues to the Trinity have already been culled from Plato and subsequent writers of his school in the *Preparation*, we must take this statement to mean that the Greeks had only an obscure presentiment of this 'second god',[16] perhaps derived from a reading of the Hebrew scriptures. Yet Plato, whom Eusebius purposely echoes here, maintains that God must create because he is good;[17] since the scriptures also teach that God alone is good, it follows that the more highly we exalt him—the more we insist upon his superiority to every name, and even to the monad itself (4.1.5)—the more necessary it is to attribute to him a will to create (4.1.6). A tacit refutation of Plotinus, who denies to the One any consciousness of the world, may be intended here, but Eusebius goes so far with the philosophers as to acknowledge that creation out of nothing is inconceivable. Where they, however, had posited matter as the eternal substrate, Eusebius avers that God requires no other substrate than his will (4.1.7).

At the same time, since there cannot be any meeting of the eternal and transcendent with the contingent and mundane, it was also necessary that God should rule this world through his image, which in accordance with Proverbs 8.22, is characterized as the perfect creature of a perfect creator. The scriptures also authorise the use of the title Son, and hence of the adjective 'begotten', though neither of these implies any alienation or division of the divine substance (4.2). What is rather implied is the fullness of the divine attributes: the Son is not only the product of intellect, Logos and wisdom, but intellect itself, Logos itself and wisdom itself. (4.2.1). Although he is posterior to the Father in the order of generation, he was born before all the ages (4.3.13); as the breath and effulgence of the Father he is in no way inferior to him in his attributes (4.3.10).[18] The world being one, the power that sustains its heterogeneous elements must also be one (4. 5); the unity of Christ the only-begotten is not belied by the infinite variety of works that he performs in the lower sphere, any more than the plurality of our limbs and senses belies the unity of

[16] For the qualification 'second' see 4.3.6, 4.3.7

[17] *Preparation* 4.1.6 echoes *Timaeus* 29e.

[18] 4.3.4 and 4.3.10, citing Hebrews 1.3 and Wisdom 7.25.

the 'demiurgic power' that rules them (4.5.4, 4.5.9). Eusebius does not identify the Son with the world-soul of the Platonists, though there may be a glancing allusion to Heraclitus in his observation that fire remains one element whether it hardens clay, dissolves wax, melts lead, dries wood, or purifies gold (4.5.8). Nevertheless, for all that is said in his honour, it must be remembered that the Father alone is God Most High, and that the Logos who is also *kurios* (Lord) is rightly so called (*kuriolegomenon*) because he alone is second (*deuteros*) to the God over all (4.7.1).

Eusebius, who is often called an Origenist,[19] follows Origen in bestowing the compound *autologos* (Logos itself) upon the second person of the Trinity and in identifying the latter with the Wisdom of Proverbs 8.22. In accepting Hebrews 1.3 as a prooftext and collating it with Wisdom 7.25–26, he is also a pupil of Origen, yet not in all respects a faithful one. Origen had affirmed the coeternity of the Father and the Son in plain terms; Eusebius, in plainer terms, denies it, though without affirming ascribing a temporal beginning to the Son. Origen had spoken of the Father as a monad; Eusebius makes him anterior to the monad, and asserts at one point that the wisdom of the Father is preserved by the Son in his monadic character. For this reason he never implies, as Origen does at times, that the Son differs from the Father in being naturally disposed to multiplicity. It would be equally injudicious, though it is equally common, to categorize Eusebius as an Arian, for he holds none of the tenets which were anathematized when Arius was condemned in 325. He implicitly denies that the Son is eternal, but does not expressly assert that 'he was not before he was begotten'. Presupposing as he does that nothing comes from nothing, he could not say that the Son is 'out of nothing', and quotes the words of Isaiah, 'his generation who shall declare?' as a divine embargo on all such speculations. His younger contemporary Athanasius, who has come to be seen as the conscience of the Nicene Council, opined that the Son is not so much a creature of the Father's will as the very will of the Father—a difficult and innovatory teaching, as is his argument that Proverbs 8.22 does not commemorate the origin of the Word but foretells the creation of his flesh. Appealing once again to Plato's axiom that the Good must superabound, he maintains that the Second Person is an eternal projection of the Father's love, not merely his organ for the creation of the world. Yet even Athanasius can interpret Christ's saying 'the Father is greater than I' as an admission that the Father precedes the Son in the logical order of causation (*Against the Arians* 1.58–59). While the *Demonstration* is not a handbook of Nicene doctrine, it is not a mine of heresies unless we presume to determine what is heresy for ourselves.

Eusebius goes on to explain why the Word became incarnate. All nations other than Israel had been assigned to the charge of an angel,[20] and had not

[19] See Chapter 13, this volume.

[20] Cf. Deuteronomy 32.8–9 Septuagint.

been vouchsafed a knowledge of the true God sufficient to wean them from animal sacrifice and the delusive cult of images (4.8.1). The powers that God appointed have now become rebels under the captaincy of the 'apostate power' (4.9.1). In his account of the moral ruin that followed, Eusebius refers to the opening book of the *Preparation* (4.9.10), and his narrative echoes that of Porphyry's second book *On Abstinence*. But taking leave of Porphyry, Eusebius avers that the only remedy was that the God who stands midway between the Father and his creation should reveal a better way to humanity, first through Moses (4.10.4–7) and then by his incarnation. This act of condescension in no way impaired his divinity: he continued to be omnipresent even while he was in the flesh and, while he imparted a portion of his glory to the flesh with which he was mingled, he himself was not defiled by this contact, any more than the sun is defiled by the creatures on which it sheds its rays (4.10.15–16, 4.13.1);[21] it was necessary also that he should die, to prove himself master of both death and life, to cleanse our sins by becoming a curse for us, to offer a sacrifice to the Father on behalf of the world, to cofound the daemons, and to give us an earnest of the life to come (4.10.15, 4.12.1–7). Having thus performed the sacrifice to finish all sacrifices, having shown the world the one image of the divine that is not an idol, he has received the everlasting unction of the Father as king and high priest to all nations (4.15.1–24). Throughout his ministry he concealed his divinity under the human form (4.10.19); at the same time, he was at all times properly God, not man (4.15.47), and at times his acts as man were enhanced by mighty works that could proceed only from God (4.11).

In the fifth book Eusebius concludes that the Second Person is made known to us in scripture under two aspects, as the image of the unbegotten nature and as the incarnate Word who reveals God to his creatures. As a preface to his compilation of prooftexts from the Old Testament, he addresses a brusque lampoon to certain authors—meaning Porphyry, here as everywhere—who regard the Israelite prophets only as local conduits of a universal revelation. What faith can be put in oracles enjoining the slaughter of beasts and every species of political malfeasance, and whose authors are convicted of ignorance, licence and deceit by the tales that they themselves have dramatized in their own mysteries. Moses alone, and those who kept faith with him, can furnish true intelligence of the 'second Lord and God', or as the peroration to the fifth book styles him, the 'second God after the first'. This adjective does not in itself imply subordination; and while it is clear enough that the instrument of the father in Eusebius, he has taken pains in the previous book to show that he differs from the Father only in being begotten. Having read what was said against Origen, he will no doubt have been conscious that to do otherwise

[21] At *Demonstration* 4.7.1 Eusebius says that Christ is in the noetic world what the sun is in the visible world; at 4.10.15 he quotes Malachi 4.2.

would excite the suspicion of heresy; at no point does he lay stress upon the Son's inferiority to the Father, because his aim throughout this work is not to qualify but to vindicate the acclamation of the Son as God. The sixth book demonstrates that the enthronement of Christ and the calling of the nations are obscurely foreshadowed in prophecies which have now been elucidated by his ministry. The seventh undertakes to show that the prophets foresaw the birth of the Messiah in Bethlehem from the tribe of Judah, while the eighth dwells on the felicitous conjunction of circumstances that attended his nativity. Citing the chronographer Julius Africanus, Eusebius proclaims that Daniel's prophecies of redemption, which have disappointed those who took them literally, have at last become perspicuous and sure of consummation. In Book 9 he undertakes to show that the prophets anticipated every event of Christ's sojourn on earth; in Book 10 he finds auguries in the Hebrew scriptures of every indignity that Christ was to suffer, and argues that historical testimonies to his resurrection cannot be gainsaid.

Theologians had hitherto done scant justice to the salience of the cross in the oldest writings of the church. Irenaeus, following Paul, had extolled it as the climax to a life of unconditional obedience;[22] no peculiar efficacy is attached to it, however, and it is not the seat of victory over Satan.[23] Origen held that the blood of Christ was a ransom to the devil—the price with which we were bought, according to Paul—but he says the same of circumcision.[24] Apologists could plead that the death of Christ, foretold by the prophets, was the logical precondition of the new life that succeeded it; in itself, none the less, it was rather to be deplored than celebrated. Eusebius, for his part, finds that the last act of Christ's life made five things possible: the preaching to the dead, the vicarious suffering for our sins, the presentation of a sacrifice to the Father, the conquest of demons[25] and the promise of immortality to all who participate in his resurrection (4.12.6–8). In the tenth book of the *Demonstration* the mystery is condensed into two texts, John the Baptist's naming of Christ as the lamb of God (John 1.29) and the prophecy of Isaiah (53.7) that he will be led as a lamb to the slaughter (10, proem 4). Strictly construed, the first speaks of expiation but not of death and the second of death but not of expiation. Eusebius, however, discovers a conjunction of the two motifs in an utterance which he takes to be that of no ordinary mortal and therefore prophetic. The speaker in Psalm 40 begs mercy from God if he has sinned, yet pleads that he suffers for no wrong of his own and foresees with assurance the ruin of those who plot his death. (10.1.1–18). The apparent contradiction is resolved when we see

[22] Irenaeus, *Against Heresies* 5.16.2; Philippians 2.6–12.

[23] At *Against Heresies* 5.21.3 the seat of victory is the wilderness; at 5.1.1–2 it is not clear that the persuasion of apostasy means the persuasion of the devil, or that the means is a ransom.

[24] *Commentary on Romans* 2.13. See further Rashdall (1919), 77–86.

[25] 1 Peter 3.19; Galatians 3.13 and 1 Peter 3.16; 1 Corinthians 5.7 and Hebrews 13.12; Colossians 2.14.

that Christ took on our impoverished condition so that, after he had borne the capital penalty that was due to us, the body that he left on earth in the form of the church might share in both his pains and his resurrection (10.1.19–22). The plotters are Judas and his Jewish sponsors, and Eusebius goes on to multiply texts which show that God's retribution was not only just but repeatedly foretold.

In the peroration Eusebius returns to the figure of Christ, the voluntary pauper and sport of demons, betrayed and killed by those whom he came to save (10.8.103–109). The conclusion to Porphyry's allegorical treatise *On the Cave of the Nymphs* is a portrait of Odysseus, cloaking his true form under the rags of a beggar until by pain and self-denial he has placated the 'marine and material gods' whom he had offended by his blinding of Polyphemus.[26] Porphyry, on his own principles, is interpreting Homer as faithfully as Eusebius interpreted Paul and the Psalms;[27] we cannot be sure that a parody was intended or that Eusebius would have suspected one had he read this opuscule. The parallel is all the more telling because it is uncalculated: Platonism and Christianity were mutual antitypes, and it is not unusual for the antitype to become a mirror.

In this work Eusebius refrains from advancing any theological position that cannot be proved directly from the scriptures. One cannot divine, for example, whether Christ possessed a human will or a rational soul distinct from the Logos:[28] the matter was in dispute, for, while the gospels clearly ascribe the grief and perturbation of the Saviour to his passible soul, they say nothing of his hegemonic faculties. If these were exercised by the Logos alone, it would appear that he was incapable of the free deliberation and moral choice that we deem essential to our humanity; on the other hand, if we grant these capacities to him, how could God himself be sure that Jesus the man would remain obedient to the incarnate Word?[29] If we reply that the Word and the man are not two agents but one, must we not conclude, as the Council of Antioch seems to have urged against Paul of Samosata, that the Word simply took the place of the inner man?[30] Origen had indeed maintained that Christ possessed both a human soul and a human spirit, but in certain quarters Origen's name was already synonymous with heterodoxy. It is possible that Juvencus, whose work will occupy the second half of this chapter had no head for such technicalities; Eusebius, when obliged to canvass them in his later writings, takes shelter in silence or equivocation. His theological axiom, in the

[26] *Cave of the Nymphs*, p. 80 Nauck.

[27] *Demonstration* 10.1.1 + Psalm 40.1; 10.1.13 is reminiscent of Philippians 2.6–7.

[28] Strutwolf (1999), 233–45 adduces passages from the commentaries of Eusebius which illustrate the 'psychology' of the incarnate Christ. Few of them, however, do more than reproduce biblical references to the soul of Christ, with the usual caveat that his divine nature remains immune to his human affliction.

[29] See further Wiles (1965). [30] See further Lang (2000).

Demonstration as in the *Preparation*, is that nothing can be an article of faith unless it has clear scriptural warrant; in the next chapter we shall see how this axiom was tested in an age when the peace of the church was felt to depend on the enunciation of strict norms of belief.[31]

IUVENCUS: *HISTORIA EVANGELICA*

The multiplication of codices must have fostered a wider knowledge of the scriptures. At the same time, the audience that Constantine had won for them by his patronage of the church must have included many who felt that the Spirit ought to have written better. Educated neophytes, accustomed to Ciceronian cadence, Tacitean undertones and the opalescent brevity of Seneca, would not find even regular grammar or purity of diction; there was also, as Athanasius and Augustine knew, a public that preferred to read theology in metre. It was for their satisfaction, we may assume, that Vettius Aquilinus Juvencus, one of the earliest Christian poets in any language, undertook the first comprehensive account of the life of Christ in verse. Jerome tells us that he came from Elvira in Spain.[32] Of his date we know only as much as he communicates in an epilogue, where he praises Constantine as the 'ruler of the wide world,[33] who alone of kings abhors the weight of the sacred name *qui solus regum sacri sibi nominis horret/Imponi pondus* (4.807–809)'. This may mean that he shunned the name of king[34] or that he did not imitate his predecessors in assuming the name of his patron deity;[35] it may also be taken as a discreet apology for taking Christ as the subject of his panegyric, rather than any mortal dedicatee. The life of Christ, as he boasts in his proem, not only outshines all others, but is the only one with which the poet is not required to mingle his own inventions. Simply to reduce to a single narrative the memoirs of four independent but concordant witnesses will entitle him to everlasting fame:

> Quod si tam longam meruerunt carmina famam,
> Quae veterum gestis hominum mendacia nectunt,

[31] To avoid tedium, I have postponed my discussion of the *Theophany* of Eusebius to an appendix.

[32] *On Famous Men* 84, with the marginal addition from MS 22 recorded by Fontaine (1959), 8. See also Jerome, Letter 70.5.

[33] On the translation see Green (2006), 4n.14, Jerome allots a date of 329 to Juvencus in his *Chronicle*. The objection of Marold (1890), 329 that this accolade could be given to him only after his conquest of the Goths in 332 would be captious, even if it were literally true that Constantine became the ruler of the entire world through this victory.

[34] So Green (2006), 5–6, noting also the suggestion of Fontaine (1984), 131–41 that Constantine declined the title invictus (uncounquerable) or *comes solis* (companion of the sun).

[35] Or perhaps the bare appellation *deus*, as Von Albrecht (1997), 1354 proposes.

Nobis certa fides aeternae in secula laudis
Immortale decus tribuet, meritumque rependet. (1.15–18)

[But if such long renown has been earned by songs that mingle falsehoods with the deeds of men of old, my sure faith will secure me the imperishable glory of eternal praise through the centuries, repaying my desert.]

The result is an epic in four books, each of about 800 lines. It hardly justifies the poet's confidence, as even the indefatigable Edward Raby spares it only a page and half in his *History of Christian Latin Poetry*. He pronounces it 'clear and unadorned, but thoroughly Virgilian'.[36] The following discussion will suggest that this tepid compliment ignores the plain demerits of the poem without doing justice to a number of curious features which deserve the attention of scholars.

JUVENCUS AND THE CANON

Irenaeus of Lyons, towards the end of the second century, was the first to maintain that the four beasts who surround the throne of God at Revelation 4.6–7 are emblems of the four evangelists (*Against Heresies* 3.11.8). In his exegesis the man corresponds to Matthew, the eagle to Mark, the calf to Luke, and the lion to John. Victorinus of Petau demurred, assigning the lion to Mark and the eagle to John. In the opening lines of his *Historica Evangelica*, however, Juvencus shows himself a pupil of Irenaeus:

Matthaeus instituit virtutum tramite mores
Et bene vivendi iusto dedit ordine leges.
Marcus amat terras inter caelumque volare
Et vehemens aquila stricto secet omnia lapsu.
Lucas uberius describit praedia Christi,
Iure sacer vitulus, quia vatum munia fatur.
Iohannes fremit ore leo, similisque rugienti
Intonat aeternae pandens mysteria vitae. (1.1–8)

[Matthew enjoined conduct by the path of virtues, and gave precepts in due order for living well. Mark loves to fly between heaven and earth, and as an impetuous eagle cuts through everything in his unswerving plunge. Luke describes the spoils of Christ more amply—rightly a sacred calf, because he rehearses the duties of prophets. John is a lion who chafes at the mouth and, as though he were roaring, thunders as he opens the mysteries of eternal life.]

In fact these four are represented very unequally. The poem contains no matter from the Gospel of Mark which is not also to be found in Matthew's

[36] Raby (1953), 17.

Gospel.[37] The inconsequential story of the young man who fled Gethsemane leaving a linen shift in the hands of his pursuers is omitted, as are two healings peculiar to Mark, in which Jesus is obliged to make use of spittle or mud and does not meet with success at his first attempt.[38] In Juvencus, as in Matthew, Jesus declares that it is not for us to know the date of the Second Coming; he does not add, as he does at Mark 13.32 that this knowledge is hidden even from the Son. Matthew and Mark agree in ascribing to Jesus the aphorism that we cannot be defiled by what goes into us (3.147–151; cf. Matthew 15.11); the poet does not follow Mark when he adds that by this saying all foods are made clean (Mark 7.19). In Matthew the woman who touches the hem of Jesus' garment is called forth from the crowd and healed with a word (Matthew 9.20–22); the reader of Juvencus' faithful paraphrase (2.385–395) would not have guessed that there was another account in which she is healed at once by the touch and then identified only by her own confession (Mark 5.25–34). These omissions do not betoken ignorance of Mark's Gospel; they indicate only that Juvencus shared the common opinion of his time that Mark's was the slightest of the four, and that his recognition of human frailties in Jesus was not so much a clue to history as a difficulty for faith. When even the learned Origen had forgotten that Jesus is said to have been a carpenter at Mark 6.3, it was hardly a mark of bad faith or bad scholarship in Juvencus to concur with Matthew in softening the jibe to 'son of a carpenter'.[39] On the other hand, the practice of his contemporaries did not lend such authority to the poet's decided preference of Matthew to Luke wherever the two diverge.

Few parables of Jesus are better known, or more admired, in the modern world than those of the rich man and the beggar, the prodigal son and the Good Samaritan. All are found only in Luke and not one is reproduced by Juvencus. Matthew's parable of the master who pays the same wage, without regard to the length of service, to every labourer in his vineyard, is retold with elaboration (3.551–583; cf. Matthew 20.1–16), as is the more inconsequential story of the man who has two sons, one of whom defies him in word but not in act while the other makes false professions of obedience (3.692–703; cf. Matthew 21.28–31). A catena of parables from the thirteenth chapter of Matthew is versified at 2.374–3.16, always in the form attested by that chapter rather than by the fourth chapter of Mark's Gospel. The parable of the talents is told in Matthew's version, according to which a different sum is entrusted to

[37] Though *Sancti filius* (son of the Holy One) at 3.271 is more reminiscent of Mark 14.61 than of any Matthaean counterpart. For tabulation of all gospel references se Green (2006), 28–9. As he observes on p. 26, the theory that the four books correspond to the number of gospels 'does not impose itself', *pace* Thraede (2001), 882.

[38] See Mark 7.31–37 (vestigially represented at Matthew 9.32 and Luke 11.14); 8.22–26; 14.51–52.

[39] At 3.25, as elsewhere (1.8, 1.62, 3.341, etc.), the word *suboles* ('offspring') is poetic rather than biblical, recalling *Eclogue* 4.29, *Aeneid* 4.328, etc.

each of three servants (25.15–16), rather than in Luke's adaptation, where each of ten servants receives a single pound (19.13). In the narrative of Christ's infancy, where Matthew and Luke are simply irreconcilable, Juvencus interlards the two, commencing with the first chapter of Luke.[40] In his account of the passion, on the other hand, Matthew is his sovereign witness. We hear of the intercession of Pilate's wife, the washing of the governor's hands, the acceptance of guilt by the populace (4.622), the crucifixion between two thieves (4.666), the earthquake and return of the dead at the hour of the crucifixion (4.704–709), the opening of the tomb by the angel (4.746), the bribing of the guards (4.775–782), and the glorious manifestation of Christ, first to three women (4.766) and then to a multitude of disciples (4.784–800).[41] But of Christ's words of forgiveness from the Cross (Luke 23.34), the penitent thief (23.42), the yielding of Christ's spirit to the Father (23.46), and the oblique disclosure of his resurrection on the road to Emmaus (24.13–35)—of all these famous episodes there is not a vestige in this Latin digest of the Gospels. Luke's testimony can serve Juvencus only when Matthew fails him, and is no more admissible than that of Mark whenever it threatens to dim the majesty of Christ.[42]

The temptations of Christ are related in the order preserved by Matthew (1.366–408).[43] At 1.591 the Lord's Prayer is addressed to 'our father in heaven', as at Matthew 6.6, and not simply to the Father, as at Luke 11.2. Juvencus follows Matthew, against Mark and Luke,[44] in recognizing adultery as the one ground (other than death) for the dissolution of a marriage (1.533). Where Luke is his guide he allows himself more liberty with the order of events. Luke sees temporarily through Mary's eyes when he writes that after the homage of the shepherds she 'kept these things and pondered them in her heart' (2.19). The child grows strong in spirit and full of wisdom (2.40), and when he reaches the age of twelve his parents, missing him in the homeward

[40] Birth of John the Baptist at 1.1–51; annunciation to Mary at 1.52–79; visit of Mary to Elizabeth at 1.80–104; naming and consecration of the Baptist at 1.105–132. After the intercalation of Joseph's dream at 1.133–143 (cf. Matthew 1.18–25), Juvencus recounts the journey of Mary and Joseph to Bethlehem, the cradling of Jesus in the manger, the homage of the shepherds, the circumcision and the prophecies of Simeon and Anna (1.144–222, closely following Luke 2.1–30). Next come the adoration of the Magi, the flight to Egypt and the return to Nazareth (1.223–277; cf. Matthew 2.1–23), and then the teaching in the temple, the last excerpt of any length from Luke (1.278–306).

[41] See Matthew 27.25, 27.38, 27.51–53, 28.2–3, 28.12–15, 28.9, 28.16–19.

[42] Note, on the other hand, that when translating Matthew 5.8 ('Blessed are the pure of heart') the Latin speaks of those who 'cherish heaven in a pure heart' (*puro qui caelum corde tuentur*: 1.463), perhaps in allusion to Luke 17.20 ('the kingdom of heaven is within [or among] you').

[43] Contrast Matthew 4.1–11 with Luke 1.1–13. At 1.409 the imprisonment of John marks the inception of a new narrative, as at Matthew 4.12; Luke's story of the reading in the synagogue at Nazareth (4.16–22) is omitted.

[44] See Matthew 19.9 against Mark 10.11 and Luke 16.18, though it is possible that Matthew is referring to sexual congress before the marriage.

journey after the Passover, return to Jerusalem and find him teaching in the temple (2.41–49). At the end of chapter 2 (as we divide the text[45]) Mary ponders his sayings once again while he continues to increase in wisdom and age (or perhaps in stature: 2.52). Juvencus, not illogically, is content to say once, having increased in age and wisdom (1.278–280), Jesus revealed the first-fruits of his maturity in the temple; it is Mary alone who discovers him there (1.287–295), and only when all these episodes from his childhood have been recounted is she left to ponder them (1.304). It is in the age of Constantine that the acclamation of Mary as Theotokos, or 'God-bearer', is first securely attested in the writings of Eusebius of Caesarea and Alexander of Alexandria. Manuscripts of Constantine's *Oration to the Saints* preserve an expression of similar import—a maid was the *mêtêr theou* (mother of God)—though this is bracketed in the printed text of Heikel.[46] Juvencus affords further evidence of its currency in the west when he substitutes for 'mother of my Lord' at Luke 2.43 the more orotund *mater numinis alti*, mother of the Exalted Power (1.89).

In a work that proclaims the divinity of Christ with such grandiloquence, one is surprised to meet no echo of the prologue to John's Gospel.[47] A seamless tract of this occupies the first half of the second book,[48] and the resurrection of Lazarus, a miracle peculiar to this Gospel, is recounted in the fourth book with little modification of the original (4.306–402; cf. John 11.1–46). Elsewhere Juvencus makes only desultory use of sayings and incidents from this text,[49] and seldom tries to bring its narrative into harmony with Matthew's. John's story of the healing of the noblemen's son is commonly regarded as a variant of the healing of the centurion's son or servant in Matthew and Luke, but these events figure in different parts of the epic as unrelated miracles.[50] More generous to John than to Luke, Juvencus records the protest of the crowd that they will have no king but Caesar (4.616–617) and the solders' casting of lots for the robe of Christ (4.662–663);[51] he has nothing to say, however, of Christ's injunctions from the Cross to his mother and the beloved disciple (19.25–27), of the role of Nicodemus in his burial (25.39) or of his subsequent appearances in a manner that tested the insight of his followers (20.11–29 and 21.1–14). Nicodemus remains anonymous in his

[45] We should note that the transitions from Luke to Matthew and from Matthew to Luke in the epic are apt to coincide with our division of chapters.

[46] See Heikel, *Leben Constantins* (Bibliography A), 168.25 with Girardet, *Oratio ad Sanctos* (Bibliography A), 166.

[47] The expression *terrarum lumen* (light of the world) at 2.75 is reminiscent of John 1.14, but also of 8.12 and 9.5.

[48] From 2.99 to 2.346 he paraphrases John 1.43–4.33 with few omissions, though at 1.198 John 4.24 has been translated prematurely as a gloss on Jesus' reference to the Spirit at 3.8.

[49] See e.g. 2.637–691, corresponding to John 5.19–47.

[50] See 1.741–766 (cf. Matthew 8.5–13); 2.326–46 (cf. John 4.47–53).

[51] See John 19.12, 19.24.

dialogue with Jesus (1.178; cf. John 3.1), and there are other conversations in the Gospel which are wholly unrepresented in the epic. Jesus does not wash the feet of his disciples (John 13.1–17), intone a long prayer at the Last Supper or say 'Before Abraham was, I am' (John 8.58). Whereas the Baptist denies that he is Elijah at John 1.21, and at Matthew 17.12 the disciples are left to infer from a gnomic saying of Jesus that he was Elijah after all, Juvencus makes him say explicitly that Elijah 'assumed the body of John as his abode' (1.544).

For Juvencus, therefore, John stands next, and clearly second, to Matthew among the four canonical gospels. There are few signs of dependence on apocryphal texts, though the clothes in which Christ awaits his execution are described in a variation of Matthew's text which recurs in other Latin witnesses, but appears to derive from a second-century harmony of the gospels:

> Matthew 27.28: They stripped him and put on him a scarlet robe.
>
> Iuvencus 4.644: *Purpureamque illi tunicam clamidemque rubentem/Inducunt* ['They put upon him a purple tunic and a robe'.]

More interesting is a prophecy of Christ's return from the underworld, which is more reminiscent of a fantastic scene in the *Gospel of Peter* than of any canonical narrative:

> Rise, and be strong; tread down ignoble fear. And let not the present vision be disclosed in words until the Son of Man brings back his glittering trophies from the lair of death, carrying them up into the light. (3.339–342)
>
> Cf. *Gospel of Peter* 9.38–41. While they were yet telling them the things which they had seen, they saw three men coming out of the sepulchre, and two of them sustaining the other, and a cross following after them. And of the two that they saw that their heads reached up to heaven, but of him that was led by them it overpassed the heavens.[52]

Consultation of apocryphal gospels might account for the cryptic embellishments to the words that pass between Jesus and the disciple who betrays him. Judas, as the eponym of his people, might be expected to receive no quarter in a narrative that tends to excise whatever the evangelists say in honour or exculpation of the Jews. Although the Decalogue remains in force, Jesus can speak of it already as a portion of the old law.[53] Nathanael's faith is praised as that of a *vir*, a man—no longer an Israelite, as at John 1.47—'in whom there is no guile' (2.111). Caiaphas is still, as in John, the chief mover of plots against Jesus (4.405), but is no longer animated by the fear of a bloody reprisal by the Romans against the whole people (John 11.49–52). Judas, by contrast, when he asks whether he is the one whose treachery has just been foretold by Jesus,

[52] Translation James (1924).

[53] See 3.504: there is no authority at Matthew 19.18 for the phrase *vetus lex*. It may be observed, however, that at 2.255 it is the Samaritans, not the Jews (as at John 4.9) who are held responsible for the ban on intercourse between the two peoples.

receives the answer, 'I hear you say it' (4.445), whereas in Matthew he says only 'the words are yours' (26.25). When Judas reveals the identity of Jesus with a kiss, his act provokes not merely a reproachful greeting—'Friend, why have you come?' (Matthew 26.50) but an enigmatic word of resignation:

> Totum complere licebit,
> Huc venisse tuo quaecumque est causa paratu. (4.519–520)

[All will be permitted to reach its term, whatever is the cause of coming hither by your contrivance.]

In the Gospel of John the crime is perpetrated not only with the full knowledge of Jesus but at his bidding (13.26); in the newly discovered gospel that is named after him, Judas is not so much a traitor as a secret accomplice in the consummation of his master's destiny. Juvencus follows neither of these sources, but is it possible that he is consciously preserving a lost tradition which assigns a secret, and not entirely ignominious place in God's design to this Jew of the Jews?

STYLE AND INTENT

The style of Juvencus is seldom pleasing, except where he steals bodily from Virgil.[54] When he forgets to plagiarize, the marriage of classic diction and biblical matter is often incongruous: if *mater numinis alti* is a curious pleonasm for 'mother of God', how was a Christian, knowing only the Bible, to divine that *aether* is heaven, and Tonans ('thunderer') an alias for the Father?[55] Conversely, there are expressions which mean nothing to those unacquainted with the scriptures: *proles hominis*, as a synonym for 'son of man' (4.153), does not become more decipherable because it is succeeded three lines later by *hominis natus* (4.156) and after another thirty by *filius hominis* (4.186).[56] We can understand, none the less, that to such a reader the poet might seem at times to have improved on his original. In his rendering of the parable of the sheep and goats, for example, he assigns each flock to its

[54] E.g. *tantae molis* at 3.326; *lumen ademptum* at 2.411. Cf. also the Lucretian *in luminis oras* (into the coasts of light) at 2.342. Subtler appropriations are detected by Van der Nat (1973) on the substitution of *Christo* at 1.27 for *Phoebo* at *Aeneid* 6.66.2; Green (2006), 10 on the relation between 2.142 and *Aeneid* 7.124; Ratkowitsch (1986) on the storm at 2.25–42. See generally Roberts (2004).

[55] At 4.533 *summi per regna tonantis* ('through the kingdoms of him who thunders on high') is a periphrasis for 'by the living God' at Matthew 26.63. It might be argued, however, that in fact a Jewish priest would used a metonym rather than a term explicitly denoting God.

[56] Cf. *suboles hominis* at 4.320.

pasture, and thereby brings the scene before the eye in a manner characteristic of pastoral, though foreign to the practice of biblical writers:[57]

> Ut pastor pecoris discernit pascua mixti,
> Lanigeris dextri permittens mollia prati
> At laevos hirtis dumos tondere capellis. (4.264–266)

[As a shepherd allocates pastures to a mixed flock, assigning to the woolly sheep the smooth field on the right, but to the goats the left-hand brambles.]

Nor is the pastoral colour entirely inapposite, for at least one allusion to the Fourth Eclogue silently endorses the reading of it as a Messianic prophecy which had been advanced in clearer terms by Constantine and Lactantius:[58]

> At tu parve puer sanctus dignusque propheta
> Diceris et Dominum mox progrediere viando
> Illius et populum duces per lumen apertum. (1.125–127)

[But you, infant boy, will be called holy and worthy of the prophet, and soon you will be the Lord's harbinger in the way and will lead his people in the open light.]

In certain cases (not the majority), circumlocution acts as a gloss on texts that admit of more than one construction. According to Matthew, the reply of Jesus to the high priest's question 'Are you the Christ, the Son of God?' was 'You have said it' (26.63), a repetition of his last words to Judas. At Luke 22.70 this becomes 'You [plural] say that I am.' These words could imply denial or affirmation, but the rendering of Juvencus leaves no doubt that Jesus returned the clear affirmative that we find in the Gospel of Mark:[59]

> Istaec sola tibi procedunt pectore verba
> Vera tuo. (4.556–557)

[These words of yours are the only true ones that have issued from your breast.]

On the other hand, when Pilate demands of Jesus, 'Are you the king of the Jews?', and receives the same response—'You say it'—in all four gospels,[60] the Latin paraphrase now conveys an equally emphatic negative: *Vestris haec audio verbis*, 'the words that tell me this are yours' (4.593). At times Juvencus expands not merely the diction but the theological import of a saying. In

[57] Note also that at 1.683–685, the way of virtue is not merely strait, as at Matthew 7.13–14, but high and rugged like the path enjoined by virtue in Prodicus' fable of the choice of Heracles.

[58] Cf. Virgil, *Eclogue* 1.18 (*at tibi prima, puer*) and 1.60 (*incipe, parve puer*). Note, however, that the object of this eulogy is not Jesus but the Baptist. Compare also *ordine saeclorum* at 2.826 with *ordo saeclorum* (the roll of centuries) at *Eclogue* 4.5; *fraudis vestigia* at 2.435 with *priscae vestigia fraudis* at *Eclogue* 4.31. The term *fraus* denotes religious infidelity in Juvencus, failure of probity in Virgil.

[59] See Mark 14.61–62, where the priest is also more circumlocutory in his reference to God.

[60] Matthew 27.11, Mark 15.2, Luke 23.3, John 18.37.

Matthew the assertion that God is not the God of the dead but of the living signifies, in refutation of the Sadducees, that there will be a resurrection (22.32). Juvencus turns it into an intimation that there are some who will die and some who will live eternally—in other words, that some are destined for heaven and some for hell:

> Nor does God wish to make himself lord of those who in their baseness have merited baneful death, but rather of those who are able to apprehend the light of life. (4.35–37)

Jesus taught his disciples to pray for bread that is described in Greek by the hitherto unknown compound *epiousion*. Origen, deriving this from the noun *ousia*, concludes that the bread is the knowledge of that which truly is; earlier Latin authors, preferring an etymology from the future of the verb which means 'to come', had arrived at the sense 'bread for tomorrow', or as we say 'daily bread'. Juvencus interjects the word *substantia* to show that he concurs with Origen:[61]

> In caelo et terris fiat tua clara voluntas,
> Vitalisque hodie sancti substantia panis
> Proveniat nobis. (1.594–596).

> [May thy august will be done in heaven and earth, and may the vital essence of holy bread be provided for us.]

He may also have inherited from Origen the principle that the sense of a term in any text of scripture is germane to its interpretation in any other text. Certainly his figurative reading of this article in the Lord's Prayer is foreshadowed in the epic by Christ's refusal to create his own daily bread:

> Nam memini scriptum, quoniam non sola tenebit
> Vitam credentis facilis substantia panis. (1.379–380)

> [For I recall that it is written that the life of the believer is not sustained by the pliable essence of bread alone.]

Whether or not this implies that every Christian meal is a Eucharist, the unity of doctrine in the New Testament is illustrated by the proleptic appearance of the talents in elaborated texts from the Gospel of Matthew. Where the latter has 'lay not up treasure for yourselves on earth' (Matthew 6.19), Juvencus writes 'it is vain to keep watch over talents buried in the earth' (1.611). Perhaps the most obscure of Matthew's parables is one that enjoins us to 'make peace with our enemy in the way lest we be thrown into a jail from which we shall not emerge until we have paid the last farthing' (Matthew 5.25–26). This for Juvencus is an allegory in which the enemy personifies the body:

[61] Cf. Colombi (1997), 37.

Always at odds with you, moreover, is the power of the body. This should be tended with keen love of chastity as it travels with you along the paths of a fleeting life. For the impure use of the body will be your accuser and will set you in chains before the Most High Judge. When you are condemned, the angels will hurry you into harsh confinement, and you will not be released from the shadows of the dark prison until the last piece of the smallest coin has been repaid. (1.511–517)

Believers are admonished at Matthew 10.28 to fear not those who are able to kill the body but the one who has power to destroy both body and soul in hell. Interpreters are divided as to whether this tormentor is God or the devil, but Juvencus resolves the question in two lines by crediting him with unlimited power, including the power to unlock the heart:

Illum sed potius cordis secreta pavescant,
Corporis est animique simul cui cuncta potestas. (2.488–489)

[But let the secrets of the heart rather fear him to whom is all power at once over body and mind.]

Iuvencus suits the moral application of Jesus' sayings to a time when the church was almost reconciled to the world, but the life of the individual believer was portrayed in monastic literature as a truceless war against Satan. On the one hand, then, he iterates the word *pax* when reproducing the command at Matthew 10.13 that the missionary should 'leave his peace' with a household that proves worthy of the gospel (2.446–450), and he modifies Matthew 22.43 to make Jesus say that a *placida gens*, a 'people of peace' will receive the inheritance of the Jews (3.736). On the other hand, greater austerities are inculcated where the Master himself had spoken only of prayer and fasting:

Nam genus hoc morbi precibus sine fine fidesque
Multaque robusti ieiunia pectoris arcent. (3.379–80; cf. Matthew 18.21)

[For a malady of this kind is averted by the faith and repeated fasting of a strong breast with endless prayers.]

Again, in this age when every sin had its place in a tariff of penances, Jesus' exclamation that the publicans and harlots would enter heaven before the Pharisees was intelligible only if their admission was made contingent on repentance:

Namque fidem potius meretricum pectora certam
Hauserunt sordesque animi posuere pudendas.
At vos tantorum scelerum nil paenitet umquam.

[For the hearts of prostitutes have drunk more deeply of faith, in some measure, and have put aside the shameful filth of the mind. For your part, great as your sins are, you never repent of them.]

Thus Christ in metre teaches Christianity by numbers. The best poet of his time is a man of the church, who achieves his harmony in the same manner as Eusebius, neglecting Mark and favouring the most didactic of the four evangelists in order to delineate a hero who can be weighed triumphantly against the gods and demigods of pagan myth.

A POET OF HIS AGE?

One might suppose that a poet who speaks so militantly of his enterprise at the outset, and salutes the universal reign of Constantine in his epilogue, would not be silent regarding the perils from which the church had recently been delivered. In fact Juvencus makes no explicit reference to the atrocities of the Tetrarchs or to the wars that put an end to them. Green observes that Christ and his disciples are often characterized by the adjective *justus* '(righteous'),[62] and this is not only the term applied to both Christ and Joseph of Arimathea by Luke (23.47.50) but the one that Apollo chose in an oracle that inspired the Great Persecution.[63] We may wonder, none the less, how any readers of the Latin poet would have been familiar with this utterance; they would certainly be aware of recent schisms in the empire, but when Juvencus renders the saying in Matthew, 'a kingdom divided against itself cannot stand' (20.26), he adds nothing to the text beyond the redundancy that always accompanies metrical paraphrase.[64] It is equally hard to find any verse in which he unequivocally gives his suffrage to the Nicene Creed against Arius. He omits one, but not both of the passages in which Luke says that Christ increased in wisdom;[65] he softens any hint in the biblical text that Christ was not divine and asserts, where the text does not say so, that he was begotten of the Father; at one point an allusion to Virgil tacitly invites the reader to add the word 'god' to the biblical question, 'Who is this that commands the wind and waves?'[66] But anyone who was truly a follower of Arius, rather than an Athanasian caricature, would insist that Christ was God and that he was begotten: the question was not whether he was god and son of God, but in what sense.

If this poem, so classical in diction and so biblical in content is in any sense of its time, it is not by echoing past events but by holding up a mirror to the present conditions that have resulted from them. Christians were no longer a people in exile, but the new masters in Egypt, with the duty of passing on the

[62] Green (2006), 118.

[63] Green (2006), 122 aptly cites Lactantius, *Institutes* 2.15.3 and *Deaths of the Persecutors* 9.11.

[64] *Pace* Green (2006), 125 on 6.605–607.

[65] Green (2006), 118 notes the omission of Luke 2.52, but not the paraphrase of Luke 2.49 at 1.279–280.

[66] See Green (2006), 62 on 2.40 ('What great power had been granted to him'), where the prototype at Aeneid 9.97 (*cui tanta deo permissa potestas*) means 'to what God such power is granted'.

arts that were still the required concomitants of prosperity. What Virgil had been to the Romans a poet with worthier matter could be to the Christian empire: he had no more fear of tedium in his readers than of censorship from the magistrate, so long as he adhered to the sacred narrative which, thanks to the munificence of the emperor, was now more widely known than the tale of Aeneas had been to readers of Virgil. By versifying this tale, he could achieve more than a sweetening of the medicine, a smoothing of the cornerstone that had hitherto been a rock of offence for cultivated readers. Constantine's panegyrists had saluted him in the words that Virgil addressed to Augustus after he had vanquished his last rival; Constantine and Lactantius had maintained that the Saviour prophesied in the Fourth Eclogue is no Roman but the prince of Peace whom a Roman governor had put to death. Just as the apologists had fought rhetoric with rhetoric in the second century, so the composition of this epic, only a few years after Constantine had reunited the empire, gave ancestral sanction to the new Christian polity, and at the same time—did Constantine himself see this?—proclaimed that the mortal rulers of this polity were mere legates for one whose kingdom will have no end.

CONCLUDING NOTE ON IMAGES

The passion of Christ could not fail to occupy a conspicuous place in any narrative based on the gospels; we have also seen, however, that both Eusebius and Athanasius chose to dwell at hitherto unusual length on the purpose of his death and the theological reasons for the manner of it. We have noted that the depiction of the cross in Christian art became under Constantine, but this tolerance was extended to representations of the living Christ, which were still held to be forbidden by the Decalogue. Eusebius himself, if a letter preserved by the iconoclasts of the eighth century is authentic and rightly ascribed to him, was one of the chief enforcers of this prohibition.[67] At no time, however, was it extended to statues of the emperor, since Constantine could not expect to be revered where his image was not present. An anecdote, too late and too tendentious to carry much authority, tells us that he was able to bear the defacement of his likeness with equanimity;[68] Eusebius, on the other hand, maintained that if the Son is the perfect image of the Father he must enjoy parity of honour, though neither he nor Athanasius argues from this to unity of substance.[69] Some would say that the simile was deployed in support of an obsolescent Christology; if it is true, however, that the secular use of statues helped to weaken the opposition to religious sculpture in the late fourth

[67] See Barnes (2010b). [68] Edwards (2006b), 156.
[69] Eusebius, *Demonstration*, proem 24–25; Athanasius, *Against the Arians* 3.6.

century,[70] it is possible that, whether he would have wished it or not, the analogical reasoning of Eusebius contributed to the early development of Christian art.

For all that, the plastic image is no rival to the text. The arch of Constantine was a public chronicle of his victories, but it would be illegible now if we possessed no written record of those victories.[71] When Constantine decreed that his place of interment should be surrounded by monuments to the twelve apostles (Eusebius, *Life of Constantine* 4.60), an observer could not know whether he was claiming to be the thirteenth of Christ's acolytes or a second incarnation. Eusebius, on the other hand, depicts his hero unambiguously as a latter-day Moses, driving his enemy Maxentius into the Tiber as the Israelite had overwhelmed Pharaoh's chariots in the Red Sea (*Life* 1.38). The typology recurs at *Life* 2.4, where it is Licinius who imagines that a rabble of Egyptian jugglers and soothsayers can defeat the anointed minister of God. A loftier comparison, which could never have been reproduced in the art of the day, is drawn by the *Tricennalian Oration* in praise of Constantine, where, as we shall see in chapter 14, no model can be found below the heavens for this indomitable servant of the Father, the sun of righteousness on earth.

[70] L'Orange and Unger (1984).

[71] Elsner (2000b) contrasts this memorial, in which Constantine collected the spoils of the imperial past, with the mausoleum in which he was unable to draw on any tradition of Roman iconography.

APPENDIX

The Theophany

The *Theophany*, which is generally reckoned to be a later work than both the *Preparation* and the *Demonstration*, offers a synthesis of the arguments which he developed separately in these longer writings.[72] The objection to be answered, here as in his *Preparation* and *Demonstration of the Gospel*, is the one that every pagan thought conclusive: how can Christianity, as a religion of yesterday, set aside the consensus of the nations and pretend to knowledge that was not vouchsafed to the founders of the more ancient religions at a time when human beings enjoyed immediate communion with the divine? His reply—not a new one, but never so clearly enunciated before him—is that Christianity is in fact the most ancient of all religions, because it worships the creative Word who endowed humankind with reason. This Word is the author of every truth that was discovered by philosophy or revealed by the prophets before the incarnation; since he has come among us, those who have turned to him are in possession of the fullness of truth for the first time in the world's history, while those who deny him—Greeks and Jews alike—are guilty of mistaking the provisional for the eternal, the adumbration for the fact.

The *Theophany* survives in its entirety only in Syriac, without dedication or preface. In the opening paragraph a salvo of ridicule and invective greets the reader who doubts that the universe is governed by a single benign intelligence (pp. 39*–40* Gressmann);[73] in the second the author turns from the atheists, as he styles them, to the polytheists, whom he represents (like Paul and Aristides before him[74]) as worshippers of the elements (40*–41*). Having disposed of this obvious confusion of the artefact with the artificer, he falls into a more biblical vein, affirming that all that lives or moves with purpose is animated by the omnipresent Word. The very multiplicity of phenomena, the diversity of habitat, anatomy and behaviour in the natural world, the incommensurability of human laws and customs all bear witness to the unity of the Word, since if there were not one power upholding it the universal fabric would dissolve (41*–45*). Those who mistake this Word for fate, an immanent principle blindly working out its ends without justice or any rational design, are also atheists and idolaters, for the processes which the Word sustains did not come into being of themselves but owe their creation to the same inscrutable God who is the father and wellspring of the Word himself (44*–45). As the wisdom and power of God (46*; cf. 1 Corinthians 1.24), it is he who proclaims the mystery of the Father's will, and who at his bidding holds the reins of the cosmos, at once the helmsman of all and the universal saviour (46*–47*). More reminiscent of Origen than of Paul is the intercalation of an angelic choir between the Word and his visible creatures, with the duty on

[72] On its relation to earlier writings (the *Prophetic Selections* and *General Elementary Introduction*) see Johnson (2013b), 19–20 and 46–9.

[73] For this edition see Bibliography A. For the Greek of this passage, see 3* Gressmann.

[74] For Aristides see Bibliography A, and cf. Galatians 4.9.

the one hand of intoning ceaseless hymns to God and on the other of welcoming the saints to their imperishable abodes (59*). Humans, though incarnate in this lower world, bear within them the bodiless image of the pure Intellect that shaped them, and it is by the intellect, not through the senses, that we discern the rational harmony of the world and deduce the existence of an incorporeal God (61*–70*). Humans alone construct their own abodes and form societies by contract; they alone can scan the heavens, number the notes of the scale, and shape the letters of the alphabet to leave records of their own deeds (66*–67*). Had we but allowed our reason to guide us, we should long ago have attained to our full stature (70*–71*); even now we see in the growth of children a presage of that transformation which awaits the elect in heaven (74*–75*). The Word himself, whose secret operations fill the cosmos (60*) is the seed of that immortality which will clothe the children of God when they come of age (78*–80*).[75]

In the next book the errors of paganism are reduced to six heads: the deification of the carnal appetites; the cult of the infamous dead; the attribution of divine sentience to the elements; the manufacture of images for worship; the murder of innocent beasts for the pleasure of demons; and the attempt to master these hidden masters by the use of magic. (82*–84*). All pretence of system, however, is then thrown to the winds in a diffuse and repetitive catalogue of atrocities, where human sacrifice, homoerotic fornication and false beliefs about the afterlife are mingled so promiscuously that we cannot tell whether demons or bygone men are the authors of them, and the Attic tragedians cast their toils about us almost before we have finished ogling the sacred prostitutes of Baalbeck (85*). Twice within a few paragraphs we are told, as though we had not heard it before, that the Phoenicians made a hecatomb to Saturn of their own 'friends' (105*–106*). While the learning in this farrago is worthy of Eusebius, and there are passages which find parallels in other works that are certainly his, he is never so chaotic and repetitive in the arrangement of his matter; we must therefore assume that, if he wrote it at all, the original plan has been obscured by a poor translator or an officious scribe.

It is certainly in the manner of Eusebius to sneer that the pagan gods were no philosophers, then proceed to show that even the philosophers have aggravated the vices that they ought to have restrained. He cannot be blamed for republishing stock caricatures of the Epicureans as atheists (101*), the Stoics as pure materialists (97*) and the presocratics as ancestors of both these blasphemies (91*). Again, it is characteristic of him to think Plato half a Christian when he subordinates the temporal to the eternal and maintains that all souls will undergo posthumous judgment (98*), and equally characteristic of him to be deaf to the comic intent of Plato's remark that we cannot disbelieve what the children of the gods say about their fathers.[76] Athenagoras had already turned this quip into an apologetic weapon, and Constantine holds a similar view of Plato as a thinker on the way to monotheism who allowed himself to be ambushed by the religion of the mob.[77] The nucleus of the case against paganism in the theophany is that its putative deities, if they were ever embodied, dispensed no gifts to their votaries but war and superstition (135*–136*); Christ, by contrast, came to release the world from its prostration by the preaching of peace and the worship of

[75] Cf. Irenaeus, *Against Heresies* 4.38.
[76] *Timaeus* 40d, cited at 93*–94*.
[77] Athenagoras, *Embassy* 23; Constantine, *Oration* 10. *Oration* 7 on fate and 11 on the miracles of Christ are other passages in this text which invite comparison with the *Theophany*.

the true God. Eusebius postpones to the following book the observation (also found in his *Church History*) that the peace of the Augustan age in which Christ was born was a providential arrangement for the diffusion of the gospel (126*). On the other hand, this is not the only book in which he argues that the oracles were silenced by the nativity, though it may be the only one in which he cites the destructibility of temples as a sign that Christ, who was with the father before all worlds, will not divide his glory with other gods (115*–117*).

Thus the *deus ex machina* enters the wings in the second act; in the third we are hurried towards the resolution of the tragedy. Since minds debauched by the cult of idols cannot be induced to worship an immaterial deity, it was necessary that he who is second only to the Father, the creator and king of all, should manifest himself in a body (119*–121*). In the third book Eusebius offers a circumstantial account of this visible ministry. The incarnate word permitted his divine power to be seen in his walking on water (147*), his feeding of the multitude and raisin of the dead; by resisting the temptation in the wilderness he put an end to Satan's dominion over the human soul (150*–152*). Nevertheless, it was necessary also that the body in which he had triumphed should suffer a public execution, in order that he might prove his own immunity to death, give an assurance of his power to confer that immunity on others, and expiate by his sacrifice the sin which gave rise to death in the beginning (153*–155*). All three ends were accomplished by his resurrection, another public event, deferred for two days lest the reality of his death should be contested (158*–159*). By this vindication of his divinity he has achieved more conquests after death than any battle-lord could gain through a life of unbroken victories; throughout the world his bloodless altars stand where demons were once enthroned (161*–162*). Recapitulating his syllabus of pagan errors, Eusebius proclaims that through the ministry of the Word the human race has now been delivered from its bondage to passion, its fear of the dead, its adulation of matter and the chicanery of demons. The very persecutors who made war on him have confessed his invincibility (134*).[78] Even the shrines of demonolatrous Egypt—a scandal to Porphyry, as Athens was to Paul—have now been cleansed (131*). The Roman Empire brought the world under one sceptre, but it is Christ who unites the Greek with the Persian, the Scythian with the Italian, the Indian with the Syrian in the worship of the true God (163*–164*).

In Book 4 the spread of faith is complemented by the incipient punishment of unbelievers. In accordance with the prophecies that he came to fulfil, Christ gave miraculous proofs of his divinity, lamented the fall of Jerusalem before it occurred and sent his first disciples into Galilee as harbingers of a universal mission. His words to the centurion (Matthew 8.10–12) show that his plan was never limited to the Jews, whose intransigence he had always foreseen (167*); in summoning fishermen to be his apostles (Luke 5.10), this revealer of things invisible made prescient use of the strength that is hidden in weakness (171*; Greek at 16*–17*). The tone is at once apologetic and minatory: if pagans ask why God destroyed his own house, they have failed to observe that after 250 years the temple in Jerusalem is still a magnificent ruin, while in the meantime many a pagan shrine has come to dust (191*–198*). It is not clear whether this is an allusion to recent acts by Constantine or to damage that might be inflicted at any time by a freak of nature or the decay of superstition. In any case it is tacitly

[78] An allusion, no doubt to Galerius' repeal of the persecution in 311.

implied that the horrors recounted by Josephus in his history of the Roman sack of Jerusalem prefigure those which await all infidels after the day of judgment (198*–201). By contrast the church has prospered year by year: Jerusalem could boast fifteen Jewish bishops before the dispersion of the people and the refoundation of the city as a Roman colony in AD 135.[79] The gospel has been carried as far as Britain,[80] while the sees which Peter founded in Antioch, Rome and Caesarea, together with the one established by his disciple Mark in Alexandria, have survived both schism within and persecution from without (173*–174*). Christ himself foretold both, and warned that both would trouble the faith of many: consequently, no argument can be made against his teaching from the proliferation of heresy or the apostasy of weak souls under duress. His own parables have warned us that the wheat and the tares will not be separated in this world (Matthew 13.6–43 at 214*).

Nothing remains to be answered in the fifth book but the stale argument that, unless the apostles were liars, their master can only have been a magician.[81] What magician, Eusebius retorts, would have made it the business of his life to expose and confound his demonic allies (229*–230*)? Why would he give the credit for his miracles not to himself, or to a false god, but to the invisible Creator (220*–223*)? How did he communicate the power of working miracles to his followers, not one of whom has been convicted of sorcery (223*–224*)? What magician has ever wrought so many works of healing and largesse, and with such facility? If he learned these arts from his teachers, why are they not equally celebrated (227*–228*)? If his detractors say that the stories told of him are fictitious, they must assume that many witnesses have conspired to deceive (240*); but why should they conspire to bring themselves into danger and infamy, seeking martyrdom at the extremities of the empire, in Armenia, Persia, Scythia, and Britain (228*–229*)? If men of no worldly account, and with visible weapons but their own faith and virtue (236*), have induced whole cities to burn their magical books[82] and forsake their idols, how could any diabolic or human artifice account for their success? What could it be, in fact, but the resurrection of Christ that made his death not a source of shame and consternation, but the seed of a kingdom which has not ceased to grow?[83]

The triumphant coda in the fifth book implies that apologetic, if it is still to be written at all, must acquire new functions as the menace of the law recedes and numbers are daily added to the church. For the most part, however, this is an apology in the conventional style, which could not meet the expectations of the fourth century. It makes no attempt, for example, to demonstrate the harmony of the four gospels, the truth of the resurrection and the fulfilment in Christ's human life of the prophecies that he had uttered beforehand as the Word. Like the *Demonstration*, however, it firmly gives the lie to those who assert that the incarnation of Christ was of little account to Eusebius.[84] It would surely be truer to say, with Christopher Beeley,[85] that

[79] *Theophany* 202*; cf. *Church History* 4.5.3.

[80] *Theophany* 170*—perhaps the first attestation of Christianity in Britain.

[81] See also Book 4, 209*, citing Matthew 12.24.

[82] Acts 19.19, quoted at 224*.

[83] See John 12.23–24 at Book 4, 203*; Matthew 13.3–8 and 18–23 at 211*–212*; Book 5, 238* and 255*. Cf. Origen *Against Celsus* 8.43.

[84] Walker (1990), 83 and Kee (1982), *passim*.

[85] Beeley (2012), 57–73 on the *Church History*.

his Christology is omnipresent even in those works which are not expressly theological in tenor; it is one of at least three texts[86] in which he dares to raise the question that hitherto had been heard more often on the lips of the unbeliever—the question why it was necessary for God's own Son to die.

[86] In addition to the *Demonstration* see *Tricennial Oration* 15 with Beeley (2012), 76.

13

From Origen to Arius

So far as is known, no Hermetist or alchemist, no Mithraist or devotee of Isis was ever subject to a strict rule of belief which had been framed by a consensus of recognized teachers. The Platonists had one master, whose ambiguous texts gave rise to impassioned seminars and caustic ebullitions of midnight oil; even for them, however, there was no hegemonic body which could determine the right view or even the opinion of a majority. Christian theologians, on the other hand, had been accustomed since the second century to invoke a rule of faith which, though unwritten, was implicit in every discourse from the pulpit, except on the rare occasions when the bishop or one of his presbyters had erred. Theologians and historians of the church agree that the Council of Nicaea in 325 marks the watershed between the age of latent norms and the age of conciliar legislation; the best students, however, do not fall into the error of supposing that the concept of orthodoxy was born at Nicaea or that its content was fixed for ever. We shall see in the present chapter that the dispute surrounding Origen, twenty years before the council, rested on theological presumptions which were shared both by his critics and by his admirers; it was only after the council that Eusebius and Marcellus, still disputing the orthodoxy of Origen, offered rival accounts of the teaching of the church. Since both subscribed to the Nicene Creed, it cannot be maintained that this document represents either the defeat or the vindication of the Origenists; by the end of this chapter it ought indeed to be obvious that no neat bifurcation of the combatants—into Arians and Nicenes, for example, or even into Eusebians and pro-Nicenes—will do justice to the diversity of their opinions or account for the multiplication of ecclesiastical parties after the signing of the creed.

THE ORIGENIST CONTROVERSY

Origen was the first Christian to merit a hagiography without undergoing martyrdom.[1] A panegyric attributed to Gregory Thaumaturgus relates that the

[1] On the authorship and date of the work, which appears to have been written in Origen's lifetime, see Rizzi (2002), 9–10.

author himself was one of the pagans weaned from error by Origen, who were able to master all the elements of the Greek philosophies in his school. It was Origen's maxim, indeed, that one cannot be become a deep scholar in theology without a philosopher's training. Compendious though his curriculum was, his favoured method in pedagogy was that of Plato's Socrates, who set out to cajole the truth from his interlocutor by the cross-examination of his 'rude and inopportune' notions. His lodestar was the maxim 'know thyself', which had been commended to Socrates by the Delphic Oracle; like the same philosopher in the *Republic*, he led his charges to dialectic through the study of physics, geometry, and astronomy; and while he never held that the pupil and the teacher should be in love as Plato enjoins, his students were bound to him by a chaste passion resembling that of David and Jonathan (p. 142 Rizzi). Origen the pastor, in short, is Origen the Platonist, though not the stereotypical Platonist that he has become for modern exponents of this thesis. Philosophy is for Gregory, as for Origen and for Socrates before him, not so much a system as a way of life. In the more famous account of Origen's career that dominates Book 6 of the *Church History* by Eusebius, he is a Christian ascetic, whose instructor in philosophy, one Ammonius, is declared, in the teeth of pagan testimony, to have been a Christian throughout his life.[2] Eusebius himself, born some years after Origen's death, was the pupil of a pupil, and conscious that Origen's reputation as a teacher had been impugned by other Christians. In reply he dwells on his labours as an exegete, the facility with which he dictated his copious works to a bevy of amanuenses, and the assistance that he rendered to episcopal synods on numerous occasions by his exposure and confutation of real heresies. It is therefore not Origen but his detractors who have impaired the unity of the Church.

What those who were not Origenists thought of Origen we learn from the *Apology* by Pamphilus, his Caesarean disciple, which Eusebius completed after the death of Pamphilus in 309.[3] The *Apology* commences with a severe reflection on those who will hear no voice but their own on points that scripture leaves undetermined, and who therefore suppose, when Origen seals a charitable armistice between two equally tenable positions, that he has no rule for discerning good from evil (*Apology* 1–13). After citing Origen's unexceptionable pronouncements on the transcendence of the Father, the divinity of the Son and the ubiquity of the Holy Spirit,[4] Pamphilus turns to

[2] See especially *Church History* 6.19.8–12.

[3] Schott (2013b) compares this work with Porphyry's *Life of Plotinus* as an exercise in the 'embodiment' of the chief character through texts.

[4] *Apology* 23–25, citing *First Principles* proem 2–10. For commentary see Röwekamp (Bibliography A), 244–52. At *Apology* 30 Pamphilus cites a disquisition on the term 'heretic' from the lost commentary on Titus; at 40 he cites *First Principles* 1.1–14 on the Fatherhood of God; at 45 *First Principles* 2.6.1 on the divinity of the Son; at 48–64 a series of other texts on the generation of the Son; at 65–82 a series of texts on the procession of the Spirit and its activity in the saints.

an inventory of the nine false charges which make up his brief as an apologist, beginning with the most heinous and concluding (as he says) with the most refutable (*Apology* 87). The first charge is that Origen accorded to the Son all the Father's attributes, including that of being unbegotten. The second answers the question, what he might have supposed him to be if not begotten, by imputing to him the doctrine of his infamous predecessor Valentinus, that the Son is an emanation or projection from the substance of the Father. The third—clean contrary to the former two, in the apologist's submission—is that he robbed the incarnate Saviour of his Godhead, representing him as a mere man. The fourth, again at odds with its predecessor, is that he slighted the humanity of Christ, reducing all accounts of his work in the flesh to allegory.[5] The contradiction is mitigated by the fifth indictment, that Origen (like a number of the Gnostics) posited two Christs, denying to each the predicates of the other.[6]

It is not our business here to inquire whether these accusations are true or whether Pamphilus and Eusebius have succeeded in rebutting them. That they chose to rebut them at all is proof of common ground between them and their opponents: they were debating not the norms of belief, but whether Origen held them. It is clear that orthodoxy at this time frowned on teachings which appeared to compromise the simplicity and immateriality of the Father or his priority to the Son. Nothing is said to imply that the subordination of the Son to the Father would have been deemed erroneous, let alone Platonic; there is no intimation, in fact, that Platonism was Origen's heresy.[7] Error was recognized by its proximity to the views of Gnostic teachers,[8] who had been condemned before Origen by Irenaeus, Hippolytus, Tertullian, and Clement. At one point his apologists are obliged to explain a passage from his *Commentary on Hebrews*, where the Son is compared to a vapour that remains *homoousios*, or consubstantial, with the ointment that exhales it.[9] Far from being a diagnostic of orthodoxy, *homoousios* here is a suspect term which must be shown to mean that the Son derives his being from the Father, but with no diminution of the latter's substance. It seems to have been another recognized tenet of orthodoxy that to ascribe a human soul to Christ was to leave no room for a genuine incarnation of the Logos:[10] that is the foundation of the fifth indictment, for Origen had certainly maintained that the Logos assumed not only a human body but a human soul and a human spirit. Eusebius, who notoriously fails to assert this in his dogmatic writings, is in

[5] Addressed at *Apology* 113–115. [6] Addressed at *Apology* 116–122.

[7] See Edwards (2002) and (2009), on the inversion of the indictment after Nicaea, when the assumptions of Origen's earlier critics were redefined as heresies and attributed to him.

[8] Coupling Hebrews 1.3 with Wisdom 7.25–26. See *Apology* 102–108 on Origen's supposed endorsement of the Valentinian term *prolatio* ('emanation'), whose Greek antecedent *probolê* is adopted with the necessary caveats by Tertullian, *Against Praxeas* 12.

[9] See *Apology* 94–101 and Edwards (1998). [10] See *Apology* 123–127.

this respect at one not only with Origen's accusers, but with almost every Christian theologian of his time.

The last four charges rehearsed by Pamphilus all concern the destiny and constitution of the human agent, and any one of them, if proved, would have carried the day for Origen's critics, in his own century and thereafter. It was alleged (6) that he denied the empirical truth of every narrative in the scriptures that purports to be historical;[11] (7) that he treated the resurrection of the body, with its associated penalties and prizes, as an edifying fable;[12] (8) that he entertained false opinions with regard to the soul; and (9) that the most culpable of these was his espousal of the Platonic doctrine of transmigration, according to which the soul, when it quits one corporal tenement, passes not into heaven or hell but into the body of another beast or human. The last two of these are easily rebutted;[13] the first two can be shown from Origen's writings to be not so much false as extravagantly phrased.

In fact we learn most about Origen's doctrine of the resurrection from a book by Bishop Methodius of Olympia, which survives now only in excerpt and epitome.[14] Among the erroneous tenets ascribed to Origen are: (1) that the coats of skins which God contrived for Adam and Eve are Biblical symbols of the flesh which attires the fallen soul;[15] (2) that the man of whom Paul says 'I was alive before the law' (Romans 7.9) is the heavenly prototype whom God created before he fashioned his earthly tenement;[16] (3) that while the soul survives death, the body is not renewed;[17] (4) that the bodies of those who rise in glory will be limbless;[18] (5) that after death the soul retains only the incorporeal form or *morphê* of the abandoned body.[19] These charges, as they stand, are not coherent, and the third is leveled not at Origen but at 'Origenists'. The first charge is brought against Origen by a number of ancient witnesses,[20] though it cannot be verified from his extant writings;[21] the complaint is not, as it might be in modern scholarship, that he tempers an

[11] See *Apology* 113–115.

[12] See *Apology* 128–150.

[13] See *Apology* 151–162 on posthumous chastisement; 163–176 on the nature of soul; 177–188 on transmigration.

[14] Reconstructed in N.P. Bonwetsch, *Methodius: Werke* (Bibliography A). Patterson (1989) observes that Origen may not be the sole target.

[15] See especially pp. 111, 122, 137–8, and 277 in Bonwetsch's edition.

[16] See pp. 175–77 Bonwetsch, where it is alleged that Origen took the speaker to be Adam, lamenting his fall into the embodied state.

[17] Hence the wearisome demonstrations at pp. 165–75 that the term 'resurrection' applies pre-eminently to bodies, that if the soul is the proper cause of sin it would not be just that only the body should die, and that the torments foretold for the damned in scripture are manifestly corporeal.

[18] Methodius, p. 272 Bonwestch. This may imply incorporeality rather than the spherical form which was later said to have been ascribed by Origen to the resurrection body.

[19] See especially 99.14 Bonwetsch, though at 124.2 it is Methodius himself who applies the term *morphê*, without reservation, to the hylomorphic union of body and soul.

[20] See p. 289 in Bonwetsch's edition.

[21] See Clark (1992), 85; Heidl (2003).

anthropomorphism by allegory, but rather that he seeks the literal counterpart of the skins in mere corporeality, not in the mortality and corruption entailed by sin. The second charge is corroborated in part by Origen's reading of the two accounts of the making of humanity in Genesis, which he takes, with his characteristic 'literalism', to signify first the creation of the inner man and next the fashioning of his carnal envelope (*Genesis Homilies* 1). The pretext for the fourth charge is to be found in Origen's statement that the spherical form is an element in the perfection of heavenly bodies (*On Prayer* 31.3); the fifth would be just if Origen's term *eidos* ('form') were understood in the sense in which he intended it. As Crouzel has demonstrated, his *eidos* is not the ideal form of Plato nor the 'entelechic' form of Aristotle;[22] while it signifies something more enduring, and for that reason far less tangible, than the shape of the physical body, it is not wholly independent of corporeality or materiality. For all that was said to the contrary by Jerome and others,[23] these properties are expressly said by Origen to be indispensable conditions of individuation, in the next life as in this (*First Principles* 1.6.4; *Against Celsus* 5.18–21).

After Nicaea it was no longer heretical to affirm that Christ the Son was *homoousios* with the Father and assumed a human soul in his incarnation. For Origen the perverse result of this revolution was that he fell under censure for holding opinions which in his own time were presuppositions of orthodoxy. One of his critics, however, escaped the chronological fallacy by convicting him of unfaithfulness to his own hermeneutic premises.[24] In his treatise *On the Pythoness*, Eustathius of Antioch rejected Origen's literal exegesis of an episode in the first Book of Kings,[25] in which the fugitive Saul induces a witch to raise the ghost of the Samuel, only to hear his own doom pronounced by the man of God. Origen had concluded that the vision, like the prophecy, was veridical, notwithstanding the objections of those who urged that it was the witch herself, and not the inspired narrator, who gave a name to the apparition. Eustathius retorts that even if there were no suspicion of her sincerity, the devil is the invariable companion of the sorcerer, and capable of deceiving men who are closer to God than Saul (12–13).[26] Origen had maintained that, since the prophecy was true, it could not proceed from the mouth of Satan; Eustathius reminds him that even Caiaphas was an oracle for a day in the Gospel of John (24.4; John 11.50–51). If it were impious to suppose that the devil can simulate the form of a prophet, it is even more impious to suppose,

[22] Crouzel (1972), 690–1. For the relevant passages in Origen see p. 101 on Bonwetsch's edition (following Proclus).

[23] See Crouzel (1972), 713 on Jerome, Letter 96.15.

[24] Parvis (2006), 57 and Beeley (2012) suggest that Eustathius consciously reinforced the criticisms of Methodius and Eutropius of Adrianople.

[25] 1 Kings 28: see Origen, *Homily 5 on Kings* in Greer and Mitchell (2007), 32–61.

[26] For text see Greer and Mitchell (2007), 62–157.

with Origen, that the saints before the incarnation dwelt in the nether world under his dominion (17). Origen himself attached the saints as well as the angels to the retinue of Christ, yet he did not believe that the angels were forced to await his coming in hell (20). Origen was notorious for his attempts to find meanings in scripture that were hidden from the simple: it is all the more remarkable, says this forerunner of the Antiochene school, that he himself should have failed to penetrate such a transparent fraud (21.1).

ARIUS AND HIS ANTECEDENTS

According to the orthodoxy which Pamphilus and Origen's detractors held in common, therefore, the Son is not the equal of the Father and cannot be said, except by a bold analogy with the created order, to be *homoousios* or consubstantial with him. In the first years of the fourth century, even such critics of Origen as Methodius were happy to reiterate his teaching that the Son is the Wisdom of God, who was created before all other works from no other matter than the Father's will. Within two decades, these were suspect doctrines in his native Alexandria, and posterity associates them with Arius, a presbyter of that city, whose defiant espousal of them in opposition to his own bishop precipitated the Council of Nicaea in 325. Although, as we shall see, this council quickly agreed to condemn the Arian tenets that the Son is 'out of nothing' and that 'before he was begotten, he was not', it was more than half a century before its proclamation that the Son is *homoousios* with the Father received the sanction of a second general council. In the course of the intervening conflict, the name of Origen was invoked both by Athanasius, the champion of Nicaea, and by Eusebius of Caesarea, who signed the creed with diffidence, having once been named by Arius as an ally. In certain quarters the texts that could once have been urged in defence of Origen furnished new articles of indictment. At the same time, those who arraigned him were confessedly in debt to him as a scholar and exegete, although they may not have known how much of his theology they had imbibed by their subscription to the doctrine of Nicaea.

The first sentence of Arius' letter to Alexander asserts that God is eternal and without beginning.[27] Neither term is scriptural, but neither would have been contested by any Christian of the fourth century. The name 'God' is used here to denote the Father, in accordance with the usage of the New Testament. Arius adds that God is the only good, the only true, the only wise, and the only immortal. For the origin of these terms we need look no further than the

[27] For discussion of the chronology of the letters of Arius see Williams (2001), 48–81.

scriptural texts which conferred upon them an indisputable legitimacy.[28] When he goes on to asseverate that the Father has a son, begotten in truth and not in semblance, in perfect accordance with the Father's will and before the ages which the Father created through him,[29] Arius was not consciously inviting contradiction. Even those who did not equate the Son with the Wisdom of Proverbs 8.22, who was with God in the beginning before the creation, would accept on the authority of Hebrews 1.2 that the Son is the one through whom God 'made the ages'. The caveat that the Son was begotten according the Father's will was understood by some of his critics to signify that the Father was not predisposed to beget a son by nature; from what follows, however, it appears to have been intended as a rebuttal of the Valentinian teaching that the Wisdom who created the world had introduced division into the Godhead by a reckless act which resulted in her involuntarily bringing forth a son.[30] We are not to join Valentinus, the letter proceeds, in describing the offspring as a material projection from the Father, nor to say, with the Manichees, that he is a consubstantial (*homoousios*) portion of the Godhead.[31] This was the second, if not the third, occasion on which a Christian had denied the orthodoxy of this term; in contrast to the Council of Antioch in 269,[32] Arius treats it as a Manichaean neologism, presupposing a materialistic notion of divine substance. Third in his list of heresies to be shunned is that of Sabellius, who 'divided the monad'; comparison with other reports of Sabellius suggests that the division came about when the Father duplicated himself in a human body. Finally he rejects the conceit that the Son is born like a flame from a flame. We know little of the Hieracas to whom he imputes this error,[33] but the image is derived from a letter of Plato and had commended itself to Justin Martyr.[34] It is curious that the same letter has been adduced to show that the relation between the Father and the Son in the thought of Arius is homologous to, and therefore dependent on, the relation between the First and the Second God in Roman Platonism.[35]

[28] Mark 10.18; John 17.3; Romans 16.27; Timothy 6.16.

[29] On the paradox that the Son, though not eternal, is timelessly begotten, see Meijering (1974); for precedents in Methodius, *On Free Will* 9 and 11, see Pattison (1966).

[30] Cf. Williams (2000), 174. The *Thalia*, cited by Athanasius, *Synods* 15, asserts that Wisdom is wisdom by the will of the Father who is wise; Valentinus, by contrast, taught that the creation was the outcome of Wisdom's alienation from her consort Thelema, or Will. On the primacy of the Father's will in Methodius see Patterson (1966) and Behr (2001), 45–9.

[31] Lyman (1989) points out that Mani echoes Athanasius in the Acts of Archelaus (p. 501) and suggests that Arius and Alexander were 'rival polemicists against the same heresy' (p. 503).

[32] Athanasius, *Synods* 16.

[33] See Clark (1992), 97 and epiphanies, *Panarion* 67.

[34] Justin, *Dialogue with Trypho* 61. But cf. Irenaeus, *Against Heresies* 2.17.4, which suggests a Gnostic origin for the image.

[35] That the arguments mirror those that divided Platonists with respect to the origin of the visible world and the participability of the highest principle has been shown by Stead (1964) and Williams (2001), 215–29. On the essentially biblical character of Arius' teaching nevertheless, see Wiles (1962).

And yet it is a truism (or it ought to be) that homology is no proof of dependence. If it were, the endeavours of early Christian writers to prove that Plato stole from Moses would not have been misdirected. The opening chapter of Genesis had affirmed the likeness of man to God long before Plato stipulated that this was the goal of philosophy. Plato had also attributed the creation of the one world to a single god, and even the heavenly paradigm which guides the demiurge has its biblical antecedent at Exodus 25.9. Christians did not hesitate to adopt the logical methods and the technical vocabulary of the pagan schools: it was therefore inevitable that, in reasoning from premisses which they appeared to share with Plato, they would sometimes arrive at thoughts which bore a specious resemblance to those of his disciples. The mark of Platonism in a Christian author is thus not mere resemblance, but the presence of some article of belief or mode of thinking which is characteristic of this school but alien to the scriptures. If there were any such shibboleth in Arius, it would be his designation of the First Person as a monad and the second as a dyad in the *Thalia*, a poem that now survives only in the tatters that were left behind by the hostile commentary of Athanasius.[36] Certainly this is a conjunction of terms which has a long philosophical ancestry, but is there any trace of this ancestry in its Arian usage? In Platonic and Pythagorean numerology, the Monad stands for limit and the Dyad for the unlimited or infinite; had Arius drawn any such antithesis, infinity would have been a salient predicate of the Father. Nowhere is he known to have asserted that the Son would be lacking in form were it not for the finitude imposed on him by the Father. It is therefore likely, as G. C. Stead proposed, that Arius yielded to the constraints of metre in substituting 'monad' and 'dyad' for the ordinals 'first' and 'second' which he would have employed in prose.[37] The term 'monad' had already been annexed by two renowned apologists, Athenagoras and Origen; if Origen was a Platonist, it does not follow that everyone who imitated his usage was also a Platonist. Arius would have no wish to be known as the disciple of a man who had maintained the coeternity of the Father and his Wisdom and had deduced from the title 'Son' that the Second Person is of the same nature as the First.[38]

In the second half of his letter to Alexander, Arius cites the formula 'three hypostases', which has never been condemned in the east since Origen first employed it, some decades before it was smuggled into Porphyry's edition of Plotinus. But Arius goes on to disown one tenet which was certainly held by Origen—that the Son is coeternal with the Father—and another that had been attributed to him—that the Father and the Son are two ungenerated beings. Origen would not doubt have concurred with him in treating the terms 'begotten' and 'created' as synonyms when we apply them to the origin of

[36] For the reconstruction of the *Thalia* see Stead (1978), with the criticisms of West (1982).
[37] Stead (1964), 19. [38] See Origen, *First Principles* 1.2.

the Son. The source of the former adjective is Psalm 2.7 ('Thou art my son, this day have I begotten thee'), and that of the latter Proverbs 8.22, where Wisdom declares that she was created by the Father in the beginning of his ways. Both would have held that either term is a poor approximation to the ineffable, and Arius affirms as clearly as Origen that the Son's generation was not a temporal process. But Origen had removed the Son from time into eternity, whereas Arius states belligerently that before he was begotten 'he was not'. The Father alone is eternal,[39] because he alone is the monad, uncompounded and hence immune to any change or alienation of his substance.

It follows, in fact, though Arius does not say this to Alexander, that he is 'from nothing';[40] in his letter to Alexander's rival Eusebius of Nicomedia,[41] he complains that it is for this belief that he is persecuted. His meaning, he explains, is that the Son is not a portion of the Father or of anything that exists; it is blasphemous to speak, as Alexander and his satellites do, of emanation or eructation in God or to posit two ingenerate beings. Again he asserts that before the Son was begotten, created, founded, or established, he was not. As scholars have remarked, it was now mandatory for Christians to affirm that the world is 'from nothing', and for many this would be all the more reason not to affirm the same thing of the Son. On the other hand, no such position was entertained by a Platonist regarding either the world or any principle that mediates between the world and the One. In 325 the Council of Nicaea anathematized the Arian doctrines that the Son is 'out of nothing' and that he 'was not before he was begotten'. If it supposed that it was condemning Arius when it affirmed the Son's divinity, it was mistaken, for in his letter to Eusebius the recalcitrant presbyter numbers *theos*, 'god' among his titles. In this respect he is closer to Origen and to the Nicene Council than the majority of today's New Testament scholars, who can deny that the Son in the Gospels is either equal to the Father or 'of the same nature' without incurring the suspicion of Platonism.

THE CREED OF ALEXANDER OF ALEXANDRIA

The tormentor of Arius, Bishop Alexander of Alexandria,[42] evades the traps that his adversary has laid for him not by dividing the monad or postulating a

[39] The Son is none the less born timelessly. The thought is obscure, for as Sorabji (1983), 98–130 demonstrates, Greek thought admitted eternity without timelessness, but not timelessness without eternity.

[40] See further Stead (1998).

[41] Theodoret, *Church History* 1.5. On Eusebius' refusal to affirm that the Son is 'from the *ousia* of the Father' see Bardy (1936), 298–315.

[42] His strategy is characterized by Beeley (2012), 117 as a 'redeployment of Origenism'.

first and second god, but by crediting the Father with a 'nature' that can be shared by emanation. The encyclical against Arius which begins with the words *henos somatos* ('of one body') commences with a polemic against Eusebius of Nicomedia, in whom Arius had found a willing protector.[43] Next Alexander rehearses in brief the errors of Arius and his partisans. They allege (he says) that there was a time when the Father was not yet Father; that, as there was a time when the Son was not, the Father made him out of nothing; that the Son is therefore both a creature and a thing made, not like the Father in *ousia* or essence, and not in truth or nature either his Word or his Wisdom. Possessing these appellatives only in an improper sense, he is subject (on the Arian view) to change and alteration, and has neither a perfect vision of the Father nor essential knowledge of him. He is indeed the Father's instrument, brought into being only that others might be made through him (Socrates, *Church History* 1.6.10).

For Alexander himself the Son is coeval with the Father, like in essence (as he expressly says[44]) and hence no creature, fully endowed with the vision and knowledge of the Father. Alexander goes on to demonstrate that every doctrine that he ascribes to Arius is confounded by the scriptures (Socrates, *Church History* 1.6.12–16). How can have been a time when the Word was not, when the Gospel tells us that he was 'with the Father from the beginning' (John 1.3)? How can the one through whom all things have come into existence be a creature? How can he be from nothing, when the father says of him 'My Heart has disgorged a goodly word' (Psalm 45.1)? Can he of whom it is said that he is the same yesterday, today and for ever (Hebrew 12.8) submit to any change? If he were unlike the Father in essence (1.6.16), would it be said that he is the Father's perfect image or his radiance. Can he for whose sake all things were made be made for the sake of another, and can his knowledge be circumscribed when he himself declares 'as the Father knows me so I too know the Father?' Alexander concludes in a lengthy peroration that one would not have thought such perversity conceivable had not the Apostle warned of heresies in days to come (1.6.24–26, citing 1 Timothy 4.1).

The other surviving work by Alexander of Alexandria is a voluminous epistle to his namesake, Alexander of Byzantium.[45] Its strictures on Eusebius of Nicomedia are eked out by comparisons with Paul of Samosata, the first great prelate to be deposed by an assembly of his peers from the neighbouring provinces,[46]

43 Socrates, *Church History* 1.6. Stead (1988) offers reasons for supposing that Athanasius was the true author.

44 Socrates, *Church History* 1.6.10, p. 8.1–2 Hansen.

45 Theodoret, *Kirchengeschichte* 1.4, ed. L. Parmentier and G. C. Hansen (De Gruyter: Berlin, GCS, neue folge 5, 1998), 8–25.

46 See Lang (2000) on the Council; on its reprobation of the term *homoousios* see Loofs (1924), 149–53 and Athanasius, *Synods* 43.

and with Lucian of Antioch,[47] who was known to have been the common teacher of Arius and Eusebius of Nicomedia, though not regarded on all sides as a heretic. It is in this letter that Alexander expressly declares the Son to be 'from the Father' (0.14.45) in opposition to those who (as he complains repeatedly) suppose him to have been created in time and out of nothing. He now asserts not so much a likeness of essence as a community of nature (1.4.31),[48] which he appears to deem equivalent to—we ought not to say, reducible to—a parity of honour (1.4.40). Nor is it any diminution, either of his Godhead or of his majesty, to style him the peerless image of the Father, for if the archetype is eternal so is the image (1.4.27f., 1.4.48). The one prerogative which is denied to the Son is that of being unbegotten. It is by virtue of being born without mediation from the Father that he shares the Father's nature; the birth is affirmed, and the unity of nature is not concealed, when he confesses that 'the Father is greater than I' (1.4.52; John 14.28). In expounding the words and acts of the Son on earth, we must beware of losing the manhood in the divinity and of burying the divinity in the manhood: to uphold the integrity of the incarnate Christ is not to confound the two natures in the one hypostasis (1.4.36–38).[49] The same heresies are unmasked as in *henos sômatos*, the same texts adduced against them from the scriptures; in a notable foreshadowing of later controversies, Alexander confers on Mary the title *theotokos*, 'mother of God' (1.4.53).

These two letters then contain *in nuce* the Trinitarian theology of the Alexandrian patriarch in the years preceding the Council of Nicaea. We see that, in opposition to those who regard the Son as a creature of the Father, he postulates a direct emission, comparable to the issuing of a word from the speaker's heart. He can tolerate no denial of a community of nature or likeness of essence between the Father and the Son. We cannot, therefore, be sure that he shared the aversion of Arius to the term *homoousios*; he may have eschewed it for fear of the invidious construction which would be put on it by those of the opposite party.

THE FIRST OECUMENICAL COUNCIL

The practice of holding councils set Christianity apart from other religions and philosophies of the empire. The first such assembly, if Acts 15 can be trusted, took place in Jerusalem under the presidency of James, the brother of Jesus,

[47] Arius styles himself a fellow-Lucianist in the letter to Eusebius: on the brotherhood see Bardy (1936), 185–216.

[48] Barnes (2007), 197 appears to deny that *ousia* and *phusis* are equivalent terms for Alexander, but I am not aware that this position represents a scholarly consensus.

[49] The occurrence of this 'Antiochene' formulary in a document that no semantic vagary can deny to be 'Alexandrian' has too often escaped the attention of historians.

was addressed by two apostles and determined the conditions on which Gentiles could be admitted to the church. The synods over which Cyprian presided as Bishop of Carthage legislated on matters touching the organization and discipline of the church, observing the pattern aid down for meetings of the Senate. A different procedure was followed in trials for heresy, where the interrogation was generally performed by a presbyter before an audience of bishops. It had never been common for delegates to come far to attend these gatherings, and obstacles to travel were increased by persecution. Even the controversy inspired by Arius came to a head less quickly than it might have done had not Licinius placed a ban on synods in his final years as emperor of the east. Yet even in years of tribulation local parliaments met and dared to issue decrees, though it is seldom possible to say who was present and how their utterances were published. The Council of Elvira in Spain (*c.*306) excommunicated prostitutes, actors, and gladiators, forbade the use of pictures in churches and defined the circumstances in which communion could be administered to heinous sinners. The Councils of Ancyra and Neocaesarea took place when the Roman world was amicably divided between Licinius and Constantine. The first provides for the chastisement and reconciliation of those who have sacrificed under duress, connived at idolatry, broken vows of celibacy, succumbed to lust, contracted a second marriage or revealed Manichaean sympathies by abstinence from meat. The second took measures for the restraint of bigamy, polygamy, adultery, fornication, second marriage, and irregular ordination. The Council of Arles in 314 is in many respects a variant of the same type, but differs in two important features: it was summoned by the emperor, who may have been present in person, and the Acts record the names of the Italian and Gallic bishops who took part. It appears that a Sicilian bishop, Chrestus, had declined the imperial summons;[50] the decision of Pope Silvester to remain in Rome to honour the memorials of the apostles is quietly ridiculed in the letter that he received from his fellow-bishops at Arles, but the precedent was faithfully observed by his successors.[51] The longest journey to Arles was made by another Pope, Caecilian, whom the council, upholding the verdict of a Roman synod in the previous year, pronounced to be the true Bishop of Carthage. Constantine, despite his professions of reverence for the bishops, did not endorse this judgement until he had held his tribunal. Though satisfied that Caecilian was innocent of the charges brought against him by the 'party of Donatus', he continued to cultivate the support of the Donatists, not only to secure the peace of Africa but to ensure that they would not halt between two masters when he went to war against Licinius.

[50] He is the addressee of a summons preserved by Eusebius, *Church History* 10.5, but does not appear in the list of assembled bishops in Optatus, appendix 4.

[51] Optatus, *Against the Donatists*, appendix 4.

The policy of Constantine after reuniting the Roman world in 324 was to govern the church in the east as he had governed in the west, through bishops whose disputations he did not control but might see fit to amend. The Council of Arles had announced that it was more than a provincial synod by issuing a canon which prescribed that Easter was to be celebrated everywhere according to the calendar of the Roman church[52]—that is, on the Sunday following the full moon after the vernal equinox, whether or not this day coincided with the Jewish Passover. This was a ratification of the protocol drawn up in the second century between Bishop Victor of Rome and a number of his eastern colleagues;[53] Constantine discovered none the less that it had failed to become a universal law for eastern Christendom outside Egypt. Egypt itself was afflicted by a schism comparable to that of the Donatists in Africa. Once again the causes are obscure, but it appears that Bishop Melitius of Lycopolis, having acted as surrogate to Peter of Alexandria during his imprisonment in the era of persecution, was not prepared to surrender his office after Peter died and Alexander was installed as his successor. Thus schism and inconsistency in worship, two distempers that had been treated at Arles with unequal success, awaited the ministrations of a similar assembly in the east, It was bound to be larger and likely to be more turbulent, as the Christian population of the east was much more numerous, and no one see could boast a pre-eminence comparable to that of Rome in the west.

To Constantine the theological controversy between Alexander and Arius was at first of little moment. In a letter to both he deplored the contumacy of Arius, but reproached Alexander for pressing him into an indiscreet confession.[54] Late in 324 or early in 325, the question came before synod in Antioch under the presidency (if the acts have been correctly restored) of Hosius of Cordova.[55] These acts, or the remnants of them, do not suggest that the emperor was present to witness the excommunication of Narcissus of Neronias and Eusebius of Caesarea for holding that there was more than one *ousia*, or being, in the Trinity. It may have been Narcissus alone who affirmed that there are three, but Eusebius never retracted his assertion that the Son and the Father are two distinct *ousiai* in his subsequent controversy with Marcellus of Ancyra. His sentence, however, like the vindication of Caecilian at Arles, remained provisional, and it may have been his good fortune that the Council

[52] Canon 1 at Jonkers (1954), 23.

[53] Eusebius, *Church History* 5.23–24.

[54] On the authenticity of this missive see Baynes (1931), 89.

[55] See Chadwick (1958), dating the council to 325. De Clerq (1954) inclines to January of that year. Abramowski (1992b) is content with a date of 324/5. The creed which she discusses in this article insists that the son is begotten, not a creature, although his birth is an unfathomable mystery. In styling the son the true *kharaktêr* (impression) of the Father, it intimates that Hebrews 1.3 was still a cardinal text for this assembly, as it had been for Tertullian and Origen; it was only at Nicaea that the formula 'from the ousia of the Father' replaced its biblical precursor 'from the *hypostasis* of the Father' (Tertullian, *Against Praxeas* 7.9).

which was charged with reviewing it took place not at Ancyra, as first intended, but at Nicaea in Bithynia. Perhaps it was also fortunate for Marcellus, for this proved to be the first of several councils in the fourth century which ended by deposing the bishop of the city in which they were convened.[56] Whatever the motive for the choice of venue, the Council of Nicaea opened in June 325 with a hortatory address by Constantine, although the president was Hosius of Cordova. Of the few other bishops from the west, the most distinguished was Caecilian of Carthage, Silvester of Rome being represented by two legates, Vitus and Vincentius. Their names stand first in the lists of those who signed the creed, but of the remainder (about 250) almost all were from the east.[57] The provinces of Asia Minor, populous as they were and close to Nicaea, were abundantly represented; there were numerous delegations from the Syrian region, the Balkans and the Danubian provinces; Alexandria led a formidable cohort from Egypt. No see outside the borders of the empire is named, though one of the delegates may have been a Goth.[58]

The comprehensive purpose of the council is illustrated by its canons.[59] Canon 1 excludes eunuchs from the clergy, unless they have suffered involuntary castration at the hands of doctors or barbarians; Canon 2 prohibits the ordination of neophytes and Canon 3 the harbouring of women, other than members of his family, in a clergyman's home. The fourth requires that a bishop shall be consecrated, where possible, by all the other bishops of his province, and the fifth that an excommunication imposed by one bishop will be honoured by others, unless it is found on scrutiny to be capricious. The sixth confirms the pre-eminence of Antioch and Alexandria in their respective provinces; a dispute now obscure to us may have prompted the seventh, which provides that honour should be accorded to Jerusalem but without prejudice to the metropolitan status of Caesarea Settling a controversy of the third century, which had been reanimated by the Donatists, Canon 8 decides that clergy ordained among the schismatic Cathari, or Novatianists,[60] may serve as clergy in the catholic church if they subscribe without reservation to its doctrines; according to Canon 19, on the other hand, those who have been baptized by heretics must be baptized again before they can be admitted. Canons 9 and 10 allow for the revocation of orders which have been conferred in ignorance on criminals or apostates; Canons 11, 12, 13, and 14 lay down terms of penance for those who have lapsed, permitting them to receive the Eucharist in the hour of death even if they have not been reconciled. Eusebius

[56] Logan (1992) contends that he was one of the framers of the Nicene Creed; on the contrary, Honigman (1942–3) believes that the primitive lists of signatories to this creed are those in which his name does not appear.

[57] See Gelzer, Hilgenfeld, and Cuntz (1995).

[58] See Gelzer, Hilgenfeld, and Cuntz (1995), 70.

[59] Jonkers (1954).

[60] That is, those whose clerical orders descended from novatian, who had set himself up as arrival to Cornelius in Rome during the Decian persecution.

of Nicomedia, formerly Eusebius of Berytus, may be the object of Canon 15, which forbids the translation of bishops from one see to another; the same curb is applied to presbyters and deacons in Canon 16. Usury is forbidden to the clergy in Canon 17, the tendering of the Eucharist by deacons to presbyters in Canon 18, and kneeling at prayer in Canon 20. A synodal letter resolves the Melitian schism with tact: Melitius is not to ordain again in Alexandria, but those already ordained by him may retain their posts so long as they submit to Alexander.

No ruling on Easter survives in this collection,[61] but a canon associated with the Dedication Council of Antioch in 341 anathematizes those who observe another date for the festival than the one fixed by the 'great and holy council at Nicaea'.[62] Eusebius preserves a letter in which Constantine exhorts the eastern bishops to abide by the Nicene ruling on Easter and not to retain a calendar which would leave the church in thrall to the machinations of the Jews who murdered Christ.[63] He does not reproduce any letter recording the council's verdict on Arius, though we learn from other witnesses that this was temporarily enforced by Constantine.[64] And yet within a few years of the council, on receiving a confession of faith from Arius which omitted the term *homoousios*, he instructed the Alexandrian church to restore him to communion. If his aim was peace, as Socrates tells us, this was not contemptible theology; nevertheless, he did not show the same indulgence to the Novatianists, who, having denied the right of the Bishop of Rome to pardon apostates in the third century, continued to deny the authority of any bishop who assumed the same powers of forgiveness. They are condemned along with far more aberrant heretics in a general interdict which spares the followers of Arius. With regard to him too, however, there was one more tergiversation—a sulphurous, self-aggrandizing and at times barely comprehensible invective which denounces him as a Porphyrian. In the chapter on Platonism I have discussed the tortuous reasoning that might have lent colour to this accusation; here we need only observe that, like those who kept the wrong date for Easter, Arius is condemned not so much for violating a norm as for making common cause with an enemy of the faith.

EUSEBIUS OF CAESAREA AND THE NICENE CREED

Our evidence regarding the evolution of the creed at the Nicene council is sparse; if we cannot rely on the testimony of Eusebius of Caesarea we know

[61] Its absence is discussed by L'Huillier (1996), 22–6.

[62] Jonkers (1954), 47; but on the uncertain date of this and other decrees attached to this council see Burgess (2000).

[63] Socrates, *Church History* 1.10.

[64] See Eusebius, *Life of Constantine* 64.1 with *Theodosian Code* 16.5.2 and Hall (1986). Baptisms by Novatianists are not deemed invalid in the canons of Nicaea.

nothing. It is often held that his letter to his own congregation at Caesarea, preserved by Athanasius and Theodoret,[65] is an exercise in camouflage; yet no ancient witness says so, and we must remember that, had it been patently disingenuous, he would not have escaped the penalties which fell on dissident prelates like his namesake of Nicomedia or Theognis of Nicaea. Eusebius undoubtedly aggrandizes his own part in the proceedings and omits much information, including names, that we should prefer him to have disclosed. That is to say that, when writing of affairs in which he was engaged, he is as tendentious as a Thucydides or a Caesar, but not that his work is any less useful to the modern historian than theirs.

According to his account, it was his own recitation of the baptismal creed of Caesarea that confirmed his own orthodoxy and furnished the council with a prototype for the creed.[66] Passing over numerous discrepancies between his own creed and the one that was promulgated by the council, he urged that nothing of substance had been added to the received faith of the church. The word *homooousios* was an innovation, but its defenders 'affirmed that it signified that, while he is from the Father, he does not exist as a part (*meros*) of the Father', thereby intimating that the term excluded the heresies that Arius had condemned. They added that the expression '*homoousios* with the Father' was not to be understood in the way that applies to bodies, or as in the case of living beings which are mortal; nor was it to be understood of a division or abscission of essence, or of any accident, change or alteration in the father's power. On the contrary, it 'signifies that the Son of God bears no resemblance to creatures that have come into being, but uniquely resembles in all respects the Father who begot him'. The last proviso leaves little doubt that one of the unnamed apologists is Alexander of Alexandria; another we may assume, on the testimony of Philostorgius, to have been Hosius of Cordova, the confessor of Constantine.[67]

It was Constantine himself, we are informed, who persuaded the council to endorse the *homoousion*:[68]

> When I had set out this faith, there was no room for contradiction. Indeed, it was our sovereign, most beloved of God, who first bore witness that its contents were perfectly sound, affirming that he himself was of the same mind. He exhorted all to agree and subscribe to the teachings with unanimous assent, with the addition of the one word *homoousios*. This word he interpreted, saying that it is not with respect to bodily accidents that he is *homoousios*, and that he does not owe his

[65] Appended to Athanasius, *On the Decrees of Nicaea*; cf. Socrates, *Church History* 1.8; Theodoret, *Church History* 1.5.

[66] See further Von Campenhausen (1976).

[67] Philostorgius, *Church History* 1.9; see Edwards (2012).

[68] Theodoret. *Church History*, p. 50 Parmentier and Hansen. Cf. Socrates, *Church History* 1.8.46–47, pp. 25–6 Hansen.

> existence either to division or to some abscission from the Father. For it cannot be that the nature which is immaterial, intellectual and incorporeal should be subject to any bodily accident; one should rather conceive such things in divine and ineffable terms. (Theodoret, *Church History* 1.12.7)[69]

The resultant declaration of faith, according to Eusebius, ran as follows:[70]

> We believe in one God, the Father almighty, maker of all that is, seen and unseen; and in one Lord Jesus Christ, *monogenês*,[71] that is, from the substance (*ousia*) of the Father, God from God, light from light, true God from true God,[72] consubstantial (*homoousios*) with the Father; by whom all things were made, who for us and our salvation came down, was enfleshed and became a human being. He underwent the passion and on third day rose again and ascended into heaven, whence he shall come to judge the living and the dead. And in the Holy Spirit. But those who say "there was when he was not" or "he was not before he was begotten" or "out of nothing" or "from another *hypostasis* or *ousia*" or "changeable" or "alterable" [or "created"]—these the holy catholic and apostolic church anathematizes.

Can we believe in Constantine's intervention? Hard as it is to believe that that such an episode could have been invented in a public document, it is almost harder still to credit the Emperor with the dialectical aptitude or even the command of Greek that would have been required of an interlocutor at this conference. 'God from God' is attested in his *Oration to the Saints*, but not the *homoousion*. From the silence of Eusebius Beatrice infers that he intervened without prompting, and that the bishops acquiesced without conviction.[73] Such an imposition upon the clergy would have been a departure from the stated principles of an emperor who is reported to have said on another occasion, 'You are asking me to judge when I await the judgment of God?'[74] Furthermore, we have still to explain, on this hypothesis, why the man who forced the term *homoousion* on 250 bishops should have been ready to waive it, less than a decade later, in his dealings with the two friendless presbyters Arius and Euzoius (Socrates, *Church History* 1.26); nor can one easily understand why the prelates who accepted the *homoousion* only in deference to imperial fiat in 325 should have become vociferous in their espousal of it, not under Constantine, but under his heir Constantius, who was commonly

[69] According to Theodoret, *Church History* 1.12.17 (not found in Socrates), this included the explanation that Christ is latent in the father before his emergence in actuality, a foreshadowing of Marius Victorinus which would certainly not have been interpolated by Eusebius.

[70] Following Theodoret, *Church History* 1.12, with matter in square brackets from Athanasius, *On the Nicene Decrees*, appendix (Socrates, *Church History* 1.8).

[71] John 1.18, 3.16, etc. The gloss excludes the rendering 'unique'.

[72] Applying John 17.3 to the Father and 1 John 5.20 to the Son.

[73] Beatrice (2002), 156.

[74] Optatus, *On the Donatists* 1.23. Corcoran (202), 157 opines that this is in fact a quotation from Constantine's letter to the bishops at Arles, on the authenticity of which see Odahl (1993).

regarded as an enemy of the council. It is surely more probable that, as the traditional theory argues, they eschewed it for the sake of peace so long as it was not openly condemned, but made it a shibboleth when it seemed to them that without it they could not preserve the substance of the creed.

It would lessen our difficulties to suppose that Constantine acted on the advice of his ecclesiastical mentors.[75] This would account on the one hand for his hardihood in enjoining this new term on the assembly, and on the other for his readiness to waive it when he received a confession from Arius, in the presence of different counsellors, and after an interim which had made it clear that the *homoousion* could not guarantee the unity of the Church. Philostorgius informs us that a draft of the Creed, containing the word *homoousios*, had been submitted to Constantine by Hosius of Cordoba and Alexander of Alexandria after the latter had heard of a letter[76] in which his enemy Eusebius of Nicomedia had said that to hold Alexander's views would be to make the son *homoousios* with the Father.[77] Philostorgius is not one to tell the truth without a good reason, but in this case he is supported by the testimony of Ambrose that a letter by Eusebius was read to the Nicene council, thus enabling his orthodox rivals to impale him with his own sword by inserting the word *homoousios* into.[78] We need not doubt that Theodoret, a third and independent witness, was speaking of the same missive when he wrote that the creed of Eusebius was 'read out and condemned'.[79]

Notwithstanding the striking unanimity of these reports, Pier Franco Beatrice contends that the word *homoousios* is in fact not of Christian but of Hermetic provenance.[80] That accounts for the zeal with which it was taken up by the Egyptian party at Nicaea; the rest is the mere confabulation of authors who either do not know the facts or have reason to misrepresent them. It is certainly true that all are tendentious witnesses; they do not all, however, represent the same tendency, and the fact that they quote the Creed in different variants gives us all the more cause to believe them when their narratives converge. In his rewriting of this narrative, Beatrice not only

[75] O. Skarsaune, 'A Neglected Detail in the Creed of Nicaea', *Vigiliae Christianae* 41 (1987) has detected the handiwork of Alexander in almost every line of the Creed, and accepts the report of his pact with Hosius before the council.

[76] Cf. the letter of this Eusebius to Paulinus of Tyre, in which he denies that the Son is from the *ousia* of the father. This must have been written before the Council of Nicaea, since as Lohr (2005), 548 n. 83 shows, Paulinus was dead before it took place.

[77] Philostorgius, *Church History* 1.7. Edwards (2012), 498 observes that the draft attributed to Alexander and Hosius concludes with an anathema on those who hold that the Son is a creature (*ktiston*). As Wiles (1991) demonstrates, this is lacking in all versions of the final promulgation except those which stem from Athanasius. If the latter was the author of the draft, we may suppose that he did not intend to deceive but was cheated by his own memory.

[78] Ambrose, *On the Faith* 3.15.151. See further Edwards (2012), 500–1.

[79] Theodoret, *Church History* 1.8.1; see further Stead (1973).

[80] Beatrice (2002).

discounts their evidence without justification but assumes without warrant that the Hermetic writings are immune to Christian influence or scribal interpolation. He also takes too little notice of Christian precedents for the *homoousion*. Origen had likened the relation between the Father and the Son to that of two consubstantial entities;[81] Dionysius of Alexandria was denounced by some of his suffragans as a heretic because he refused to apply the term *homoousios* to the persons of the Trinity;[82] within a few years, however, it had been condemned by the council which deposed Paul of Samosata in Antioch.[83] Origen's critics alleged that he had learned his nomenclature from the Valentinians, and there is no doubt that this Gnosticizing school of Christians found an audience in the second century; of the audience of the Hermetica in this period, if the Hermetica existed, we know nothing.

EUSEBIUS AND MARCELLUS

As we have seen, Eusebius did not append his signature to the creed without hesitation; the fact that his name appears fifth in the list of Palestinian bishops, although his see was the metropolis, suggest that he was more dilatory than Macarius of Jerusalem, whom Arius regarded as an enemy. Nevertheless, he signed the creed and is therefore not an Arian; those who have branded him with this name forget that he repudiated the most distinctive tenet of the Alexandrian presbyter, that the Son is 'out of nothing'. So long as we bisect his world into Arians and Nicenes, he will be a schizoid figure: when he extols the Son as the unique and perfect image of the Father he is taking Alexander's side against Arius, yet he will not go so far as to say, with Alexander, that the Son is coeternal with the Father. On the whole, it is only by his silence that he falls short of what we now call orthodoxy; as Michel Barnes opines, he may have been more representative of his age than Athanasius, who is remembered as the champion of Nicaea.[84] If he makes no reference to the council in his subsequent polemics against Marcellus, the same is true of his adversary, whose doctrines, if they are fairly represented by Eusebius, were far more heterodox than those of Arius himself.[85] It lies beyond the scope of the present volume to examine the modern apologies for Marcellus or the speculations that credit him with the authorship of the Apostles' Creed and a diatribe

[81] Edwards (1998). [82] Athanasius, *On the Opinion of Dionysius*; Abramowski (1992a).
[83] See Hanson (1988), 69–72. [84] Barnes (1998), 52–4.
[85] Parvis (2006) presents the teaching of Marcellus as an idiosyncratic rejoinder to Arius. On p. 65 her summary is as follows: 'he teaches one hypostasis, two *phuseis* and *dunameis* and *pragmata* and *prosôpa* (natures, powers, entities, persons), regards the incarnate Christ rather than the Word as the image of God, and avoids the language of *ousia* (essence) altogether in positive statements'.

against polytheism falsely attributed to Justin Martyr.[86] The following analysis of the treatise *Against Marcellus* by Eusebius is designed to show only what an intelligent churchman, who was well aware of his public notoriety, felt entitled to affirm as orthodox doctrine in the wake of the Nicene Council. The fact that this work has been preserved entire is sufficient evidence that he was claiming no more latitude than his colleagues had intended to concede.

Eusebius begins, perhaps unfairly, by locating the Bithynian see of Ancyra in the region which the New Testament calls Galatia, a nest of heresy even in that golden epoch. The gadflies of this region were its Judaizers, men who (like Marcellus) understood only the carnal meaning of the scriptures; Paul made them aware of the divinity of Christ by styling him a mediator, not between God and man (1 Timothy 2.5) but between the Father and the angels. The prooftext here is Galatians 3.19, which states that the Law was given to the Israelites through the hand of a mediator (*mesitês*): through the centuries scholars who differed on everything else have agreed that the *mesitês* is not Christ but Moses. Eusebius, however, has the commentator's way of assuming his own deductions to be irresistible; Marcellus, by contrast, raises one mist after another, forgetting the diverse histories of the two Joshuas who prefigure Jesus of Nazareth in the Old Testament, and confounding the words of St Michael to the devil himself—'the Lord rebuke thee, Satan' (Zechariah 3.2)—with the admonition, 'Get thee behind me, Satan', which was addressed by Christ to Peter, the future cornerstone of his church (Matthew 16.33 etc.). When such a man, mistaking the Proverbs of Solomon for prophecies, avers that the figure of Wisdom in Proverbs 8 is too enigmatic to be identified as Christ, the second person of the Trinity, we learn only that a text which is luminous to everyone else is obscure to him. A wordy demonstration that we cannot grasp the force of a secular proverb if we are ignorant of its history is quoted as evidence that his puerile learning has left Marcellus blind and deaf to the testimony of the Spirit, which (as every Christian knows) is to be interpreted by his testimony elsewhere in Holy Writ, and not by the recitation of dubious histories.

A catena of excerpts from Marcellus follows, in each of which he opposes the plain construction of a scriptural text to the 'dogma' which has been wrung from it by one of his interlocutors. Eusebius of Nicomedia, appealing to the orthodoxy of the 'most wise fathers', asserts that it is only by referring the birth of the Son to the will of the Father (rather than to his essence or nature) that we escape 'somatic and passible' notions of his origin (1.4.10). The perversity of his arguments becomes evident, says Marcellus, when they are eked out with false inferences from scripture by his acolyte Asterius. The latter (surnamed 'the sophist' by later adversaries) maintains that if the Father is to

[86] Kinzig and Vinzent (1999); Riedweg (1994).

be truly Father, the Son truly Son and the Spirit truly Spirit (1.4.6), we must attribute the 'unbegotten nature' to the Father alone (1.4.11), while confessing that the Son, as his image, is of a different nature, just as any statue differs in nature from its prototype (1.4.30). Marcellus, denying his premiss that 'first-born' and 'only-begotten' are biblical synonyms,[87] retorts that a son is always of one nature with his father (1.4.33–34), while an image is defined above all by its function of showing us that which we cannot see (1.4.31–32). The image of the Father therefore resides in the flesh of the incarnate Logos; if any of the 'most wise fathers' said otherwise, they are fathers only to Asterius and his fellow-heretics (1.4.15). The name of Origen has been adduced by Paulinus of Tyre, a correspondent of Eusebius who contends that the Son is a creature (1.4.49); Marcellus objects that the treatise *On First Principles*, where Origen insists on the eternal generation of the Second Person, derives not only its title but its opening sentence from the works of Plato, who is no guide for a Christian.[88]

The philippic now turns against two bishops who had been condemned at Antioch a few months before the Council of Nicaea. Narcissus of Neronias, who admits no more than a harmony of 'words and works' between the three distinct *ousiai* in the Godhead,[89] is a disciple of Plato and Marcion (1.4.41). Eusebius of Caesarea, on the other hand, follows Hermes in affirming the existence of 'another god' or of two gods who differ 'in *ousia* and *dunamis*', in essence and power (1.4.59), as though Christ were not the *dunamis* of the Father. Since he also characterizes the Father as the 'one true god'[90] and the Son as the 'mediator' who holds a middle rank between this God and his creatures (1.4.57), he also falls incongruously into the 'psilanthropism' of Paul of Samosata, whose doctrine that the Saviour is a 'mere man' had been condemned by eighty fathers at Antioch in 268.[91]

Eusebius finds it easy enough to reciprocate all these strictures. This man who reviles the holy fathers and the pious Origen does not know the scriptures well enough to distinguish the 'dogmas' of men from the inspired words of the apostles. Had he read as far as Genesis 5.3 he would learn that Adam had fathered Seth 'after his own image' (1.4.35–36);[92] as it is he himself denies the Son of God by allowing him neither filial nor iconic status before the nativity.

[87] Asterius at *Marc.* 1.4.12–13, collating Col 1.15 with John 1.18 etc.

[88] *Marc.* 1.4.18–20 cites Origen, *Princ.* 4.1.28; 1.4.22–23 cites *Gen.Comm.* 1.1; 1.4.26 cites Plato, *Gorgias* 454d–e.

[89] See *Marc.* 1.4.39 and 1.4.55. At 1.4.53 it is only Narcisssu who is said to have enumerated first and a second god, no doubt because Eusebius, though he employs both terms, avoids the juxtaposition.

[90] *Marc.* 1.4.51, citing John 17.3; at 1.4.52 the Son and the Father are contrasted as begotten and unbegotten.

[91] *Marc.* 1.4.62; on Paul see Eusebius, *Church History* 6.29–30.

[92] Cf. Origen, *First Principles* 1.2.6.

For him the Logos is properly 'in the Father'; when he is told at John 1.1 that the Logos was 'with the Father in the beginning', he takes this preposition to indicate not a hypostatic distinction between the two persons but the exercise of a 'drastic energy' which permits us to speak of the world as the joint creation of the Father and his Word (2.2.43). When he hears Wisdom proclaiming that 'the Lord created me in the beginning of his way', he absurdly maintains that this creation is predicated only of the flesh that the Word assumed in Bethlehem (2.2.3–21). Had he reflected, however, on our own creation in the image of God, he would have perceived that it is only in our incorporeal element, the soul or inner man, that we can be said to bear any likeness to our invisible Maker. If the incarnate Logos is assumed to act in Jesus as our own soul acts in us, a hypostatic distinction from the father must be admitted (4.4.26) if his flesh was animated only by 'drastic energy', from above, how does his sonship differ from ours? (4.4.27). In one respect Marcellus sets him apart to his disadvantage: he opines that, since the flesh is unworthy of God, the Son will be relieved of his body on the last day (4.4.28). Thus he will be deprived of the immortality that is promised to his creatures, and will have no place in the everlasting kingdom of the saints. No wonder that the man who emitted such blasphemies was anathematized, with reluctance by the bishops who gathered from Pontus, Cappadocia, Asia, Phrygia, Thrace, and even his own Bithynia to judge the orthodoxy of the document which he himself voluntarily submitted to the Emperor (4.4.29–30). Thus, when he hoped to witness the judgment of others, he was sentenced by the great judge whom he refused to confess as God (4.31).

In his *Ecclesiastical Theology* Eusebius turns an old forensic weapon against his adversary by imputing to him the errors of known heretics. Arius had menaced Alexander with a fourfold innuendo; Marcellus had intimated that Eusebius himself was a Valentinian, a Hermetist, or a Samosatene. Eusebius distinguishes three heresies into which theologians stumble for fear of duplicating the Godhead or deifying a man. The first is to deny the reality of Christ's human flesh; the second is to reduce Christ to a 'mere man' in the manner of Paul of Samosata; the third is to identify the son with Father in order that there may be no 'second god' (1.3). Eusebius too professes to abhor the ditheism which is implied by this locution, just as he abhors the Arian tenet that the Son is 'out of nothing'. We can avoid these blasphemies, however, without denying the Son his hypostatic character before the incarnation; Marcellus in taking this position follows Sabellius even while pretending to refute him (1.5); in limiting the sonship to the time of his earthly ministry, he is guilty of the Samosatene teaching that he ascribes to Eusebius (1.14). The unity of the Godhead is preserved if we affirm that the Son was begotten before all ages by the Father, as very Word, very Wisdom, very Life—in short, as god from God as radiance flows from the source of light.[93] He is thus, as Proverbs 8.22 implies, a distinct hypostasis before the creation, not (to judge by the silence of Eusebius) coeternal with the Father, nor strictly his equal, since a mediator was needed to protect the fragile world from the infinite majesty of the Godhead.

One of the indiscretions of Marcellus, says Eusebius, is his statement that the Logos had no other name before the incarnation. The prologue to the Fourth Gospel would apprise him that 'in the beginning' the second person was already god beside God, the universal instrument of creation, the light that illuminates the world—none of which could be said of him were he not hypostatically distinct from the Father (1.20.90). Even in the Fourth Gospel the title Son is commoner than Logos, and not only Son of Man, as Marcellus avers. Nor can it be maintained that he became Son of God through the incarnation, for this event was the consequence of God's decision to give the world his only-begotten Son (1.20.18–19; John 3.16). Four ways of accounting for the incarnation are open to us: to have the Father himself take flesh, to grant the second person his own hypostasis, to make Christ nothing more than a body endowed with soul, and to make him a *sôma apsukhon*, an automaton with no principle of life (1.20.41). The fourth of these possibilities is unthinkable; the first is Sabellian and the third Samosatene (1.20.42–44). The second way, to acknowledge the discrete character of the Son before the ages, is the only one that is left to us. The summary rejection of the third way has raised a doubt as to whether the Logos takes the place of a human soul in the Christology of Eusebius; as Strutwolf demonstrates, however, the purpose of his argument is to overreach Marcellus, not to satisfy the historian's curiosity on a question which few authors of this period cared to answer.[94] Our bafflement here should warn us that when later texts forbid us to think of Christ as a *sôma apsukhon*, they are simply disavowing an obvious heresy, and fall well short of affirming the presence of a human soul.

The second part of the *Ecclesiastical Theology* is a medley of old indictments, new exposures, fatal inferences and deft insinuations. It had also pronounced an anathema on those who held the Son to be subject to change and alteration; Eusebius hints that his enemy falls into this error by positing an expansion of the Godhead to allow for the incarnation. He alleges, with little support from his own quotations, that Marcellus imagined an epoch of divine silence before the procession of the Logos (2.9.4–5); this quiet imputation of Valentinianism is reinforced by the argument that the emission of the Logos from the Father would deprive him of his wisdom (2.9.11). Because Marcellus denies that the eternal Word was eternally the Son (2.23.1), he is vulnerable to the charge that was laid against Origen, of teaching 'two unbegotten ones

[93] *Ecclesiastical Theology* 1.20.68–69, citing Hebrews 1.3 and 1 Timothy 6.16.
[94] Strutwolf (1999), 223–33.

(*agennêta*)';[95] at the same time, Eusebius throws suspicion on his adversary's representation of God as a simple 'monad', although this term also is found in Origen.[96] When Origen's neologism *autotheos* is taken up by Eusebius, it no longer denotes the Father alone in contrast to the Son;[97] in his cryptic parlance the Godhead is *autotheos, autologos,* and *autosophia*—very God, very Word, and very Wisdom—while the Son is *autos theos, autos logos, autos sophia*—'himself God, word and wisdom'—by virtue of his unique origination from the Father (2.14.5–7). Himself no more a faithful Origenist than an ardent Nicene, Eusebius hopes to show that his opponent is no Nicene at all, and not an Origenist either, except insofar as all that was falsely said of Origen can be truly said of him.

To Eusebius it is a manifest absurdity that the Logos of Marcellus should be now *endiathetos*, immanent to the Father as thought, and now *prophorikos*, issuing forth as speech (2.11.1, 2.14.20). Marcellus maintains that to posit two hypostases before the incarnation is to compromise the unity of the godhead (2.16.2); he fails to perceive—and this is once again a Nicene doctrine—that one who is born of God is god. Even if we could doubt that the Son is the hypostatic Wisdom of God at Proverbs 8.22, the exordium to the Fourth Gospel could not be clearer. In the beginning was the Word, and the Word was with God (*pros ton theon*), and the Word was god (*theos*). The preposition is 'with', not 'in', as it would have been had the evangelist been of one mind with Marcellus. Furthermore, the noun *theos* is coupled with the definite article only when it refers to the Father, because the latter is the one who is properly God, whereas the Son (once again) is god by virtue of his origination (2.17.1–3). Marcellus opines that the Logos was so called in the beginning as the archetype in the mind of God of the *logikoi,* or rational beings, whom he had not yet created (2.16.1; cf. *Against Marcellus* 2.4.26); according to Eusebius, he is so called as the one through whom the Father spoke to create the world, and through whom it is now governed and redeemed. If the Jews knew nothing of him, that is because it was not possible for the Spirit to reveal the whole truth to those who had not yet witnessed the incarnation; nevertheless, as Christians now perceive, he revealed his hypostatic difference from the Father when he appeared to Abraham and the other patriarchs in the semblance of a man.

After a few more broadsides against the errors and inconsistencies of Marcellus the second section ends. In the third Eusebius argues at length that the Wisdom of Proverbs 8 is a true hypostasis, not a reified attribute of the

[95] It was this fear, according to Robertson (2007), 51, 57–8, and 164 which led Eusebius to insist repeatedly that the Son 'points to' the sublime Godhead of the Father above him. See *Preparation* 14.6–9; *Ecclesiastical Theology* 2.17; *Tricennalian Oration* 11. Beeley (2012), 91–2 argues that thus use of the term 'eternity' to express the Father's priority need not preclude an eternal generation of the Son.

[96] *Ecclesiastical Theology* 2.6.1–4.

[97] Cf. Origen, *Commentary on John* 2.1.17.

Father. When she declares that the Lord created her as the beginning of his works (Proverbs 8.22) the verb 'created' metaphorically signifies 'appointed for the purpose of creating the visible cosmos'. The Hebrew reading 'possessed' is to be welcomed because it implies that the second person is proper (*oikeios*) to the first (3.2.15–26).[98] On the other hand, to apply Proverbs 8.22 to the incarnation, as Marcellus does, is to flirt with the error of Marcion, who denied that the events recounted in the Old Testament were works of God. Eusebius goes on to tax Marcellus with denying not only the hypostatic character of the Spirit but his procession from the Father. Marcellus, he says, took the dictum 'God is Spirit' (John 4.24) to mean that the Holy Spirit cannot be one of three distinct persons in the Godhead (3.19–22); his readers would recall that the Nicene Council had affirmed its belief in the Spirit in the last sentence of the Creed. Finally, Eusebius repeats the charge that Marcellus has robbed Christ of his immortal flesh and his everlasting kingdom.[99] By now it should be obvious that those who profess to see 'at a glance' that Eusebius was an Arian after Nicaea owe this work a second glance. The peculiar tenet of Arius, that the Son is 'from nothing', is repudiated just as sharply as its Gnostic and Sabellian alternatives; at the same time, Eusebius does not explicitly teach the doctrine of his beloved Origen, that the Son is coeternal with the Father. Against Marcellus he takes the side of Asterius the sophist, Narcissus of Neronias, Paulinus of Tyre, and Eusebius of Nicomedia: the last had proved to be dangerous company at the Nicene Council, but the Caesarean Eusebius is as dexterous a trimmer in these subsequent writings against Marcellus as he was at the council itself. He contrives indeed to suggest that it is Marcellus who has contravened its decrees. The outcome of his exegetic casuistry (another term for theological acumen in this period) is a Christology which, while it is certainly not that of his younger contemporary Athanasius, would have been at least as acceptable as that of Athanasius to many of his co-signatories at Nicaea.

CONCLUDING REFLECTIONS

If we compare the Nicene Creed with the syllabus of charges laid against Origen, we shall find that the creed is silent on many points in this indictment, including some that would have been answered differently by theologians writing after the Council. Thus Eustathius of Antioch, although he found fault with Origen's use of allegory, would have urged that it was not he but his

[98] On the meaning of the Hebrew, which is still in dispute, see Holdrege (1996), 133–5.
[99] *Ecclesiastical Theology* 3.14–15 on 1 Corinthians 15.28.

detractors who had fallen into heresy when they denied a soul to Christ.[100] A ruling by the Council on the origin and destiny of our own souls might have forestalled a number of questions that were to occupy the more philosophic minds of the church for a century to come. On the other hand, the decisions that were made at Nicaea did not put an end to controversy because the employment of new terms without definition gave rise to new perplexities and dissensions. If the Son was from the *ousia* of the Father, did it follow that the *ousia* was a thing distinct from God? If the word *homoousios* was borrowed from the realm of material objects, how could be applicable to the incorporeal persons of the Trinity? If the incarnate Christ was still *homoousios* with the Father, was this true of his flesh or only of his Godhead? How were the nouns *hypostasis* and *ousia* to be differentiated in the anathemas? The assumption that they were synonyms at the Council of Sardica in 343 was to be a source of embarrassment to Athanasius in 362. He himself has been accused of adulterating the creed because he quotes an anathema on the word *ktiston* (created) which is unknown to other ancient witnesses.[101]

The study of Christian thought in the Roman era (or, as theologians say, the patristic era) has yet to escape from a teleological notion of development, according to which diversity and error were pruned by council after council until at last a tenacious orthodoxy emerged which did not admit of further growth or ramification. In its oldest form, this narrative represented the development as the unfolding of the bud from the flower, the evolution (to put it in Latin) of the implicit truth into the explicit formulation.[102] In John Henry Newman's redaction, the validity of preservative additions is acknowledged, so long as a uniform principle of accretion is followed and the original type is not obscured.[103] Anglicans have endorsed the early chapters of this modified hagiography; German Protestants, fearing that every advance upon the scriptures is a step towards Roman hegemony, have been apt to regard the increasing complication of Christian teaching under the influence of philosophy as something akin to the progress of a virus, or have written the tale of the Reformation backwards to produce a dismal catalogue of the victories of intrigue over innocence and the extinction of freedom by authority.[104] In American histories, written in the shadow of Foucault, the triumph of orthodoxy is represented as the supersession of rival ideologies by the one that enjoys the countenance of the most powerful institution;[105] the triumph is not disputed but is differently appraised. In short, it is still the rule that theologians write the history of theology as scientists write the history of science; the

[100] Grillmeier (1975), 299–302. [101] Wiles (1991).
[102] Still the assumption of Grillmeier (1975) and Kelly (1977).
[103] Newman (1845). [104] Harnack (1957); Bauer (1971). [105] Pagels (1979).

scientists, however, have the excuse that an acquaintance with the history of their own discipline is seldom required for the practice of that discipline today. Theology, by contrast, has always been understood as the passing on and refinement of tradition, and it is therefore not desirable that the study of this tradition should be burdened by assumptions which, though far from ancient, are already antiquated.

14

Retrospectives, Christian and Pagan

The only extant panegyric on Constantine in Greek was delivered years after the four which survive in Latin.[1] Being the work of the indefatigable Eusebius, it is not so much a eulogy of the man as a vindication of his religion and a prose hymn to the god who has raised him to the imperial throne. Dating the reign of Constantine from his seizure of the purple at York in 306, it offers no reply to those who denounced him as a usurper; nor is any other event in his career a subject either for boasting or for apology in this oration. It commences instead with a prayer to God, the creator of all, whose sovereign will sustains the order of seasons, the harmonious revolution of the heavens and the subordination of the natural realm to that one being on whom he has impressed his own image. That image resides in the human reasoning faculty, whose counterpart above is the Logos, the Word or reason of God, who in the scriptures is styled his Son. As the one sun nourishes and illumines all below it (1.5), so the one Word of God informs and governs the inanimate creation; as the invisible source and norm of ratiocination, he is able to sow the seeds of truth in every human intellect (2.4), teaching us that the one sacrifice that pleases the Father is purity of soul (2.6). In the latter days, however, he has taken a visible form so that the true gospel may be published to all the nations, and that these nations may in turn be gathered under the all-seeing eye of his vicegerent Constantine:[2]

> Now the unique Word of God,[3] ruling as his Father's colleague from ages without beginning , will continue for infinite and endless ages; while the one who is dear to him, led by royal emanations from above and empowered by the one who bears the title of divinity, rules the things on earth for long spans of years. (*Tricennial Oration* 2, p. 199 Heikel)

[1] Dated by Barnes (1977), 342 to 25 July 336; Drake (1975) proposed December 335.

[2] At 3.2 the emperor and his co-regent sons form a Trinity (cf. chapter 6); at 3.5 Constantine too is likened to the sun.

[3] Kee (1982), 29–30 complains that the Logos of this oration is never the incarnate Christ. He appears to have forgotten that it is addressed to the empire, not to the church alone, and that the incarnation is hardly neglected in the other writings of Eusebius.

In chapter 9 Eusebius recalls the emperor's vision and commends the church which he built to house a figure of the cross on the site of the Holy Sepulchre (9.16–18). In the eleventh chapter, which is generally held to mark the beginning of a different speech,[4] he addresses himself to pagans for whom this edifice is nothing but a memorial to a deceased quack and an affront to ancestral custom. His reply is a second harangue on the fall of the nations into idolatry, with its inevitable consequence that the Creator was forgotten and the laws which maintain the peace of human society were annulled. By taking flesh and dying for our sins, the Word of God revealed both the incorrigibility of human malice and the inexhaustibility of his own love. The church that now adorns the site of his tomb is not an idol but a standing testimony to the new life that he won on our behalf by his resurrection. Offering himself as a sinless victim to the Father, he rose again in an incorruptible body so that the image of the Father might be displayed in all its glory and the nations might be weaned from the worship of demons at the altars of the dead.

In this episcopal mirror for princes, the peace of the realm goes hand in hand with the renunciation of idols. As the first section of this chapter will show, however, Constantine's reign did more to increase the distempers of the church than to allay them, as factions who had hitherto been restrained by fear of persecution began to vie acrimoniously for his favour. One of the most vociferous petitioners, Athanasius of Alexandria, was heard to say in the next reign, 'What has the emperor to do with the church?' (*History of the Arians* 52); we shall see in the second section that his apologetic writings, though as caustic as those of Eusebius in their ridicule of pagan cults, do not take up his argument that if God is one the nations should be united under his human deputy. Pagans were circumspect in their expressions of dissent, and it is only in recent years that the gnomic epigrams of Palladas, briefly considered in the third section, have been quoted by scholars as evidence for a thoroughgoing destruction of images under Constantine. Finally we shall learn from the tract of Firmicus Maternus *Against the Error of Profane Religions* how much certain Christian expected of their champion, and how much, in their eyes, remained undone at his death.

CONFORMITY AND NON-CONFORMITY

Whether or not the *Church History* of Eusebius passed through more than one redaction,[5] it was one of its pervasive themes that the church and the empire

[4] Drake (1971), 31–3; Barnes (1977). It is probable, as Barnes argues, that this appendix is the speech, or one of the speeches, to which Eusebius refers at *Life of Constantine* 4.33, 4.45.3, and 4.46.1; it seems to me equally probable that it was he, not a blundering scribe, who was responsible for the contamination of the two panegyrics.

[5] See the introduction to Schwarz's edition of the *Church History* (Bibliography A). Barnes (1981a), 148–63 and (1981b) places the first edition before the persecution. This thesis is

are always at peace when the latter is well-governed; another is that ecclesiastical discord is invariably the result of duress from without or of private ambition, never of fissiparous tendencies in the church as a whole. In illustrating the first theme, he invites pagan readers to sympathize with the martyrs who poured out their blood under Nero, Domitian, Decius, Maximinus Thrax, Valerian, and the late Tetrarchs; the edict of Marcus Aurelius which preceded the popular riot against the Christians of Lyons in 177 is wishfully ascribed to the ignoble Lucius Verus.[6] The thesis might seem to founder on the martyrdom of Ignatius under Trajan, were it not that Trajan's letter to Pliny gives evidence of a more lenient policy (3.33). The letters of Ignatius also exemplify the second theme, for they inculcate obedience to the bishop as the precondition of unity and fellowship in Christ (3.36). Bishops, like others, have their personal frailties, and Eusebius takes pains to show that Origen, the most brilliant theologian of the church, was also the lodestar of orthodoxy and a staunch confuter of heresies, his exile from Alexandria being attributable solely to the jealousy of the bishop who happened to be his contemporary (6.8.4). When strife breaks out in Rome between Cornelius and Novatian, the cause is the latter's thirst for power, acidified by the recent persecution (6.43.1); Cornelius shows a broader understanding of his office by maintaining communication with the bishops of the east (6.43.7–20).

Rome is often the healer, never the origin of schism: even Bishop Victor's chastisement of the Asiatics who would not conform to his date for the Easter festival was only an intemperate application of an oecumenical ruling (5.23.2), and Irenaeus was able to remind him that his predecessors had always followed more pacific counsels (5.24.12–17) Rome was an instrument of peace in the late third century both to Alexandria and to Antioch: in the latter case, the task imposed upon her by the Emperor Aurelian was to fill the see left vacant after a council of eighty bishops from different provinces had unanimously concurred in the deposition of the tyrannical bishop, Paul of Samosata (7.30.19). Eusebius, though he intimates that Paul had lost sight of the difference between himself and Christ, says nothing of the theological arguments that were exchanged on this occasion;[7] when he comes to the Great Persecution, he passes silently over the schisms that it engendered in Alexandria and Carthage, dwelling only on the fortitude of the martyrs. In the *Life of Constantine* he reckons the abolition of ecclesiastical synods among the errors of Licinius which made it necessary for Constantine to overthrow him. The

disputed by Louth (1990), while Burgess (1997) is widely held to have established that the Chronicle which preceded the composition of the *History* cannot have been appeared before 306. Nevertheless the first Anglophone scholar of recent times to have denied that there was more than one redaction is Johnson (2014), 104–12.

[6] Though it is possible that, at 4.18.2 and elsewhere, he is calling the emperor whom we know as Marcus Aurelius by one of the names that he bore before his accession.

[7] Compare *Church History* 7.30.11 with Lang (2000) on the *Acts of Malchion*.

summoning of the Council of Nicaea in 325 is one of Constantine's first measures after assuming the sole government of the empire, and it leads to an almost unanimous agreement on the date of Easter, together with general concord in the church except in Egypt, where dissent is stirred by a few men of evil will. As for the theological altercation which the Nicene Creed purports to resolve, it enters the record obliquely through the reproduction of a letter from Constantine to Alexander and Arius, rebuking both for their failure to agree on a point that is of so little consequence to the faithful. As Socrates the historian noted, an emperor desires peace above all things (*Church History* 1.10).

But peace was not the immediate fruit of the Council of Nicaea. The Novatianists who had severed themselves from the main church when it began to issue pardons for sins that they deemed unforgivable, were not reconciled by the canons, though they found nothing to offend them in the creed.[8] Eusebius of Caesarea had won the freedom to expound his own theology; Eusebius of Nicomedia was deposed for his refusal to sign the Creed (or perhaps the anathemas), but restored on his recantation.[9] Eustathius of Antioch, who impugned the orthodoxy of both Origen and the Caesarean Eusebius, was deposed on political charges which our principal witness, Athanasius, declares to be factitious.[10] Above all the Melitians of Alexandria—that is, the clergy ordained in the city by Melitius of Lycopolis during the episcopates of Peter and Alexander—were only partially reconciled. According to Epiphanius (a hostile redactor of sources that were more generous to the schismatics), the quarrel began when Melitus denounced the lenient policy of Peter of Alexandria toward those who had lapsed under persecution; when he himself was imprisoned in 306, his rival seized the opportunity to excommunicate him. The story fits an all too familiar template, but we have no other evidence that Peter treated the lapsed with more indulgence than Melitius. His encyclical letter of 306 suggests that his offence, in the eyes of Melitius and other Alexandrian confessors, was to deny them the right of granting absolution.[11] Accordingly, modern scholars have interpreted the secession as a protest against the concentration of power in the hands of the bishop;[12] yet Peter was doing no more than Cyprian had done in Carthage fifty years earlier,

[8] Socrates, *Church History* 1.10.

[9] Perhaps at a second session of the Council in 327: Baynes (1931), 22 and 90 n. 66. See Socrates, *Church History* 1.8; Sozomen, *Church History* 1.21; Philostorgius, *Church History* 1.9–10 and Gwynn (2007), 117–88 nn. 40–1.

[10] Chadwick (1948) surmises that the council which deposed him was held at Antioch some months after Nicaea under the presidency of Eusebius of Caesarea. Burgess (2000) proposes 328, with some reservations. Parvis (2006), 106 deduces from Theodoret, *Church History* 1.11.6 that his deposition was a local and clandestine affair to which of which Eusebius of Nicomedia initially knew nothing. In contrast to Elliott (1992b) and Maraval (2005), Parvis holds that the notion of an 'Arian reaction' after Nicaea is not fanciful.

[11] Hauben (1989), 270–3.

[12] Hauben (1998).

and a man in the position of Melitius will always be suspected of resenting not the episcopal prerogative but the exercise of it by another man.

The Nicene Council decreed that Alexander was to be recognized as bishop, and in turn should recognize the orders of those ordained by Melitius who submitted to his authority.[13] The truce, if it held at all, did not survive the installation of Athanasius as successor to Alexander in 328.[14] The Melitians declared that he was not yet thirty, and therefore not of an age to hold a bishopric; we cannot test the truth of that claim, but we know that Athanasius vindicated his authority with a high hand.[15] For this he was arraigned in his absence at a synod in Caesarea,[16] and then in person at Tyre. Reckless charges of murder, mutilation and consorting with a prostitute were deflected with comic adroitness (so Athanasius informs us), but these acquittals throw into relief the unrefuted interrupting the grain supply from Alexandria and deploying an army of monks to club the dissenters into communion. The discovery of a papyrus containing a detailed indictment of Athanasius cannot prove that these accusations are true,[17] but if they were reckoned credible at the time, they give us a measure of the political power that had now come into the hands of the Alexandrian patriarch. At Tyre he was condemned, and while his enemies celebrated this judgment in Jerusalem, he made his way in haste to Constantinople. Finding the emperor mounted in public, he grasped the bridle of his horse to obtain a hearing.[18] His story that he was the victim of a conspiracy orchestrated by Eusebius of Nicomedia was partially verified by the swift arrival of the latter. Constantine, as a man of peace, suspended Athanasius without pronouncing him guilty or depriving him of his office. After his death, however, his son Constantius II confirmed the deposition of Athanasius and made Eusebius bishop of Constantinople, in place of the incumbent Paul and in clear defiance of the Nicene canon which forbade the translation of any bishop to a second see.

The Egyptian recusants had few allies abroad, and the surviving inventory of Melitian sees does not corroborate the theory that they drew their support primarily from disaffected Copts.[19] The Donatists of Africa, on the other hand, were not only irrepressible in their own province but won the favour

[13] Hauben (1987). [14] See further Hauben (1981).

[15] On Athanasius' charge that the Melitians formed an unscrupulous alliance with the Arians see Gwynn (2007), 128–33 and Williams (1986).

[16] Sozomen, *Church History* 2.25; Bell (1914), 47.48. On chronological difficulties in the narrative see Barnes (1993), 19–33.

[17] Bell (1914), 53–71, noting inaccuracies on p. 67. On the charge of breaking a chalice, which Athanasius purports to have rebutted, see p. 46. For differing appraisals of the papyrus see Barnes (1981a), 235; Arnold (1991), 84–9; Hauben (2001).

[18] See Drake (2000), 3–12 on the political significance of this public appeal and Constantine's response.

[19] Hauben (1989–90); Wipszycka (1996), 9–61, esp. 51–52, and on the more general question Jones (1959).

of the eastern bishops in 343 when east and west held separate councils.[20] The public rupture took place in 311, when after the death of Mensurius of Carthage, a number of Numidian bishops declined to recognize his deacon Caecilian as his successor. In 313 a synod was convened at Rome by Constantine, and the party of Donatus (as they were now called after their leader) alleged that Felix of Abthugni, one of the three bishops who had consecrated Caecilian, was a *traditor*—that is, he had given copies of the scriptures to pagan inquisitors who had instructions to burn them.[21] Apologists for Caecilian, however, professed to know that the plot had been laid some years before at the instance of Lucilla, a spiteful woman whom he had once forbidden to venerate the bones of a spurious martyr.[22] On the other side, Donatist literature had a further impeachment to bring against Caecilian: during the persecution, certain Christians who were imprisoned awaiting trial had starved to death because Caecilian, as the agent of Mensurius, had intercepted the supplies of food that had been procured for their sustenance by their fellow-saints.[23] These were not matters for the synod of 313, and the bishop of Rome, Miltiades, announced the acquittal of Felix.[24] In 314, however, another verdict was sought from the council of Arles,[25] and when this too had exonerated Caecilian, Constantine held his own review of the case.[26] Although the subsequent course of events is obscure, it is clear that Constantine decided to favour the church over which Caecilian presided; this, henceforth was the Catholic Church, while the Donatists lacked for subsidy and were periodically curbed by force of arms. Only when he needed Christian levies for the war against Licinius did Constantine grant funds for the erection of a Donatist church;[27] and even after this it was Caecilian who represented Carthage at Nicaea in 325.

Overmatched in arms, the Donatists fought back with words. Vituperation reaches its height in a sermon commonly thought to have been delivered in 316 or 317 in the wake of a punitive massacre of Caecilian's opponents.[28] After giving a circumstantial account of Caecilian's treachery during the

[20] For discussions of the chronology of the schism see Millar (1977), 584–90; Barnes (1982), 238–47.

[21] Optatus, *Against the Donatists* 17 and 22. Barnes (1975) maintains that the petition from the Donatists recorded here was in fact presented after the Roman synod and secured a new hearing at the Council of Arles. See further Edwards (1997), 22–3.

[22] Optatus, *Against the Donatists* 1.16; Augustine, *Against Cresconius* 3.33; Dolger (1932).

[23] See *Passion of the Abitinensian Martyrs* at Maier (1987), 57–91. Tilley (1996), 26n suggests that this account was written before the elevation of Caecilian to the bishopric.

[24] Optatus, *Against the Donatists* 1.24.

[25] Optatus, appendix 4.

[26] Optatus, *Against the Donatists* 1.26; Augustine, *Against Cresconius* 3.80–83; Edwards (1997), 26.

[27] See Optatus, appendix 9; Maier (1987), 240.

[28] Maier (1987), 201–11; Tilley (1996), 51–60.

persecution, the preacher derides the terms 'schismatic', 'heretic', and 'Donatist', which fall so easily from the lips of the self-styled 'catholic' party. Our name for them, he says, is 'Caecilianists', and since we gathered the severed limbs of our wives and children from the basilica, it is a name that signifies only persecution. Those who style themselves catholics are the Gentiles; those in whom the Spirit is truly at work are the saints on whom they have conferred the glory of martyrdom. The murderers prate of unity, and there is indeed one church, our holy mother, oppressed on all sides by the wicked yet still undefiled, whose members after their numerous trials are destined to receive the crown of virginity from the Saviour; there is one church of the one Christ, and both are ours.

As we observed in a previous chapter, few scholars now endorse—few scholars have ever endorsed—the theory of Frend that the Donatists represent a fierce, indigenous strain of Christianity, barely weaned from the barbarous cult of Saturn.[29] It is common enough, however, to contrast the rigorism and fanaticism of the African rebels with the moderation, if not laxity, of the catholic party. Such judgements would be anachronistic in the early fourth century: whatever catholicism came to signify for Augustine, the Caecilianists and the Donatists differed only in their appraisal of the facts, and neither proposed that the facts should be blotted out for the sake of brotherhood. The assumption of both sides at the Roman synod of 313 was that if Felix was guilty Caecilian's consecration was invalid; and this, in law, was the only point at issue. The catholics were not, so far as the evidence goes, more lukewarm in their veneration of martyrs; it does not follow that no martyrs are genuine because one is false. The truth behind the story that was told against Caecilian is now irretrievable; if, however, he abandoned the prisoners because he thought them heretics, voluntary martyrs or desperadoes, he was taking the course that might have been taken by Cyprian, a hero to both parties. The Donatists might none the less have put an invidious colour upon his action to justify an enmity born of other causes. The catholics after 313 were the party of Rome; the notion that the Donatists drew their following chiefly from the less Romanized areas of North Africa is not confirmed by the archaeological record. We must not exaggerate their insularity or their rusticity: they gained Parmenianus from abroad before the catholics found Optatus,[30] while Tyconius and Petilian were a match for every African mouthpiece of the catholic cause before Augustine.

[29] Frend (1952). See further Rebillard (2013).

[30] It is his list of the notes or characteristics of the true church that Optatus modifies at *Against the Donatists* 2.1–8. For the Donatists this list includes the font, the Spirit, the priesthood and the altar, but it must have been the catholics who added the chair of Peter and his keys, while refusing to treat the altar as a note distinct from the priesthood.

We may raise one final question: did her position as arbiter in this controversy enhance Rome's claim to primacy in the church?[31] In 343, some thirty years after the synod under Miltiades, the western Council of Sardica conferred on Rome the right to set up a new trial for a case that had been decided in another province. Two years earlier Julius I had annulled the verdict on Athanasius and summoned the judges to his own tribunal in Rome (though the summons was ignored). In 313, however, the Donatists were permitted to contest the Roman decision; Aurelian seems to have countenanced no such process when he left it to Rome to appoint a successor to Paul of Samosata. In 314 the Council of Arles, having disappointed the Donatists once again, dispatched an ironic account of its proceedings to Silvester, the successor of Miltiades, lamenting his absence but making it clear that if he preferred to stay at home by the graves of Peter and Paul, their decrees had equal force without him.[32] After Constantine's capture of Rome his panegyrists descanted on his love for the ancient capital, and his prodigal donations to its churches are enumerated in the *Book of Pontiffs*.[33] Nevertheless—and notwithstanding the fanciful *Acts of Silvester* and the fictitious Donation of Constantine—we possess no credible account of the emperor's relations with the Roman bishop after 313. History records that in 317, on capturing Serdica from Licinius, he transferred the seat of his government to that city and declared it his second Rome.

ATHANASIUS AND THE LIVING IMAGE

In the eyes of posterity, the theological norm was this age was set not by Eusebius but by his younger contemporary Athanasius, who treated his rules only with as much deference as they displayed to him. The *Contra Gentes*, or *Against the Nations*, of Athanasius, is the first part of a double work, the second part of which is his more famous treatise *On the Incarnation*.[34] Both have been regarded as early productions, since they make no allusion to Arius,

[31] Pietri (1976), 16–167 suggests that Constantine was following the policy of Aurelian in referring the case of the Donatists to Rome.

[32] Optatus, *Against the Donatists*, appendix 4. Silvester alleged that his duty was to honour the memorials of the apostles in the city: on the publication of a calendar of saints in 336 see Pietri (1991), 32–3.

[33] See also Curran (2000), 90–115 on the Lateran, St Peter's and lesser foundations. The *Book of Pontiffs* (Liber Pontificalis), section 34, which is not above suspicion, enumerates the churches of St Peter, St Paul, St Agnes and St Lawrence and SS Marcellinus and Peter the exorcist, together with the Lateran and a church which housed a relic of the Cross. It also lists generous grants of land and implausibly credits Constantine with an official commination of certain heretics, including Pope Callistus.

[34] See Bibliography A.

who began to propound his heresy that the Son is 'out of nothing' around 318, as Athanasius was reaching the age of twenty.[35] No great theologian has been so precocious, and if silence were any test of date at all, it would be more persuasive to argue that Athanasius composed these works at the end of a long career when the hubbub raised by Arius had subsided. We need not suppose, however, that he had forgotten his bugbear merely because he fails to mention him. The theology of the second treatise is manifestly opposed to that of Arius since it assumes that, if the Son is to transform us into the image and likeness of God, he must be God in the fullest sense. By representing this as the elementary and universal teaching of the church, he tacitly implies that there is no legitimate choice between him and Arius and that a Christian who is not an Athanasian is no Christian at all.[36]

Athanasius presents idolatry as an apostasy from the One God at the instigation of demons who by setting up effigies of beasts and corpses throughout the world, having persuaded the nations to turn away from their Creator, the Second Person of the Trinity, losing sight of the divine image which he himself implants in every human soul. Polytheism is thus not only rebellion but folly, a forsaking of that which has power for that which has none. Reason alone, without the aid of revelation, teaches us that it is blasphemy to posit a *dunamis* equal to God (*Contra Gentes* 6); for the last three hundred years, however, the infidel has defied not only reason but the visible manifestation of the Word, who is the *dunamis* and wisdom of God (40), in fact the *autodunamis* of the Father (47). Extending his *dunameis* throughout the creation (42), he moves the stars and regulates the motion of the heavens, sustaining even those invisible powers who have betrayed him (44). Every denizen of the cosmos is bound to worship him according to its own *dunamis* (43); because this power has been perverted in the fallen soul (8), it was necessary for the Word to recover and renew his creation through the *dunamis* of the Cross (1). Now that this has filled the world (1), there is no excuse for those who go on urging that cultic statues 'have been fashioned and modelled for the invocation of divine messengers and powers (*dunameis*), in order that being made manifest by these means they may inform them about the knowledge of God. And they are like letters for men, they say, by reading which they can come to an understanding of God from the appearance through them of the divine messengers'.[37]

[35] Van Winden (1975) argues for an early date; for arguments to the contrary see Pettersen (1982) and Beatrice (1990). Kannengiesser (2006), 23 places the work shortly after the exile to Trier which followed the condemnation of Athanasius at Tyre.

[36] As Meijering (2010), 176 observes, Athanasius joins issue with (unnamed) heretics who deny the immortality of the soul or impute the creation to another god than the Father of Jesus Christ.

[37] *Against the Nations* 19, trans Thomson (Bibliography A), 55. Cf. ch. 21.

Whether or not Athanasius is a philosopher, there is no doubt that his opponent here is the Neoplatonist Porphyry, numerous fragments of whose treatise *On Statues* are preserved in the *Preparation for the Gospel* by Eusebius.[38] At 3.7.1 we learn that the exordium ran as follows: '*I shall speak to those for whom it is right; close the doors, ye uninitiated.* I shall make known the teachings of theological wisdom, by which men have revealed God and the *dunameis* of God through images naturally adapted to vision, figuring things invisible in manifest creations for those who have learned to read truths about the gods from images as one reads letters from books. But it is no wonder if those who are wholly unlearned should suppose that these effigies are mere wood and stone, just as those who are ignorant of letters imagine stelae to be mere stones, writing tablets mere wood and books mere woven papyrus.' Eusebius was much the older and the learned man, and we might suspect that Athanasius is merely quarrying the researches of his co-religionist.[39] It is clear, however, that the *Preparation for the Gospel* cannot be the source of all the elements in this ensemble, though the ensemble itself is eminently Porphyrian. It is thus not improbable that Athanasius, like many of his contemporaries,[40] knew Porphyry at first hand.

Eusebius, who had witnessed the Great Persecution as an adult, records with indignation that the bodies of those who died in it had been disinterred and cast into the sea by the authorities to ensure that no cult would develop around their tombs (*Church History* 8.6.7). Against the cult itself he has nothing to say, although he reproduces a letter in which the Christians of Lyons aver that the pagans were misinformed when they drowned the bodies of those who died in the massacre of 177 for fear that they were would be venerated by the survivors (5.1). He seems to concur with another Christian's judgment that the bones of the martyred Polycarp were of more worth than precious stones (4.15.43). Athanasius, in an invective against the Melitians, maintains that it was they who were now responsible for the exhumation of the sleeping martyrs, and that they were even guilty of selling the corpses that they had stolen from catholic graves.[41] The *Life of Antony* puts into its hero's mouth a valedictory speech in which he warns his fellow-ascetics not to embalm his corpse for public display, as such acts do no honour to the holy man but flout the ancient custom which the apostles themselves observed when they left the body of the Saviour in its tomb (*Life* 90). From this we may infer that Pharaonic usages were being adapted to new beliefs by the Christians of Egypt; it is wholly characteristic of Athanasius to oppose such pagan

[38] Bidez, (1913); Smith (Bibliography A).
[39] On his obvious debt to the *Theophany* see Beeley (2012), 126.
[40] See Simmons (1995); Digeser (2000); Chapter 2 of the present volume.
[41] *Festal Letter* 41: see further Wortley (2006), 23–4.

survivals by appealing to the example of Christ, who, because he is the image of God on earth, is the sovereign paradigm for all who are being refashioned in that image.

The 'incarnation of the Word' is the subject of the sequel to the treatise *Against the Nations*. Following the precedent of Constantine and Eusebius, Athanasius begins with the creation of the world, the subjection of all other creatures to the one whom the Word has moulded in his own image, and the universal deformation of this image by human disobedience (4). Since the penalty decreed for this trespass was nothing less than death, it was necessary for God to enforce this sentence without blotting out his own image from the creation (7). The expedient by which this was accomplished was the incarnation of that very Word who has stamped the image upon humanity, in order that by the exemplification of consummate virtue he could reform us from within (15) and that by subsuming us in his death he could restore to us the life that Adam lost. The Cross which had now become a regal ensign under Constantine, and whose victories are extolled in the interdiction to the treatise *Against the Nations*, becomes the centrepiece of this second volume, as Athanasius undertakes to demonstrate the necessity, not only of Christ's death, but of his dying in this public, abrupt and ignominious manner. A death that was less widely witnessed might have been denied (23); a natural death would have been incongruous with his character as God (19). The Cross which made his premature death a spectacle to the world also enabled him to spread his arms over those who had rejected him, and became an unforeseen instrument of warfare against those powers of the air who imagined that by slaying his body they could retain possession of our souls (25).

In chapter 9 the Saviour's presence is likened to that of a king who takes up residence in a city, thereby putting an end to crime and molestation in the vicinity of his new dwelling. This simile would most naturally have suggested itself to the author at one of those infrequent periods of his life when he was on good terms with the emperor—in his closing years, for example, or under Constantine before the Council of Tyre. On the other hand, he does not imitate Eusebius in representing the monarch on earth as the Vicar of Christ above; he does not deduce from the sovereignty of the one God that it is fitting for the Roman world to have only a single ruler. In the course of his career he was moved to exclaim, as Eusebius never did, that a human overlord has no right to meddle in the affairs of the church. Constantine is said to have expressed the same opinion, yet his competence was not contested by either party when Athanasius sought his protection in Constantinople. The Alexandrian patriarch knew well enough that the dominion of the Cross would not have been so widely acknowledged had it not been inscribed on the shields of the troops who prevailed at the Milvian Bridge.

THE NEW PALLADAS

Athanasius sets the living image against the dead idol, and exults in the sure destruction of the latter. One of the most admired of the later poets in the Palatine Anthology is Palladas, who, when he is not penning lampoons or eulogies on unnamed contemporaries, is denouncing the new evils of his age with equally cryptic brevity. One of his epigrams refers to a woman named Hypatia, and an editorial rubric in the Anthology identifies her with the pagan philosopher who was torn apart by an Alexandrian mob in 415.[42] Although other poems reveal that Alexandria was the native city of Palladas, it is now agreed that he cannot have been writing in the fifth century, since by the year 380 a number of his epigrams had already been translated into Latin by ageing and distinguished poets. For over half a century it has been assumed that a shift of date by one or two generations would suffice to explain a handful of poems, obsequious in tone but perhaps ironic in tenor, which seem to play on the name Theophilus, 'beloved of God'.[43] The name suggests a Christian, and Theophilus was a man of no little consequence, to judge by the overtures that the poet addressed to him at the age of 72 when he found himself without a position. He has been identified as the patriarch of Alexandria, who took office in 385; another poem alluding to the incineration of statues has been interpreted as a satire on his spoliation of a pagan temple in 391, and thus to the train of events that culminated in the destruction of the Serapeum.[44] This chronology yields a date of 313 at the earliest for the birth of Palladas;[45] yet this too has proved untenable for two reasons. Firstly, it would not give Palladas time to acquire the celebrity that would warrant his translation into Latin by 380;[46] secondly, a manuscript containing some of his epigrams to Theophilus has been confidently dated by palaeographers to the first half of the fourth century. Kevin Wilkinson argues that in this period the man most likely to be addressed or praised as the 'god-beloved' was the emperor Constantine, on whom this epithet was constantly bestowed by such admirers as Eusebius. If that is so,

[42] *Palatine Anthology* 9.400; Wilkinson (2009), 37–8. The editorial rubrics also assert that AP 11.292 was written in praise of the philosopher Themistius and that 9.528 extols the house of Marina, the daughter of the Emperor Arcadius. If both annotations were accurate, the career of Palladas would span the years from 380 to 425, but neither is verified by the poet's own words.

[43] *Palatine Anthology* 10.90 and 10.19: see Lacombrade (1953), 17–26 and Keydell (1957), 1–3.

[44] Wilkinson (2009), 44 n.47 cites numerous allusions to Constantine as a 'god-beloved' man; at (2010), 184–5 he gives reasons for applying *Palatine Anthology* 10.90 to the destruction of the Tychaion in Constanntinople, which may have occurred at the time of its foundation.

[45] Bowra (1959), 266 infers from PA 10.97, where Palladas is said to have been 72 at the end of his career as a grammarian, that he was born in AD 319.

[46] On the Epigrammata Bohiensia see Cameron (1993), 90–1.

the following squib will have been inspired by some desecration of pagan images long before 391:[47]

> The owners of Olympian abodes dwell here unscathed, having now become Christian; for the pot that brings forth the life-giving follis[48] will not commit them to the flames.

The poem refers to the preservation of statues at a time when these relics of paganism were being melted down. Wilkinson surmises that the images which 'became Christians' and therefore escaped the furnace were those that, according to Eusebius, were spared by Constantine so that they could be 'playthings' to the Christian populace of Constantinople after 330. Eusebius' *Life of Constantine* supplies him with a gloss on another couplet, in which the poet laments the foundering of all that he once held dear:

> Are we not dead, men of the Greeks, only seeming to live, now that we have fallen into calamity, limning our life as a dream? Or can we be alive when life has perished? (*Palatine Anthology* 10.82)

Such plaints would be well-suited to the times described or imagined by Eusebius, when statues, divination and sacrifice had all been forbidden.[49] It may be objected that certain of the historian's assertions remain unverified; yet Palladas himself reminds us that what we fear is real to us while we fear it:

> If Rumour is a deity, she too is enraged with the Greeks, deceiving them with footloose tales. Yet when you suffer, all of a sudden Rumour is proved to be true; and often the swiftness of events overtakes even Rumour. (*Palatine Anthology* 10.89)

Wilkinson compares the letter of Constantine to the 'people of the east', in which he declares that if the times were favourable he would carry out the plan for the abolition of all the temples which is falsely imputed to him by the pagans.[50] He suggests, therefore, that Palladas is anticipating rather than describing the widespread desecration of ancient shrines that in fact took place (with imperial prompting) in the last decade of the fourth century, but was prophesied with menaces sixty years earlier in the edicts of the first Christian emperor.

The argument for an early dating of Palladas is decisive; Wilkinson's elucidations of particular epigrams are conjectural, though seductive.[51] The

[47] *Palatine Anthology* 9.528, Wilkinson conjectures that the editor names the house of Marina because this was a building of the Constantinian era in which pagan images were preserved in his own day as works of art.

[48] Most probably a coin, though in Latin the word means 'bellows': see Salamon (1995), 91–101; Pontani (2006–7), cited by Wilkinson (2009), 38 n.12.

[49] Wilkinson (2009), 53, citing Eusebius, *Life of Constantine* 4.23 and 25.

[50] Wilkinson (2009), 53–4.

[51] Note also Wilkinson (2009), 49–50, where he finds an allusion at *Palatine Anthology* 11.378 to the legal penalties which are attached to divorce at *Theodosian Code* 3.16.1; Wilkinson (2010), 185–9, where he associates a poem put into the mouth of Nikai or 'victories' (*Anth.* 16.282) with

paucity of the evidence forbids us to assume that the circumstances of composition will always be recoverable, and the likelihood—it is no more than a likelihood—that Theophilus is Constantine does not make it impossible for Palladas to have written under Constans and Constantius. Nothing in Wilkinson's argument entitles us to cite Palladas as a witness to any legislative act which aimed at the universal suppression of pagan cults. To conclude that he is describing what he had seen, and not merely what was threatened or presaged, we must assume that his epigrams can date themselves and explain themselves without corroboration or illumination from other sources. And this is an assumption to which a century of scholarship on Palladas gives the lie.

A VALEDICTION TO PAGANISM

Firmicus Maternus has already come before us an astrologer and as a satirical commentator on profane religion. In this, the later of his surviving works, he writes without disguise as a Christian, and with the object of persuading the Emperors Constans and Constantius, sons of Constantine, to suppress these parodies of the Christian sacraments.[52] It does not represent itself as the work of a convert (though we cannot know what he said of himself in the preface, which is lost), and it is certainly not the work of a man who is new to his religion. His exposition of its cardinal tenets in the closing chapters is brief and declamatory, yet it encompasses the fall, the incarnation, the passion, the resurrection and the reward of the saints, and thus permits us to entertain none of the doubts that we might entertain regarding the theological education of Lactantius or Arnobius. Moreover, he reveals a wider acquaintance with apologetic literature by grounding his indictment of the mysteries on three premises, all of which underpin the Greek polemics against idolatry in the second century. Firstly, he asserts that every nation worships an element, improving a hint from Paul which had been take up by the Christian philosopher Aristides in a speech exploding the claims of each of the elements in turn.[53] Secondly, like Tatian and Athenagoras before him,[54] he assumes that it is the demons who have an interest in promoting the worship of matter. Thirdly, he maintains that the demons achieve their ends by promoting the

Constantine's use of the title Victor after 324; and 189–91, where he argues that the twelve new gods ironically acclaimed at *Anth.* 10.56.17–18 are the twelve apostles who surrounded Constantine at his burial.

[52] *Error* 6.1, 8.4, 17.1, 20.7, etc. The date of publication must fall between 343 and 350, since Constans was overthrown in that year.

[53] See the edition with commentary by Pouderon (Bibliography A). Cf. Galatians 4.9.

[54] Tatian, *Oration* 12; Athenagoras, *Embassy* 26.

cult of the dead. Finally, he attributes their success to their proficiency in counterfeiting the mysteries of the church.

In his *Mathesis* Firmicus subscribes to the common astrological principle that the character of a people is determined by the climate and the physical geography of the region that it inhabits.[55] He applies this principle to the first of the mysteries that he denounces in his later work: the Egyptians, who dwell by the Nile, are predisposed to worship Osiris as the personification of its nutritive waters (*Error* 2.1, 2.5). Yet at the same time he asserts that the real Osiris was a man and the brother of a real woman, Isis, with whom he had incestuous relations, and who set up the Egyptian rites in his honour when the crime was detected and brutally punished by her husband Typhon (2.2). Likewise Cybele, the idol of the Phrygians, was a queen who caused the death of a youth named Attis after he spurned her overtures (2.1), but then repented and instituted an annual ceremony of mourning. If her votaries identify Cybele with the earth, they merely show themselves more conscious than other pagans that they are worshipping gods of stone (3.5). The Assyrians pay their devotions to a nameless goddess who represents the air (4.1–2), while Mithras, the god of the Persians, is worshipped under the form of fire (5.2). In neither case, however, is the latitude said to account for the choice of element, and once again we are given to understand that these nations commemorate the sufferings of real humans who committed inhuman crimes. Although it is he who identifies each deity with one of the elements, Firmicus consistently treats the physical explanation of myth as a palliative stratagem, devised by others and easily exploded, since nothing is gained by hiding the well-known facts of nature under tales of lechery and murder. When he turns to Greek cults, the tribulations of Bacchus and Persephone are recounted at prurient length, and with some innovative details that explain away the miraculous elements of the original story (*Error* 6–7). Pliny the Younger had echoed Livy's account of the suppression of the Bacchanals to justify his own measures against the Christians;[56] Firmicus, recalling the same event, laments that Romans now condone enormities which their pagan forebears knew to be intolerable (6.9).

Firmicus proceeds to expose the obscene cults of Adonis (9), the Cyprian Venus (10), Jupiter Sabazius (10), the Kabiri (11), and Serapis (13.1–5). The scriptures unmask the origin of this last cult, for Serapis is clearly Joseph, the saviour of Egypt in her years of want (13.2); even Porphyry, a notorious patron of idolatry, admits that Serapis appeared in human guise (13.4). Having played long enough on the Roman contempt for eastern superstitions, Firmicus turns his harangue against the capital, where fire is worshipped under the name of Vesta (14.3). When you lay food and drink before your Penates or ancestral

[55] Cf. Ptolemy, *Tetrabiblos* 4.10.

[56] Pliny, Letter 96; Livy, *Histories* 39.8–9; Grant (1948).

spirits, scoffs Firmicus, you are obviously unaware of Christ's admonition to the devil in the wilderness,[57] that human beings live not by bread alone but by God's word (14.2). Mocking the veneration of the Palladium which failed to protect either Troy or Rome (15), Firmicus proceeds to denounce five cults of Minerva (16)[58] and briefly recapitulates his argument that all cults originate in the worship of matter (17).

In his closing chapters Firmicus begins to expound the true faith, not in the words of an official creed (he was a layman, after all) but in a series of ripostes to the best-known watchwords of the pagan mysteries. 'I have eaten from the drum, I have drunk from the cymbal, I have borne the dish; I have entered the bridal chamber',[59] says the initiate; or, as the Latin of Firmicus has it (18.1), 'I have been schooled in the secrets of religion (*religionis secreta perdidici*)'. The Christian polemicist rejoins that there is poison in this cup, and that the 'bread of Christ' is the one food that can heal the sick, raise the fallen and avert the death to which our sins have doomed us (18.2). Although he gives no particulars of the rite,[60] this plain allusion to the Eucharist as the antidote to pagan secrecy indicates that the old positions have been reversed, that the church is now the one religious guild that cannot be suspected of covert sacrilege—the only one, we may add, that would not be forbidden to the virtuous astrologer in the *Mathesis*—and hence that a Christian sovereign must be as vigilant in the cause of God as his pagan forebears were in that of Satan.[61] Another salutation of unknown provenance—'hail, bridegroom, hail the new light' (19.1)—is answered by a salvo of texts which prove that Christ alone is the light of the world, the lord of the nuptial chamber, the sun of righteousness who will shine forth for his saints in heaven, 'decked as a bridegroom for his bride'.[62] Mithraists may prate of a 'god from a rock', but his birth was hallowed by no prophecies like those which foretold that Christ would be laid as a cornerstone in Zion.[63] If he remains a rock of offence to many,[64] the error lies with those who go on singing the exequies of the two-horned serpent Dionysus[65] while the horns of the Cross are spreading

[57] Matthew 4.4; Luke 4.4; Deuteronomy 8.3.
[58] Cf. Cicero, *Nature of the Gods* 2.59; Clement, *Protrepticus* 2.28.
[59] Clement of Alexandria, *Protrepticus* 2.15. For reconstructions of the original formula and (speculative comparisons) see the edition of Pastorino (1956), 188–90.
[60] He quotes as prooftexts Genesis 27.37; Isaiah 65.13–15; Psalm 33.9; and John 6.46.
[61] The emperors are addressed with fervour at 20.7.
[62] Revelation 21.9; Psalm 18.6; John 8.12; Joel 2.15; and Jeremiah 7.34 are also quoted.
[63] *Error* 20.1–2, citing Isaiah 28.16. Pastorino (1956), 204–6 notes that the formula is described as a *sacramentum* and compares the use of the same term at *Mathesis* 2.12.21 and 2.14.27. For the birth of Mithras from a rock see Justin, *Trypho* 70.
[64] *Error* 20.2 citing Psalm 17.22–23.
[65] See *Error* 21.2, with Pastorino (1956), 215; Euripides, *Bacchae* 90; Clement, *Protrepticus* 2.12; Plutarch, *Greek Questions* 299a. See *Error* 5.1 on the cult of the serpent in Persia and 10 on the serpentine character of Serapis.

throughout the world.[66] It is the victim of this cross who saved us by his resurrection: the mourners who anoint themselves for the funerary rites of Attis are falsely taught that he rises again each year,[67] but this proves only that the devil has his antichrists as Christ has his elect (22.4).

It was now a common tenet of Christianity that the saviour had descended to the underworld in the three days between his burial and his return, in order to free those who had died before his advent.[68] Firmicus, recounting his assault with unprecedented vigour, declares that, as the veil of the temple was rent in two, the iron gates below collapsed at Christ's command and the elements shook in concert (24.2–5). This martial imagery befits an age in which the Cross had become the talisman of a Christian conqueror. Apostrophizing the royal sons of Constantine (25.1), Firmicus undertakes to crown his denunciation of the pagan mysteries with an account of God's benign dealings with his own people. He commences with the fall, an event that ought to have been familiar enough to rulers who had ascended the throne as Christians (25.2); in contrast to Athanasius and Eusebius, however, he treats Adam and Eve as two distinct individuals and blames their trespass not on their natural frailty but on the cunning of the serpent who has been unmasked by stages in this treatise as the author and object of all idolatry (26.1–2). Again it was a commonplace that false cults are the work of demons, though the history of deception and not hitherto been carried back so picturesquely to Eden. This new aetiology of false religion appears to contradict the thesis that the gods are personified elements; Firmicus may, however, have been aware that Athenagoras had characterized the devil as the prince of matter, explaining his promotion of idolatry as a means of extending his perverse dominion to the soul.[69] The same author opined that the tempter, being too wise to reveal his own form to his votaries, had taken on the semblance of the dead; in marrying the Euhemeristic theory to the other two, therefore, Firmicus is guilty of no logical incoherence, and is stripping his pagan opponents of every possible excuse. If they accept the allegorical reading of their own myths, their gods are illusory; if they adopt the euhemeristic view, the gods are real but unworthy of worship. In either case, who but the lying spirit would persuade us to adore beings who do not offer us immortality or any balm for our spiritual distempers?

Although it might seem that his work has reached its peroration, Firmicus returns to the attack on the pagan mysteries, contrasting the wood of the cross with its pagan counterfeits and the immolation of the Paschal lamb with the Taurobolium,[70] or immersion in the blood of a bull, which Christian imagined

[66] *Error* 21.4, citing Habakkuk 3.3–5.

[67] *Error* 22.1. This is the earliest text in which Attis is said to have lived again. The liturgical formula is here described as a *symbolum*.

[68] See e.g. Eusebius, *Demonstration* 4.12.5.

[69] Athenagoras, *Embassy* 24.

[70] *Error* 27.8.

to be typical of the rites of Cybele and Mithras (27.1–2). Thus he gives pride of place to the favoured symbol of Constantine and to the festival at which he had preached his *Oration to the Saints* (27.5). In a final appeal to the emperors, he reminds them that the Deuteronomic code prescribes the extirpation of all sacrilegious cults (29.3; Deuteronomy 13.12–18).

CONCLUDING NOTE: WHAT NEXT?

We do not know whether the measures urged by Firmicus were put into execution, but the Theodosian Code records that a general decree against sacrifice was issued by the two emperors to whom he addressed his treatise. They imply that they are upholding their father's policy, though Eusebius and Optatus, as we have seen, are the only witnesses who attribute such a law to Constantine. It is possible that Constans and Constantius gave a more elastic character to the old but potent charge of superstition, once employed against the Christians, and reserved by Constantine himself for those cults that he judged sacrilegious or obscene.[71] There is evidence, as we have seen in Chapter 6, that a number of the cults against which Firmicus inveighs had passed their heyday by the beginning of the fourth century; the Mithraic *taurobolium*, for example, would appear to have survived only as a private rite, and prudent scholars regard the vivid description of it in Prudentius as an exercise of poetic imagination.[72] The epigrams of Palladas were written at a time when pagan sentiment was strong enough to deplore, but not to resist, the desecration of the ancestral places of worship; if this time was the reign of Constantine, as Wilkinson argues, Palladas must be struck from the list of writers who bear witness to the survival or recrudescence of pagan sentiment in the last years of the fourth century. So must the *Asclepius*, which, since the discovery of a Coptic version at Nag Hammadi, can no longer be regarded as a lament for the destruction of the Egyptian temples under Theodosius I.[73]

In a recent book by Alan Cameron,[74] the pagan population of Rome after Constantine shrinks to a *côterie*. At the same time paganism was not yet extinct, for we know what it cost the Christians of the fifth century to overthrow the temples of Marnas in Gaza, of Serapis in Alexandria, and of Asclepius in Athens. Constantine too was not chasing ghosts in his legislation: the rites that he suppressed had come to his notice because they were popular, though

[71] Salzman (1987). Here and in (2011), 169 she suggests that the edict of Constans and Constantius was directed only to Italy and that it may have been enforced only with respect to divinatory sacrifices.

[72] McLynn (1996). [73] See Chapter 7, this volume. [74] Cameron (2010).

his measures may have hastened the end of other institutions that were already in decay. These measures may have tempted pagan remonstrants into hyperbole, but their protests foreshadow the aggravated severities of emperors who had learned from Eusebius to think of Constantine as a thirteenth apostle[75] and Christ's vicegerent on earth.

[75] See the account of the monument that he erected for his burial at Eusebius, *Life of Constantine* 4.60.

Epilogue

This epilogue is for the most part a summary of the foregoing pages. If at times I pass from the mere rehearsal of phenomena to what may be called appraisal or explanation, it is always on the assumption that in human affairs there is no inevitability, and that scholarship can at best reveal the circumstances, not the determining causes, of a process or event. Shakespeare could not have been a product of the twentieth century nor Dadaism of the seventeenth; on the other hand, it cannot be said that the First World War inevitably gave rise to Dadaism or that Shakespeare was the predestined child of the English Reformation. Although the career of Constantine was in some sense prepared by the evolution of Christian thought and the tribulation of the church under Diocletian, the historian cannot usurp the role of the theologian by declaring his appearance at this time to be providential. We can hope to show at best that the phenomena were explicable; I do not know why we would even wish to demonstrate that the course of events was fore-ordained by God or by some immanent law of history. The universal premiss of all revolutions, after all, is that things could be other than they are.

PHILOSOPHICAL VARIATIONS

The first Christian appeals to the pagan world were rhetorical exercises, bearing such titles as 'Embassy', 'Apology', and 'Oration'. Following the conventions of that epoch which became known as the 'second sophistic', they cite few philosophers other than the founders of the great Athenian schools, and having once quoted a dictum they are content to applaud or reprimand it without inspecting the grounds on which it is held. We cannot be certain that any second-century apologist knew even Plato at first hand. Polemic gives way in Origen and Clement to criticism which is still far from dispassionate and to polymathy which stops a little short of their own generation. The pagan interlocutor of the eight books *Against Celsus* had published his invective about a decade before the birth of Origen. Eusebius, like the first apologists, took up his pen in the wake of persecution; if the fifteen books of his *Preparation for the Gospel* exceeded even the *Stromateis* of Clement in breadth of reference, one reason was that he had at his disposal not only the works of Clement himself but those of his older contemporary, the erudite Porphyry of Tyre, whose attack on Christianity may have appeared on the very eve of the persecution. In undertaking to demonstrate from his own words that this doyen of the Platonic school was also an idolater, a plagiarist, a sycophant to demons, and a vacillating critic of ancestral rites, Eusebius preserves many texts by Porphyry that would otherwise have been lost. No such windfalls come to us from his Latin contemporaries, though it has been persuasively argued that the apologies of Lactantius and Arnobius were also designed, in part at least, as refutations of Porphyry. Both are compendious in their erudition: Lactantius, who presents his work as an institution or manual of instruction, mingles classic texts which were regularly employed in didactic literature with extracts from Euhemerus and Hermes, while Arnobius cites material that is foreign and unfamiliar to his readers, in order to prove that Rome has disowned the traditions of her fathers and succumbed to the vices of those whom she believed herself to have conquered. Less encyclopaedic than Eusebius, and more studiously rhetorical, they share his conviction that if the pagan world is induced to open its books again, it will rediscover the everlasting gospel.

Philosophers exhibit no reciprocal interest in the Christianity of this era. For Iamblichus the dialogues of Plato contain the whole world of truth, in which the monad, the dyad, and the triad define the anatomy of all being. His exegesis makes no allowance for levity, development or abortive speculation; there are no two thoughts that cannot be harmonized, no speaker, however, recalcitrant, who does not at some time utter the thoughts of Plato. His disciple Theodorus of Asine was, if anything, still more prone to extravagance in his desire to complete the system. The Christian appropriation of Plato was less scholastic, as their object was not merely to interpret the text but to turn it to account. Chalcidius, perhaps the first Christian Platonist, compounds a hybrid theology from Platonic myth and biblical revelation. Eusebius finds an analogue to the Trinity in the three gods of Numenius, though apart from the phrase second god his own doctrine borrows little from this alleged precursor. The *Symposium* of Methodius is a feast without food, a series of discourses in praise not of love but of its renunciation, delivered not by men in the heat of desire but by chaste members of the sex to which Plato denied the use of reason. This challenge to the master through his own art, however, suggests that he has caught the ludic spirit of the dialogues which entirely escaped the sworn admirers of Plato in late antiquity.

In opposing Plato Christians declared that they too were philosophers; in common with all ancient thinkers, they understood by philosophy not merely a system of thought but an all-encompassing rule of life. Iamblichus, as we have seen in Chapter 4, acknowledged this fact when he composed a long biography of Pythagoras, with an account of the discipline that he imposed on is pupils, as a preface to the expository portions of his Pythagorean encyclopaedia. I have argued that this work contains tacit allusions to the gospels; an acquaintance with Christian literature (to say no more) is also discernible in the *Mathesis* of the astrologer Firmicus Maternus, who echoes Lactantius, flatters Constantine and describes the creation of humanity in a style reminiscent of the Mosaic scriptures. By contrast, it was not with any goodwill to Christianity that Sossianus Hierocles set him up as a pagan foil to Christ; its contents are known to us only from the polemical tract *Against Hierocles* attributed to Eusebius, the one Greek work by a Christian before the mid-fourth century which achieves the eloquence of a professional sophist. Both eloquence and the philosophy of the schools are alien to the new patterns of the ascetic life—one solitary at first, the other always cenobitic—which are reviewed in Chapter 5. Both Anthony and the disciples of Pachomius may be suspected of seeking physical affliction as an end in itself, without asking that it should be conducive to any more palpable good; their example was none the less followed by many unlettered folk who could never have grasped the principles of philosophy even if they could have paid the teacher's fee. Since the population of the Egyptian desert continued to grow under all political conditions, we cannot say that the movement was encouraged either by persecution or by the repeal of persecution; in the first half of this chapter I have noted that even Christians in common life were required to submit to unexplained restrictions on their choice of profession and their sexual conduct.[1] However distasteful some of its manifestations may be to modern eyes, we should not be too quick to throw the charge of madness at a community of equals who (in contrast to most philosophers) supported themselves by the labour of their own hands.

RELIGIOUS PLURALITY

In the chapter on the religions of the vanquished, we discovered little evidence that the cults denounced by Firmicus Maternus enjoyed wide patronage in Roman circles of the early fourth century. We are rightly warned by Ramsay Macmullen against inferring anything but our ignorance from the paucity of inscriptions; at the same time, if the marketplace of religions in antiquity has

[1] One always hesitates to judge ancient phenomena by grand theories based on modern observations, but it may be pertinent here to recall the comment of Durkheim (1961), 335–6 that in all religions the few who exceed the prescriptive standard of conduct help to sustain the adherence of the many to that standard.

an archaeology like any other, we cannot ignore the superior abundance of the wares that I have assembled in the following chapter under the title 'religions of transformation'. The ancients spoke of the mysteries of Mithras and his fellow-deities, never of 'Mithraism' as a philosophy that exercised unqualified dominion over the lives and thoughts of its adepts. We know little of the demands that it imposed on the initiate, and we know that it was not always thought to preclude the veneration of other gods. It did not compete with Christianity, therefore, as Christianity competes with Platonism. The Manicheans, on the other hand, were an alternative church, and this was also true of those Gnostic movements which had crystallized as sects. Of Hermetism and alchemy we cannot speak so confidently, but the texts which remain to us can be described as scriptures insofar as they set out a way of salvation to which all other goals must yield. It is here that we find the rivals to Christianity—or more properly, to the Christianity of the New Testament and its interpreters, for this literature was written for the most part by men who thought of themselves as Christians, and cannot be shown to have found any readers outside Christian circles.

Yet these religions also spoke of mysteries, just as the church did: have we sufficient proof that Mithraism and Hermetism were not only distinct religions but distinct species of religion? Zosimus appears to rank Zoroaster second to Hermes in authority, and there was a time when the eastern cults were invoked in Gnostic preaching almost as often as the Jewish or Christian scriptures. The Naassene sermon of the second century incorporates a commentary on a more ancient hymn to Attis, which Wilamowitz believed to have been the core of the whole composition.[2] The cosmologies of the Mithraists and the Ophites, as the pagan Celsus reported them in the same period, are so alike as to warrant the speculation that they were practising the same religion, what we call Mithraism being nothing but the iconographic representation of what we call Gnosticism. This theory, however, would find no support in the Nag Hammadi Codices, in which the only matter that purports to be oriental is an allusion to a patently spurious book of Zoroaster. The Gnosticism of the fourth century is less syncretistic than that of the second, and more obviously an esoteric form of Christianity. Far from preserving elements that could be plausibly characterized as oriental, it contributed by its metamorphosis to their extinction. From the evidence that remains to us, then, it appears—with due apology for the crude and provisional character of the inference—that the rivals to catholic Christendom in the age of Constantine were those that made the same promises that the church made and which might be embraced without conscious repudiation of Christianity.

[2] Wilamowitz-Moellendorf (1902).

It need hardly be said that Judaism was the one religion of eastern provenance which proved itself equally durable under all vicissitudes. In Chapter 8 I have noted that Christian literature of the Constantinian era is uniformly hostile to the living Jew, and that when Constantine took measures to protect or adorn a holy place, he invariably transformed it into a Christian preserve. A law forbidding the forcible circumcision of slaves can hardly be called tyrannical, but when it is reinforced by maledictions, which reappear in a letter enforcing the Nicene decision on Easter, the modern accusations of anti-Semitism may not be anachronistic. Since Jews were not compelled to abjure their religion or to perform any act in violation of the Mosaic law, it can be said that they enjoyed more toleration under Constantine than had been extended to Christians in the last years of Diocletian; we cannot acquit him, however, of contributing to the erosion of a Jewish culture in Palestine which was far from effete at the time of his rise to power.

CHRISTIAN POLYPHONY

Constantine's religion has been a topic of debate for more than a century, and I do not pretend in my chapter to shine a lamp into his conscience. I argue instead what I take to be the common view and the commonsensical one—that a ruler who makes it his stated aim to propagate Christianity, confessing his own adherence to that religion on all occasions when such a confession would be apposite (and on some when it would not), has done enough to demonstrate his sincerity according to every canon that we are wont to apply to European monarchs. Few would now applaud Burckhardt's portrait of him as a political opportunist without convictions, who professed only what he needed to profess in order to reconcile his most discontented subjects. It is still, however, held in certain quarters that he was either too much a statesman or too ignorant of theology to keep his Christianity free of pagan elements. I agree with those who find in the *Oration to the Saints* a demonstration of his acquaintance with the exclusive character of Christianity; if one of the early dates that I and Girardet propose is found acceptable, it will be clear that he understood the consequences of his own conversion from the outset. Some who assign a later date to the speech detect an inclination to the Arian teaching which was defeated at Nicaea; others, of whom I am one, find nothing in it that is at odds with the doctrines of the Catholic Church. The policy of Constantine throughout the Arian controversy is that of a man who aimed at 'nothing but peace'; before we call this temporization, we should reflect that every ruler has a duty to be a father to all his people and not only those whom he hopes to rejoin in heaven. His legislation too bespeaks a policy of governing as a Christian without treating the governed as Christians: he is not an oppressor, but neither is he tolerant on any religious or philosophic principle. I believe that most scholars today will concur with this judgement; I am perhaps behind the fashion, however, in my reluctance to accept that Constantine's sign from heaven was a solar halo. I do not doubt the reality of his conversion, but it does not become more real to me when we reduce it to a natural anomaly, which is plainly not the event related in any of our conflicting narratives.

Notwithstanding the silence of the Theodosian Code, it would be rash to discount the statement of Eusebius that Constantine abolished pagan sacrifice. In Chapter 10 I cited Optatus as a neglected witness to the belief that he did so, and not only in Italy. I have also pointed out that the reign of Constantine coincided with a triangular debate on the legitimacy of sacrifice, in which Arnobius amplified and refined the philippics of his Christian predecessors, while Porphyry and Iamblichus drew opposing inferences from Plato's teaching on the intermediate status of the daemon. It is certain at least that sacrifice became obsolete in the fourth century, whether through legislation or by natural atrophy. In a recent monograph Guy Stroumsa has maintained that in the wake of its cessation the public religion of the empire was obliged, like Judaism after the ruin of the temple, to define itself by its liturgy, its texts and its disciplines rather than by the practice of immolation.[3] The asymmetry is obvious, since Jews and pagans alike would have offered sacrifice had the Christians not proscribed it; Eusebius would have added that the church was now the true celebrant of the Passover, no longer presenting the lamb to God but receiving the divine flesh and blood in return for the oblation of bread and wine.

That Constantine promoted the distribution of the New Testament as a written norm, is attested by Eusebius, the bishop of the city in which fifty new codices were prepared at the emperor's behest. This action may have contributed to the emergence of a standard text, though no decree could secure the same uniformity in the transmission of this text that had been secured by the Nicene Council's ruling on the date of Easter. It may have seemed to Eusebius that the imperial letter restored to Caesarea the pre-eminence that it was losing to Jerusalem; be that as it may, his own commentaries on both testaments are informed by a profound reverence for the text in all its variants, and his hermeneutic premiss, as I have shown by my brief sampling of his works in chapter 11, is that the true sense of the text can be elicited only by the most minutely literal reading. In fact, it is when he is at his most pedestrian that he surprises modern exegetes by declaring that the text speaks only of Christ and not of its ostensible subject. I have noted in the same chapter that his namesake Eusebius of Emesa sometimes arrives at the same conclusion,

[3] Stroumsa (2009).

notwithstanding his professed distaste for allegory. It did not seem profitable to compare the method so of the Eusebii with those of their Platonic contemporaries, since the commentaries of Iamblichus and Theodorus now survive only in fragments. It will none the less be obvious to the reader of Chapter 3 that both the Christians and the Platonists of this epoch were led to results that strike us as fanciful today by their determination to charge every word with a meaning that would cohere with the meaning of every other word in the sacred corpus.

At the centre of the liturgy, and at the centre of both Testaments for all catholics of this period, stood the figure of Christ eternal and incarnate. Jews denied his Messianic pretensions; pagans scoffed at his miracles and urged that no god would have undergone such a death. Eusebius, as befits a historian, urged in his *Demonstration of the Gospel* that the veracity of the witnesses is beyond reproach, that therefore there can be no doubt of the miracles, and that the miracles, being wrought in fulfilment of the ancient prophecies, show Jesus to be the anointed one of God. Then prominence that Constantine had given to the Cross made it all the more necessary for Christian apologists to account not only for the death of Christ but for his suffering and abasement; Eusebius develops his theology of the atonement at greater length than any writer before him, pre-empting the more famous exposition of Athanasius. In Chapter 12 I juxtaposed this work with the versified harmony of the gospels by Juvencus. This imitator of Virgil, we may say, is no dogmatician, but he has found a better way of courting the interest of the educated Roman. Arnobius and Lactantius had set out to convert the pagans from their own libraries: Juvencus adds a new book to these libraries, completing the epic promised in the exordium to the Fourth Eclogue, as though the prophecies of the Sibyl had been delivered to Rome but intended for the church.

To judge by his own report and the position of his signature, Eusebius was a straggler at the Council of Nicaea in 325, where the creed was signed without hesitation by his rival Macarius of Jerusalem. Since he completed Pamphilus' *Apology for Origen* and wove a hagiographic account of that theologian's life into the sixth book of his *Church History*, he is often represented as the spokesman of an 'Origenist' party which struggled against the outcome of the Council. As I hope to have shown in Chapter 13, however, Eusebius was never a servile follower of Origen, and if the term 'Origenism' connoted anything in his time, it was not the subordination of the Son but his coeternity with the Father—a tenet that Arius vigorously denied. If it was Constantine, as Eusebius tells us, who ensured that the creed would take a form unpalatable to Arius, he too, on this view, was an anti-Origenist; a few years later, he must have become an Origenist when he endorsed the lukewarm recantation of Arius, but returned to his former position when he shot the heretic down with a hot-headed quiverful of invective. I have granted that the story of his enforcing the *homoousion* is more credible than the theory that it found its way into the Creed from the Hermetica; his apparent vacillations, however, betoken only his desire to govern his realm in peace, which (as we have noted) is the first duty of any sovereign, whatever his religion. Whatever its origin, the Creed prevailed, and my analysis of his writings against Marcellus after the council does not indicate that Eusebius had found himself obliged to give up or dissemble his old beliefs.

Was the peace of the realm enhanced or impaired by the emperor's policies? Eusebius testifies that Christian numbers had increased after his accession[4]—how could they not?—and in the laudatory oration of 336 which supplies to the preface to Chapter 14 he represents Constantine as the surrogate on earth of the Word in heaven, under whose patronage all nations have been gathered into one commonwealth of believers. Nevertheless, the Donatists had not been repressed in Africa, and the immediate result of the Nicene council had not been to establish unity but to aggravate the penalties of discord. Athanasius crowed that the idols had been banished by the manifestation of the living Word, and the complaints of Palladas, if he is indeed a voice of this era, suggest an orchestrated spoliation of the pagan temples. Yet victors and victims are equally prone to exaggerate, and the exhortations of Firmicus Maternus to the sons of Constantine can also be read as a confession of their father's failure to uproot paganism.

But of course we do not expect to see all the consequences of a great innovation during the lifetime of the author. Inveterate habits and entrenched convictions cannot be erased by fiat; the habits and convictions that the legislator hopes to foster will grow up only when his laws have been in force for so long that the new generation remembers no others. Constantine, like Henry VIII, was succeeded by a son in whose reign his measures were imitated with less tact and more tenacity; Julian the pagan successor of Constantius, being even more short-lived than Edward's successor Mary Tudor, could not reverse the trend that had been established, and he had no pagan heir. We need only suppose that Constantius had been a pagan, or that Julian had reigned longer, to persuade ourselves that Constantine's conversion did not necessitate the conversion of the empire. Nevertheless, it was he who initiated that conversion, and only an obstinate predestinarian would argue that the triumph of Christianity was inevitable even if he had not become a Christian. Nor, on the other hand, would his own espousal of Christianity have been more than an aberration in Roman history had he acted alone, without any cultural or political stimulus and without the support of a well-governed multitude. If the Christian population had been smaller, if the catholic church had not yet been established in every province, if the spokesmen of this church had not been able to hold their own in learned company, if there had been

[4] *Life of Constantine* 4.36, cited in chapter 11.

some other philosophy which united itself with a cult that was open to all—we need not paint imaginary scenarios, as we have only to compare the fortunes of Constantine with those of Akhenaten. Some change in the equilibrium of religious forces was, no doubt, inevitable, just as it was inevitable that relations between the church and the crown would change when England found herself in conflict with two other commercial empires, each more capable of bending the Pope to its will. But just as it is thanks to Henry VIII (whatever his aims) that the British monarch now swears an oath to uphold the protestant religion, so it was thanks to Constantine (whatever he accomplished in his own time) that Christianity became the professed religion of a majority in the Empire, that its tenets were openly cited in imperial legislation and that the church which enjoyed a legal monopoly of the name 'Christian' was the one whose clergy had ratified the Nicene Creed.

Bibliography

Primary Literature

Contains texts which are not available in the Loeb Classical Library. Where the title employed in this book differs from that of the printed edition, it is added here in square brackets.

Alexander of Lycopolis, *Contra Manichaei opiniones disputatio* [*Against the Manichees*], ed. A. Brinkmann (Leipzig: Tebner, 1895).

Aphthonius, *Progymnasmata*, ed. H. Rabe (Leipzig: Teubner, 1926).

Aristides of Athens, *Apologie* [*Apology*], ed. B. Pouderon (Paris: Cerf, 2003).

Arnobius, *Adversus Nationes* [*Against the Nations*], ed. A. Rifferscheid (Vienna: Gerold, 1875).

Arnobius, *Contre les Gentils livres VI–VII* [*Against the Nations 6–7*], ed. and trans. B. Fragu (Paris: Belles-Lettres, 2010).

Athanasius, *Lettere Festali* [*Festal Letters*], ed. A Camplani (Milan 2003).

Athanasius, *Vie d'Antoine* [*Life of Antony*], ed. G.M. Bartelink (Paris: Cerf, 2004).

Athanasius, *Werke, 3.1: Dokumente zur Geschichte des arianischen Streites, ed.* H.-F. Brennecke, U. Heil, A von Stockhausen, A. Wintjes (Berlin: De Gruyter, 2007).

Athenagoras, *Legatio* [*Embassy*] and *De Resurectione*, ed. and trans. W. R. Schoedel (Oxford: Clarendon Press, 1972).

Augustine, *De Civitate Dei* [*City of God*], ed. E. Hoffmann, 2 vols (Turnhout: Brepols, 1899).

Augustine, *Contra Cresconium* [*Against Cresconius*], ed. M. Petschanig (Vienna: Tempsky, 1909).

Aurelius Victor, *De Caesaribus* [*Caesars*], ed. F. Pichlmayr (Leipzig: Teubner, 1911).

Chalcidius, *Commentarium in Timaeum* (*Plato Latinus* IV) [*Commentary on the Timaeus*], ed. J. H.Waszink (Leiden: Brill, 1974).

Chaldaean Oracles, ed. with translation and commentary by R. Majercik (Leiden: Brill, 1989).

Clement of Alexandria, *Werke*, 4 vols, ed. O. Staehlin, L. Früchtel and U. Treu (Berlin: Akademie Verlag, 1970–1980).

Collatio Legum Mosaicarum Et Romanarum, ed. T. Mommsen in *Collectio Librorum Iuris ante-Justiniani*, vol. 3 (Berlin: Weidmann, 1890), 107–98.

Cologne Mani Codex. See Gnoli (2003).

Constantine, *Oratio ad Sanctum Coetum/Rede an die Versammlung der Heiligen* [*Oration to the Saints*], ed. and trans. K. Girardet (Basel: Herder, 2013).

Cyprian, ed. G. F. Diercks and G. W. Clark (Turnhout: Brepols, 1972).

Cyril of Jerusalem, *Catechesis Quarta* [*Fourth Catechetical Oration*], in Heurtley (Bibliography B), 62–80.

Damascius, *Dubitationes et Solutiones* [*Doubts and Solutions*], ed. C. A. Ruelle (Amsterdam: Hakkert, 1966).

Eusebius, *Das Leben Constantins, Constantins Rede an die Heilige Versammling, Tricennatsrede an Constantin* [*Life of Constantine, Oration to the Saints, Tricennial Oration*], ed. I. A. Heikel (Leipzig: Hinrichs, 1902).

Eusebius, *Kirchengeschichte* [*Church History*], ed. E. Schwartz, 3 vols (Leipzig: Hinrichs, 1903–1909).

Eusebius, *Onomasticon/Theophanie*, ed. E. Klostermann and H. Gressmann (Leipzig: Hirichs, 1904). *Theophanie* re-edited by A. Laminski (Berlin: De Gruyter, 1992).

Eusebius, *Demonstratio Evangelica* [*Demonstration of the Gospel*], ed. I. A. Heikel (Leipizzig: Hinrichs, 1913).

Epiphanius, ed. K. Holl, 3 vols (Leipzig: Hinrichs, 1915–1933).

Eusebius, *Praeparatio Evangelica* [*Preparation for the Gospel*], 2 vols, ed. K. Mras (Berlin: Akademie Verlag, 1954–56).

Eusebius, *Gegen Markell/Über die Kirchliche Theologie* [*Against Marcellus, On Ecclesiastical Theology*], etc., ed. E. Klosterman (Berlin: De Gruyter, 1972).

Eusebius, *Jesajakommentar* [*Commentary on Isaiah*], ed. J. Ziegler (Berlin: Akademie Verlag, 1975).

Eusebius, *Contre Hiéroclès* [*Against Hierocles*], ed. M. Forrat and E. Des Places (Paris: Cerf, 1986).

Eusebius, *Reply to Hierocles*, ed. and trans. C. P. Jones in *Philostratus: Apollonius of Tyana* III (Cambridge, MA: Harvard University Press, 1986), 147–257.

Eusebius, *De Vita Constantini/Das leben Konstantins* [*Life of Constantine*], ed. and trans. B. Bleckman (Turnhout: Brepols, 2007).

Eusebius, *Commentarium in Lucam* [*Commentary on Luke*], in *Patrologia Graeca* 24.

Eusebius, *Commentarium in Psalmos* [*Commentary on Psalms*], in *Patrologia Graeca* 23 and 24.

Firmicus Maternus, *De l'erreur des religions païennes* [*On the Error of Profane Religions*], ed. R. Turcan (Paris: Belles Lettres, 1982).

Firmicus Maternus, *Mathesis*, ed. P. Monat, 3 vols (Paris: Belles Lettres, 1992–1997).

Gelasius of Cyzicus, *Kirchengeschichte* [*Church History*], ed. G. C. Hansen (Berlin: De Gruyter, 2002).

Gregory Thaumaturgus, *Remerciement à Origène* [*Panegyric on Origen*], ed. and trans. H. Crouzel (Paris: Cerf, 1969).

Hermetica, ed. and trans. W.B. Scott, 4 vols (Oxford: Clarendon Press, 1925–1936).

Hermetica ed. and trans. A. D. Nock and A. -J. Festugière, 2 vols (Paris: Belles Lettres, 1945).

Hermetica ed. and trans. P. Scarpi (Florence: Lorenzo Valla institute, 2011).

Hippolytus, *Refutatio Omnium Haeresium* [*Refutation of all Heresies*], ed. M. Marcovich (Berlin: De Gruyter, 1986).

Iamblichus, *De Vita Pythagorica* [*On the Pythagorean Life*], ed. L. Deubner (Leipzig: Teubner, 1937).

Iamblichus, *Commentariorum Fragmenta*, ed. and trans. J. M. Dillon (Leiden: Brill, 1973).

Iamblichus, *De Communi Mathematica Scientia Liber* [*On the Common Science of Mathematics*], ed. N. Festa and U. Klein (Stuttgart: Teubner, 1975).

Iamblichus, *Protrepticus*, ed. E. Des Places (Paris: Belles Lettres, 1989).

Iamblichus, *De Anima* [*On the Soul*], ed. and trans. J. F. Finamore and J. M. Dillon (Leiden: Brill, 2002).

Iamblichus, *De Mysteriis* [*On the Mysteries*], ed. and trans. J. M. Dillon, E. Clarke and J. Hershbell (Atlanta: Society of Biblical Literature, 2003).
Iamblichus, *I Frammenti delle epistole*, ed. D. Taormina and R. M. Piccione (Rome: Bibliopolis, 2011).
Irenaeus, *Demonstration of the Apostolic Preaching*, trans. from Armenian by J. A. Robinson (Cambridge: Cambridge University Presss, 1920).
Irenaeus, *Contre les Hérésies* [*Against Heresies*], 10 vols, ed. A. Roussau, J. Doutreleau and others (Paris: Cerf, 1965–82).
Jerome, *Regula Pachomii* [*Rule of Pachomius*], in J.-P. Migne (ed.), *Patrologia Latina* 23 (Paris: Vrayet, 1845), 67–82.
Jerome, *De Viris Illustribus* [*On Famous Men*], ed. W. Herding (Leipzig: Teubner, 1879).
Jerome, *Epistulae* [*Letters*], ed. I. Hilberg, 3 vols (Vienna: Tempsky 1910–1918/1996).
Jerome, *Die Chronik des Hieronymus* [*Chronicle*], ed. R. Helm, in Eusebius, *Werke* 7 (Berlin: De Gruyter, 1956).
Jerome, *Vita Pauli* [*Life of Paul*], ed. I. Kosik (Mouint Vernon, NY: King Lithographers, 1968).
Justin Martyr, *Dialogue cum Tryphone* [*Dialogue with Trypho*], ed. M. Marcovich (Berlin: De Gruyter, 1997).
Justin Martyr, *Apologies*, ed. and trans. D. Minns and P. Parvis (Oxford: Oxford University Press, 2009).
Juvencus, *Libri Evangeliorum IIII*, ed. C. Marold (Leipzig: Teubner, 1886).
Lactantius, ed. S. Brandt and G. Laubmann, 2 vols (Venna: Tempsky, 1890–3).
Lactantius, *Les morts des persécuteurs* [*Deaths of the Persecutors*], ed. J. Moreau (Paris: Cerf, 1954/2004).
Lactantiused. A. Städele (Turnhout: Brepols, 2003).
Libanius, ed. R. Foerster, 4 vols (Leipzig: Teubner, 1903–7).
Liber Pontificalis [*Book of Pontiffs*], ed. L. Duchesne (Paris: Thorin, 1886).
Macarius Magnes, *Le Monogénès*, ed. and trans. R. Goulet, 2 vols (Paris: Vrin, 2003).
Marcellus of Ancyra. *Die Fragmente, Der Brief an Julius von Rom*, ed. M. Vinzent (Leiden: Brill, 1997).
Methodius, *Schriften*, ed. N. Bonwetsch (Leipzig: Böhme, 1891).
Methodius, *Le Banquet* [*Symposium*], ed. and trans. H. Musurillo and V.-H. Debidour (Paris: Cerf, 1963).
Musici Scriptores Graeci, ed. K. von Jan (Leipzig: Tuebner, 1895).
Nag Hammadi Codices, *The Coptic Gnostic Library*, general editor J. M. Robinson, 5 vols (Leiden: Brill, 2000).
Numenius, *Fragments*, ed. E. Des Places (Paris: Belles Lettres).
Optatus, *Contre les Donatistes* [*Against the Donatists*], ed. J. Labrousse, 2 vols (Paris: Cerf, 1997).
Origen, *Vom Gebet/Gegen Celsus* [*On Prayer, Against Celsus*], ed. P. Koetschau (Leipzig: Hinrichs, 1899).
Origen, *De Principiis* [*First Principles*], ed. P. Koetschau (Leipzig: Hinrichs, 1913).
Origen, *Homilien zu Samuel, zum Hohelied und zu den Propheten* [*Homilies on Samuel, Commentary and Homilies on Song of Songs, Homilies on the Prophets*], ed. W. Baehrens (Berlin: De Gruyter, 1925).

Origen, *Sur le libre arbitre: Philocalie 21–27* [*Philokalia*], ed. E. Junod (Paris: Cerf, 1976).

Origen, *Römerbriefkommentar* [*Commentary on Romans*], vol. 1, ed. C. P. Hammond Bammel (Freiburg: Herder, 1990).

Origen, *Kommentierung des Buchs Genesis* [*Commentary on Genesis*], ed. K. Metzler (Berlin: De Gruyter, 2010).

Orphic Argonautica, in H. Abel, *Orphica* (Leipzig, Teubner, 1885).

Pamphilus, *Apologia pro Origene* [*Apology for Origen*], ed. G. Röwekampf (Turnhout: Brepols, 2005).

Panegyrici Latini [*Latin Panegyrics*], ed. R. B. Mynors (Oxford: Clarendon Press, 1964).

Philostorgius, *Kirchengeschichte* [*Church History*], ed. J. Bidez (Leipzig: Hinrichs, 1913).

Porphyry, *De Philosophia ex Oraculis Haurienda* [*Philosophy from Oracles*], ed. G. Wolff (Berlin: Springer, 1856).

Porphyry, *Opuscula Selecta* [*History of Philosophy, Life of Pythagoras, Cave of the Nymphs, On Abstinence, Letter to Marcella*], ed. A. Nauck (Leipzig: Teubner, 1886).

Porphyry, *Lettera ad Anebo* [*Letter to Anebo*], ed. A. Sodano (Naples: L'arte tipografia, 1952).

Porphyry, *In Timaeum Commentarium* [*Commentary on Timaeus*], ed. A. Sodano (Naples L'arte tipografia, 1964).

Porphyry, *Sententiae ad Intelligibilia Ducentes*, ed. E. Lamberz (Leipzig: teubner, 1975).

Porphyry, *Vie de Plotin* [*Life of Plotinus*], ed. L. Brisson, 2 vols (Paris: Vrin, 1982).

Porphyry, *Fragmenta*, ed. A. Smith (Leipzig: Teubner, 1993).

Porphyry, *Contra I Cristiani* [*Against the Christians*], ed. A. von Harnack and G. Muscolini (Milan: Bompiani, 2009).

Proclus, *Commentarium in Timaeum* [*Commentary on Timaeus*], ed. W. Diehl, 3 vols (Leipzig: Teubner, 1903–1906).

Proclus, *Commentarium in Parmenidem* [*Commentary on the Parmenides*], ed. R. Klibansky (London: Warburg Institute, 1953).

Prolegomena to *Platonic Philosophy*, ed. and trans. L. G. Westerink (Amsterdam: North Holland Publishing Co., 1962).

Psellus, Michael, *Philosophica Minora: Opuscula*, ed. J. M. Duffy and D. J. O'Meara, 2 vols (Leipzig: Teubner, 1989).

Rufinus, *Commentarium in Symbolum Apostolarum* [*Commentary on Apostles' Creed*], in Heurtley (Bibliography B), 121–73.

Sallustius, *Concerning the Gods and the World*, ed. and trans. A. D. Nock (Cambridge: Cambridge University Press, 1926).

Socrates, *Kirchengeschichte* [*Church History*], ed. G. C Hansen (Berlin: Akademie Verlag, 1995).

Sozomen, *Kirchengeschichte* [*Church History*], ed. J. Bidez (Berlin: Akademie Verlag, 1960).

Suidae Lexicon (*Suda*), ed. A. Adler, 5 vols (Leipzig/Berlin: Teubner, 1928).

Tatian, *Oratio ad Graecos* [*Oration to the Greeks*], ed. and trans. M. Whittaker (Oxford: Clarendon Press, 1982).

Tertullian, *Opera*, ed. A. Gerlo, 2 vols (Turnhout: Brepols, 1950–54).

Theodore of Asine. *Sammlung der Testimonien*, ed. W. Deuse (Wiesbaden: Franz Steiner).
Theodoret, *Haereticarum Fabularum Compendium*, ed. K. Gutberlet (Munich: Bibliothek der Kirchenvater, 1926).
Theodoret, *Kirchengschichte* [*Church History*], ed. L. Parmentier (Berlin Akademie Verlag, 1998).
Theologoumena Arithmeticae [*Theology of Arithmetic*], ed. V. de falco (Leipzig: Teubner, 1922).
Theophilus of Antioch, *Ad Autolycum* [*To Autolycus*], ed. and trans. R. M.Grant (Oxford: Clarendon Press, 1970).
Zosimus, *Histoire Nouvelle [New History*], Livres I-Ii, ed. F. Paschoud (Paris: Belles Lettres) 1971.
Zosimus of Panaopolis, *Mémoires Authentiques* [*Authentic Memoirs*], ed. M. Mertens, in *Les Alchimistes grecs* IV (Paris: belles Letters, 1985/2002).

Secondary Literature

Abramowski, L. (1992a), 'Dionysius of Rome (d. 268) and Dionysius of Alexandria (d. 264/5) in the Arian Controversies of the Fourth Century', in Abramowski, *Formula and Context: Studies in Early Christian Thought* (Aldershot: Variorum), vol. 11, 1–35.
Abramowski, L. (1992b), 'The Synod of Antioch 324/5 and its Creed', in Abramowski, *Formula and Context: Studies in Early Christian Thought* (Aldershot: Variorum), vol. 3, 1–12.
Abramowski, L. (2007), 'Audi ut dico: Literarische beobachtungen und chronologische Erwägungen zu Marius Victorinus und den 'platonisierenden' Nag Hammadi Traktaten', *Zeitschrift für Kirchengeschichte* 117, 145–68.
Adamson, P. (2007), '*Porphyrius Arabus* on Nature and Art: 463F Smith in Context', in G. Karamanolis and A. Sheppard (eds), *Studies on Porphyry* (London: Institute of Classical Studies), 141–63.
Adamson, P. (2008), 'Plotinus on Astrology', *Oxford Studies in Ancient Philosophy* 35, 265–91.
Addey, C. (2014), *Divination and Theurgy in Neoplatonism* (Farnham: Ashgate).
Alföldi, A. (1937), *A Festival of Isis in Rome under Christian Emperors of the IVth Century* (Budapest).
Aldridge, R. E. (1999), 'Peter and the Two Ways', *Vigiliae Christianae* 53, 233–64.
Alexander, D. (2006), *Saints and Animals in the Middle Ages* (Woodbridge: Boydell).
Angelov, A. (2014), 'Bishop over "Those Outside": Imperial Ideology and the Boundaries of Constantine's Christianity', *Greek, Roman and Byzantine Studies* 54, 274–92.
Arjava, A. (1996), *Women and the Law in Late Antiquity* (Oxford: Clarendon Press).
Arnold, D. (1991), *The Early Episcopal Career of Athanasius* (Chicago: University of Notre Dame Press).
Assmann, J. (2003), *Die mosaische Unterscheidung oder der Preis des Monotheismus* (Munich: Hanser).
Athanassiadi, Polymnia. 'Antiquité Tardive: Construction et Déconstruction d'un Modèle historiographique', *Antiquité Tardive* 14 (2006), 211–24.

Aufferth, C. (2012), 'Le rite sacrificial antique: la longue durée et la fin du sacrifice', *Kernos* 25, 297–303.

Avi-Yonah, M. (1976), *The Jews of Palestine: A Political History from the Bar-Kochba War to the Arab Conquest* (Oxford: Blackwell).

Bagnall, R. (1982), 'Religious Conversion and Onomastic Change in Early Byzantine Egypt', Bulletin of the American Society of papyrologists 19, 105–24.

Baldwin, B. (1976), 'Vergilius Graecus', *American Journal of Philology* 97, 361–8.

Bardill, J. (2012), *Constantine, Divine Emperor of the Christian Golden Age* (Cambridge: Cambridge University Press).

Bardy, G. (1936), *Recherches sur s. Lucien d'Antioche et son école* (Paris: Beauchesne).

Barnes, M. (1998), 'The Fourth Century as Trinitarian canon', in L. Ayres and G. Jones (eds), *Christian Origins: Theology, Rhetoric and Community* (London: Routledge), 47–67.

Barnes, T. D. (1971), *Tertullian* (Oxford: Clarendon Press).

Barnes, T. D. (1973a), 'Porphyry, *Against the Christians*: Date and Attribution of the Fragments', *Journal of Theological Studies* 14, 424–42.

Barnes, T. D. (1973b), 'Lactantius and Constantine', *Journal of Roman Studies* 63, 29–46.

Barnes, T. D. (1975), 'The Beginnings of Donatism', *Journal of Theological Studies* 26, 13–22.

Barnes, T. D. (1976a), 'Sossianus Hierocles and the Antecedents of the "Great" Persecution', *Harvard Studies in Classical Philology* 80, 239–52.

Barnes, T. D. (1976b), 'The Emperor Constantine's Good Friday Sermon', *Journal of Theological Studies* 27, 414–23.

Barnes, T. D. (1976c), 'Imperial Campaigns A.D. 285–311', *Phoenix* 30, 174–93.

Barnes, T. D. (1977), 'Two Speeches by Eusebius', *Greek, Roman and Byzantine Studies* 18, 341–45.

Barnes, T. D. (1978), *The Sources of the Historia Augusta* (Brussels).

Barnes, T. D. (1979), 'Methodius, Maximus and Valentinus', *Journal of Theological Studies* 30, 47–55.

Barnes, T. D. (1981a), *Constantine and Eusebius* (Cambridge, MA: Harvard University Press).

Barnes, T. D. (1981b), 'The Editions of Eusebius' *Ecclesiastical History*', *Greek, Roman and Byzantine Studies* 22, 191–201.

Barnes, T. D. (1982), *The New Empire of Diocletian and Constantine* (Cambridge, MA: Harvard University Press).

Barnes, T. D. (1986), 'Angel of Light or Mystic Initiate? The Problem of the Life of Anthony', *Journal of Theological Studies* 37, 353–68.

Barnes, T. D. (1993), *Athanasius and Constantius* (Cambridge, MA: Harvard University Press).

Barnes, T. D. (1994), 'Scholarship or Propaganda? Porphyry's *Against the Christians* and its historical setting', *Bulletin of the Institute of Classical Studies* 39, 53–65.

Barnes, T. D. (1997), 'The Constantinian Settlement', in H. Attridge and G. Hata (eds), *Eusebius, Christianity and Judaism* (Leiden: Brill), 635–57.

Barnes, T. D. (2001a), 'Monotheists all?', *Phoenix* 55, 142–62.

Barnes, T. D. (2001b), 'Constantine's *Speech to the Assembly of the Saints*', *Journal of Theological Studies* 52, 26–36.

Barnes, T. D. (2004a), Review of Edwards, *Constantine and Christendom*, *Journal of Theological Studies* 55, 351–5.
Barnes, T. D. (2004b), 'Constantine's Prohibition of Pagan Sacrifice', *American Journal of Philology* 105, 69–72.
Barnes, T. D. (2007), Review of N. Lenski (ed.), *The Cambridge Companion to the Age of Constantine*, *International Journal of the Classical Tradition* 14, 184–220.
Barnes, T. D. (2009), 'The Exile and Recalls of Arius', *Journal of Theological Studies* 60, 109–29.
Barnes, T. D. (2010a), *Early Christian Hagiography and Roman History* (Tübingen: Mohr Siebeck).
Barnes, T. D. (2010b), 'The Letter of Eusebius to Constantia (*CPG* 3503)', *Studia Patristica* 46, 313–17.
Barnes, T. D. (2011), *Constantine: Dynasty, Religion and Power in the Late Roman Empire* (Chichester: Wiley).
Barnes, T. D. (2013), 'The First Christmas in Rome, Antioch and Constantinople', *Studia Patristica* 64, 77–83.
Barton, T. S. (1994), *Power and Knowledge: Astrology, Physiognomics and Medicine under the Roman Empire* (Ann Arbor: University of Michigan Press).
Battifol, P. (1914), 'Les documents de la *Vita Constantini*', *Bulletin d'ancienne literature et d'archéologie chrétiennes* 4.
Bauckham, R., with J. Davila and a. Panayotov (2013), *Old Testament Pseudepigrapha. More Non-Canonical Texts*, vol. 1 (Grand Rapids,MI: Eerdmans).
Bauer, W. (171), *Orthodoxy and Heresy in Earliest Christianity* (Philadelphia, PA: Fortress Press).
Baumgarten, A. (1981), *The Phoenician History of Philo of Byblos. A Commentary* (Leiden: Brill).
Baynes, C. (1933), *A Coptic Gnostic Treatise Contained in the Codex Brucianus* (Cambridge: Cambridge University Press).
Baynes, N. H. (1931), *Constantine the Great and the Christian Church* (London: Milford).
Beard, M. (1990), 'Priesthood in the Roman Republic', in M. Beard and J. North (eds), *Pagan Priests* (Ithaca, NY: Cornell University Press), 17–48.
Beatrice, P. F. (1989), '*Quosdam libros Platonicos*: the Platonic readings of Augustine in Milan', *Vigiliae Christianae* 43, 248–81.
Beatrice, P. F. (1990), 'La croix et les idoles d'après l'apologie d'Athananse contre les païens', in A. Gonzalez (ed.), *Cristianesimo y aculturcion en tiempo del Imperio Romano* (Murcia: University of Murcia), 159–77.
Beatrice, P. F. (2002), 'The *Homoousion* from Hellenism to Christianity', *Church History* 74, 243–72.
Bechtle, G. (1999), *The Anonymous Commentary on the Parmenides* (Bern: Haupt).
Beck, R. (1988), 'The Mysteries of Mithras: A New Account of their Genesis', *Journal of Roman Studies* 88, 115–28.
Beck, R. (1994), 'In the Place of the Lion: Mithras in the Taurctony', in J. R. Hinnells (ed.), *Studies in Mithraism* (Rome: Bretschneider), 29–50.
Beck, R. (2006), *The Religion of the Mithras Cult in the Roman Empire* (Oxford: Oxford University Press).

Beduhn, J. (2002), *The Manichaean Body. Its Discipline and Ritual* (Baltimore, MD: Johns Hopkins University Press).

Beeley, C. (2012), *The Unity of Christ* (New Haven, CT: Yale University Press).

Behr, J. (2001), *The Nicene Faith*, vol. 1 (New York: St Vladimir's Seminary).

Belayche, N. (2010), '*Deus deum . . . summorum maximus* (Apuleius): ritual expressions of distinction in the divine world in the imperial period', in S. Mitchell and P. van Nuffelen (eds), *One God. Pagan Monotheism in the Roman Empire* (Cambridge: Cambridge University Press), 141–66.

Bell, H. I. (1914), *Jews and Christians in Egypt. The Jewish Troubles in Alexandria and the Athanasian Controversy* (London: Oxford University Press/British Museum).

Berchman, R. M. (2005), *Porphyry against the Christians* (Leiden: Brill).

Berrens, S. (2004), *Sonnenheit und Kaisertum von den Severern bis zu Constantin I* (Stuttgart).

Berthier, A. (1942), *Vestiges du Christianisme antique dans la Numidie central* (Algiers).

Bévenot, M. (1979), '*Sacerdos* as Understood by Cyprian', *Journal of Theological Studies* 30, 413–29.

Bianchi, U. (1975), 'Mithraism and Gnosticism', in J. R. Hinnells (ed.), *Mithraic Studies* (Manchester: Manchester University Press), 457–65.

Biddle, M. (1999), *The Tomb of Christ* (Scarborough: Sutton).

Bidez, J. (1913), *Vie de Porphyre* (Ghent: van Goethem).

Bidez, J. (1919), 'Le philosophe Jamblique et son école', *Revue des Études grecques* 32, 29–40.

Bidez, J. and F. Cumont (1938), *Les mages hellénisés*, 2 vols (Paris).

Bleckmann, R. (1997), 'Ein Kaiser als prediger: zur Datierung der konstantinischen "Rede an die Versammling der Heiligen" ', *Hermes* 125, 183–202.

Bochet, I. (2011), 'Les *quaestiones* attribuées à Porphyre dans la letter 102 d'Augustin', in Morlet, *Le traité*, 371–94.

Böhlig, A. (1994), 'Die Bedeutung der Funde von Medinet Madi für die Erforschung des Gnostizismus', in A. Böhlig and C. Markschies (eds), *Gnosis und Manichäismus: Forschungen und Studien zur Texten von Valentin und Mani sowie zu den Bibliotheken von Nag Hammadi und Medinet Madi* (Berlin: De Gruyter), 135–71.

Bolhius, A. (1956), 'Die Rede Konstantins des Grossen an die Versammlung der Heiligen und Lactantius, *Divinae Institutiones*', *Vigiliae Christianae* 10, 25–32.

Borgehammar, S. (1991), *How the True Cross Was Found: From Event to Medieval Legend* (Stockholm).

Borzi, S. (2003), 'Sull'autenticità del *Contra Ieroclem* di Eusebio di Ceasrea', *Augustiniaum* 43, 397–416.

Borzì, S. (2013), 'Il *Filaletes* di Ierocle e l'*Apocriticus* di Macario Magnes', *Augustinianum* 53, 393–425.

Bousset. W. (1923), *Apophthegmata. Studien zur geschichte des ältesten Mönchtums* (Tübingen: Mohr).

Bowersock, G. (2002), 'The Highest God with Reference to North Pontus', *Hyperboreus* 8, 353–63.

Bowra, C. M. (1959), 'Palladas and Christianity', *Proceedings of the British Academy* 45, 255–67.

Box, G. H. (1917), *The Apocalypse of Ezra* (London: Haymarket).
Brakke, D. (1994), 'The Greek and Syriac Versions of the *Life of Antony*', *Le Muséon* 107, 29–53.
Brakke, D. (1995), *Athanasius and the Politics of Asceticism* (Oxford: Oxford University Press).
Brakke, D. (2006), *Demons and the Making of the Monk. Spiritual Combat in Early Christianity* (Cambridge, MA: Harvard University Press).
Brakke, D. (2011), *The Gnostics. Myth and Diversity in Early Christianity* (Cambridge, MA: Harvard University Press).
Brenk, F. (1977), *In Mist Apparelled. Religious Themes in Plutarch's Moralia and Lives* (Leiden: Brill).
Bril, A. (2006), 'Plato and the Sympotic Form in the *Symposium* of St Methodius', *Zeitschrift für Antike Christentums* 9, 279–302.
Brown, T. S. (1946), 'Euhemerus and the Historians', *Harvard Theological Review* 39, 259–74.
Brown, P. (1971), 'The Rise and Function of the Holy Man in Late Antiquity', *Journal of Roman Studies* 61, 80–101.
Brown, P. (1978), *The Making of Late Antiquity* (Cambridge, MA: Harvard University Press).
Brown, P. (1988), *The Body and Society* (London: Faber).
Bruun, P. (1966), *Roman Imperial Coinage VI* (London: British Museum).
Buchinger, H. (2005), *Pascha bei Origenes*, 2 vols (Innsbruck and Vienne: Tyrolia).
Budischevsky, M. -Chr. (1977), *La diffusion des cultes Isiaques autour de la Mer Adriatique* (Leiden: Brill).
Burckhardt, J. (1853), *Die Zeit Constantins des Grossen* (Basel: Schweighauser). English translation, Moses Hadas (New York: Doubleday, 1949).
Burgess, R. W. (1997), 'The Dates and Editions of Eusebius' *Chronici Canones* and *Ecclesiastical History*', *Journal of Theological Studies* 48, 471–504.
Burgess, R. W. (2000), 'The Date of the Deposition of Eusebius of Antioch', *Journal of Theological Studies* 51, 150–60.
Burkert, W. (1983), *Homo Necans. The Anthropology of Ancient Greek Sacrificial Ritual and Myth*, trans. P. Bing (Berkeley: University of California Press).
Buzási, G. (2009), 'An Ancient debate on Canonicity: Julius Africanus and Origen on Susanna', in K. Dobos and M. Kozhegy (eds), *With Wisdom as a Robe. Qumran and Other Studies in Honour of Ida Fröhlich* (Sheffield: Phoenix), 438–50.
Cameron, Alan (1968), 'The Date of Iamblichus' Birth', *Hermes* 96, 374–6.
Cameron, Alan (1993), *The Greek Anthology from Meleager to Planudes* (Oxford: Clarendon Press).
Cameron, Alan (2010), *The Last Pagans of Rome* (New York: Oxford University Press).
Cameron, Averil (1997), 'Eusebius' *Vita Constantini* and the Construction of Constantine', in M. J. Edwards and S. C. R. Swain (eds), *Portraits* (Oxford: Clarendon Press), 245–74.
Cameron, Averil (2000), 'Form and Meaning: The *Vita Antonii* and the *Vita Constantini*', in T. Hägg and P. Rousseau (eds), *Greek Biography and Panegyric in Late Antiquity* (Berkeley: University of California Press), 73–88.

Cameron, Averil, and S. G. Hall, trans. (1999), *Eusebius: Life of Constantine* (Oxford: Clarendon Press).

Campbell, J. (1968), *Mithraic Iconography and Ideology* (Leiden: Brill).

Canfora, L. (1990), *The Vanished Library* (Berkeley: University of California Press).

Canfora, L. (1993), *Studi di storia della storiografia romana* (Bari: Edipuglia).

Carleton Paget, J. (1994), *The Epistle of Barnabas: Outlook and Background* (Tübingen: Mohr Siebeck).

Chadwick, H. (1948), 'The Fall of Eustathius of Antioch', *Journal of Theological Studies*, 27–35.

Chadwick, H. (1958), 'Ossius of Cordoba and the Presidency of the Council of Antioch', *Journal of Theological Studies* 9, 292–304.

Chadwick, H. (1972), 'The Origin of the Title "Oecumenical Council"', *Journal of Theological Studies* 23, 132–5.

Chalupa, A. (2008), 'Seven Mithraic Grades: An Initiatory or Priestly Hierarchy?', *Religio* 16, 178–201.

Chastagnol, A. (1981), 'L'inscription constantinienne d'Orcistus', *Mélanges de l'école francaise de Rome* 93, 381–416.

Chesterton, G. K. (1960), *St Francis of Assisi* (London: Hodder).

Chitchaline, Y. (1992), "À propos du titre du traité de Plotin περὶ τῶν τριῶν α'ρχικῶν ὑποστασείων̆, *Revue des Études Grecques* 105, 253–61.

Chitty, D. (1954), 'Pachomian Sources Reconsidered', *Journal of Ecclesiastical History* 5, 38–77.

Chitty, D. (1966), *The Desert a City* (New York: St Vladimir's Seminary).

Clark, E. A. (1992), *The Origenist Controversy* (Princeton, NJ: Princeton University Press).

Clark, G. (1993), *Women in Late Antiquity* (Oxford: Clarendon Press).

Clark, G. (1998), 'Bodies and Blood: Late Antique Debate on Martyrdom, Virginity and Renunciation', in D. Montserrat (ed.), *Changing Bodies, Changing Meanings. Studies on the Human Body in Antiquity* (London: Routledge), 99–115.

Clark, G. (2004), *Christianity and the Roman World* (Oxford: Oxford University press).

Clark, G. (2005), 'The Health of the Spiritual Athlete', in H. King (ed.), *Health in Antiquity* (London: Routledge), 216–29.

Cleary, T. (1999), *Sex. Health and Long Life: Manuals of Taoist Practice* (Boston, MA: Shambala).

Clemen, C. (1901), 'Zu Firmicus Maternus', *Rheinisches Museum* 73, 350–8.

Cohen, S. (1999), *The Beginnings of Jewishness* (Berkeley: University of California Press).

Colombi, E. (1997), '*Paene ad verbum*: gli *Evangeliorum libri* di Giovenco tra parafrasi e comento', *Cassiodorus* 3, 9–36.

Cook, J. G. (1998), 'A Possible Fragment of Porphyry's *Contra Christianos* from Michael the Syrian', *Zeitschrift fur Antikes Christentum* 2, 113–22.

Copenhaver, B. (1992), *Hermetica: The Greek Corpus Hermeticum and the Latin Asclepius in a New English Translation with Notes and Introduction* (Cambridge: Cambridge University Press).

Corcoran, S. P. (1993), 'Hidden from History: the Legislation of Licinius', in Harries and Wood, 97–119.

Corcoran, S. P. (2000), *The Empire of the Tetrarchs, AD 284–324* (Oxford: Clarendon Press).
Courcelle, P. (1953), 'Les sages de Porphyre et les "viri novi" d'Arnobe', *Revue des Études Latines* 31, 157–71.
Cox, P. (1983), *Biography in Late Antiquity* (Berkeley: University of California Press).
Cremer, F. W. (1969), *Die Chaldäischen Orakel und Jamblich De Mysteriis* (Meisenheim am Glan: Hain).
Croke, B. (1983), 'Porphyry's Anti-Christian Chronology', *Journal of Theological Studies* 34, 168–85.
Crouzel, H. (1972), 'Les critiques adressées par Méthode et ses contemporains à la doctrine origénienne du corps ressuscité', *Gregorianum* 53, 649–716.
Cumont, F. (1896–99), *Textes et Monuments Relatifs aux Mystères de Mithra* (Brussels: Lamertin).
Cumont, F. (1911), *The Oriental Religions in Roman Paganism* (Chicago: Open Court).
Cumont, F. (1975), 'The Dura Mithraeum', in J. R. Hinnells (ed.), *Mithraic Studies* (Manchester: Manchester University Press), 151–214.
Curran, K. (2000), *Pagan City and Christian Capital* (Oxford: Clarendon Press).
Davies, P. S. (1989), 'The Origin and Purpose of the Persecution of 303', *Journal of Theological Studies* 40, 66–94.
Dearn, A. (2004), 'The Abitinian Martyrs and the Outbreak of the Donatist Schism', *Journal of Ecclesiastical History* 55, 1–8.
De Clerq, V. (1954), *Ossius of Cordova: A Contribution to the History of the Constantinian Period* (Washington, DC: Catholic University of America).
De Decker, D. (1978), 'Le discours a l'assemblée des saints attribuée a l'Constantin et l'oeuvre de Lactance', in J. Fontane and M. Perrin (eds), *Lactance et son temps. Recherches actuelles* (Paris: Beauchesne), 75–87.
Den Boeft, J. (1970), *Calcidius on Fate: His Doctrine and Sources* (Leiden: Brill).
Den Boeft, J. (1977), *Calcidius on Demons (Commentarius 127–136)* (Leiden: Brill).
Detienne, M. (1979), *Dionysos Slain* (Baltimore, MD: Johns Hopkins University Press).
Dieterich, A. (1923), *Eine Mithrasliturgie* (Lepzig: Teubner).
Dietz, M. (2010), *Wandering Monks, Virgins and Pilgrims. Ascetic Travel in the Mediterranean World*, 300–800 (University Park: Pennsylvania State University Press).
Digeser, E. D. (2000), *The Making of a Christian Empire. Lactantius and Rome* (New York: Cornell University Press).
Digeser, E. D. (2002),'Porphyry, Julian or Hierocles? The Anonymous Hellene in Macarius Magnes', *Journal of Theological Studies* 53, 466–502.
Digeser, E. D. (2004), 'An Oracle of Apollo at Daphne and the Great Persecution', *Classical Philology* 99, 57–77.
Dillon, J. M. (1973), 'The Concept of Two Minds: A Footnote to the History of Platonism', *Phronesis* 18, 176–85.
Dillon, J. M. (1987), 'Iamblichus of Chaclis', *Aufstieg und Niedergang des römischen Welt* II.36.2, 862–909.
Dix, G. P. (1945), *The Shape of the Liturgy* (London: A. and C. Black).
Dodds, E. R. (1965), *Pagan and Christian in an Age of Anxiety* (Cambridge: Cambridge University Press).

Dodds, E. R. (1970), 'Tradition and Personal Achievement in the Philosophy of Plotinus', *Journal of Roman Studies* 2, 1–7.

Dodds, E. R. (1973), *The Ancient Concept of Progress and Other Essays on Greek Literature and Belief* (Oxford: Clarendon Press).

Doergens, H. (1915), *Eusebius von Cäsarea als Darsteller der phönizischen Religion* (Paderborn: Schöningh).

Dolger, F. (1932), 'Das Kultvergehnder Donatistin Lucilla von Karthago', *Antike und Christentum* 3, 245–52.

Dolger, F. (1934), '*Sacramentum Infanticidii*: Die Schlachtung eines Kindes und der Genuss seines Fleisches und Blutes als vermeintlicher Einweihungsakt im ältesten Christentum', *Antike und Christentum* 4 (Münster: Aschendorff), 188–224.

Doresse, J. (1960), *The Secret Books of the Egyptian Gnostics* (London: Hollis).

Dorival, G. (2013), 'Origen', in J. Carleton Paget and J. Schaper (eds), *The New Cambridge History of the Bible. From the Beginnings to 600* (Cambridge: Cambridge University Press), 605–28.

Dornsieff, F. (1922), *Das Alphabet in Mystik und Magik* (Leipzig: De Gruyter).

Dörrie, H. (1967), *Wort und Stunde* (Göttingen: Vandenheok und Ruprecht).

Dothan, M. (1983), *Hammath Tiberias: Early Synagogues and the Hellenistic and Roman Remains* (Jerusalem: Israel Exploration Society).

Douglas, L. (1996), 'A New Look at the *Itinerarium Burdigalense*', *Journal of Early Christian Studies* 4, 313–33.

Downing, F. G. (1992), *Cynics and Christian Origins* (London: Bloomsbury).

Draguet, R. (1980), *La vie primitive de S. Antoine conservée en syriaque* (Louvain: CSCO).

Drake (1971), *In Praise of Constantine: A Historical Study and new Translation of Eusebius' Tricennial Orations* (Berkeley: University of California Press).

Drake, H. A. (1975), 'When Was the "De Laudibus Constantini" Delivered?', *Historia* 24, 345–56.

Drake, H. A. (1976), trans., *In Praise of Constantine* (Berkeley: University of California Press).

Drake, H. A. (1985a), 'Eusebius on the True Cross', *Journal of Ecclesiastical History* 36, 1–22.

Drake, H. A. (1985b), 'Indications of Date in Constantine's *Oration to the Saints*', *American Journal of Philology* 106, 335–49.

Drake, H. A. (2000), *Constantine and the Bishops* (Baltimore, MD: Johns Hopkins University Press).

Drijvers, J. W. (1992), *Helena Augusta: The Mother of Constantine the Great and the Legend of her Finding of the True Cross* (Leiden: Brill).

Dunand, F. (1963), 'Les noms théophores en–ammon', *Chronique d'Egypte* 38, 134–46.

Dunand, F. (1977), 'L'Oracle du Potier et la formation de l'apocalyptique en Égypte', in M. Philonenko (ed.), *L'Apocalyptique* (Paris: Guenther), 41–67.

Durkheim, E. (1961), *The Elementary Forms of the Religious Life* (New York: Collier).

Duthoy, R. (1969), *The Taurobolium: Its Evolution and Terminology* (Leiden: Brill).

Edwards, M. J. (1989), '*Aidôs* in Plotinus: *Enneads* II.9.10', *Classical Quarterly* 39, 573–8.

Edwards, M. J. (1990), 'Porphyry and the Intelligible Triad', *Journal of Hellenic Studies* 110, 14–25.
Edwards, M. J. (1992), 'Some Early Christian Immoralities', *Ancient Society* 23, 71–82.
Edwards, M. J. (1993), 'Two Images of Pythagoras', in H. J. Blumenthal and G. Clark (eds), *The Divine Iamblichus* (London: Bristol Classical Press),
Edwards, M. J. (1993b), 'Porphyry and the Cattle-Stealing God', *Hermes* 121, 122–5.
Edwards, M. J. (1997), *Optatus: Against the Donatists* (Liverpool: Liverpool University Press).
Edwards, M.J. (1998), "Did Origen Apply the Word Homoousios to the Son?", *Journal of Theological Studies* 49, 658-670.
Edwards, M. J. (1999), 'The Constantinian Circle and the *Oration to the Saints*', in M. J. Edwards, M. D. Goodman, and S. R. F. Price (eds), *Apologetics in the Roman Empire* (Oxford: Clarendon Press), 251–76.
Edwards, M.J. (2000), *Neoplatonic Saints. The Lives of Porphyry and Plotinus by their Students* (Liverpool: Liverpool University Press).
Edwards, M. J. (2002), *Origen against Plato* (Farnham: Ashgate).
Edwards, M. J. (2003), *Constantine and Christendom* (Liverpool: Liverpool University Press).
Edwards, M. J. (2004), 'Dating Arnobius: Why Discount the Evidence of Jerome?', *Antiquité Tardive* 12, 263–71.
Edwards, M. J. (2006a), 'Nicene Theology and the Second God', *Studia Patristica* 40, 191–5.
Edwards, M. J. (2006b), 'The Beginnings of Christianization', in N. Lenski (ed.), *The Cambridge Companion to the Age of Constantine* (Cambridge: Cambridge University Press), 137–58.
Edwards, M. J. (2007a), 'Notes on the Date and Venue of the *Oration to the Saints*', *Byzantion* 77 (2007), 149–69.
Edwards, M. J. (2007b), 'Porphyry and the Christians', in G. Karamanolis and A. Sheppard (eds), *Studies on Porphyry* (London: Institute of Classical Studies, BICS supplement 98), 111–26.
Edwards, M. J. (2011), 'Greeks and Demons in the Great Persecution', in G.A. Cecconi and C. Gabrielli (eds), *Politiche religiose nel mondo antico e tardocantico* (Bari: Edipuglia), 217–34.
Edwards, M. J. (2012), 'Alexander of Alexandria and the Homoousion', *Vigiliae Christianae* 66, 482–502.
Edwards, M. J. (2013a), 'Plotinus: Monist, Theist or Atheist?', in L. Nelstrop and S. Podmore (eds), *Christian Mysticism and Incarnational Theology* (Farnham: Ashgate), 13–26.
Edwards, M. J. (2013b), 'Why Did Constantine label Arius a Porphyrian?', *L'Antiquité Classique* 82, 239–47.
Ehrhardt, C. (1980), '"Maximus", "Invictus" und "Victor" als Datierungskriterien auf Inschriften Konstantins des Grossen', *Zeitschift für Papyrologie und Epigraphik* 49, 177–81.
Ehrman, B. and Z. Pleše (2011), *Apocryphal Gospels: Texts and Translation* (New York: Oxford University Press).
Eliade, M. (1977), *Forgerons et Alchimistes* (Paris: Flammarion).

Elliott, T. G. (1992a), 'Constantine's Explanation of his Career', *Byzantion* 62, 212–34.
Elliott, T. G. (1992b), 'Constantine and the Arian Reaction after Nicaea', *Journal of Ecclesiastical History* 43, 169–94.
Elliott, J. K. (2005), *The Apocryphal New Testament* (Oxford: Oxford University Press).
Elm, S. (1994), *Virgins of God* (Oxford: Clarendon Press).
Elm., S. (2012), *Sons of Hellenism, Sons of the Church* (Cambridge: Cambridge University Press).
Elsner, J. (2000a), 'The *Itinerarium Burdigalense*: Politics and Salvation in the Geography of Constantine's Empire', *Journal of Roman Studies* 90, 181–95.
Elsner, J. (2000b), 'From the Culture of *Spolia* to the Cult of Relics: The Arch of Constantine and the Genesis of Late Antique Forms', *Papers of the British School at Rome* 68, 149–84.
Festugière, A. -J. (1940), 'La doctrine des *viri novi* sur l'origine et le sort des âmes', *Memorial Lagrange* (Paris: Gabalda), 97–132.
Festugière, A. -J. (1954), *Personal Religion among the Greeks and Romans* (Berkeley: University of California Press).
Finamore, J. (1985), *Iamblichus and the Theory of the Vehicle of the Soul* (Atlanta: Society of Biblical Literature).
Finn, R. (2009), *Asceticism in the Graeco-Roman World* (Cambridge: Cambridge University Press).
Fontaine, J. (1959), *Isidore de Seville et la culture classique dans l'Espagne Wisigothique* (Paris: Études Augustiniennes).
Fontaine, J. (1984), '*Dominus lucis*: un titre singulier du Christ dans le dernier vers de Juvencus', in E. Lucchesi and H. D. Saffrey (eds), *Memorial André-Jean Festugière* (Geneva:), 131–41.
Fowden, G. (1993), *The Egyptian Hermes. A Historical Approach to the Late Pagan Mind* (Princeton, NJ: Princeton University Press).
Fowden, G. (1994), 'Constantine's Porphyry Column: The earliest Literary Allusion', *Journal of Roman Studies* 81, 119–31.
Fragu, B. (2010), *Arnobe: Contre les Païens Livres VI–VII* (Paris: Belles Lettres).
Frakes, R. M. (2006), 'The Dynasty of Constantine to 363', in N. Lenski (ed.), *The Cambridge Companion to the Age of Constantine* (Cambridge, Cambridge University Press), 91–107.
Franzmann, M. (2003), *Jesus in the Manichaean Writings* (London: Bloomsbury).
Frede, M. (1999), 'Eusebius' Apologetic Writings', in M. J. Edwards, M. D. Goodman and S. R. F. Price (eds), *Apologetics in the Roman World* (Oxford: Oxford University Press), 223–50.
Frend, W. H. C. (1952), *The Donatist Church. A Movement of Cultural Protest in Roman North Africa* (Oxford: Clarendon Press).
Galor, K. and H. Bloedhorn (2013), *The Archaeology of Jerusalem: From the Origins to the Ottoman Period* (New Haven, CT: Yale University Press).
Gardner, I. (1995), *The Kephalaia of the Teacher* (Leiden: Brill).
Gardner, I. and S. N. C. Lieu (2004), *Manichean Texts from the Roman Empire* (Cambridge: Cambridge University Press).
Gascou, J. (1967), 'Le réscrit d'Hispellum', *Mélanges d'archéologie et d'histoire* 79, 609–59.

Gelzer, H., with H. Hilgenfeld and O. Cuntz (1995), *Patrum Nicaenorum Opera*, revised edition (Leipzig: Teubner).
Gerlach, K. (1998), *The Ante-Nicene Pascha* (Leuven: Peeters).
Gersh, S. (1978), *From Iamblichus to Eriugena* (Leiden: Brill).
Girardet, K. (2013), 'Ein spätantiker "Sönnenkönig" als Christ', *Göttinger Forum für Altertumswissenchaft* 16, 371–81.
Girardet, K. M. (2008), 'L'invention du dimanche: du jour du soleil au dimanche. Le Dies Solis dans la legislation et la politique de Constantin le Grand', in J-N. Guinot and F. Richard (eds), *Empire chrétien et Église aux IVe et Ve siècles* (Paris: Cerf, 2008), 341–70.
Gnoli. G. (2003), *Il Manicheismo* I: *Mani e il Manicheismo* (Florence: Lorenzo Valla Institute).
Goddard, C. J. (2010), 'Un principe de différenciation au Coeur des processus de Romanisation et de Christianisation: quelgues reflexions autour du culte de Saturne en Afrique romaine', in H. Inglebert, S. Destephen and B. Dumézil (eds), *Le problème de la christianisation du monde antique* (Paris), 115–45.
Goehring, J. (1986), *The Letter of Ammon and Pachomian Monasticism* (Berlin: De Gruyter).
Goehring, J. (2001), 'The Provenance of the Nag Hammadi Codices Once More', *Studia Patristica* 35, 234–53.
Goehring, J. (2005), 'The Dark Side of Landscape: Ideology and Power in the Christian Myth of the Desert', in D. B. Martin and P. C. Miller (eds), *The Cultural Turn in Late Ancient Studies: Gender, Asceticism and Historiography* (Durham, NC: Duke University Press), 136–49.
Goodman, M. D. and P. Alexander (2010), *Rabbinic Texts and the History of Late-Roman Palestine* (New York: Oxford University Press for the British Academy).
Goulet, R. (2010), 'Cinq nouveaux fragments nominaux du traité de Porphyre 'Contre les chrétiens", *Vigiliae Christianae* 64, 140–59.
Graf, F. (1995), 'Aphrodite', in K. van der Torn, B. Becking and P. W. van der Horst (eds), *Dictionary of Deities and Demons in the Bible* (Leiden: Brill), 118–25.
Grafton, A. and M. Williams (2006), *Christianity and the Transformation of the Book* (Cambridge, MA: Belknap Press).
Grant, R. M. (1948), 'Pliny and the Christians', *Harvard Theological Review* 41, 273–4.
Grant, R. M. (1975), 'Eusebius and his Lives of Origen', in *Forma Futuri Studi in Honore del Cardinale Michele Pellegrino* (Turin: Erasmo), 635–49.
Graves, R. (1956), *The Greek Myths*, 2 vols (Harmondsworth: Penguin).
Green R. P. H. (2006), *Latin Epics of the New Testament: Juvencus, Sedulius, Arator* (Oxford: Oxford University Press).
Greer, R. and M. M. Mitchell (2007), *The Belly-Muther of Endor. Interpretations of 1Kingdoms 28 in the Early Church* (Atlanta: Society of Biblical Literature).
Grégoire, H. (1927–28), 'L'étymologie de "Labarum"', *Byzantion* 4, 477–82.
Griffiths, J. G. (1970), *Plutarch, De Oside et Osiride* (Oxford: Clarendon Press).
Griffiths, J. G. (1975), *The Isis-Book of Lucius Apuleius* (Leiden: Brill).
Grig, L. and G. Kelly (2012), *Two Romes: Rome and Constantinople in Late Antiquity* (Oxford: Oxford University Press).
Grigg, R. (1977), 'Constantine the Great and the Cult without Images', *Viator* 8, 1–32.
Grillmeier, A. (1975), *Christ in Christian Tradition* I (London: Mowbray).

Grubb, J. E. (1993), 'Constantine's Imperial Legislation on the Family', in Harries and Wood, 120–42.

Gwynn, D. (2007), *The Eusebians: The Polemic of Athanasius of Alexandria and the Construction of the Arian Controversy* (Oxford: Oxford University Press).

Gwynn, D. (2012), *Athanasius of Alexandria: Bishop, Theologian, Ascetic* (Oxford: Oxford University Press).

Hadot, P. (1968), *Porphyre et Victorinus*, 2 vols (Paris: Études Augustiniennes).

Hägg, T. (1992), 'Hierocles the Lover of Truth and Eusebius the Sophist', *Symbolae Osloenses* 67, 138–50.

Hahneman, G. M. (1992), *The Muratorian Fragment and the Dating of the Canon* (Oxford: Clarendon Press).

Halkin, F. (1979), 'Une vie inédite de Saint Pachôme, BHG 1401', *Analecta Bollandiana* 97, 5–55 and 241–87.

Hall, S. G. (1986), 'The Sects under Constantine', in W. J. Shield and D. Wood (eds), *Voluntary Religion* (Oxford: Oxford University Press), 1–13.

Hall, S. G. (1998), 'Some Eusebian Documents in the *Vita Constantini*', in S. N. C. Lieu and D. Montserrat (eds), *Constantine: History, Historiography, Legend* (London: Routledge), 86–104.

Hanson, R. P. C. (1973), 'The *Oratio ad Sanctos* Attributed to the Emperor Constantine and the Oracle at Daphne', *Journal of Theological Studies* 24, 105–11.

Hanson, R. P. C. (1985), *Studies in Christian Antiquity* (Edinburgh: T. and T. Clark).

Hanson, R. P. C. (1988), *The Search for the Christian Doctrine of God* (Edinburgh: T. and T. Clark).

Harmless, W. (2004). *Desert Christians. An Introduction to the Literature of Early Monasticism* (New York: Oxford University Press).

Harnack, A. von (1908), *The Mission and Expansion of Christianity*, vol. 1, trans. J. Moffatt (London: Williams and Norgate).

Harnack, A. von (1916), *Porphyryius, 'Gegen die Christen', 15 Bücher: Zeugnisse, Fragmente und Referate* (Berlin: Prussian Academy).

Harnack, A. von (1957), *Outlines of the History of Dogma* (Boston: Beacon Press).

Harries, J. and I. Wood (1993), *The Theodosian Code: Studies in the Imperial Law of Late Antiquity* (London: Duckworth).

Hauben, H. (1981), 'On the Melitians in P. London VI (P. Jews) 1914. The Problem of Papa Heraiscus', in R. S. Bagnall, G. M. Browne, A. E. Hanson and L. Koenen (eds), *Proceedings of the Sixteenth International Congress of Papyrology, New York, 24—31 July 1980* (Chico, CA), 447–56.

Hauben, H. (1987), 'La réordination du clergé mélitien imposé par le Concile de Nicée', *Ancient Society* 18, 203–7.

Hauben, H. (1989), 'La première année du schism mélitien (305/6', *Ancient Society* 20, 267–80.

Hauben, H. (1989/90), 'Le catalogue mélitien réexaminé', *Sacris Erudiri* 31, 155–67.

Hauben, H. (1998), 'The Melitian "Church of the Martyrs"', in T. W. Hillard, R. A. Kearsley, C. E. V. Nixon and A. M. Nobbs (eds), *Ancient History in a Modern University* (Cambridge: Cambridge University Press), 329–49.

Hauben, H. (2001), 'Le Papyrus London VI (P. Jews) 1914 dans son contexte historique', in I. Andorlini, G. Bastiani, M. Manfredi and G. Manci (eds), *Atti del XXII Congresso Internazionale di Papirologia*, Florance, 23–29 August 1998 (Florence), 605–18.

Hayward, R. (2010), 'Targum', in Goodman and Alexander, 235–52.

Heck, E. (1972), *Die dualistiche Zusätze und die Kaiseranreden bei Lactantius* (Heidelberg).

Hegedus, T. (2007), *Early Christianity and Ancient Astrology* (Bern: Peter Lang).

Heidl, G. (2003) *Origen's Influence on the Young Augustine: A Chapter in the History of Origenism* (Piscataway, NJ: Gorgias Press).

Henry, P. (1935), *Recherches sur la Préparation Évangelique d'Eusèbe et l'edition perdue des Oeuvres de Plotin publié par Eustoce* (Brussels: L'édition universelle).

Henry, P. (1948), *Études potiniennes II: Les manuscits des Ennéades* (Brussels: L'edition universelle).

Heurtley, C. A. (1911), *De Fide et Symbolo* (Oxford: Parker).

Holdrege, B. (1996), *Veda and Torah: Transcending the Textuality of Scripture* (New York: SUNY Press).

Hollerich, M. J. (1999), *Eusebius of Caesarea's Commentary on Isaiah* (Oxford: Clarendon Press).

Holmberg, B. (2013), 'The Syriac Collection of Apophthegmata Patrum in MSSin. Syr.46', *Studia Patristica* 55.3, 35–57.

Honigman, E. (1942–3), 'The Original List of the Members of the Council of Nicaea, the Robber synod and the Council of Chalcedon', *Byzantion* 16, 20–80.

Hopkins, K. (1998), 'Christian Number and its Implications', *Journal of Early Christian Studies* 6, 186–225.

Hordern, J. H. (2002), *Timotheus of Miletus* (Oxford: Clarendon Press).

Hughes, D. D. (2013), *Human Sacrifice in Ancient Greece* (London: Routledge).

Hughes, E. J. (1986), *Wilfrid Cantwell Smith: A Theology for our Time* (London: SCM).

Humfress, C. (2011), 'Bishops and Law Courts in Late Antiquity: How (Not) to Understand the legal Evidence', *Journal of Early Christian Studies* 19, 375–400.

Humphries, M. (2008), 'From Usurper to Emperor: the Politics of Legitimation in the Age of Constantine', *Journal of Late Antiquity* 1, 82–100.

Hunink, V. (1996), 'Apuleius and the *Asclepius*', *Vigiliae Christianae* 50, 288–308.

Hunt, E. D. (1982), *Holy Land Pilgrimage in the Later Roman Empire, A.D. 312–462* (Oxford: Clarendon Press).

Hunt, E. D. (1993), 'Christianizing the Roman Empire: the Evidence of the Code', in J. Harries and I. Wood, *The Theodosian Code. Studies in the Imperial Law of Late Antiquity* (London: Duckworth), 143–60.

Hutton, R. H. (1999), *The Triumph of the Moon. A History of Modern Pagan Witchcraft* (Oxford: Oxford University Press).

Igal, J. (1981), 'The Gnostics and the Ancient Philosophy in Plotinus', in H. J. Blumenthal and R. A. Markus (eds), *Neoplatonism and Early Christian Thought* (London: Variorum), 138–49.

Ison, D. (1985a), 'The Constantinian *Oration to the Saints*—Authorship and Background', Ph.D. thesis, University of London.

Ison, D. (1985b), '*Pais theou* in the Age of Constantine', *Journal of Theological Studies* 38, 412–19.

Jacobson, H. (1983), *The Exagoge of Ezekiel* (Cambridge: Cambridge University Press).

Jackson, H. M. (1978), *Zosimus of Panopolis on the Letter Omega* (Atlanta, GA: Society of Biblical Literature).

Jackson, H. M. (1985), *The Lion Becomes Man. The Gnostic Leontomorphic Creator and the Platonic Tradition* (Atlanta, GA: Society of Biblical Studies).

Jackson, H. M. (1990), 'The Seer Nikotheus and his Lost Apocalypse in the Light of Sethian Apocalypses from Nag Hammadi and the Apocalypse of Elchasai', *Novum Testamentum* 32, 250–97.

James, M. R. (1924), *The Apocryphal New Testament* (Oxford: Ooxford University Press).

Jensen R. (2005), 'Towards a Christian Material Culture', in M. Mitchell and F. M. Young (eds), *The Cambridge History of Christianity* I (Cambridge: Cambridge University Press), 568–85.

Jeremias, J. (1955), *The Eucharistic Words of Jesus* (New York: Macmillan).

Johnson, A. (2006), *Ethnicity and Argument in Eusebius' Praeparatio Evangelica* (New York: Oxford University Press).

Johnson, A. (2013a), *Religion and Identity in Porphyry of Tyre* (Oxford: Oxford University Press).

Johnson, A. (2013b), 'The Author of the *Against Hierocles*: A Response to Borzì and Jones', *Journal of Theological Studies* 64, 574–94.

Johnson, A. (2014), *Eusebius* (London: I.B. Tauris).

Jones, A. H. M. (1959), 'Were Ancient Heresies National or Social Movements in Disguise?', *Journal of Theological Studies* 10, 280–98.

Jones, A. H. M. (1964), *The Later Roman Empire*, 2 vols (Oxford: Clarendon Press).

Jones, A. H. M. (1966), *The Decline of the Ancient World* (New York: Holt, Rinehart and Winston).

Jonkers, E. J. (1954), *Acta et Symbola Conciliorum quae Seculo Quarto Habita Sunt* (Leiden: Brill).

Jung, C. G. (1967), 'The Visions of Zosimus', trans. R. F. C. Hull, in *Alchemical Studies* (London: Routledge and Kegan Paul), 57–108.

Kakosy, L. (1995), 'Probleme der Religion im römerzeitliche Âgypten', *Aufstieg und Niedergang der römischen Welt* II.18.5, 2894–3049.

Kalligas, P. (2001), 'Traces of Longinus' Library in Eusebius' *Praeparatio Evangelica*', *Classical Quarterly* 51, 584–98.

Kamesar, A. (1993), *Jerome, Greek Scholarship and the Hebrew Bible* (Oxford: Clarendon Press).

Kane, J. P. (1975), 'The Mithraic Cult Meal in its Greek and Roman Environment', in J. R. Hinnells (ed.), *Mithraic Studies* (Manchester: Manchester University Press), 313–35.

Kannengiesser, C. (2006), 'The Dating of Athanasius' Double Apology and the Three Orations against the Arians', *Zeitschrift fur Antkes Christentum* 10, 19–33.

Kaplan, A. (1990), *Sefer Yetzirah: The Book of Creation* (York Beach: Samuel Weiser).

Kee, A. (1982), *Constantine versus Christ: The Triumph of Ideology* (London: SCM).

Kee, H. C. (1988), *Medicine, Miracle and Magic in New Testament Times* (Cambridge: Cambridge University Press).

Kelly, J. N. D. (1977), *Early Christian Doctrines* (London: A. and C. Black).

Keydell, P. (1957), 'Palladas und das Christenum', *Byzanteinische Zeitschrift* 50, 1–3.

King. C. (2005), *Origen on the Song of Songs as the Spirit of Scripture* (Oxford: Clarendon Press).

King, K. L. (2005), *What Is Gnosticism?* (Cambridge, MA: Harvard University Press).
Kingsley, P. (1993), 'Poimandres: the Etymology of the Name and the Origins of the Hermetica', *Journal of the Warburg and Courtauld Institutes* 56, 1–24.
Kinzig, W. (1994), *Novitas Christiana. Die Idee des Fortschritts in der Alten Kirche bis Eusebius* (Göttingen: Vandenhoek and Ruprecht).
Kinzig, W. and M. Vinzent (1999), 'Recent Research on the Origin of the Creed', *Journal of Theological Studies* 50, 535–59.
Kirk. K. E. (1931), *The Vision of God* (London: Longmans, Green and Co.).
Kofsky, A. (2002), *Eusebius of Caesarea against Paganism* (Leiden: Brill).
Kraft, K. (1955), *Kaiser Konstantins religiöse Entwicklung* (Tübingen: Mohr).
Krämer, B. and J. C. Shelton (1987), *Das Archiv des Nephoros und Verwandte Texte* (Mainz am Rehn).
Kurfess, A. (1936), 'Die griechischen Übersetzervon Vergils vierter Ekloge in Kaiser Konstantins rede an die versammlung der heilger', *Zeitschrift für die Neutestamentliche Wissenschaft* 35, 97–100.
Lacombrade, C. (1953), 'Palladas d'Alexandrie ou les vicissitudes d'un professeur-poète à la fin du IVième siècle', *Pallas* 1, 17–26.
Laeuchli, S. (1972), *Power and Sexuality: The Emergence of Canon Law at the Synod of Elvira* (Philadelphia, PA: Temple University Press).
Lane Fox, R. (1986), *Pagans and Christians* (Harmondsworth: Viking/Penguin).
Lang, U. M. (2000), 'The Christological Controversy at the Synod of Antioch in 268/9', *Journal of Theological Studies* 51, 54–80.
Larsen, L. (2013), 'On Learning a New Alphabet: the Sayings of the Desert Fathers and the Monostichs of Menander', *Studia Patristica* 55.3, 59–77.
Laurin, J. R. (1954), *Orientations maîtresses des apologistes chrétiens de 270 à 361* (Rome: Analecta Gregoriana)
Lefort, L.-T. (1933), 'S. Athanase, écrivain copte', *Le Muséon* 46, 1–33.
Lefort, L.-T. (1954), 'Les sources coptes pachômiennes', *Le Muséon* 67, 217–29.
Leglay, M. (1966), *Saturne africain* (Paris: De Boceaud).
Lewis, N. (1983), *Life in Roman Egypt* (Oxford: Clarendon Press).
L'Huillier, P. L. (1996), *The Church of the First Councils* (New York: St Vladimir's Seminary).
Lieu, S. N. C. (1992), *Manichaeism in the Later Roman Empire and Mediaeval China* (Tübingen: Mohr Siebeck).
Lieu, S. N. C. (2007), 'Christianity and Manichaeism', in A. Casiday and F. W. Norris (eds), *The Cambridge History of Christianity 2: Constantine to c. 600* (Cambridge: Cambridge University Press), 279–98.
Lieu, S. N. C. and D. Montserrat (1996), *From Constantine to Julian* (London: Routledge).
Lilla, S. R. (1971), *Clement of Alexandria: A Study in Christian Platonism and Gnosticism* (Oxford: Clarendon Press).
Linder, A. (1987), *Jews in Roman Imperial Legislation* (Detroit: Wayne State University).
Linder, A. (2006), "The Legal Status of Jews in the Roman Empire", in S.T. Katz (ed.), *The Cambridge History of Judaism*, vol. 4 (Cambridge: Cambridge University Press), 128–173.
Lightfoot, J. L. (2003), *Lucian: On the Syrian Goddess* (Oxford: Oxford University Press).
Lightfoot, J. L. (2007), *The Sibylline Oracles* (Oxford: Oxford University Press).
Linforth, I. M. (1941), *The Arts of Orpheus* (Berkeley: University of California Press).

Logan, A. H. B. (1992), 'Marcellus of Ancyra and the Councils of AD 325: Antioch, Ancyra and Nicaea', *Journal of Theological Studies* 43, 428–46,, 441–446.

Lohr, W. (2005), 'Arius Reconsidered: Part I', *Zeitschrift für Antikes Christentums* 9, 214–60.

Loofs, F. (1924), *Paulus von Samosata* (Leipzig: Hinrichs).

L'Orange, P. and R. Unger (1984), *Das spätantike Herrscherbild von Diokletian bis zu den Konstantin-Söhnen, 284-361 n. Chr* (Berlin: Akademie Verlag).

Louth, A. (1988), 'St Athanasius and the Greek Life of Antony', *Journal of Theological Studies* 39, 504–9.

Louth, A. (1990), 'The Date of Eusebius' *Historia Ecclesiastica*', *Journal of Theological Studies* 41, 111–23.

Lowe, M. (1976), 'Who Were the *Ioudaioi*?', *Novum Testamentum* 18, 101–30.

Lyman, R. (1989), 'Arians and Manichees on Christ', *Journal of Theological Studies* 40, 493–503.

McDonald, L. (1995), *The Formation of the Christian Biblical Canon* (Peabody, MA: Hendrickson).

Machen, A. (2011), 'The Bowmen', in *The White People and Other Stories* (Harmondsworth: Penguin), 213–16.

McLynn, N. (1996), 'The Fourth-Century Taurobolium', *Phoenix* 50, 312–30.

Macmullen, R. (1968), 'Constantine and the Miraculous', *Greek, Roman and Byzantine Studies* 9, 82–96.

Macmullen, R. (1981), *Paganism in the Roman Empire* (New Haven, CT: Yale University Press).

Macmullen, R. (1990), *Changes in the Roman Empire* (Princeton, NJ: Princeton University Press).

Macmullen, R. (2006), *Voting about God in Early Christian Councils* (New Haven, CT: Yale University Press).

Magny, A. (2014), *Porphyry in Fragments. Reception of an Anti-Christian Text in Late Antiquity* (Fanham: Ashgate).

Maier, J. -L. (1987), *Le dossier du Donatisme* (Berlin: Akademie Verlag).

Malaise, M. (1972), *Les conditions de penetration et de diffusion des cultes égyptiens en Italie* (Leiden: Brill).

Mango, C. (1985), *Le développement urbain de Constantinople (IVe-VIe siècles)* (Paris: Centre de recherché d'histoire).

Mansfeld, J. (1992), *Heresiology in Context. Hippolytus' Elenchus as a Source for Greek Philosophy* (Leiden: Brill).

Maraval, P. (2005), 'Constantin est-il devenu arien?', *Theophylion* 10, 371–84.

Maraval, P. (2013), 'La religion de Constantin', *Anuario de Historia de la Iglesia* 22, 17–36.

Markschies, C. (2010), 'The Price of Monotheism: Some New Observations on a Current Debate about Late Antiquity', in S. Mitchell and P. van Nuffelen (eds), *One God. Pagan Monotheism in the Roman Empire* (Cambridge: Cambridge University Press), 100–11.

Marold, K. (1890), 'Ueber das Evangelienbuch des Juvencus in seine Verhältniszum Bibeltext', *Zeitschrift für Wissenschafliche Theologie* 33, 329–41.

Marx-Wolf, H. (2010), 'Third-century Daimonologies and the *Via Universalis*', *Studia Patristica* 46, 207–15.

Mastandrea, P. (1979), *Un neoplatonico latino. Corneli Labeone* (Leiden: Brill).
Matthews, J. (1991), *Taliesin. Shamanism and the Bardic Mysteries in Britain and Ireland* (London: Aquarius Press).
Mazzarino, S. (1974), 'Antico, tardantico ed era Constantino I', *Storia e Civilta* 13, 98–150.
McCracken, J. (1949), *Arnobius of Sicca: The Case against the Pagans* (New York).
Meigne, M. (1975), 'Concile ou collection d'Elvire?', *Revue de'Histoire Ecclésiastique* 70, 361–87.
Meijering, E. P. (1974), ''HN 'OTE OYK 'HN 'O 'YIOΣ: A Discussion on Time and Eternity', *Vigilae Christianae* 38, 161–8.
Meijering, E. P. (2010), 'Athanasius on God as Creator and Redeemer', *Church History and Society* 90, 175–98.
Mercati, G. (1901), *Note di letteratura biblica e cristiana antica*, in *Studi e Testi* (Rome: Vatican Press, 1901).
Meredith, A. (1980), 'Porphyry and Julian against the Christians', *Aufstieg und Niedergang der römischen Welt* II.23.2, 1120–50.
Metzger, B. (1987), *The Canon of the New Testament: Its Origin, Development and Significance* (Oxford: Clarendon Press).
Meyer, M., ed. (2007), *The Nag Hammadi Scriptures: The Revised and Updated Translation of Sacred Gnostic Texts* (New York: Harper).
Michel, A. (2005), 'Aspects du culte dans les églises de Numidie au temps d'Augustin: état de la question', in S. Lancel (ed.), *Saint Augustin, la Numidie et la société de son temps* (Bordeaux), 67–108.
Millar, F. (1977), *The Emperor in the Roman World* (London: Duckworth).
Millar, F. (2010), 'The Palestinian Context of Rabbinic Judaism', in M. D. Goodman and Philip Alexander (eds), *Rabbinic Texts and the History of Later-Roman Palestine* (London: Oxford University Press for the British Academy), 25–49.
Mirecki, P. (2006), 'Manichaean Literature', in W. Barnstone and M. Meyer (eds), *The Gnostic Bible* (Boston: Shambala), 569–654.
Mitchell, S. (1999), 'The Cult of Theos Hypsistos between Pagans, Jews and Christians', in P. Athanassiadi and M. Frede (eds), *Pagan Monotheism in Late Antiquity* (Oxford: Oxford University Press), 81–148.
Mitchell, S. (2010), 'Further Thoughts on the Cult of Zeus Hypsistos', in S. Mitchell and P. van Nuffelen (eds), *One God. Pagan Monotheism in the Roman Empire* (Cambridge: Cambridge University Press), 167–208.
Mommsen, T. (1894), 'Firmicus Maternus', *Hermes* 29, 468–72.
Monceaux, P. (1905), *Histoire littéraire de l'Afrique chrétienne* (Paris).
Moreschini, C. and C. Tommasi (2007), *Opere teologice di Mario Vittorino* (Turin).
Morison, K. (1992), *Understanding Conversion* (Charlottesville: University Press of Virginia).
Morlet, S. (2008), 'Un Nouveau témoignage sur le *Contra Christianos* de Porphyre?', *Semitica et Classica* 1, 157–66.
Morlet, S. (2009), *La Démonstration Évangélique d'Eusèbe de Césarée: Étude sur l'apologétique chrétienne à l'époque de Constantin* (Paris: Études Augustiniennes).
Morlet, S. (2010), 'Le *Démonstration Évangelique* d'Eusèbe de Césarée contient-elle des fragments du *Contra Christianos* de Porphyre? À propos du frg 73 Harnack', *Studia Patristica* 46, 59–64.

Morlet, S., ed. (2011), *Le traité de Porphyre contre les chrétiens* (Paris: Institute d'Études Augustiniennes).
Mosshammer, A. (1979), *The Chronicle of Eusebius and the Greek Chronographic Tradition* (London: Associated University Presses).
Munnich, O. (2011), Recherche de la source Porphyrienne dans les objections 'païennes' du *Monogénès*", in Morlet, *Le traité*, 75–104.
Muro M. S. and T. B. Villena (2005), *El Concilio de Elvira y su tempo* (Granada).
Murphy-O'Connor, J. (2008), *The Holy Land: An Oxford Archaeological Guide* (Oxford: Oxford University Press).
Nasrallah, L. (2011), 'The Embarrassment of Blood; Early Christians and Others on Sacrifice, War and Rational Worship', in J. W. Knust and Z. Varhelyi (eds), *Ancient Mediterranean Sacrifice* (New York: Oxford University Press), 142–65.
Nautin, P. (1950), 'Trois autres fragments du livre de Porphyre *Contre les Chrétiens*', *Rheinisches Museum* 57, 49–416.
Needleman, J. (2009), *The New Religions* (New York: Tarcher).
Neusner, J. (1999), *The Transformation of Judaism: From Philosophy to Religion* (Baltimore, MD: Johns Hopkins University Press).
Newman, J. H. (1845), *An Essay on the Development of Christian Doctrine* (London: Toovey).
Nicholson, O. P. (1984), 'The Date of Arnobius' *Adversus Gentes*', *Studia Patristica* 15, 100–7.
Nilsson, M. (1945), 'Pagan Divine Service in Late Antiquity', *Harvard Theological Review* 38, 63–9.
Nixon, C. V. and B. S. Rodgers (1994), *In Praise of Later Roman Emperors* (Berkeley: University of California Press).
Nock, A. D. (1933), *Conversion: The Old and the New in Religion from to Alexander the Great to Augustine of Hippo* (Oxford: Clarendon Press).
North, J. (1992), 'The Development of Religious Pluralism', in J. N. Lieu, J. North, and T. Rajak (eds), *The Jews among Pagans and Christians* (London: Routledge), 174–93.
North, J. (2010), 'Pagan ritual and monotheism', in S. Mitchell and P. van Nuffelen (eds), *One God. Pagan Monotheism in the Roman Empire* (Cambridge: Cambridge University Press), 34–52.
Odahl, C. M. (1993), 'Constantine's Epistle to the Bishops of the Council of Arles', *Journal of Religious History* 17, 274–9.
Odahl, C. M. (2003), *Constantine and the Christian Empire* (London: Taylor and Francis).
Ogilvie, R. S. (1978), *The Library of Lactantius* (Oxford: Clarendon Press).
O'Meara, D. J. (1989), *Pythagoras Revived: Mathematics and Philosophy in Late Antiquity* (Oxford: Clarendon Press).
Opitz, H.-G. (1934), *Urkunde zur Geschichte des arianischen Streites* (Leipzig: Teubner).
Pagels, E. (1979), *The Gnostic Gospels* (New York: Vintage).
Parkes, J. (1961), *The Conflict of the Church and the Synagogue* (New York: Meridian Books).
Parvis, S. (2006), *Marcellus of Ancyra and the Lost Years of the Nicene Controversy* (Oxford: Clarendon Press).

Pastorino, A. (1956), *Iuli Firmici Materni De Errore Profanarum Religionum* (Florence: Nuova Italia).

Patai, R. (1994), *The Jewish Alchemists* (Princeton, NJ: Princeton University Press).

Patterson, L. G. (1966), 'The Creation of the Word in Methodius' *Symposium*', *Studia Patristica* 9, 240–50.

Patterson, L. G. (1989), 'Who Are the Opponents in Methodius' *De Resurrectione*?', *Studia Patristica* 19, 221–9.

Patterson, L. G. (1993), 'Methodius, Origen and the Arian Dispute', *Studia Patristica* 17, 912–23.

Pearson, B. (1981), 'Jewish Elements in *Corpus Hermeticum* I (*Poimandres*)', in R. Van den Broek and M. J. Vermaseren (eds), *Studies in Gnosticism and Hellenistic Religions presented to Gilles Quispel on the Occasion of his Sixty-Fifth Birthday* (Leiden: Brill), 336–48.

Perczel, I. (1999), 'Mankind's Common Intellectual Substance: A Study in the Letters of St Antony and his Life by St Athanasius', in B. Nagy and M. Sebők (eds), *The Man of many Devices, Who Wandered Full Many Ways* (Budapest: Central European University), 197–213.

Petropoulou, M. (2008), *Animal Sacrifice in Ancient Greek Religion, Judaism and Christianity, 100 BC to AD 200* (Oxford: Oxford University Press).

Pettersen, A. (1982), 'A Reconsideration of the Date of the *Contra Gentes—De Incarnatione* of Athanasius of Alexandria', *Studia Patristica* 17, 1030–40.

Pietri, C. (1976), *Roma Christiana* (Rome: Pontifical Institute).

Pietri, C. (1980), 'La mort en Occident dans l'épigraphie latine: de l'épigraphie païenne à l'épitaphe chrétienne, 3e-6e siècles', *La Maison Dieu* 144, 25–48.

Pietri, C. (1983), 'Constantin en 324. Propagande et théologies impériales d'après les documents de la *Vita Constantini*', in *Crise et redressement dans les provinces européennes de l'Empire (milieu du IIIe- milieu du IVe siècle). Actes du colloque de Strasbourg 1981*, 63–90.

Pietri, C. (1985), 'Épigraphie et culture : l'évolution de l'éloge funérairedans es textes de l'Occident chrétien (IIIe-VIe siècles)', in *La trasformazioni della cultura nella tarda antichità* (Rome; proceedings of colloquium of Catana 1982), 157–83.

Pietri, C. (1991), 'La conversion de Rome et la primauté du Pape', in *Il primate del vescovo di Roma nel primo millennio: Richerche e testimonianze* (Vatican: Pontifical Institute), 23–47.

Piganiol, C. (1932), 'Dates Constantiniennes', *Revue d'Histoire et de Sciences Religieuses* 12, 360–72.

Pontani, A. (2006–2007), 'Ancora su Pallada, AP IX 528, ovvero il bilinguismo al prova', *Incontri triestini di filologia classica* 6, 175–210.

Potter, D. (2013), *Constantine the Emperor* (New York: Oxford University Press).

Raby, E. (1953), *A History of Christian-Latin Poetry from the Beginnings to the Close of the Middle Ages* (Oxford: Clarendon Press).

Rackham, R. B. (1891), *The Text of the Canons of Ancyra* (Oxford: Clarendon Press).

Radhakrishnan, S. (1935), *The Thirteen Principal Upanishads* (London: Allen and Unwin).

Rahner, K. (1979), 'The "Spiritual Senses" according to Origen', in *Theological Investigations* 16: *Experience of the Spirit*, trans. D. Morland (New York: Crossroads), 81–103.

Rapp, C. (1998), 'Imperial Ideology in the Making: Eusebius of Caesarea on Constantine as "Bishop"', *Journal of Theological Studies* 49, 685–95.

Rashdall, H. (1919), *The Idea of Atonement in Christian Theology* (London: Macmillan).

Rasimus, T. (2009), *Paradise Reconsidered in Gnostic Mythology: Rethinking Sethianism in the Light of the Ophite Evidence* (Leiden: Brill).

Rasimus, T. (2010), 'Porphyry and the Gnostics: Reassessing Pierre Hadot's Thesis in the light of Second- and Third- Century Sethian Treatises', in K. Corrigan and J. Turner (eds), *Plato's Parmenides and Its Heritage* (Leiden: Brill), vol. 2, 81–110.

Ratkowitsch, C. (1986), 'Vergils Seesturm bei Iuvencus und Sedulius', *Jahrbuch für Antike und Christentum* 29, 40–58.

Rebillard, E. (2013), 'William Hugh Clifford Frend (1916–2005): The Legacy of *The Donatist Church*', in M. Vinzent (ed.), *Studia Patristica* LIII: *Former Directors* (Leuven: Peeters), 55–71.

Reichman, R. (2010), 'The Tosefta and its Value for Historical Research', in Goodman and Alexander, 117–28.

Reitzenstein, R. (1904), Poimandres. Studien zur griechisch-ägyptischen und frühchristlichen literature (Leipzig: Teubner).

Reitzenstein, R. (1914), *Der Athanasius Werk über das Leben des Antonius* (Heidelberg: Winter).

Reitzenstein, R. (1916), *Historia Monachorum und Historia lausiaca. Eine Studie zur Geschichte des Mönchtums* (Göttingen).

Reydams-Schils, G. (2002), 'Calcidius Christianus?', in T. Kobusch, M. Erler and I. Männlein-Robert, *Metaphysik und Religion* (Munich/Leipzig:), 193–211.

Reydams-Schils, G. (2010), 'Calcidius', in G. L. Gerson (ed.), *The Cambridge History of Philosophy in Late Antiquity* (Cambridge: Cambridge University Press), 498–508.

Reynolds, J. and R. Tannenbaum (1987), *Jews and Godfearers at Aphrodisias* (Cambridge: Cambridge Philological Society).

Richard, M. (1949), 'Un opuscule méconnu de Marcel évêque d'Ancyre', *Mélanges de Science Religieuse* 6, 5–24.

Richardson, G. P. (2004), *Building Jewish in the Roman East* (Waco: Baylor University Press).

Riedweg, C. (1994), *Ps.-Justin (Markell von Ankyra?) Ad Graecos de vera religione* (Basel).

Rist, J. M. (1967), 'Integration and the Undescended Soul in Plotinus', *American Journal of Philology* 88, 410–22.

Rives, J. B. (1995a), *Religion and Authority in Roman Carthage from Augustus to Constantine* (Oxford: Clarendon Press).

Rives, J. B. (1995b), 'Human Sacrifice among Pagans and Christians', *Journal of Roman Studies* 85, 68–85.

Rives, J. B. (1999), 'The Decree of Decius and the Religion of the Empire', *Journal of Roman Studies* 89, 135–54.

Rives, J. B. (2011), 'The Theology of Animal Sacrifice in the Ancient Greek World: Origins and Developments', in J. W. Knust and Z. Várhelyi (eds), *Ancient Mediterranean Sacrifice* (New York: Oxford University Press), 187–202.

Rizzi, M. (2002), *Encomio di Origene* (Milan:).

Robert, L. (1971), 'Un oracle grave à Oinoanda', *Comptes rendus des séances de l'Académie des Inscriptions* 115, 597–629.
Roberts, C. H. (1938), *Catalogue of Papyri in the John Rylands Library Manchester*, vol 3 *Theological and Literary Papyri* (Manchester).
Roberts, M (2004), 'Vergil and the Gospels: The *Evangeliorum Libri IV* of Juvencus', in R. Rees (ed.) *Romane memento: Vergil in the Fourth Century* (London:), 47–62.
Robinson, J. M. (1977), 'The Jung Codex: The Rise and Fall of a Monopoly', *Religious Studies Review* 3, 17–30.
Robinson, J. M. (1981), 'From the Cliff to Cairo: The Story of the Discoverers and Middlemen of the Nag Hammadi Codices', in B. Barc (ed.), *Colloque international sur les textes de Nag Hammadi (Québec: 22–25 août 1978)* (Louvain: Peeters), 21–58.
Robertson, J. M. (2007), *Christ as Mediator. A Study of the Theologies of Eusebius of Caesarea, Marcellus of Ancyra and Athanasius of Alexandria* (Oxford: Clarendon Press).
Rohrbacker, D. (2013), 'The Sources of the *Historia Augusta* Re-examined', *Histos* 7, 146–80.
Rousseau, P. (1978), *Ascetics, Authority and the Church in the Age of Jerome and Cassian* (Oxford: Oxford University Press).
Rousseau, P. (2000), 'Antony as Teacher in the Greek Life', in T. Hägg and P. Rousseau (eds), *Greek Biography and Panegyric in Late Antiquity* (Berkekely: University of California Press), 89–109.
Routh, M. (1846), *Reliquiae Sacrae* (Oxford: Oxford University Press).
Rubenson, S. (1995), *The Letters of St Antony* (Minneapolis, MN: Fortress Press).
Rubenson, S. (2006), 'Antony and Pythagoras: A Reappraisal of the Appropriation of Classical Biography in Athanasius' *Vita Antonii*', in D. Brakke et al. (eds), *Beyond Reception* (New York: Lang), 191–208.
Rubenson, S. (2013), 'The Formation and Re-formations of the Sayings of the Desert Fathers', *Studia Patristica* 55.3, 5–22.
Rubin, Z. (1982), 'The Church of the Holy Sepulchre and the Conflict between the Sees of Caesarea and Jerusalem', *Jerusalem Cathedra* 2, 79–105.
Saffrey, H.-D. (1971), 'Abamon, pseudonyme de Jamblique', in *Philomathes. Studies and Essays in the Humanities in Memory of Philip Merlan* (The Hague: Nijhoff), 227–39.
Saffrey, H.-D. (1984), 'Le "philosophe de Rhodes": est-il Théodore d'ASsine?', in E. Lucchesi and H. -D. Saffrey (eds), *Memorial A.-J. Festugière* (Geneva), 65–76.
Saffrey, H.-D. (1988), 'Connaissance et inconnaissance de Dieu: Porphyre et la Théosophie de Tübingen', in *Gonimos: Studies Presented to Leendert G. Westerink at 75* (Buffalo, NY:), 3–20.
Salamon, M. (1995), 'Coinage and Money in the Epigrams of Palladas', in S. Stabryla (ed.), *Everyday Life and Literature in Antiquity* (Cracow: Classia Cracovieniensia).
Salzman, M. R. (1987), '"Superstitio" in the *Codex Theodosianus* and the Persecution of Pagans', *Vigiliae Christianae* 41, 172–88.
Salzman, M. R. (2011), 'The End of Public Sacrifice: Changing Definitions of Sacrifice in Post-Constantinian Rome and Italy', in J. W. Knust and Z. Várhelyi (eds), *Ancient Mediterranean Sacrifice* (New York: Oxford University Press), 167–86.

Sanchez, M. J. L. (2008),'L'état actual de la recherche sur le concile d'Elvire', *Revue des sciences religieuses* 82, 517–46.
Scarpi, P. (2011), *La Rivelazione secreta di Ermete Trismegisto*, vol. 2 (Florence: Lorenzo Valla Institute).
Schäfer, P. (2010), 'Hekhalot Literature and the Origins of Jewish Mysticism', in Goodman and Alexander, 264–80.
Schmidt, C. (1896), 'Ein vorirenaische gnostiches Originalwerke', *Abhandlungen des kgl. preussischen Akademie des Wissenschaft*, 839–947.
Scholem, G. (1987), *Origins of the Kabbala* (Princeton, NJ: Jewish Society Publications).
Schott, J. M. (2013a), *Christianity, Empire and the Making of Religion in Late Antiquity* (Pennyslvania University Press).
Schott, J. M. (2013b), 'Plotinus' Portrait and Pamphilus' Prison Notebook: Neoplatonic and Early Christian Textualities at the Turn of the Fourth Century C.E.', *Journal of Early Christian Studies* 21, 329–62.
Schwartz, H. (1975), 'Cautes and Cautopates, the Mithraic Torchbearers', in J. R. Hinnells (ed.), *Mithraic Studies* (Manchester: Manchester University Press), 406–23.
Scott, W. B. (1936), *Hermetica*, vol. 4 (Oxford: Clarendon Press).
Scotti, M. Horsfall (2000), 'The Asclepius: Thoughts on a Re-Opened Debate', *Vigiliae Christianae* 54, 396–416.
Shaw, G. (1995), *Theurgy and the Soul: The Neoplatonism of Iamblichus* (University Park: Pennsylvania University Press).
Sheppard, A. (1982), 'Proclus' Attitude to Theurgy', *Classical Quarterly* 22, 212–24.
Simmons, M. B. (1995), *Arnobius of Sicca* (Oxford: Oxford University Press).
Simmons, M. B. (2009), 'Porphyrian Universalism: A Tripartite Soteriology and Eusebius's Response', *Harvard Theological Review* 102, 169–92.
Simon, M. (1986), *Verus Israel* (New York: Oxford University Press).
Skarsaune, O. (1987), 'A Neglected Detail in the Creed of Nicaea (325)', *Vigiliae Chiristianae* 41, 34–54.
Smith, A. (1987), 'Porphyrian Studies since 1913', *Aufstieg und Niedergang der Römischen Welt* II.36.2, 717–73.
Smith, J. Z. (1987), 'Dying and Rising Gods', in M. Eliade (ed.), *Encyclopedia of Religion*, vol. 4, 521–7.
Smith, M. D. (1997), 'The Religion of Constantius I', *Greek, Roman and Byzantine Studies* 38, 187–209.
Smith. W. C. (1978), *The Meaning and End of Religion* (London: SPCK).
Snyder, G. (2000), *Teachers and Texts in the Ancient World: Philosophers, Jews and Christians* (London: Routledge).
Solomon, N. (2009), *The Talmud: A Selection* (Harmondsworth: Penguin).
Sorabji, R. (1983), *Time, Creation and the Continuum* (London: Duckworth).
Sperber, D. (1978), *Roman Palestine 200–400 A.D. The Land, Crisis and Change in Agrarian Society as Reflected in Rabbinic Sources* (Ramat Gan: Bar-Ilan University Press).
Stanley, A. O. (1970), *Lectures on the History of the Eastern Church* (London: Dent).
Stark, R. (1997), *The Rise of Christianity* (San Francisco: Harper).
Stead, G. C. (1964), 'The Platonism of Arius', *Journal of Theological Studies* 15, 16–31.
Stead, G. C. (1973), 'Eusebius and the Council of Nicaea', *Journal of Theological Studies* 24, 85–100.

Stead, G. C. (1978), 'The *Thalia* of Arius and the Testimony of Athanasius', *Journal of Theological Studies* 29, 20–52.
Stead, G. C. (1988), 'Athanasius' Earliest Written Work', *Journal of Theological Studies* 39, 76–91.
Stead, G. C. (1998), 'The Word "From Nothing"', *Journal of Theological Studies* 49, 671–84.
Stemberger, G. (2000), *Jews and Christians in the Holy Land* (Edinburgh: T. and T. Clark).
Stemberger, G. (2010), 'Halakhic Midrashim as Historical Sources', in M. D. Goodman and P. Alexander (eds), *Rabbinic Texts and the History of Later-Roman Palestine* (London: Oxford University Press for the British Academy), 129–42.
Stenhouse, P. (1995), 'Fourth-Century Date for Baba Rabba Re-examined', in A. D. Crown and L. Davey (eds), *Essays in Honour of G. D. Sexdenier: New Samaritan Studies of the Société d'études Samaritaines III–IV* (Sydney: Mandelbaum), 317–26.
Stern, S. (2010), 'The Talmud Yerushalmi', in M. D. Goodman and P. Alexander (eds), *Rabbinic Texts and the History of Later-Roman Palestine* (London: Oxford University Press for the British Academy), 142–64.
Stevenson, J. (1929), *Studies in Eusebius* (Cambridge: Cambridge University Press).
Stewart, A. (1887), *Itinerary from Bordeaux to Jerusalem: The Bordeaux Pilgrim* (London: Palestine Pilgrimage Text Society).
Strack, H. A. and G. Stemberger (1991), *Introduction to the Talumd and Midrash* (Edinburgh: T. and T. Clark).
Stroumsa, G. (2009), *The End of Sacrifice* (Chicago: University of Chicago Press).
Strutwolf, H. (1999), *Die Trinitätslehre und Christologie des Euseb von Caesarea* (Göttingen: Vanderhoeck and Ruprecht).
Syme, R. (1971), 'Ipse Ille Patriarcha', in Syme, *Emperors and Biography* (Oxford: Clarendon Press), 17–29.
Tardieu, M. (1996), *Recherches sur la formation de l'Apocalypse de Zostrien et les sources de Marius Victorinus* (Louvain: Peeters).
Taylor, J. (1993), *Christians and Holy Places: The Myth of Jewish-Christian Origins* (Oxford: Oxford University Press).
Taylor, J. (2003), *Jewish Women Philosophers in Ancient Alexandria* (Oxford: Oxford University Press).
Taylor, T. (1821), *Iamblichus on the Mysteries* (London).
Ter Haar Romeny, R. B. (1997), *A Syrian in Greek Dress. The Use of Greek, Hebrew and Syriac Texts in Eusebius of Emesa's Commentary on Genesis* (Leuven: Peeters).
Testa, E. (1972), *I graffiti della casa di San Pietro* (Jerusalem: Franciscan Printing Press).
Thomassen, E. (2006), *The Spiritual Seed: the Church of the 'Valentinians'* (Leiden: Brill).
Thompson, E. A. (1963), 'Christianity and the Northern Barbarians', in A. Momigliano (ed.), *The Conflict between Paganism and Christianity in the Fourth Century* (Oxford: Clarendon Press),
Thraede, K. (2001), 'Iuvencus', in *Reallexicon für Antike und Christentum*, 19, 881–906.
Thümmel, H. -G. (1992), *Die Frühgeschichte der ostkirchlichen Bilderlehre Texte* (Berlin:

Tilley, M. (1996), *Donatist Martyr Stories* (Liverpool: Liverpool University Press).

Torjesen, K. (1986), *Hermeneutical Procedure and Theological Method in Origen's Exegesis* (Berlin: De Gruyter).

Toutain, J. (1920), *Les cultes païens dans l'empire Romain* (Paris: Leroux).

Trapp, M. (1997), 'On the Tablet of Cebes', in R. Sorabji (ed.), *Aristotle and After* (*Bulletin of the Institute of Classical Studies* supplement 68), 159–80.

Trombley, F. R. (2001), *Hellenic Religion and Christianization*, 2nd edition (Leiden: Brill).

Turcan, R. (1975), *Mithras Platonicus* (Leiden: Brill).

Turcan, R. (1989), *Les cultes orientaux dans le monde Romain* (Paris: Belles Lettres).

Turner, J. H. (2001), *Sethian Gnosticism and the Platonic Tradition* (Leuven: Peeters).

Ulansey, D. (1989), *The Origin of the Mithraic Mysteries* (Oxford: Oxfird University Press).

Ullucci, D. (2012), *The Christian Rejection of Animal Sacrifice* (New York: Oxford University Press).

Uro, R., ed. (1990), *Thomas at the Crossroads* (London: T. and T. Clark).

Ustinova, J. (1999), *The Supreme Gods of the Bosporan Kingdom: Celestial Aphrodite and the Most High God* (Leiden: Brill).

Van Bekkum, W. J. (2010), 'The Future of Ancient Piyyut', in Goodman and Alexander, 217–34.

Van Blundel (2009), *The Arabic Hermes* (Oxford: Oxford University Press).

Van der Horst, P. and J. Mansfeld (1974), *An Alexandrian Platonist against Dualism: Alexander of Lycopolis' Treatise 'Critique of the Doctrine of Manichaeus'* (Leiden: Brill).

Van der Nat, P. G. (1973), 'Die Praefatio der Evangelienparaphrase des Iuvencus', in W. Den Boer, P. G. Van der Nat (eds), C. M. J. Sicking and J. M. C. Van Winden (eds), *Romanitas et Christianitas* (Amsterdam), 249–57.

Van Nuffelen, P. (2010), 'Pagan Monotheism as a Religious Phenomenon', in S. Mitchell and P. van Nuffelen (eds), *One God. Pagan Monotheism in the Roman Empire* (Cambridge: Cambridge University Press), 16–33.

Van Winden, J. M. C. (1959), *Calcidius on Matter: His Doctrine and Sources* (Leiden: Brill).

Van Winden, J. M. C. (1975), 'On the Date of Athanasius' Apologetic Writings', *Vigiliae Christianae* 29, 291–5.

Veilleux, A. (1980), *Pachomian Koinonia* 1 (Kalamazoo: Cistercian Press).

Veilleux, A. (1982), *Pachomian Koinonia* 3 (Kalamazoo: Cistercian Press).

Vermes, G. (2011), *The Dead Sea Scrolls in English* (Harmondsworth: Penguin).

Versnel, H. (1990), *Ter Unus. Isis, Dionysos Hermes: Three Studies in Henotheism* (Leiden: Brill).

Versnel, H. (2011), *Coping with the Gods* (Leiden: Brill).

Vessey, J. M. (1993), 'The Origins of the *Collectio Sirmondiana*: A New Look at the Evidence', in Harries and Wood, 178–99.

Vogt, J. (1924), *Die Alexandrinische Münzen* (Stuttgart: Olms).

Von Albrecht, M. (1997), *A History of Latin Literature* (Leiden: Brill).

Von Campenhausen, H. (1976), 'Das Bekenntnis Eusebs von Caesarea', *Zeitschrift für Neutestamentliche Wissenschaft* 67, 123–39.

Walker, P. W. L. (1990), *Holy City, Holy Places? Christian Attitudes to Jerusalem and the Holy Land in the Fourth Century* (Oxford: Clarendon Press).

Wallraff, M. (2002), *Christus verus sol* (Münster).

Waszink, J. H. (1974), 'Le rapport de Calcidius sur le doctrine platonicienne de la métampsychose', in *Mélanges H.-C. Puech* (Paris), 315–22.

Waterland, D. (1896), *A Review of the Doctrine of the Eucharist*, ed. W. Van Mildert (Oxford: Clarendon Press).

Weiss, P. (2003), 'The Vision of Constantine', trans. A. R. Birley, *Journal of Roman Archaeology* 16, 237–59.

West, M. L. (1982), 'The Metre of Arius' *Thalia*', *Journal of Theological Studies* 33, 98–105.

Wiedemann, T. (1995), *Emperors and Gladiators* (London: Routledge).

Wilamowitz-Moellendorf, U. von (1902), 'Lesefrüchte', *Hermes* 37, 328–32.

Wiles, M. F. (1962), 'In Defence of Arius', *Journal of Theological Studies* 13, 339–47.

Wiles, M. F. (1965), 'The Nature of the Early Debate about Christ's Human Soul', *Journal of Ecclesiastical History* 16, 139–51.

Wiles, M. F. (1991), 'A Textual Variant in the Creed of the Council of Nicaea', *Studia Patristica* 26, 428–33.

Wilken, R. (1992), *The Land Called Holy: Palestine in Early Christian History and Thought* (New Haven, CT: Yale University Press).

Wilkinson, J. (1971), *Egeria's Travels* (London: SPCK).

Wilkinson, K. (2009), 'Palladas and the Age of Constantine', *Journal of Roman Studies* 99, 36–60.

Wilkinson, K. (2010), 'Palladas and the Foundation of Constantinople', *Journal of Roman Studies* 100, 179–94.

Williams, R. D. (1986), 'Arius and the Meiitian Schism', *Journal of Theological Studies* 37, 39–52.

Williams, R. D. (2001), *Arius: Heresy and Tradition*, 2nd edition (London: SCM).

Wilson, A. I. (2005), 'Romanizing Baal: the Art of Saturn Worship in North Africa', in *Proceedings of the Eighth International Colloquium on Problems of Roman Provincial Art* (Zagreb), 403–8.

Winiarczyk, M. (2013), *The 'Sacred History' of Euhemerus of Messene* (Berlin: De Gruyter).

Winn, R. E. (2011), *Eusebius of Emesa: Church and Theology in the Mid-Fourth Century* (Washington: Catholic University of America Press).

Wipszycka, E. (1996), *Études sur le christianisme dans l'Égypte de l'antiquité tardive* (Rome: Augustinianum).

Witt, R. E. (1971), *Isis in the Graeco-Roman World* (Ithaca, NY; Cornell University Press).

Wlosok, A. (1989), 'L. Caecilius Firmianus Lactantius', in R. Herzog (ed.), *Handbuch der lateinische Literatur der Antike* 5 (Munich: Beck), 375–404.

Woods, D. (2002), review of Edwards, *Constantine and Christendom*, *Peritia* 16, 498–9.

Woods, D. (2003), 'Ammianus Marcellinus and Bishop Eusebius of Emesa', *Journal of Theological Studies* 54, 585–91.

Wortley, J. (2006), 'The Origins of the Christian Veneration of Body-Parts', *Revue de l'histoire des religions* 223, 5–28.

Woschitz, K. (1989), 'Der Mythos des Lichts und der Finsternis', in K. Woschitz, M. Hunter, K. Prenner, *Das manichäische Urdrama des Lichts. Studien zu koptischen, mitteliranischen und arabien texte* (Vienna: Herder).

Wyatt, N. (1995), 'Astarte', in K. van der Torn, B. Becking and P. W. van der Horst (eds), *Dictionary of Deities and Demons in the Bible* (Leiden: Brill), 203–13.

Young, F. M. (1997), *Biblical Exegesis and the Formation of Christendom* (Cambridge: Cambridge University Press).

Zachhuber, J. (2013), 'Modern Discourse on Sacrifice and its Theological Background', in J. Meszaros and J. Zachhuber (eds), *Sacrifice and Modern Thought* (Oxford: Oxford University Press), 12–27.

Zambon, M. (2011), 'Porfirio e Origene; uno *status quaestionis*', in S. Morlet (ed.), *Le traité de Porphyre contre les Chrétiens* (Paris: Institute des Études Augustiniennes), 107–64.

Ziegler, K. (1909), 'Zur Überlieferung der Apologie des Firmicus Maternus', *Berliner Philologische Wochenschrift* 29, 1195–9.

Zuntz, G. (1955), 'On the Hymns in *Corpus Hermeticum* XIII', *Hermes* 83, 68–92.

Index

Printed and bound by CPI Group (UK) Ltd, Croydon, CR0 4YY